Blender 3D By Example
Second Edition

A project-based guide to learning the latest Blender 3D, EEVEE rendering engine, and Grease Pencil

Oscar Baechler
Xury Greer

BIRMINGHAM - MUMBAI

Blender 3D By Example
Second Edition

Commissioning Editor: Kunal Chaudhari
Acquisition Editor: Ashitosh Gupta
Content Development Editor: Akhil Nair
Senior Editor: Hayden Edwards
Technical Editor: Shubham Sharma
Copy Editor: Safis Editing
Project Coordinator: Kinjal Bari
Proofreader: Safis Editing
Indexer: Manju Arasan
Production Designer: Alishon Mendonsa

First published: September 2015
Second edition: May 2020

Production reference: 1280520

Published by Packt Publishing Ltd.
Livery Place
35 Livery Street
Birmingham
B3 2PB, UK.

ISBN 978-1-78961-256-1

www.packt.com

Packt.com

Subscribe to our online digital library for full access to over 7,000 books and videos, as well as industry leading tools to help you plan your personal development and advance your career. For more information, please visit our website.

Why subscribe?

- Spend less time learning and more time coding with practical eBooks and Videos from over 4,000 industry professionals

- Improve your learning with Skill Plans built especially for you

- Get a free eBook or video every month

- Fully searchable for easy access to vital information

- Copy and paste, print, and bookmark content

Did you know that Packt offers eBook versions of every book published, with PDF and ePub files available? You can upgrade to the eBook version at www.packt.com and as a print book customer, you are entitled to a discount on the eBook copy. Get in touch with us at customercare@packtpub.com for more details.

At www.packt.com, you can also read a collection of free technical articles, sign up for a range of free newsletters, and receive exclusive discounts and offers on Packt books and eBooks.

Contributors

About the authors

Oscar Baechler is a CG generalist, professor, painter, photographer, open source advocate, and community organizer who teaches at Lake Washington Institute of Technology. He's published a number of mobile games with a Blender pipeline and created animation for clients both big and small. Oscar runs the Seattle Blender User Group and Ballard Life Drawing Co-op and has presented on CGI at SIGGRAPH, LinuxFest Northwest, the Blender Conference, OSCON, Usenix LISA, SeaGL, SIX, WACC, and others.

> *I want to thank my wife Roxanne, for her endless support; my kids Felix and Susan, for playing Baby Dragon with me; and my mom and dad for giving me art supplies. Also, I want to thank my friend Jacob, for his scanning help. Thanks to Lake Washington Institute of Technology, and all the students who have shared the classroom with me. Thank you Xury, for writing a book with me! Lastly, thanks to the Blender community, especially the Seattle Blender User Group, for over a decade of Blender and friendship.*

Xury Greer has been involved in digital media production for over 15 years. He got his start as an indy film director, participating in 48-hour film competitions, and creating training videos for businesses in the Greater Seattle Area. Xury earned his bachelor's degree in game design at Lake Washington Institute of Technology and graduated with the highest honors. Xury specializes in 3D characters and technical art, and he loves to share his knowledge. He has taught courses for Mount Si High School, Washington Network for Innovative Careers, DigiPen, and LWTech.

About the reviewers

Henk Kok is an experienced 3D generalist with over a decade of experience working on games, television series, and feature films. He values thriving cooperation with those around him. In 2019 he worked as the 3D animation supervisor for the groundbreaking Amazon Prime series *Undone*.

Fernando Castilhos Melo lives in Toronto, Canada, and works as a software engineer. He holds a degree in computer science. In his spare time, he works on 3D modeling using Blender and has done so since 2009. He has given some lectures about Blender and 3D modeling at some open source software events and reviewed several Blender books. He also developed an integration between Blender and Kinect to create 3D animation using body movements.

I would like to say a big thank you to:
-My wife, Mauren, for all the support
-My parents, Eloir and Miriam, for encouraging me
-My dog, Polly, for being (literally) at my side all the time during this review
-All my friends for giving me the confidence for this work

Packt is searching for authors like you

If you're interested in becoming an author for Packt, please visit `authors.packtpub.com` and apply today. We have worked with thousands of developers and tech professionals, just like you, to help them share their insight with the global tech community. You can make a general application, apply for a specific hot topic that we are recruiting an author for, or submit your own idea.

Table of Contents

Preface

What is Blender? In a nutshell, it's a free, open source 3D modeling suite. But it's also a 3D and 2D animation program. But wait! It's also a video editor. And a Python programming IDE. And a sculpting interface, a compositor, a motion tracker, and so much more. A nutshell is insufficient; Blender needs more of a watermelon to cover all its features.

I remember my first experience with Blender. After years with the commercial program Maya, I was skeptical of how free software could compare, and learning 3D programs is rarely forgiving to newcomers. But every day I used Blender, I would discover an awesome killer feature Blender had that expensive commercial 3D animation software didn't. Then a new update for Blender would launch, and the new features and workflows would leave me floored again.

Over the years, I've met so many Blender users who retell this story in their own words. The conclusion is generally the same: we can't believe how lucky we are that such phenomenal software exists, free for everyone, and supported by a robust open source community. The energy is infectious, and long-time Blender users talk about this magic piece of software with a passion usually reserved for wedding speeches.

We look forward to introducing you to Blender in this book. The chapters we've put together will help Blender beginners leap over the initial stumbling blocks of Blender's tools and interface. They'll also challenge your artistic and technical skills with advanced workflows to bring your imagination to life.

Who this book is for

This book assumes that you have a decent familiarity with computers. You should have some rudimentary skills at using a mouse and keyboard, navigating the internet, and know your way around your computer's operating system. You'll also need some grasp of your hardware. Tools such as a keyboard with a number pad, a mouse with three buttons, and a powerful CPU and GPU are helpful, but you can make some decent Blender projects using even a bare bones netbook.

Maybe you have some knowledge of other 3D programs, such as ZBrush, Maya, Cinema4D, or SketchUp. Maybe you're looking to learn Blender because the price tag appeals, the newest features blow you away, or a professional client wants you working with their Blender-centric pipeline. You'll find many concepts that have equivalencies to those programs. You can gloss over the explanations of 3D vocabulary, such as polygons, normals, and rigs, and instead jump right into Blender's tools and workflows.

For those of you who enjoy gaming, that experience will also pay off when learning Blender. Just like many AAA games, Blender's interface is heavily based on keyboard shortcuts, and navigating the 3D viewport is similar to moving the view around in games. Additionally, Blender is an excellent choice for any gamers looking to create content for their favorite game's custom mod community.

If you're more inclined toward coding, you might have experience with a game engine, such as Unity, Unreal, or Godot. This book will serve as an excellent expansion to your technical skills, showing you how to make 3D content to add to games. This book will also give you a foundation in understanding how these 3D components work, which will come in handy if you ever build out your own 3D tools.

Artists of every stripe can find their new favorite tool in Blender. Blender's 2D animation tools are perfect for artists who love drawing, anime, and experimental media. Especially when combined with Blender's native 3D interface, plus a drawing tablet, Blender has everything you need for both 3D and hand-drawn cartoons.

Whether you're completely new to Blender, or a 3D animation veteran enticed by Blender's newest features, this book will have something for you.

What this book covers

Chapter 1, *Introduction to 3D and the Blender User Interface*, explains the basics of Blender's interface, tools, and workflow conventions.

Chapter 2, *Editing a Viking Scene with a Basic 3D Workflow*, will take a look at a 3D scene and let us get used to navigating and transforming objects.

Chapter 3, *Modeling a Time Machine – Part 1*, is the beginning of a two-part project in which we will model an object based on provided reference images. We will cover many of the essential modeling tools needed for creating 3D objects.

Chapter 4, *Modeling a Time Machine – Part 2*, is the second half of the time machine project. We will build on our modeling knowledge and discover non-destructive workflows.

Chapter 5, *Modern Kitchen – Part 1: Kitbashing*, will show how to plan a complete scene and model the necessary assets to complete a kitchen layout.

Chapter 6, *Modern Kitchen – Part 2: Materials and Textures*, is a deep dive into material nodes and explains how to create all kinds of materials to decorate our kitchen with.

Chapter 7, *Modern Kitchen – Part 3: Lighting and Rendering*, is the final chapter in the kitchen series. We will produce a final rendered image complete with lighting and post-processing effects.

Chapter 8, *Illustrating an Alien Hero with Grease Pencil*, is the first of our three chapters that dives into the brand new feature set known as Grease Pencil. We will learn about character concept art workflows and how to use the basics of Grease Pencil.

Chapter 9, *Animating an Exquisite Corpse in Grease Pencil*, builds on the previous chapter's workflows and dives into animation and key frames with a loose and fun animation style.

Chapter 10, *Animating a Stylish Short with Grease Pencil*, wraps up the Grease Pencil projects in this book. We will cover more advanced workflows and explain how to animate something with more structure than the previous chapter.

Chapter 11, *Creating a Baby Dragon – Part 1: Sculpting*, is the beginning of the biggest project in this book. We'll start with an introduction to sculpting. We'll see an overview of the brushes and learn how to create our very own baby dragon design, which we will take all the way to a game-ready asset by the final chapter.

Chapter 12, *Creating a Baby Dragon – Part 2: Retopology*, is a shift into the more technical side of 3D character creation. We'll learn about shrink-wrapping, surface snapping, and rules of topology to transform the sculpted baby dragon into a low-poly mesh that can be used in a production pipeline.

Chapter 13, *Creating a Baby Dragon – Part 3: UV Unwrapping*, is where we'll prepare the model for texture painting. We'll learn how to cut seams, unwrap UVs, lay out islands, and use checker patterns to check for distortion.

Chapter 14, *Creating a Baby Dragon – Part 4: Baking and Painting Textures*, gets back to the artistic side of things. We'll start by baking texture maps that can be used as masks in our texture painting workflow. We'll use Blender's built-in texture painting tools, and we'll add some color and surface detail to the baby dragon.

Chapter 15, *Creating a Baby Dragon – Part 5: Rigging and Animation,* is the final baby dragon chapter. We'll get to see all of our hard work pay off and rig the dragon so that it can be posed and animated. To wrap it up, we'll animate a fly cycle so that we can see the character in action.

Chapter 16, *The Wide World of Blender,* shows off some of the areas that this book couldn't cover in detail. Even a book this size can barely scratch the surface of what a 3D suite such as Blender can do, but we'll have a look at some inspiring extra features before we're done.

To get the most out of this book

You will need an internet connection to download the latest version of Blender and the source files for this project (an internet connection is not required after downloading the software and the files).

Blender can be downloaded from `https://www.blender.org/download` and requires about 400 MB of storage space to install. The project files in this book are approximately 2.65 GB all together (you do not need to download them all at once). There are some projects that require additional software for digital painting / image editing such as Krita, GIMP, Affinity Photo, or Photoshop. We recommend Krita because it's free and open source, just like Blender! It can be downloaded from `https://krita.org/en/download/krita-desktop/`. The download for Krita is approximately 100 MB. It's a good idea to have at least 4 GB of additional free storage so that you can create your own 3D sculptures and texture files for the projects. In total, about 7 GB of space will be enough for everything covered in this book.

The version of Blender used in this book requires a computer that supports OpenGL 3.3. You can find the official hardware requirements on the Blender website here: `https://www.blender.org/download/requirements/` This book has been tested for the Blender 2.8 series of releases. The upcoming 2.9 and 3.0 series of releases may have different hardware requirements.

Blender works best on a computer that has a numpad because the camera navigation hotkeys are bound the numpad keys. This book uses an alternative method to teach these controls since many laptops do not have a numpad, so it is not absolutely required.

A drawing tablet with pressure sensitivity is highly recommended for the Grease Pencil projects as well as the sculpting and texturing chapters in the Baby Dragon project. There are affordable options available from `http://www.huion.com/`, premium options on offer from `https://www.wacom.com/`, or if you have a computer with a built-in stylus such as a Microsoft Surface that will work nicely as well. It is possible to complete these chapters using a mouse, but it is not recommended.

Software/Hardware covered in the book	OS requirements
Blender 2.83	Windows 10, 8.1, and 7 macOS 10.12+ Linux
Krita 4.2.9	Windows 8.1 or higher, OSX 10.12, Linux

Blender and Krita are open source and receive updates several times a year. There may be new versions available if you're picking up this book even a few months after it's published, but don't worry. The projects in this book should still be compatible.

Download the example code files

You can download the example code files for this book from your account at www.packt.com. If you purchased this book elsewhere, you can visit www.packtpub.com/support and register to have the files emailed directly to you.

You can download the code files by following these steps:

1. Log in or register at www.packt.com.
2. Select the **Support** tab.
3. Click on **Code Downloads**.
4. Enter the name of the book in the **Search** box and follow the onscreen instructions.

Once the file is downloaded, please make sure that you unzip or extract the folder using the latest version of:

- WinRAR/7-Zip for Windows
- Zipeg/iZip/UnRarX for Mac
- 7-Zip/PeaZip for Linux

The project files for the book are also hosted on GitHub at https://github.com/PacktPublishing/Blender-3D-By-Example-Second-Edition. In case there's an update to the project files, it will be updated on the existing GitHub repository.

We also have other code bundles from our rich catalog of books and videos available at https://github.com/PacktPublishing/. Check them out!

Download the color images

We also provide a PDF file that has color images of the screenshots/diagrams used in this book. You can download it here: https://static.packt-cdn.com/downloads/ 9781789612561_ColorImages.pdf.

Conventions used

There are a number of text conventions used throughout this book.

CodeInText: Indicates code words in text, database table names, folder names, filenames, file extensions, pathnames, dummy URLs, user input, and Twitter handles. Here is an example: "Rename it Top."

Bold: Indicates a new term, an important word, or words that you see onscreen. For example, words in menus or dialog boxes appear in the text like this. Here is an example: "Choose **Delete | Faces**."

 Warnings or important notes appear like this.

 Tips and tricks appear like this.

Get in touch

Feedback from our readers is always welcome.

General feedback: If you have questions about any aspect of this book, mention the book title in the subject of your message and email us at customercare@packtpub.com.

Errata: Although we have taken every care to ensure the accuracy of our content, mistakes do happen. If you have found a mistake in this book, we would be grateful if you would report this to us. Please visit www.packtpub.com/support/errata, selecting your book, clicking on the Errata Submission Form link, and entering the details.

Piracy: If you come across any illegal copies of our works in any form on the Internet, we would be grateful if you would provide us with the location address or website name. Please contact us at copyright@packt.com with a link to the material.

If you are interested in becoming an author: If there is a topic that you have expertise in and you are interested in either writing or contributing to a book, please visit authors.packtpub.com.

Reviews

Please leave a review. Once you have read and used this book, why not leave a review on the site that you purchased it from? Potential readers can then see and use your unbiased opinion to make purchase decisions, we at Packt can understand what you think about our products, and our authors can see your feedback on their book. Thank you!

For more information about Packt, please visit packt.com.

Introduction to 3D and the Blender User Interface

1

Welcome to the wonderful world of 3D graphics! This section of this book will help you jump-start your knowledge with some terminology and the basics of working in 3D. We'll keep this brief and try to get through the boring stuff as quickly as possible so you can get right into creating amazing 3D projects in Blender 2.8!

Blender 2.8 is a series of releases. There is usually an update for the software every 3 to 4 months. The first release in the series was 2.80, then 2.81, 2.82, and so on. The projects in this book can be completed with version 2.80 onward, with some optional features requiring 2.81 onward. You can read more about Blender's release cycle here: `blender.org/download/releases`.

First, we will take a look at the fundamentals of a 3D scene. We will learn how the 3D coordinate system uses three dimensional axes, as well as how 3D objects are manipulated with transformations. We will answer some basic questions, such as: what are objects? What are polygons? What is topology? What are materials and textures? What is the difference between Perspective and Orthographic views? The answers to these questions are key to working with any 3D software.

After we've provided you with some general 3D knowledge, we will learn about the specifics of Blender. We will cover how to install the software, as well as how to download the source files for this book. We will take a look at Blender 2.8's user interface. Then, we will learn about the basic 3D navigation controls, which include Rotate, Zoom, and Pan. We will also learn how to use Blender's hotkeys effectively. At the end of this chapter, we will provide an overview of the projects in this book.

We will cover the following topics in this chapter:

- Overview of the 3D workflow
- Blender 2.8's user interface
- Basic 3D navigation controls
- A brief introduction to the projects in this book

Overview of the 3D workflow

If this is your first time working with 3D software, you'll find the explanations in this section very helpful. However, if you are already familiar with 3D terminology and the composition of a 3D scene, then you may want to skip ahead to the next section of this chapter.

Some of the vocabulary terms you're about to learn might sound overwhelming at first, but don't worry – you don't have to be good at math just because we use words such as "geometry" to describe our 3D models. Luckily for us, the software does all of the complex math for us, and we get to sit back and create art without having to worry about it – hooray!

The 3D coordinate system

All 3D software uses the Cartesian coordinates system, which is made up of three-dimensional axes: the **X-Axis** (red), the **Y-Axis** (green), and the **Z-Axis** (blue). The exact unit size of this coordinate system is arbitrary and varies from one software package to another, but many packages set one unit on the grid to be equal to 1 meter in the real world:

 There is a special type of 3D software known as **Computer-Aided Design (CAD)**. This is used for engineering and conforms more closely to real-life units, but for the purposes of this book, we will not be discussing CAD software.

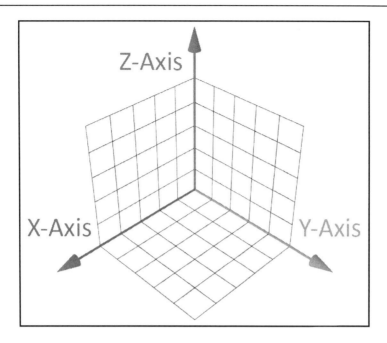

The three-dimensional axes: **X-Axis** (red), **Y-Axis** (green), and **Z-Axis** (blue)

With these three axes, we can define where an object is in a 3D space using **transforms**. There are three types of transforms:

- **Location**: (sometimes called **translation**) This determines the position of an object.
- **Rotation**: This determines the orientation of an object.
- **Scale**: This determines the size of an object.

Now that we understand the coordinate system, let's look at the 3D objects that will appear in the scene.

3D objects

An object is something that appears in a 3D scene. All objects have transforms that define their location, rotation, and scale in a 3D space. You will find several types of objects in a 3D scene:

- **Mesh**: A mesh is the most common type of object in 3D; nearly everything we make is a mesh. Meshes are 3D objects that are made up of components (sometimes referred to as the geometry of the mesh). These components are used to form geometric polygons. Polygons are the multi-sided shapes that form the visible surface of a model. Creating 3D models with this approach is called polygonal modeling.

- **Empty**: An empty is an object that doesn't have any components attached to it. Some software packages call these null objects or locators. These are useful in advanced workflows for defining and keeping track of an exact spot in a 3D space. Since an empty has transforms, it will be present in the 3D scene just like all other objects, but because it has no components, it will not be visible in the final result.

- **Light**: A light is a type of object that casts light onto the scene. Just like in the real world, you can't see without a light source. If a 3D scene had no light source, you would just see black. Most 3D software includes a light source in the scene by default so that you can see what you're doing. Often, these default lights are a type of environmental light or ambient light source that illuminates the scene without necessarily coming from a particular point in the scene.

- **Camera**: A camera is a tool that's used to create the final image from our 3D scene. We can use a 3D camera the same way we would use a camera in real life: position it, aim it at the subject, and take a picture. The picture we take with a 3D camera is called a render. Rendering creates a high-quality image of the scene. High-quality renders take much longer to process than the normal Viewport preview of the scene, so we don't usually render until we are finished creating the scene.

Now that we know what an object is, let's take a closer look at the most important type of object: a mesh. We need to understand how the components of a mesh come together to create a 3D model.

Components of a mesh

There are three basic components that we use in polygonal modeling:

- **Vertices**: The most basic piece of geometry is a vertex (the plural form is vertices). A vertex is a single point in 3D space. It has no size nor orientation; it only has a location within the mesh object. You can't do much with vertices alone, which is why we need edges.
- **Edges**: These are straight lines that are drawn between vertices, similar to a connect-the-dots puzzle. The edges that connect two points are always perfectly straight in polygonal modeling.
- **Faces**: The visible part of a polygon. Faces are created by filling in the space between three or more edges.

The following diagram shows the vertices, edges, and faces of a 3D model:

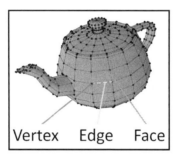

The three basic components of a mesh

Polygons can have any number of sides; three sides make up a **triangle** (**tri**), while four sides make up a **quadrilateral** (**quad**). There are lots of fancy names for specific polygons with more than four sides, such as pentagon, hexagon, and so on, but in the world of 3D modeling, any polygon with more than four sides is simply referred to as an **n-gon**. The following image shows some of the basic polygons you'll come across:

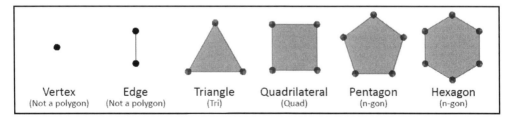

Vertex, edge, tri, quad, and n-gons

The way in which these components are connected is referred to as **topology**, a subject that we will cover in depth later in this book. There are many best practices and rules for creating a mesh with good topology. The most basic rule of topology is that quadrilaterals are the best type of polygon, triangles should be used sparingly, and n-gons should be avoided altogether. Models that don't follow the rules of good topology usually have problems in the final result. Topology is a very large and advanced subject, so we won't go into any more detail about it in this chapter.

Materials and textures

We can add color to our 3D models with a mixture of materials and textures. Materials are used to determine how light behaves when it interacts with the surface of the object. Does it look like glass? Metal? Skin? Textures are 2D images that are wrapped onto a 3D model, sort of like a candy wrapper. To make our textures line up with the model, we have to unwrap the model first. Unwrapping gives us a 2D representation of the model called a UV map (or UVs). An example of this can be seen in the following image:

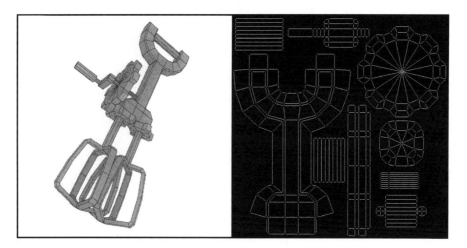

The 3D model on the left has been unwrapped to create the UVs on the right.

Once we have UVs, we can paint a texture that will be wrapped back onto the model, as shown here:

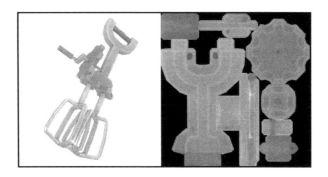

The 3D model on the left has been given a texture from the 2D image on the right

They are called UVs because all of the pieces have a U coordinate and a V coordinate, which are used to determine their positions in 2D space (very similar to graphing data on a 2D graph). Since we already used X, Y, and Z for our three-dimensional axes, our two-dimensional axes are labeled U and V. We will cover UVs, materials, and textures in detail in later chapters.

Perspective view versus Orthographic view

3D scenes can be displayed in Perspective mode or in Orthographic mode. In Perspective mode, objects are drawn with a vanishing point. As objects get farther away from us, they look smaller, which is the way things look in real life. In Orthographic mode, however, objects stay the same size no matter how far away they are from us. In this mode, everything looks flat and close together. This can be useful for making blueprints or architectural renders, but usually, we keep the view in Perspective mode because it looks more natural:

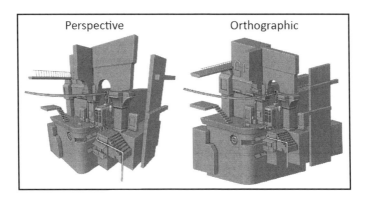

Perspective versus Orthographic

So there it is – your first introduction to 3D! We've covered a lot of new ideas in a short time, but they will all become second nature to you once you've spent a little time working on 3D projects. Next, we'll take a look at Blender's user interface.

Blender's user interface

You can download the latest version of Blender at `http://blender.org/download`. At the time of writing, the latest version is Blender 2.83. Blender is available on Windows, macOS, and Linux. It is a very similar experience on all three operating systems.

 Most of Blender's hotkeys are the same between operating systems. However, if you are following along with this book using a Mac, you need to use the *command* (*cmd*) key instead of the *control* (*ctrl*) key any time the instructions say to use the control key.

Before we learn about the current version of the user interface, it's useful to know a little bit about Blender's history. There is over a decade's worth of tutorials and resources available online. The software may look a bit different in those old resources, but if you can get past the old interface, the information is just as helpful as it always was, so let's take a look.

A brief history of Blender's user interface

Blender's **user interface** (**UI**) was very polarizing in the past. Older versions of Blender required the user to memorize dozens of hotkeys before it was possible to accomplish even basic tasks, which meant that many users found this hard to use. However, those were the days of Blender 2.49, and when Blender was updated to version 2.50, the UI got its first major facelift, which added many new features, more buttons, and a cleaner user experience.

Each release of Blender increments the version number by +0.01, which means 2.80 is 30 versions newer than 2.50 – that's a lot of versions! Many of these versions simply added small new features and bug fixes, but version 2.80 is just as big of an overhaul from version 2.79 as 2.50 was from version 2.49.

The original Blender included most of the basic requirements for a 3D modeling suite: 3D modeling, rigging, animating, and its internal "Blender Render" rendering engine. The earliest versions of the software were infamous for missing features such as undo and warning the user that data might be lost if they exited the program without saving first.

Its bright white UI with horizontal buttons, excessive use of tabs, and odd coloration was criticized by many users, but nevertheless, it was responsible for some amazing Open Movie projects such as "Elephant's Dream" and "Big Buck Bunny":

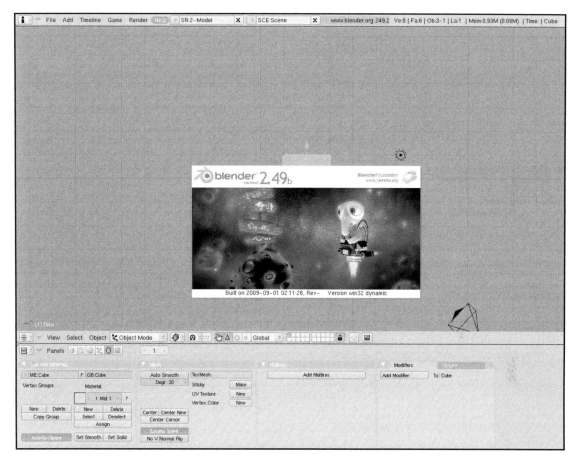

The UI for Blender 2.49

When Blender 2.50 rolled around, the UI was changed radically in response to user feedback. The Open Movie "Sintel" was created alongside the development of this new version to make sure that it included all of the features required for animation production. The 2.5 series of releases continued to introduce amazing features such as Cycles, the ray tracing rendering engine; the bMesh modeling system, which overhauled all of the modeling tools and allowed users to use n-gons; the new dynamic topology sculpting tools; and much more.

It quickly became a formidable modeling suite and gained popularity as the software grew all the way through to version 2.79:

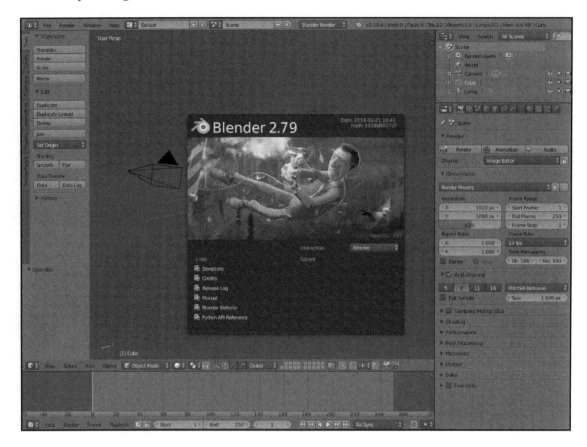

The UI for Blender 2.79

Finally, the 2.8 series came around. This highly anticipated release was in development for over 3 years and overhauled many of the underlying systems that were starting to show their age. The result was a stable, fast, customizable, and user-friendly experience that provided all the modern features you would expect in a modeling suite:

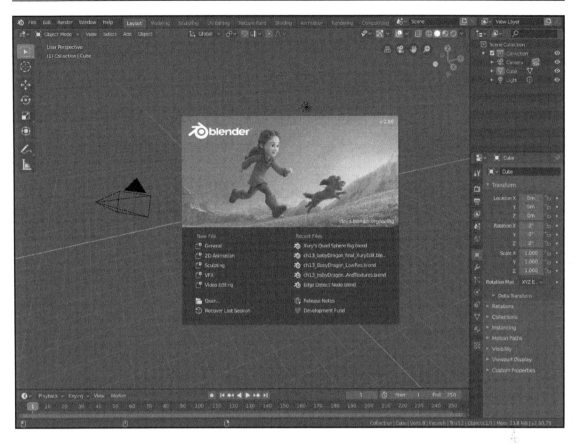

The UI for Blender 2.80

This is an excellent time to learn Blender! The Blender 2.8 series of releases comes with massive improvements to the software, among other things. The user interface has received several updates that will make it more user-friendly than ever before! There has especially been a focus on making it more accessible to new users (that's you!).

So, there's your brief history lesson on Blender's UI. Now, let's break the UI down into its different sections and learn how to use it!

Blender 2.8's user interface

When you first launch Blender, you will see the Splash Screen. This screen will show you what version of Blender you are using. It will display a piece of artwork made with Blender, and it will let you open project files that you've recently been working with:

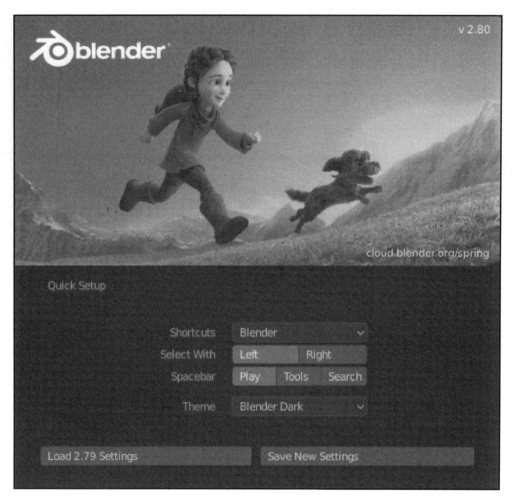

The Splash Screen for Blender 2.80

If this is your first time launching Blender 2.8, it will also ask you to choose which mouse button you would like to select objects with: left or right.

In previous versions of Blender, the default was to select objects in the Viewport with the right mouse button. Many users found this strange, so in 2.8, the new default is to use a left-click to select objects (you can change this at any time through the user preferences menu).

Believe it or not, right-click is more ergonomic in this context; your hand won't get as tired if you use right-click to select. It sounds weird, but you should give it a try! From this point on in this book, selecting objects will simply be referred to as "click to select" so that you can follow along with either a left-click select or right-click select.

When you're finished with the Splash Screen, click anywhere outside of it to dismiss it.

Blender's UI is highly customizable. By default, it is broken up into six distinct areas, as highlighted and numbered in the following image:

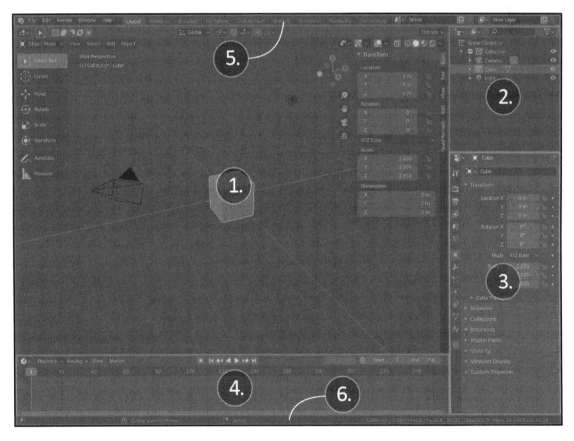

Blender's user interface, broken down into six areas

The four largest areas in the center of the UI are called **editors**. Each editor presents us with a specific way of visualizing our 3D project. There are many types of editors, but these four are open in the default workspace:

1. **3D Viewport**: The 3D Viewport is where we will be spending most of our time. It is our window onto the 3D scene. Nearly all of our 3D modeling is done here.

2. **Outliner**: The Outliner lists all of the objects in the project and helps us organize our scene.

3. **Properties**: The Properties panel contains the render settings and lets us add advanced modifiers, constraints, particles, physics, and materials to our 3D models.

4. **Timeline**: The Timeline is useful when we start animating. It keeps track of playback options and keyframes.

    Blender 2.8 includes two new major pieces of the UI: the Top Bar and the Status Bar. Most of the data that can be seen in these areas isn't new to Blender 2.8; it has just been reorganized into these two bars so that it is always visible:

5. **Top Bar**: The Top Bar is found at the very top of the user interface. The Blender logo can be seen at the top left. Clicking on it will give us the option to reopen the **Splash Screen**. The Top Bar includes the typical menu options that you'll find in most software, such as **File**, **Edit**, and so on. The most exciting feature on the Top Bar is the new Workspace presets, such as **Layout**, **Modeling**, **Sculpting**, and more. These tabs will allow us to quickly rearrange the UI for different workflows.

6. **Status Bar**: The Status Bar can be found at the very bottom of the user interface. It includes helpful hotkey reminders, tool options, a polygon count, and other useful information about the current file. Check here often for reminders of how tools work.

 In Blender 2.80, the Top Bar included a tool settings section. However, in version 2.81 and later, the tool settings have been consolidated into the header of the 3D Viewport.

We've broken down the latest version of the UI into its main sections, which means we're ready to take a look at basic navigation in the software.

Basic 3D navigation controls

The first thing you'll need to learn in any 3D software is how to navigate the 3D Viewport.

In Blender, the *X*-Axis is used for width, the *Y*-Axis is used for depth, and the *Z*-Axis is used for height. All 3D applications use the same colors for these axes; red for *X*, green for *Y*, and blue for *Z*.

 The *X*-Axis is always used for width in 3D software. However, some software such as Unity and Maya reverse the other two axes so that the *Y*-Axis is used for height and the *Z*-Axis is used for depth.

The 3D Viewport is where you will be spending the majority of your time in any 3D software, and Blender is no exception. We will need a three-button mouse to be able to navigate the 3D Viewport properly (pressing the scroll wheel down acts as a middle mouse button). The **Middle Mouse Button** (**MMB**) is used for three fundamental navigation controls:

- **Rotate** (sometimes referred to as **Orbit**): Click and hold *MMB* and drag the mouse to rotate the view.
- **Zoom** (sometimes called **Dolly**): Scroll with the *scroll wheel* to zoom in and out. If you want more precision, you can hold down the *Control* key (abbreviated to *Ctrl*) and then click and hold *MMB* and drag to zoom in and out.
- **Pan** (sometimes referred to as **Slide** or **Move**): Hold down the *Shift* key and then click and hold MMB and drag to pan the view.

If you ever forget these controls, you can always look at the Status Bar at the bottom of the screen. There, you will see reminders of these hotkeys. Alternatively, in Blender 2.8, there is a new navigation gizmo at the top-right corner of the 3D Viewport. This gizmo is particularly useful if you're using Blender with a drawing tablet or any other device with a stylus instead of a mouse:

The new navigation gizmo, along with a few helpful navigation controls

Navigating in 3D space can take some getting used to, but it is essential that you practice these controls. Every 3D project will require you to be constantly using a combination of rotate, zoom, and pan.

As long as we're talking about the essentials, let's give a quick mention to how to use Blender's hotkeys effectively. You will need to learn several important keyboard shortcuts, or hotkeys. The hotkeys in Blender only work correctly if your mouse cursor is hovering over the appropriate window when you press them.

Most of the hotkeys covered in this book are for the 3D Viewport, which means you need to make sure that your mouse is hovering over the 3D Viewport when you press a hotkey. Otherwise, the hotkeys won't do what you expect them to do.

So, now you know the basic navigation controls in Blender. You will need to know these controls before you can follow along with the projects in this book. Speaking of which, up next, we'll have a quick look at the projects in this book!

A brief introduction to the projects in this book

This book offers a wide variety of projects, so there's something for everyone: you'll start by adding horns to a Viking helmet. Then, you'll kick it up a notch by building a time machine. After that, you'll try your hand at architecture by modeling and rendering a modern kitchen in the EEVEE **physically-based rendering (PBR)** engine. Next, you'll explore 2D character design techniques with Blender's brand-new Grease Pencil tool. You'll practice 2D animation by creating a free-form surreal transformation animation, learn advanced Grease Pencil animation techniques by creating a fun 2D animated short, and finally jump back into the world of fantasy by creating a baby dragon. It is recommended that you go through these chapters in order, but you can try skipping ahead to some of the later projects if they sound more interesting to you. Here are the projects, in order:

- **Viking Helmet**: In this project, you'll dive right into Blender 2.8 and get a feel for the 3D workflow. You'll start with a scene of Viking-themed items, including a helmet that's been partially created. You'll add a nose guard, rivets, and horns to the helmet, and then place the helmet on the head of a training dummy to make a completed scene.
- **Time Machine:** Starting from scratch this time, you'll build a time machine. You'll learn about modeling tools, creating new objects, the modifier stack, and fixing shading issues in a 3D mesh.

- **Modern Kitchen:** With this project, you'll learn how to assemble a scene from premade parts to create custom materials and lighting to turn a boring grey scene into a fully rendered gorgeous final shot in the new EEVEE rendering engine.
- **Illustrating an Alien Hero with Grease Pencil:** You will design a character with the powerful new Grease Pencil tool and learn how to draw 2D images inside of a 3D scene.
- **2D Surreal Transformation Animation:** This will be your first introduction to animation, you don't have to have fantastic drawing skills for this one. You'll learn about frames and materials in Blender's Grease Pencil tool.
- **Animating a Stylish Short**: Taking your 2D skills to the next level, you'll learn how to animate a short film from start to finish.
- **Baby Dragon:** This is one of the biggest projects in this book, but don't let that scare you – you'll start off with one of the most artistic and fun parts of the 3D process: sculpting! By the end you'll have a finished character that can be used for animations and video games.

Now that we know what projects will be covered in this book, let's have a look at how to get the starter files for the projects.

Setting up the source files

This book comes with project files that you can use to follow along with each chapter. Please check the *Download the example code files* section of this book's Preface to learn how to access the project files.

There are a variety of file formats in these source files. Blender projects are labeled with the `.blend` suffix. The `.blend` files store data such as objects, materials, collections, scripts, and more. Basically, your whole project is stored inside of this single file. One exception, however, is image files. It is possible to store images inside of `.blend` files, but image files take up a lot of space on your computer, so this would make each project file huge.

By default, Blender saves projects with a relative file path, which means as long as you don't move the `.blend` file or the linked texture files out of their appropriate folders, Blender will know where the files are and everything will work properly when you open a project.

Summary

In this chapter, you learned how 3D software works and in particular, Blender. You learned the basics of the three-axis coordinate system, as well as how transforms are used to place objects in a 3D scene. You also got a glimpse of Blender's UI and looked at the list of projects that will be covered in this book.

These concepts will be the foundation of your 3D knowledge. There are so many possibilities that there's something for everyone! You can model, create materials, paint textures, sculpt, render, and much more! To learn more about Blender's features, have a look at the features page on the Blender website at: `blender.org/features`.

Now, you're ready for your first 3D project! In the next chapter, you'll be provided with a small scene full of Viking themed objects. You'll get to position objects in the scene and make some edits and additions to a Viking helmet. See you there!

Editing a Viking Scene with a Basic 3D Workflow

2

In this chapter, you'll get your first taste of the 3D workflow. Now that we've covered some basic 3D terminology, we can learn the navigation controls, menus, and a few modeling tools. Whether you're new to 3D or you've used other 3D software before, this chapter will help you get an idea of how things are done in Blender 2.8.

Many of the 3D modeling concepts we're about to learn are interdependent on one another. It would be difficult and very slow to learn in order of the smallest features to the largest features. If we take things too slowly, you'll be so bored that you'll fall asleep before getting to do anything exciting, so we're going to keep things moving. If this chapter seems like it's going fast, don't worry; we will break down these concepts in more detail in subsequent chapters.

Once we've finished the boring textbook stuff, we'll dive right in and work on our first project in Blender 2.8! This project is a little Viking themed scene with a training dummy, arrows, and most importantly, a Viking helmet! We'll get some practice transforming objects by sticking the arrows into the dummy's chest, and we'll really have some fun by adding horns and other features to the Viking helmet.

In this chapter, we will cover the following topics:

- Setting up the source files
- Using the Outliner to organize a scene
- Navigating the 3D Viewport
- Using the Toolbar
- Basic transformations in Object Mode
- Editing the Viking helmet
- Rendering the final image

Setting up the source files

For this project, you'll need the files from `Blender3DByExample_Chapter02.zip`, which can be downloaded here: `https://github.com/PacktPublishing/Blender-3D-By-Example-Second-Edition`. Download and unzip the folder. You should now have a directory called `Blender3DByExample_Chapter02` that contains the starting project file and a folder that contains all of the texture files that are required:

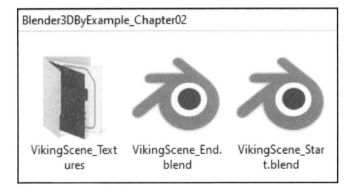

Example of the unzipped directory

Blender saves projects in a proprietary format called `.blend` – these files store everything you need for a 3D scene: models, animations, lights, you name it! `.blend` files can also include image textures, though most 3D artists choose to keep the texture files separate so that the `.blend` file will take up less room on the computer. For this chapter, the textures can be found inside the `VikingScene_Textures` folder, as you can see here:

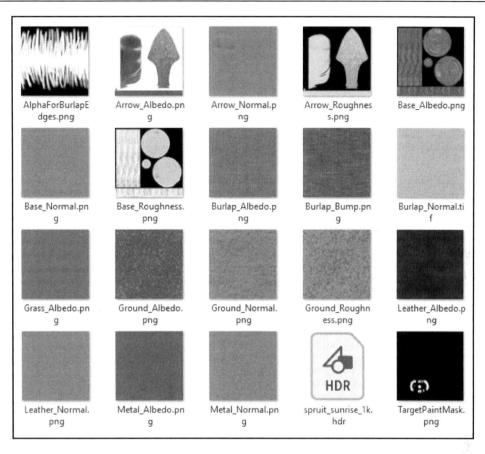

You'll find these files in the VikingScene_Textures folder

 Always keep the texture files in their original folder. Blender looks for texture files in specific locations. If the files aren't where Blender expects them to be, then they will be missing when the `.blend` file is opened. To find missing files, we can tell Blender where to look for them via the **File | External Data | Find Missing Files** option.

Now that we have our files, we can get started. Open the `VikingScene_Start.blend` file to begin this project. You can open a `.blend` file by dragging and dropping it into Blender, or by going to the **File** menu and choosing **Open**.... We will start by learning how to use the Outliner panel.

Using the Outliner to organize a scene

Welcome to your first Blender scene! We had a brief introduction to the user interface in Chapter 1, *Introduction to 3D and the Blender User Interface*, but now we can see it with our own eyes. The largest area of the UI is dedicated to the 3D Viewport (or just "Viewport" for short). You can see all of the 3D objects inside this area. This scene has been set to use the new Random Colors feature, which gives all of the objects false colors so that they are easier to identify in the Viewport, as shown in the following screenshot:

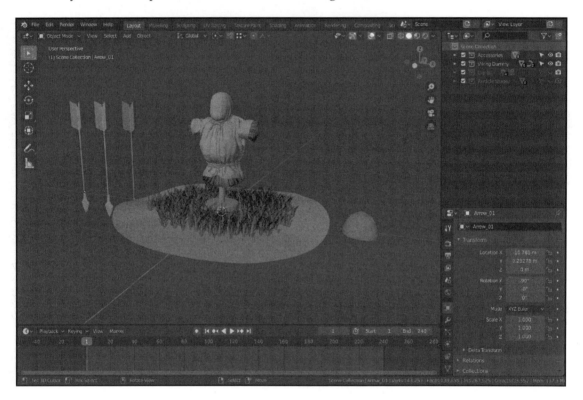

Objects in the VikingScene_Start.blend file with random colors

The random colors are helpful, but there is an even better way to discover the contents of a scene: the Outliner. The Outliner can be found in the top-right corner of the UI. Let's learn how to use it to our advantage.

We can look at the Outliner to get a sense of what's in this project file. The Outliner in Blender 2.8 has been upgraded with a new feature called Collections. Collections are similar to layers or groups in other applications. These collections are a very powerful feature as they can have any type of object grouped within them, including other collections.

Let's take a look at how this scene uses the Outliner to organize the objects. In the following screenshot, you can see that there are five collections in this `.blend` file; a top-level collection and four collections inside it:

Collections in the Outliner

The top-level collection is called **Scene Collection**. This is a default collection that contains everything else within the scene. The indentation in the Outliner shows that the bottom four collections are all grouped inside the **Scene Collection**.

Next to each collection are orange icons with little numbers that indicate how many of each type of object is inside them:

- **Accessories** has four mesh objects.
- **Viking Dummy** has six mesh objects and two curve objects.
- **Lights** has four light objects and one camera object.
- **Particle Shapes** has four mesh objects.

To the left of each collection is a little arrow that indicates that the collections are collapsed in the Outliner. Let's expand two of these collections to see the list of objects that belong to each collection:

1. Click on the little arrow to the left of the **Accessories** collection.
2. Click on the little arrow to the left of the **Viking Dummy** collection.

Good! Now, we can see the expanded hierarchy for each collection, as shown here:

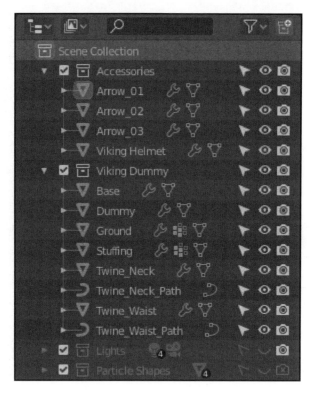

Expanded hierarchy

This Viking scene is relatively small with 21 objects in total, but it's still important to stay organized. Imagine working in a project that has hundreds of objects. The Outliner fills up really fast, so placing objects into collections is a terrific way to stay organized.

The bottom two collections are grayed-out because their visibility has been turned off. On the right-hand side of the Outliner, you can see three icons for each row, as shown in the following screenshot:

The three restriction toggle icons (the top row is the regular state, while the bottom row is the grayed-out state)

These three icons represent Restriction Toggles. From left to right, we have **Selectable**, **Hide in Viewport**, and **Disable in Renders**:

- When the **Selectable** toggle is set to its grayed-out state, the object can't be selected by clicking on it in the Viewport.
- When the **Hide in Viewport** toggle is set to its grayed-out state, the object can't be seen in the Viewport.
- When the **Disable in Renders** toggle is set to its grayed-out state, the object will not show up in the final image.

 Blender has many types of restriction toggles, but in this scene, we only have three available to us. To make more or fewer toggles appear in the Outliner, we can open the Filter pop-up menu, which we will learn about in the next project in this book.

The **Lights** collection has both its **Selectable** and **Hide in Viewport** toggles grayed-out so that the lights will not be in the way while we work in this scene. However, the **Disable in Renders** toggle has not been grayed-out, which means that the lighting will turn on for the final image.

The **Particle Shapes** collection is for storing objects that make up the particles, such as the grass on the ground and the straw that fills the dummy. Particles are an advanced feature, so don't worry about this for now – just know that this collection is still being used in the scene, even though all three of its toggles are grayed-out.

You may have noticed that the other objects in the Outliner also have little arrows and can be expanded. This is useful for advanced users because you can see all of the data associated with each object, similar to how we can see all of the objects associated with each collection. But let's not get ahead of ourselves – you're probably itching to get into the 3D scene!

Navigating the 3D Viewport

3D navigation is essential when working on any project in Blender, so let's practice what we learned in the *Basic 3D Navigation Controls* section of `Chapter 1`, *Introduction to 3D and the Blender User Interface*, before learning one more very important navigation feature.

As we have already learned, Blender's 3D navigation controls are all about using the **middle mouse button** (**MMB**). Let's start by rotating the view:

1. Move your mouse into the 3D Viewport.
2. Press and hold the middle mouse button.
3. Drag your mouse around to rotate the viewing angle.

Notice that the focal point of the view is focused on the Viking dummy in the center. When we rotate, our view always orbits around the current focal point. We'll see why this is important after we practice our other controls.

 By default, Blender uses a Turntable style for Viewport rotations. If you're more comfortable with a Trackball style, you can go to **Edit | Preferences**. Go to the **Navigation** tab, then set **Orbit Method** to **Trackball**.

Once you're comfortable with orbiting the Viking dummy, let's try panning:

1. Make sure the mouse is still in the 3D Viewport.
2. Hold down the *Shift* key, then press and hold the middle mouse button.
3. Drag your mouse around to pan the view.

Panning shifts the focal point of the Viewport. If we rotate the view now, we will orbit around the new focal point. Both orbiting and zooming are relative to the focal point. Let's give zooming a shot now:

1. Once again, make sure the mouse is in the 3D Viewport.
2. Hold down the *Ctrl* key, then press and hold the middle mouse button.
3. Drag your mouse up and down to zoom in and out.

 A second method for zooming is to simply scroll up and down on the scroll wheel. Either method works, but you may have smoother control by using the first method.

As we rotate, pan, and zoom around the scene, the focal point of the Viewport will inevitably get stuck in an awkward position. Eventually, navigating the Viewport will become very difficult and frustrating. This is a common issue in all 3D software.

To fix this issue, we can choose an object that we want to focus on, then frame it by using the **View Selected** feature (also known as the **Frame Selected** feature). First, we'll pick an object that we want to work with:

1. Select the **Dummy** object by clicking on it in the 3D Viewport or in the Outliner.

The object will have an orange outline in the Viewport to indicate that it is selected. Now, we need to frame it. There are many ways to do this, but Blender 2.8 has a new pie menu that we can use for easy Viewport navigation.

2. Move the mouse over the 3D Viewport so that the keyboard shortcuts behave correctly.
3. Press the *Tilde* key (~) to bring up the **View** pie menu.

 The tilde key can be found in the top-left of the keyboard, directly beneath the *Escape* key on most keyboards.

The **View** pie menu is one of many pie menus in Blender 2.8. When activated, pie menus bring up a quick list of menu options in a circular pattern around the mouse, as shown in the following screenshot:

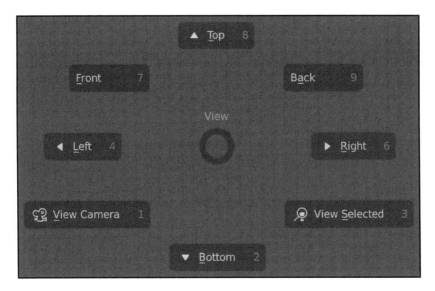

The View pie menu will appear when you press the tilde ~ hotkey

Each option on the pie menu takes up a slice of space around the mouse (like a slice of pie) and can be selected by simply moving your mouse in the direction of the menu option you want and then clicking.

We will become familiar with the other options of this pie menu later in this book, but for now, we just need the **View Selected** option:

1. Make sure the **View** pie menu is still open.
2. Move the mouse diagonally down and to the right to highlight the **View Selected** option.
3. Click while the **View Selected** option is highlighted.

The nice thing about pie menus is that you don't have to click directly on the menu option; all you have to do is aim the mouse in the general direction of the "slice" of the pie menu that you want and then click.

Pie menus are designed around speed, so if you're really, really fast, you don't even have to click! Press the key to open the pie menu, and while it's still opening, swipe the mouse in the direction of the menu option you want to choose.

Excellent – the Viewport's focal point has been reset so that the Dummy object is centered in the view. You should get familiar with using this navigation feature since it will come up over and over again in our workflow.

If you have a keyboard with a number pad, you can press the period key (.) on the number pad to activate the **View Selected** feature, without having to use the pie menu.

Play around with the navigation controls until you're comfortable with them – you'll be using them from here on out. Practice rotating, panning, and zooming. Try selecting different objects in the scene and use the **View Selected** option to frame them within the 3D Viewport. One more time, here are the navigation controls we covered:

- **Rotate**: MMB and drag
- **Zoom**: *Ctrl* + MMB and drag OR *scroll wheel*.
- **Pan**: *Shift* + MMB and drag.
- **View Selected**: *Tilde* ~ hotkey | **View Selected** OR period . on the number pad.

When you feel comfortable with these controls, you can move on to the next section of this chapter, where we'll have a look at Blender's new Toolbar.

Using the Toolbar

In Blender 2.8, there is a new user-friendly Toolbar attached to the left-hand side of the 3D Viewport. The Toolbar provides an assortment of large icons, with each icon representing a tool. By default, the Toolbar is collapsed into a single column, but we can expand it to show the names of all of the tools. Let's expand the Toolbar now:

1. Hover your mouse over the right-hand side edge of the Toolbar until your mouse turns into a double arrow.
2. Left-click and drag to the right to expand the Toolbar, as shown in the following screenshot:

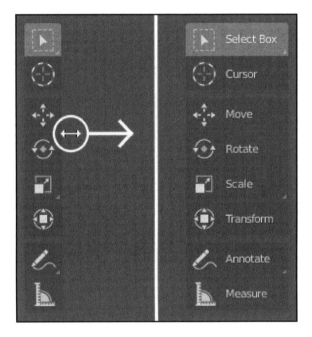

When the mouse is placed on the edge of the Toolbar, the cursor changes to the "Resize Horizontal" symbol

Now that the Toolbar has been expanded, let's learn about some of the tools.

The first tool in the Toolbar is the **Select Box** tool, which is highlighted in blue to indicate that it is active. When a tool is active, it can be used by clicking in the 3D Viewport with the **Left Mouse Button** (**LMB**). The **Select Box** tool lets us draw a box selection by clicking and dragging over multiple objects.

All of the tools on the Toolbar can be accessed with hotkeys for a faster workflow. To discover the keyboard shortcut for a tool, hover your cursor over the tool and wait for the tooltip to show up.

Directly beneath the **Select Box** tool is the **Cursor** tool. This will let us place the 3D cursor in the scene. You'll learn more about what the 3D cursor is and how to use it in the next project, so don't worry about it for now.

The next four tools are used for transformations: **Move**, **Rotate**, **Scale**, and **Transform**. The names of these tools should sound familiar from what we learned in the first chapter. Clicking on a tool in the Toolbar will activate it, and a gizmo will appear in the 3D Viewport. We use gizmos to interact with the tools from the Toolbar. The gizmos for the four transform tools are shown in the following image:

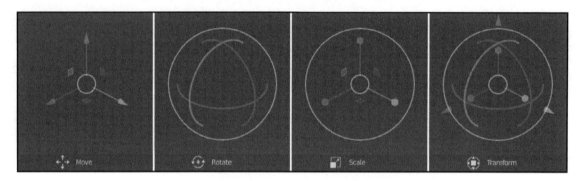

The Move, Rotate, Scale, and Transform gizmos

Let's learn more about these four gizmos:

- **Move**: The Move tool gizmo has three colored arrows, one for each axis (red for X, green for Y, and blue for Z). Clicking and dragging on these arrows will move the selected object.
- **Rotate**: The Rotate gizmo also has three colored handles, but this time they are shaped like semicircles instead of arrows. The colors still correspond to the same X, Y, and Z axes. Clicking and dragging on these semicircles will rotate the selected object.
- **Scale**: This gizmo looks almost identical to the Move gizmo but, instead of little arrows, the tips are shaped like little cubes. Clicking and dragging on these little cubes will scale the selected object.

- **Transform**: The Transform gizmo is just a combination of the previous three gizmos. Some users like to have all of these gizmos active at once, but it can be a little overwhelming.

The last few tools in the Toolbar are for advanced workflows, so we'll skip them for now. Next, we'll practice with the basic transformation tools by moving, rotating, and scaling the three arrow objects in the scene.

Basic transformations in Object Mode

Before we can edit the Viking helmet in this project, we need to practice using the transformation tools. We already learned how to activate tools, and we know what the gizmos look like, so now it's time to stick some arrows in the dummy!

1. Click on the **Move** tool in the Toolbar to activate it.
2. Select the `Arrow_01` object by clicking on it in the Outliner or in the 3D Viewport.
3. Press the tilde ~ key to bring up the **View** pie menu.
4. Choose the **View Selected** option to frame the arrow.
5. Rotate the view with the middle mouse button so that we can see the dummy in the middle of the scene, as shown in the following screenshot:

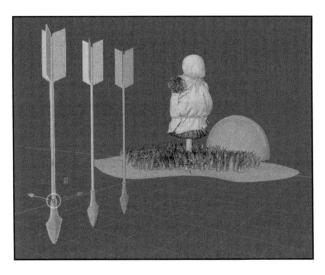

The Arrow_01 object has been selected and the Dummy object is visible

6. Left-click on the red axis arrow of the Move gizmo and drag it sideways toward the Dummy object.

7. Next, click and drag the green axis arrow of the gizmo to pull it toward the front of the Dummy object.

8. Finally, click and drag upward on the blue axis arrow to bring it up to the chest area of the Dummy object.

 As you move the arrow, you may need to refocus the view on it. Use the **View Selected** option as often as you need to.

When you're done moving the arrow along all three axes, the arrow should be positioned similarly to what's shown in the following screenshot:

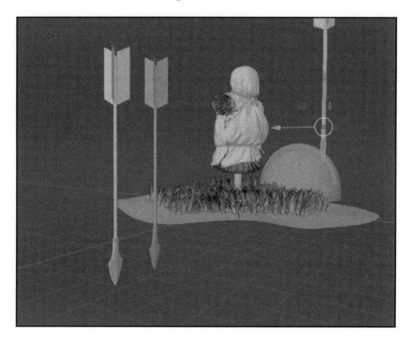

Arrow moved into position on all three axes

 Looks can be deceiving when working in 3D, so check your work from multiple viewing angles before moving on. The arrow might look like it's in place from this angle, but it could be askew.

Now that the arrow has been moved into position, it's time to rotate it. First, we'll frame the arrow in the view, and then we'll use the rotate tool:

1. Press the tilde ~ key to bring up the **View** pie menu.
2. Choose the **View Selected** option to frame the arrow.
3. Select the **Rotate** tool from the Toolbar.
4. Click and drag on the red axis of the rotation gizmo to aim the arrow at the dummy's chest, as shown in the following screenshot:

Arrow rotated along the red x-axis

This is looking good, but the arrow is way too big – it's an arrow, not a spear! Let's size it down with the Scale tool. When we scale objects, we usually want to scale along all three axes at once to keep the object's size proportional. Luckily, the scale tool makes this really easy as we can use the white circles of the gizmo. Let's give it a shot:

1. Click on the **Scale** tool in the Toolbar to activate it.
2. Hover your mouse over the Scale gizmo so that the gizmo's white circles light up.
3. Click and drag inward to make the arrow smaller.

That will do the trick! The arrow should now be a similar size to what you can see in the following screenshot:

Arrow scaled down to an appropriate size

Excellent! Now, we need to go back to the Move tool one last time and stick that arrow into the dummy's chest. Just like with the Scale tool, you can click on the Move gizmo's white circle to move the object along all three axes at once. Let's try this now:

1. Click on the **Move** tool in the Toolbar to activate it.
2. Rotate the view as needed so that we can move the Arrow_01 object toward the Dummy object.

3. Hover your mouse over the Move gizmo's white circle.

4. Click and drag the white circle toward the dummy until the tip of the `Arrow_01` object pierces the `Dummy` object, as shown in the following screenshot:

Bullseye!

Don't forget to rotate the Viewport frequently so that you can see what you're doing; if you only work from one viewing angle, you might not be placing objects correctly in the 3D space.

Good work, but there are two more arrows. Use what we just learned to finish placing all three arrows into the dummy's chest:

1. Select the `Arrow_02` object.
2. Press the tilde ~ key to bring up the **View** pie menu and choose the **View Selected** option.
3. Use the **Move** tool to move it in front of the dummy.
4. Use the **Rotate** tool to aim the arrow tip at the dummy.
5. Use the **Scale** tool to shrink the arrow down to a more appropriate size.
6. Use the **Move** tool again to stick the arrow in the dummy's chest.
7. Repeat these steps again for the `Arrow_03` object.

When you're finished placing the arrows, we can move on to editing the Viking helmet!

Editing the Viking helmet

Now that we've had some practice transforming objects, we're ready for the main event: editing the Viking helmet. This is the largest part of this chapter, so we'll break it down into a few small subsections, as follows:

- Preparing to work on the helmet
- Making changes to components in **Edit Mode**
- Adding the nose guard
- Adding the horns
- Adding the studs
- Returning to **Object Mode** to finish

We will begin by preparing to work on the helmet so that the rest of the objects in the scene don't get in the way.

Preparing to work on the helmet

Let's take a moment to prepare for working on the helmet. In a typical 3D workflow, we edit one object at a time. We can use a special view mode called Local View to temporarily hide all of the other objects in the scene. Let's do this now:

1. Select the `Viking Helmet` object.
2. Look at the header of the 3D Viewport and find the **View** menu at the top-left.

3. Click on the **View** menu to open it and choose **Local View** | **Toggle Local View**, as shown here:

View | Local View | Toggle Local View

 If you are using a computer that has a number pad, the hotkey to toggle the **Local View** is the slash (/).

4. Open the **Object** menu in the top-left of the 3D Viewport header.
5. Choose **Clear** | **Location**, as shown in the following screenshot:

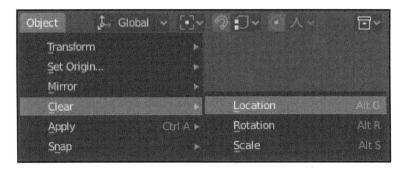

Object | Clear | Location

6. Press the tilde ~ key to bring up the **View** pie menu and choose the **View Selected** option to frame the helmet in the Viewport.

The clear location operation has moved the helmet to the center of the grid, which will make it easier to work on. Lastly, let's turn off the Random Colors so that we can see the helmet's material colors. We'll do this from the Viewport Shading pop-up menu:

1. Look at the header of the 3D Viewport and find the four circle-shaped icons in the top-right corner.
2. Click the little downward-facing arrow to the right of the four circles to open the **Viewport Shading** pop-up menu.
3. Change the **Color** option from **Random** to **Material** by clicking on the **Material** button, as shown in the following screenshot:

Viewport Shading I Color I Material

There are many ways to customize the Viewport's shading in Blender 2.8. At the end of this chapter, we'll take look at how powerful this feature can be for creating a final high-quality image. But for now, we're ready to make some changes to the Viking helmet!

Making changes to components in Edit Mode

The Viking helmet provided in this scene is already halfway done, but as we can see in the following screenshot, it's missing some details: a nose guard, pyramid studs, and horns. To add these features, we need to switch to a different Interaction Mode:

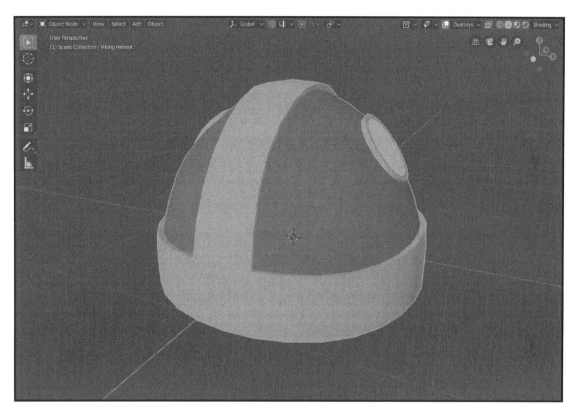

Viking Helmet in Object Mode

Blender has several interaction modes that provide us with different ways of editing our models. We can see which mode we are in by looking at the header of the 3D Viewport; at the moment, it says **Object Mode** because we have been in **Object Mode** up to this point. While we are in **Object Mode**, we can move objects around, rotate them, and scale them, but we can't make any changes to the components of the objects.

To edit the components of the `Viking Helmet` object, we need to switch to **Edit Mode**. **Edit Mode** is where we can edit the components that make up a mesh object. As you may recall from Chapter 1, the components of a mesh are vertices, edges, and faces. Let's switch to **Edit Mode**:

1. If it isn't already selected, select the `Viking Helmet` object.
2. Go to the header of the 3D Viewport and click on **Object Mode**.
3. Choose **Edit Mode** from the drop-down list:

The Interaction Mode drop-down list

 A faster way to enter **Edit Mode** is to use the *Tab* hotkey. In Blender, you will be switching between **Edit Mode** and **Object Mode** very often. Many Blender users refer to this as "Tab into **Edit Mode**," or simply "Tab in."

Once we enter **Edit Mode**, we'll see that several things have changed regarding the User Interface: the 3D Viewport header has several new options, the interaction mode now says **Edit Mode**, the Toolbar on the left contains several new tools, and the `Viking Helmet` object has dots and lines drawn all over it, as shown in the following screenshot:

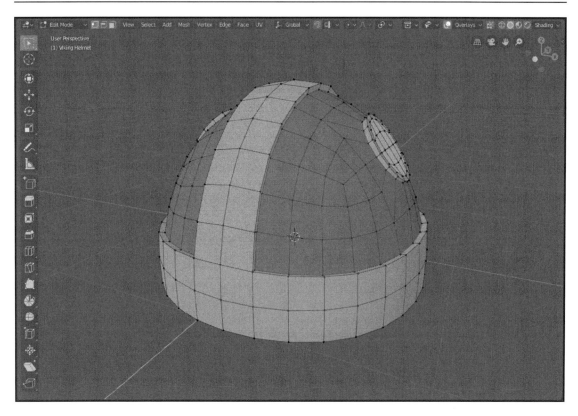

Viking Helmet in Edit Mode

These dots and lines are the vertices and edges that the mesh is made out of. While we are in this mode, we aren't limited to selecting the object as a whole; we can select the individual components instead. Take a look at the header of the 3D Viewport again. Next to where it says **Edit Mode**, you'll see three component selection types: **Vertex Select**, **Edge Select**, and **Face Select**. These are represented by the icons shown here:

Component selection modes

While we're in **Edit Mode**, we can switch between these selection modes by *clicking* on these three icons, or by pressing the *1*, *2*, and *3* hotkeys on the home row of the keyboard.

These selection modes provide us with flexibility in terms of the types of selections we can make, but they don't limit us to the types of operations we can perform on a mesh.

Most of the time, it doesn't matter which selection mode we use because when we have a face selected, all of its edges and vertices are also selected. It's even possible to activate all three selection modes at once by holding the *Shift* key before clicking on each icon. This can of course be overwhelming, so usually one at a time is enough.

We can also switch between the selection modes at any time. For example, we can make a selection in **Face Select** mode, then swap over to **Vertex Select** mode, and the selection will automatically be converted from a selection of faces into a selection of vertices (if possible).

There are a few edge cases (that's a pun) where we need to select edges but not faces, at which point **Edge Select** mode becomes very useful. But the rest of the time, we can use whichever selection mode works best for the task at hand.

We will switch between these three selection modes as needed while we're editing our models. Speaking of which, it's time to add a nose guard to the helmet!

Adding the nose guard

This is exciting! You're about to make your first edits to a 3D model in Blender! Adding the nose guard will give our little Viking dummy some much-needed protection, just like a proper helmet would!

To get started, we need to make a selection. Technically, we could use any of the three selection modes for this part, but face selection is the most efficient choice in this case:

1. Switch to face selection mode by pressing *3* on the home row of the keyboard, or by clicking the **Face Select** icon in the header of the 3D Viewport.

 Notice that the vertex dots disappear from the view because we are in face selection mode now.

2. Use the middle mouse button to rotate the view so that we can see the underside of the helmet, as shown in the following screenshot:

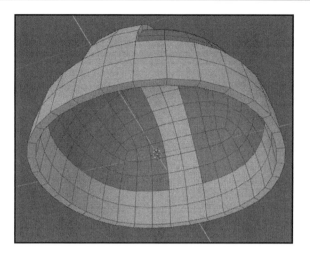

The underside of the helmet

3. Hold down the *Shift* key so that we can select multiple faces at once.
4. Click on the two faces that the nose guard will be attached to, as shown in the following screenshot:

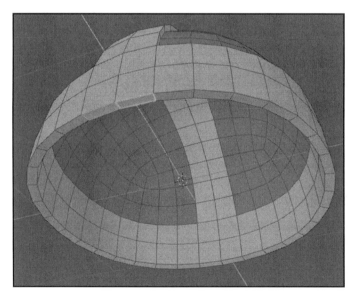

The nose guard will be added to the two faces shown here

Great – we've got our selection. To add the nose guard, we can use the most common tool in 3D modeling: **Extrude**. Extruding lets us pull new polygons out of the selected polygons. We do this very often in almost every 3D project. It's appropriate that the first modeling tool we get to use is Extrude because we will use it over and over again in the modeling workflow. There are several extrude tools in Blender, but the one we need is called **Extrude Region**. It looks like this in the Toolbar:

The Extrude Region tool as it appears in the Toolbar

Alright, let's start extruding:

1. Click on the **Extrude Region** tool on the Toolbar. The Extrude tool gizmo will appear, sticking out of the selected faces, as shown here:

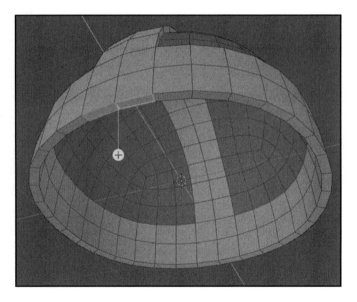

Select these polygons so we can extrude the nose guard

2. Click and drag downward on the gizmo's yellow plus (+) symbol to start creating the nose guard. Try to match the length shown in the following screenshot:

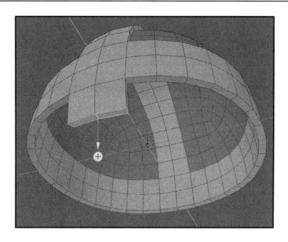

The first extruded segment of the nose guard

 New polygons will be created each time we use the yellow plus symbol. If you need to adjust the length of the extrusion, click and drag the yellow arrow part of the gizmo, NOT the plus symbol; otherwise, we'll end up with unneeded duplicate polygons, which is a common pitfall when learning to extrude.

3. Click and drag the plus symbol again to make a second extrusion. Try to match the length shown in the following screenshot:

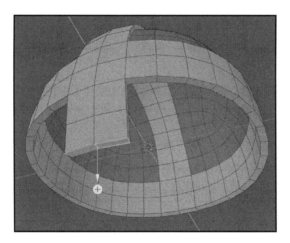

The second extruded segment of the nose guard

4. Select the face on the right-hand side of the newly extruded section.
5. Extrude the next piece of the nose guard, as shown in the following screenshot:

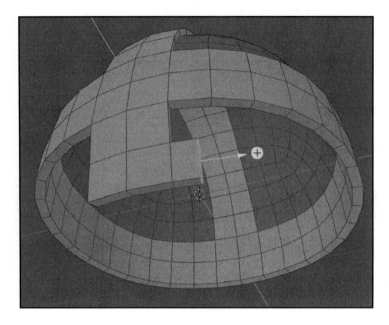

The third extruded segment of the nose guard

Looking good! Don't worry about the other side for now – we'll learn an easy way to make it symmetrical when we're finished with our other edits. We have all of the polygons that we need for the nose guard, but they aren't quite the right shape yet, so let's make some adjustments:

1. Activate the **Move** tool on the Toolbar.
2. Switch to **Edge Select** mode by pressing 2 on the keyboard, or by clicking the **Edge Select** icon in the header of the 3D Viewport.

 Notice that the edges appear slightly thicker than before to emphasize that we are in edge selection mode now.

3. Select the bottom-right corner edge of the nose guard.
4. Click and drag upward on the Move gizmo's blue arrow to raise the edge up along the Z-axis, as shown in the following screenshot:

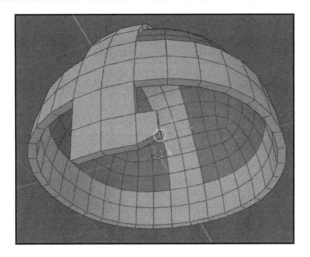

The edge of the nose guard raised up

5. Select the center edge at the bottom of the nose guard.
6. Click and drag the blue arrow downward to form the tip of the nose guard, as shown here:

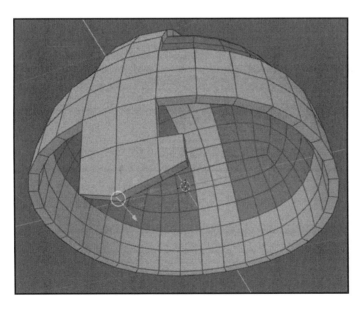

The tip of the nose guard

Awesome – now, we just need to make it symmetrical. There are several ways to make sure that our models stay symmetrical while we are making them. In this case, we did not turn on any of these features ahead of time... does that mean it's too late? Of course not! Never say never:

1. Go to the **Select** menu in the header of the 3D Viewport.
2. Choose **All** to select all of the Viking Helmet's components.
3. Go to the **Mesh** menu in the header of the 3D Viewport.
4. Choose **Symmetrize**:

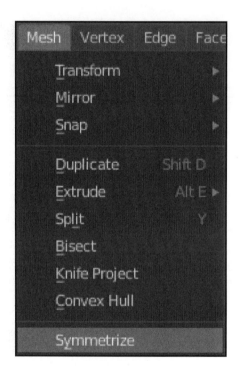

Mesh | Symmetrize

The **Symmetrize** operation should have left your model looking like this:

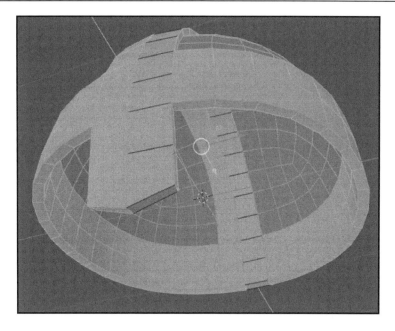

The default (backwards) result of the Symmetrize operation

It sort of worked... but it symmetrized the wrong side. To fix this, take a look at the bottom-left corner of the 3D Viewport. Here, you will see the **Adjust Last Operation** panel. You may have noticed this panel already. It appears every time we perform an operation such as extrude or move. In this case, it shows the **Symmetrize** operation that we just performed. Click on the little triangle next to the word **Symmetrize** to show the parameters for the operation:

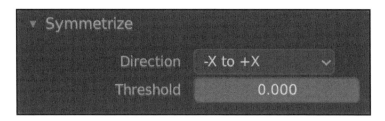

Adjust Last Operation panel displaying the Symmetrize operator

From this panel, we can adjust some options to get a different result:

1. Change the **Direction** from **-X to +X** to **+X to -X**.

The operator will now symmetrize the correct side of the helmet and complete the nose guard:

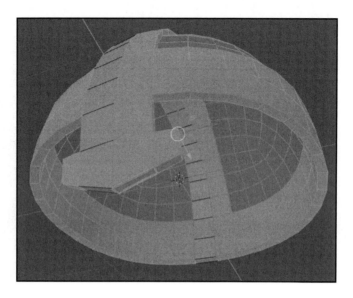

The final result of the Symmetrize operation

 You must change these parameters immediately after performing this operation. If you don't do this right away, the operator panel will disappear and you won't be able to change any of the options. If you make a mistake, undo with the *Ctrl + Z* hotkey, and then try the operation again.

Deselect everything so that we don't accidentally make unwanted changes to the selected parts. You can deselect by either clicking in the empty space near the helmet, or by pressing the *Alt + A* hotkey. Excellent! Now, our Viking helmet has a nose guard. Don't forget to rotate your view around to make sure it looks good from every angle. If you're happy with the edit you've made, save the file by going to **File** | **Save**. Alternatively, you can press the *Ctrl + S* hotkey.

We've covered a lot of ground by making these few edits to the helmet. Let's keep the momentum going and add some horns.

Adding the horns

Historically, Vikings didn't actually have horned helmets, but this is our world, so we can add whatever we want!

Remember how we mentioned that you would be using the Extrude tool over and over again? Well, guess what? We're going to extrude again here:

1. Switch to **face** selection mode by pressing 3 on the home row of the keyboard.
2. Rotate your view with the middle mouse button so that you can see the area of the helmet that the horn will be extruded from:

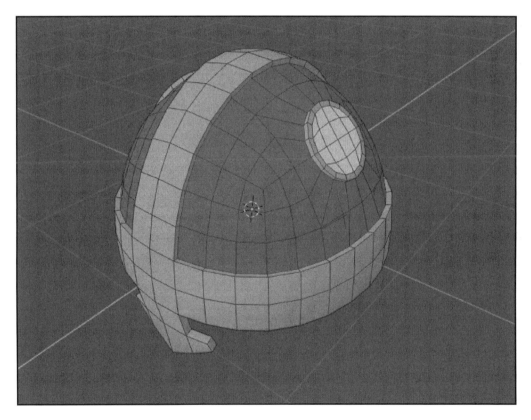

A nice view of the area that the horn will be extruded from

Just like when we extruded the nose guard, the first step is to make a selection. We have a lot of really fancy selection methods that we can use, but some of them aren't visible in the UI right now. You may have noticed that some of the tool icons on the Toolbar have a tiny arrow in the bottom-right corner.

This means that there are similar tools stacked underneath that tool. Let's try out the **Select Circle** tool, which is stacked underneath the **Select Box** tool:

1. Click and hold down the left mouse button on the **Select Box** tool to expand the list of stacked tools, as shown here:

Stacked Selection tools on the Toolbar

2. While the mouse button is still held down, hover over the **Select Circle** tool.
3. Let go of the mouse button to activate the **Select Circle** tool.
4. Hover the little selection circle over one of the Viking Helmet's round white side pieces.
5. Click and drag the circle to select all of the white polygons, as shown here:

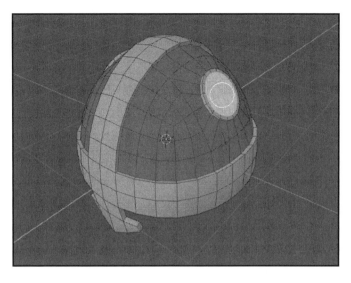

The white polygons that make up the base of the horn are selected

There! Wasn't that easy? The next step is... you guessed it, extrude!

1. Activate the **Extrude Region** tool again.
2. Click and drag the yellow plus (+) symbol on the gizmo to extrude the first piece of the horn, as shown here:

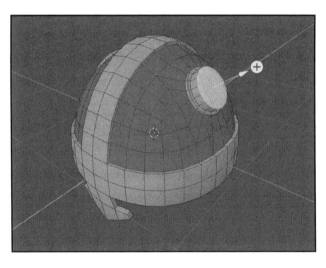

Extruding the first piece of the horn

We're off to a good start, but these horns should be curved. Unfortunately, the only way to make a 3D model curved is to add lots and lots of extra polygons, so we're going to have to extrude over and over again. The problem is that with each extrusion, we will have to make small adjustments to the position, rotation, and scale. That's going to involve a lot of back and forth between the extrude tool, the move tool, the rotate tool, and the scale tool, but there is a better way of doing this! We'll use one of the alternative extrude tools stacked underneath the **Extrude Region** tool:

1. Make sure you still have the same polygons selected from the previous step.
2. Press the *Tilde* ~ key to bring up the **View** pie menu.
3. Choose the **Front** option from the pie menu in order to rotate the view to the front of the helmet, as shown here:

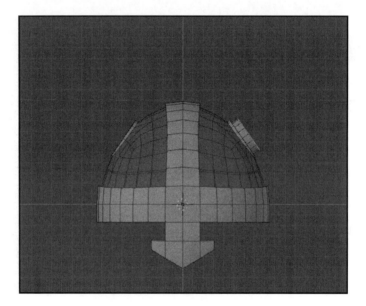

The Viking Helmet, as seen from the front view

4. Click and hold down the left mouse button on the **Extrude Region** tool to expand the list of stacked tools, as shown here:

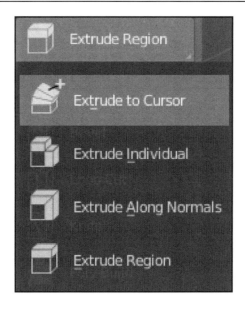

Stacked Extrude tools in the Toolbar

5. While the mouse button is still held down, hover over the **Extrude to Cursor** tool.
6. Let go of the mouse button to activate the **Extrude to Cursor** tool.
7. Hover your mouse over the position you would like to extrude the horn toward.
8. Left-click to extrude the horn to the position of the mouse, as shown here:

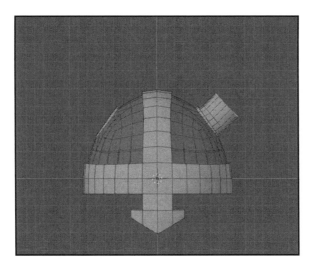

The extruded horn

Excellent – the **Extrude to Cursor** tool took care of the position and rotation at the same time as extruding! Now, all that's left is the scale. It would be nice to avoid switching back and forth between the **Extrude to Cursor** and **Scale** tools, so it's time to learn about a new hotkey. The hotkey for the scale operation is *S*. This hotkey automatically begins scaling as soon as you press it, no gizmo required:

1. Hover the mouse near (but not directly on top of) the selected polygons.
2. Press the *S* hotkey to begin scaling.
3. Drag the mouse slightly closer toward the horn so that the extruded piece tapers slightly, as shown in the following screenshot.
4. Left-click to confirm the scale operation:

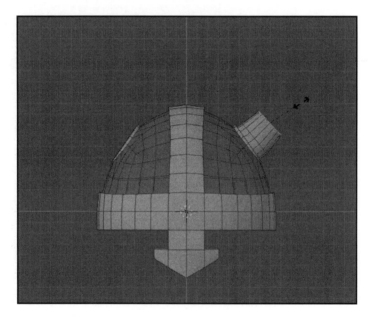

Scale the extruded section down to taper the horn

It helps to back the mouse away from the selection before pressing the *s* hotkey. The amount of scale is determined by the distance, so you will have very little control over it if your mouse is right on top of the selection when you press the hotkey.

Perfect! The great thing about using the *s* hotkey for scale is that our **Extrude to Cursor** tool remains active, so we can finish the horn without switching tools over and over:

1. While the **Extrude to Cursor** tool is still active, left-click to extrude the next small section.
2. Press the *S* hotkey to begin scaling down the newly extruded section.
3. Drag the mouse inward to shrink the selected polygons.
4. Left-click to confirm the scaling operation.
5. Repeat these steps as many times as needed to finish making the horn.

Have fun with your design! Our example turned out like this:

Finished horn

When you're finished with your horn, we can symmetrize the helmet again:

1. Go to the **Mesh** menu in the header of the 3D Viewport.
2. Choose **Symmetrize** from the **Mesh** menu.
3. Use the **Adjust Last Operation** panel to change the **Direction of the Symmetrize** operation if needed.

If you like, you can make the second horn by hand instead to get a wacky asymmetrical result. Make the horns however large or small or lopsided as you like!

Beautiful! That's a fine pair of horns. Our example turned out like this:

A fine pair of horns on our Viking Helmet

Now that we have a nose guard and horns, all that's left is to make some pyramid studs for decoration.

Adding the studs

If there's one thing we know about helmets, it's that they look cooler with pyramid studs, especially if they go all the way around the metal rim. We're going to use a couple of advanced techniques to make selections and create the studs.

In 3D modeling, we have a very useful topology concept called **Edge Loops**, which we will learn about in more detail in the next chapter. Basically, an edge loop is exactly what it sounds like: a loop of edges that run through a model. If the model has good topology (like our Viking Helmet), there will be clean edge loops all over the model. We can use these loops to our advantage in our modeling process. Let's use them to start modeling the studs:

1. Switch to **Edge Select** mode by pressing 2 on the keyboard.
2. Hover your mouse over the middle horizontal loop of the Viking Helmet's base.
3. Hold down the *Alt* key and click on any one of the horizontal edges in the loop.

The whole loop will be selected with just one click, as shown here:

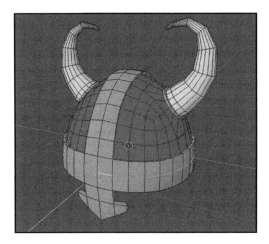

The whole edge loop around the base of the helmet is selected

Next, we want to select a part of the vertical loop that crosses over the middle of the helmet. We have to use a different method this time because the vertical edge loop runs all the way through the nose guard and underside of the helmet, which isn't ideal. Instead, we're going to use a wonderful selection feature called **Shortest Path**:

1. Hold down the *Shift* key and click to add the first edge in the vertical edge loop to the current selection, as shown here:

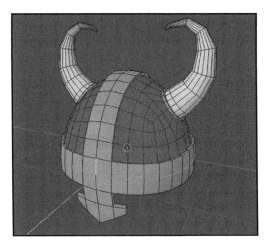

Selecting the edge above the horizontal edge loop

2. Use the middle mouse button to rotate the view to the back of the helmet.

3. Hold down the *Ctrl* key and click on the final edge in the vertical edge loop (it's in the same position as the first, but on the opposite side).

Perfect – the shortest path between the two edges has been added to the selection. Now, our selection includes a horizontal edge loop around the rim and part of a vertical edge loop across the top of the helmet, as shown here:

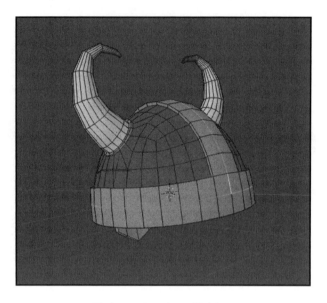

The shortest path over the top of the helmet

Selecting these edges by hand would have been a pain, but with the right approach, we were able to select them all in just three clicks.

If you're having trouble with the **Shortest Path** feature, you can select the edges one at a time by holding the *Shift* key and clicking on each edge. The way in which you make your selection will not be an issue for the following steps; just make sure you have all of the edges selected, as shown in the preceding screenshot.

We're going to use the vertices in this selection as center points for our studs, so let's switch to **Vertex Select** mode:

1. Press *1* on the home row of the keyboard to switch to **Vertex Select** mode.

That's good, but that's going to be way too many studs, so let's remove some of the vertices from the selection. Specifically, we want to remove every other vertex. That sounds like a pain, but fear not – we don't have to do that by hand either!

2. Go to the **Select** menu in the header of the 3D Viewport.

3. Choose **Checker Deselect**, as shown here:

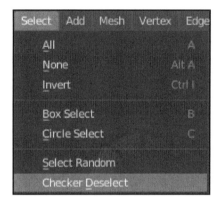

Select | Checker Deselect

Good – the selection should now look like this:

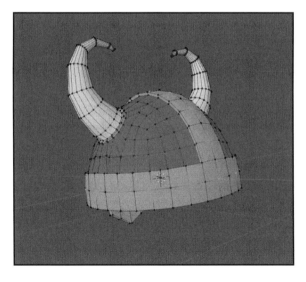

The selection after using Checker Deselect

If your selection is offset from the example shown here, then we need to make an adjustment to the **Checker Deselect** operation by using the **Adjust Last** operation, just like we did when we had to edit the parameters of the **Symmetrize** operation earlier in this project:

1. Have a look at the **Adjust Last Operation** panel in the bottom-left of the 3D Viewport.
2. If needed, increase the **Offset** to shift the selected vertices until they match the ones shown in this example.

There we go – that will make for a more manageable number of studs. Now that we've selected all of the individual spots where our studs should go, we're ready to actually make the studs:

1. Open the **Vertex** menu in the header of the 3D Viewport.
2. Choose **Bevel Vertices** from the menu:

Vertex | Bevel Vertices

This operation works similarly to how the *s* hotkey works: you have to drag the mouse to increase the amount of vertex bevel:

1. Drag the mouse outward until the vertices split into little diamond shapes.
2. Left-click to confirm the operation when the little diamonds match the example shown in the following screenshot:

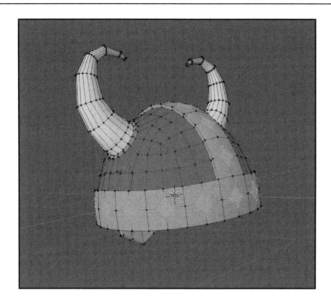

Beveled vertices

Now, we just need to turn the diamonds into pyramids.

3. Open the **Face** menu in the header of the 3D Viewport.

4. Choose **Poke Faces** from the menu:

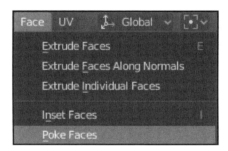

Face | Poke Faces

Remember that even though we are in **Vertex Select** mode, we can still use the operations in the **Face** menu because the highlighted faces in-between the vertices are also selected.

Poking faces sounds dangerous, but in 3D modeling, it's fun! We just need to make one more adjustment in the **Adjust Last Operation** panel:

1. Have a look at the **Adjust Last Operation** panel at the bottom-left of the 3D Viewport.
2. Increase the **Poke Offset** to make the little diamonds stick out like pyramids. 0.08m feels about right, but feel free to try other values until you get a result like the one shown in the following screenshot:

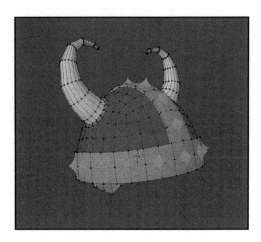

The studs are raised up with the poke offset

And there we have it – the **Poke** added an extra vertex to each face and the **Poke Offset** raised them up to form the studs. We're done!

That was a lot of work. Now, we just have to wear it proudly! And by that, we mean we have to place the helmet on the dummy's head.

Returning to Object Mode to finish

Now that we're done making our additions to the helmet, we can finish the scene. We've been spending a lot of time in **Edit Mode**, but we want to return to **Object Mode** so we can place the helmet on the dummy's head:

1. Return to **Object Mode** by using the drop-down menu in the header of the 3D Viewport, or by pressing the *Tab* hotkey.

2. Go to the **View** menu in the header of the 3D Viewport.

3. Choose **Local View** | **Toggle Local View** to leave **Local** mode and bring all of the other objects back.

You can always tell if you're still in **Local** view because the 3D Viewport will display **(Local)** in the top-left corner.

Now that we're back from the isolated **Local** view, the helmet is buried in the ground, as shown in the following screenshot:

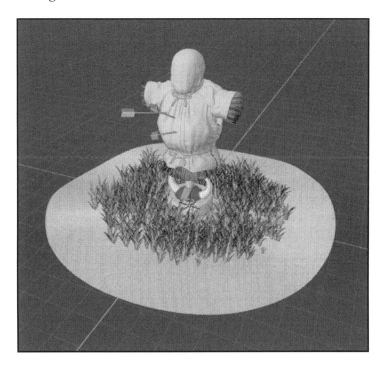

The helmet buried in the ground

Use the transformation skills you learned about at the beginning of this chapter to place the helmet on top of the dummy's head:

1. Activate the **Move** tool and move the helmet upward to the dummy's head.

2. Activate the **Rotate** tool and rotate the helmet so that it aligns with the head.

3. Activate the **Scale** tool and resize the helmet if needed.

When you're done, the helmet should fit nicely on the dummy's head (don't forget to check it from multiple camera angles). Here's how our example turned out:

The helmet fits nicely on the dummy's head

You've done an excellent job making your first 3D scene. Don't forget to save your work. Now, it's time for a reward – you'll get to see the scene in a proper render!

Rendering the final image

While we work in 3D, we tend to use low-quality preview settings for the Viewport because it's easier to see the polygons and it keeps our computers running fast while we work. So far, we have been working with low-quality preview settings, so our Viewport looks like this:

The low-quality preview of our scene

Now that we've finished making edits to the Viking scene, we can change a few settings to get a high-quality final image. A high-quality render needs a nice set of lights. Remember the **Lights** collection in the Outliner? Well, it's time to make it visible:

1. Find the **Lights** collection in the Outliner.
2. Click on the grayed-out eyeball icon to the right of the **Lights** collection.

Good – we have some lights, but a bunch of ugly lines appeared in the Viewport. These lines are part of a feature called **Overlays**. Overlays include everything from grid lines to selection highlights. They are helpful for modeling, but they get in the way for rendering. Next, let's turn off all of the Overlays so we can get a clear look at our final image:

1. Look at the header of the 3D Viewport and find the four circle-shaped icons in the top-right corner.
2. Find the button to the left of the four circles labeled **Show Overlays**.
3. Click the button to disable all of the Overlays in the Viewport.

There's one last thing we need to do, and this is the big one: we need to change the shading from Solid to Rendered to see what our finished scene looks like:

1. Look at the header of the 3D Viewport and find the four circle-shaped icons in the top-right corner.
2. Click on the fourth circle icon to activate **Rendered shading**.

And that's all there is to it. Our scene shouldn't look boring, flat, and gray anymore. Instead, we should have an image like this:

The high-quality render of our scene

 Sometimes, the materials and textures can take a long time to load. If the models don't look like the one shown in the preceding screenshot, try clicking on the third circle icon to go into **Material Preview** mode instead.

Much better, wouldn't you say? If you would like to, you can save this image by going all the way to the top bar and choosing **Render** | **Render Image**. Then, save the image to your computer. Congratulations on finishing your first Blender 2.8 project!

Summary

Wonderful! We've covered a lot of ground and you've edited your first model. We learned how to use the Outliner to organize the objects in the scene. We've built some familiarity with the 3D navigation controls. We also had a quick look at Blender's new Toolbar. Finally, we practiced basic transformations using 3D objects and components.

After doing all this, we edited a provided model with some of the most common modeling tools, such as extrude, and we learned how to select edge loops.

In the next chapter, we will learn how to start a project from scratch by making a time machine! We'll take what we learned while working on the Viking Helmet and expand on that knowledge using many more tools and workflows.

Modeling a Time Machine - Part 3 1

In this chapter, we are going to begin building a time machine! So far, we've seen a little bit of the 3D workflow by editing an existing model, but now it's time to use some of those skills to build a model from scratch. This first part of the project will introduce you to the main modeling methods we will be using to build the time machine: box modeling and modeling with modifiers.

Box modeling is one of the oldest methods of modeling in the 3D industry; it uses primitives and extrusions to build up the major forms of a model before refining them into the final form. Primitives are standard geometrical shapes that we can use as a starting point for our models— a plane, cube, sphere, cylinder, cone, and torus.

Modeling with modifiers is somewhat unique to Blender. Modifiers are a very powerful set of non-destructive tools that let us generate new geometry, deform existing geometry, and perform other complex edits to our models without damaging the underlying mesh.

Throughout this chapter, we will be expanding on the things you have already learned and developing skills to make you a more effective modeler. And of course, we'll sprinkle in some other tips and tricks along the way. We will use repetition and common workflows to learn how to build the chair for the time machine, and when we're finished with the chair, we will put those skills to use in the next chapter and finish off the rest of the time machine.

In this chapter, we will cover the following topics:

- Using transformation hotkeys
- Setting up the reference images for the time machine
- Box modeling the main section of the chair
- Destructive editing versus non-destructive editing
- Modeling the cushions of the chair
- Modeling the sci-fi rings with modifiers
- Modeling the armrests

Using transformation hotkeys

Unlike the previous chapter, we're going to start this project from scratch, so open Blender, and if you don't already have a fresh scene, go to **File** | **New** | **General**. The default scene has a default cube, a point light, and a camera.

Before we get started on the time machine, let's introduce a few important hotkeys. As stated in the previous chapter, Blender is full of hotkeys. To take full advantage of the software, you'll want to memorize several of them.

Hotkeys are especially useful for things that you will be doing over and over again, in particular, switching between the three transformation tools (move, scale, and rotate), so let's go over how to use these hotkeys so we can work faster:

- *G*: Grab (Translate / Move)
- *R*: Rotate
- *S*: Scale

As always, remember to hover your mouse inside the 3D Viewport before pressing any of these hotkeys.

Blender takes a different approach to the majority of 3D software when it comes to these transformation hotkeys; unlike the buttons in the Toolbar, which activate manipulation widgets, these three transformation hotkeys immediately begin transforming the selected objects the moment you press the hotkey. No widget required!

Give it a try:

1. Select the cube.
2. Press the *G* hotkey to grab it.
3. Move the mouse to translate the cube around the screen.

When you're done moving the cube, you need to either confirm the transformation by left-clicking or pressing the *Enter* key, or cancel the transformation by right-clicking or pressing the *Esc* key. This is true of all of Blender's hotkey operations, so take a moment to practice.

 Blender includes a handy feature called **Continuous Grab**; if you move the mouse outside of the 3D Viewport while performing an operation, the cursor will wrap back around to the other side of the screen so that you can keep going.

Next, try rotating the cube:

1. Make sure the cube is still selected.
2. Press the *R* hotkey to begin rotating it.
3. Move the mouse to rotate the cube around its origin point.
4. Confirm or cancel the rotation with the left or right mouse button, respectively.

 Using the rotation hotkey will draw a line from your mouse to the origin of the object you are manipulating. Rather than dragging the mouse left and right or up and down, you need to rotate your mouse around the object's origin point in a circular motion to achieve the desired rotation.

It's pretty easy, right? Now, let's try scaling the cube:

1. Make sure the cube is still selected.
2. Press the *S* hotkey to begin scaling it.
3. Move the mouse toward or away from the cube's origin point.
4. Confirm or cancel the rotation with the left or right mouse button respectively.

 You need to move your mouse outward or inward to scale up or down, respectively. The sensitivity and precision of this motion are based on how close your mouse was to the origin of the object when you pressed the scale hotkey. To get the best control over the motion, start with your mouse a short distance away from the object before pressing the hotkey.

Using these hotkeys is a lot faster than using the Toolbar once you commit them to memory. However, we need to combine these three hotkeys with a second set of hotkeys to get the same amount of precision as the tools in the Toolbar.

Remember, when we used the tools in the previous chapter, that we could transform our selected object along a specific axis: *x*, *y*, or *z*? Well, we can do that with hotkeys as well!

When you first press one of the three transformation hotkeys (*G*, *R*, or *S*), the transformation begins by using View Space (also known as Screen Space), and all movements are based on the current angle of the 3D Viewport. To lock the movement to one of the three axes (*x*, *y*, or *z*), all you have to do is press the corresponding letter. So, to move the cube straight up and down in Global Space (also known as World Space), press *G* to begin grabbing it, then press *Z* to lock to the *z*-axis. This is the same for any of the three axes:

- **X**: Lock transformation to the *x*-axis.
- **Y**: Lock transformation to the *y*-axis.
- **Z**: Lock transformation to the *z*-axis.

Locking to an axis works for grabbing, rotating, and scaling. You can also transform along two axes at once by holding *Shift* and pressing the letter for the axis that you don't want to include:

- *Shift* + *X*: Lock transformation to both the *y* and *z* axes.
- *Shift* + *Y*: Lock transformation to both the *x* and *z* axes.
- *Shift* + *Z*: Lock transformation to both the *x* and *y* axes.

For added precision, you can type the exact value of the transformation you wish to apply. For instance, to rotate an object 90 degrees along the *x*-axis, do the following:

1. Press the *R* hotkey to begin rotating.
2. Press the *X* hotkey to lock the rotation to the global *x*-axis.
3. Type 90 on the keyboard to rotate exactly 90 degrees.
4. Left-click or press the *Enter* key to confirm the rotation.

You can see the precise transformation values while you are performing the operation in the top-left corner of the 3D Viewport. In this case, you should see: `Rot: [90|] = 90° along global X`.

These hotkeys are meant to be intuitive since you will be using them a lot and, with a little practice, they will become second nature. From now on in this book, we will encourage you to use these hotkeys to transform objects. However, if you are more comfortable using the tools in the Toolbar, you may keep using them instead. The results will be identical, but you will work faster if you get used to using the hotkeys.

Next, we'll learn how to set up reference images in Blender so that we can see the concept art for the time machine directly in the Viewport.

Setting up the reference images for the time machine

For this workflow, our first step is to get our reference images set up. Download the reference images for the time machine from the `Blender3DByExample_Chapter03-04` folder from `https://github.com/PacktPublishing/Blender-3D-By-Example-Second-Edition`. If you would like to learn how to set up these reference images for yourself, keep reading this section. If you would rather dive right into modeling, open the `TimeMachine_Start.blend` file and skip to the *Box modeling the main section of the chair* section. There are six reference images:

- `Back_Exterior.png`
- `Back_Interior.png`
- `Front_Exterior.png`
- `Front_Interior.png`
- `Side.png`
- `Top.png`

The two "Interior" images will be helpful in modeling the inner parts of the time machine such as the chair and the clock, while the "Exterior" images will be more useful for everything else:

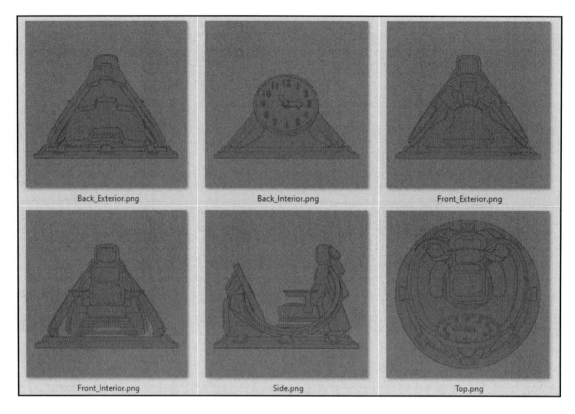

The six reference images provided for this project

Reference images like this are sometimes referred to as a **Modeling Sheet**. They are drawn with as little perspective as possible so they align nicely to the orthographic views of 3D software.

If you don't already have a fresh Blender scene, then open one. We won't need any of the default objects, so let's delete them:

1. Go to **File** | **New** | **General**.
2. Press the *A* hotkey to select all of the objects.
3. Press the *Delete* key or the *X* hotkey to bring up the **Delete** menu.
4. Click **Delete** to confirm.

The X hotkey brings up the **Delete** menu, while the *Delete* key deletes the objects immediately. You cannot use the *Delete* key on the Numpad since Blender uses the Numpad keys for a different set of hotkeys.

Blender 2.8 has streamlined the way we import reference images. Unlike previous versions of the software, reference images can be brought directly into the 3D Viewport and live in 3D space like any other 3D object. The easiest way to set this up is to turn on the Quad View:

1. Click to open the **View** menu in the top-left of the 3D Viewport.
2. Go to **Area | Toggle Quad View**.

This will give us three orthographic views—one for the top, front, and right side, as well as one perspective view. Each of the four quadrants is labeled in the top-left corner, for example, **Top Orthographic**, as you can see in the following screenshot:

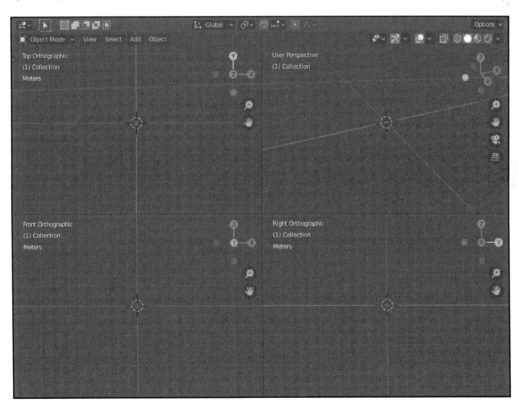

The 3D Viewport with Quad View enabled

Next, we will take advantage of Blender 2.8's new drag-and-drop feature. Simply drag and drop the images from your computer's file browser into each of Blender's Viewports:

1. Drag the `Top.png` file into the Top Orthographic view.
2. Drag the `Front_Exterior.png` file into the Front Orthographic view.
3. Drag the `Side.png` file into the Right Orthographic view.

As you drag each of these images into the Viewports, they will automatically be added to the scene as image planes. Be careful not to drag the images on top of each other as this will replace an existing image plane instead of creating a new one. Don't worry if the alignment of these images is out of whack; we'll fix that in the next step.

Unfortunately, the computer's operating system might retain focus when we drag and drop these images into Blender. If your hotkeys aren't responding, you may need to click inside the Blender software once to make the operating system give the focus back to Blender.

1. Press the *A* hotkey to select all three image planes.
2. Press the *Alt + G* hotkey to reset the positions of the selected objects.

As we know, the *G* hotkey lets us "grab" and adjust the positions of objects. In contrast, the *Alt + G* hotkey will reset the positions of objects back to 0 on the *x*, *y*, and *z* axes.

Once the images are all in place and their positions have been reset, your scene should look like this:

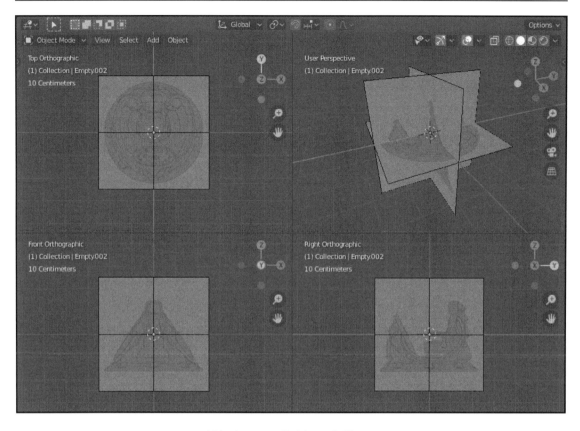

All three images centered in their respective Viewports

Let's rename these images so they are easier to find in the Outliner:

1. Select the image in the Top view.
2. Either press the *F2* hotkey or double-click the name in the Outliner to rename it.
3. Rename it `Top`.
4. Repeat these steps to name the front and right side images `Front_Exterior` and `Side`, respectively.
5. While we're at it, double-click the collection in the Outliner called **Collection** and rename it `Reference Images`.

Good, now let's go to the **Properties** panel to fine-tune some of the settings for our image planes:

1. Select the `Front_Exterior` object.
2. Go the **Object Data Properties** tab in the **Properties** panel.
3. Set the **Offset Y** to `-0.175`.
4. Set the **Depth** to **Back**.
5. Set the **Side** to **Front**.
6. Uncheck the box for **Display Perspective**.
7. Check the box for **Display Only Axis Aligned**:

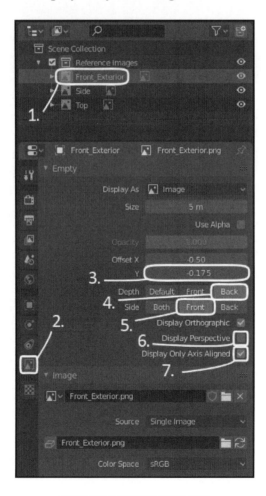

Use these settings for the front reference image

The offset has lifted the reference image up so that the base of the drawing aligns with the grid in 3D space. The depth will ensure that the reference image is always behind our 3D objects so it won't block our view of the model. The side option means the image will only be visible from its own front side, and the display axis-aligned and display perspective options have made it so that the image is invisible when we aren't looking directly at it from the Front Orthographic view.

Now, let's set similar (but slightly different) settings for the right side image:

1. Select the `Side` object.
2. Set the **Offset Y** to -0.175.
3. Set the **Depth** to **Back**.
4. Uncheck the box for **Display Perspective**.
5. Check the box for **Display Only Axis Aligned**.

Now, let's change the settings for the top reference image:

1. Select the `Top` object.
2. Set the **Depth** to **Back**.
3. Uncheck the box for **Display Perspective**.
4. Check the box for **Display Only Axis Aligned**.

Very good, but we have three additional reference images for this project that we also need to set up. One goes in the "Front" view, and the other two go in the "Back" view. Let's set them up one at a time so we don't get confused:

1. Hide the `Front_Exterior` object by clicking the eyeball icon in the Outliner next to its name.
2. Drag the `Front_Interior.png` file into the Front Orthographic view.
3. Press the *Alt + G* hotkey to recenter it.
4. Set the **Offset Y** to -0.175.
5. Set the **Depth** to **Back**.
6. Set the **Side** to **Front**.
7. Uncheck the box for **Display Perspective**.
8. Check the box for **Display Only Axis Aligned**.
9. Rename it `Front_Interior`.

Good! If you haven't figured it out already, the exterior reference image of the time machine gives us a nice view of the front, but the details of the chair are blocked. We need to see the interior of the time machine when we model the chair, so this second reference image is going to help us a lot. We have a similar situation for the back, so we need to add both our interior and exterior images of the back. However, the Quad View doesn't include a back view, so we need to use the perspective Viewport to look at the back.

We're done with the Quad View feature for now. If you prefer to keep it active, you can follow the rest of the instructions in this chapter by interacting with the top-right quadrant of the quad view. The other three quadrants take up a lot of space on the screen, so for the rest of this project, we will assume you've turned it off. We can turn Quad View back off by going to the same menu as before: **View | Area | Toggle Quad View**.

Now, let's go to the back view and add the last two reference images:

1. Press the *Tilde* (~) hotkey to bring up the **View** pie menu.
2. Choose **Back** from the pie menu.
3. Drag the `Back_Exterior.png` file into the Back Orthographic view.
4. Press the *Alt + G* hotkey to recenter it.
5. Set the **Offset Y** to `-0.175`.
6. Set the **Depth** to **Back**.
7. Set the **Side** to **Front**.
8. Uncheck the box for **Display Perspective**.
9. Check the box for **Display Only Axis Aligned**.
10. Rename it `Back_Exterior`.

Good, we have just one left:

1. Hide the `Back_Exterior` object by clicking the eyeball icon in the Outliner next to its name.
2. Drag the `Back_Interior.png` file into the Back Orthographic view.
3. Press the *Alt + G* hotkey to recenter it.
4. Set the **Offset Y** to `-0.175`.
5. Set the **Depth** to **Back**.
6. Set the **Side** to **Front**.
7. Uncheck the box for **Display Perspective**.

9. Check the box for **Display Only Axis Aligned**.
10. Rename it `Back_Interior`.

Excellent! Whenever we need to toggle the visibility of the interior and the exterior, we can click on the eyeball icons for the reference images in the Outliner.

One last thing before we move on: let's disable the selectability for the **Reference Images** collection so we don't accidentally click on it during our modeling phase:

1. Go to the Outliner.
2. Click the **Filter** button to open the pop-over menu.
3. Activate the **Selectable** button under the **Restriction Toggles:** section (it's a button that looks like a mouse cursor).
4. Move your mouse away from the pop-over menu to close it.
5. Click the new little mouse cursor icon next to the **Reference Images** collection to disable selectability for the collection.
6. Click on the **Scene Collection** collection in the Outliner to highlight and activate it.

 When we add new objects, they will be added to the active collection, so make sure that **Scene Collection** is the active collection before moving on. You can see the name of the current active collection in the top-left corner of the 3D Viewport.

Excellent! Now we can use these reference images as a guide for modeling the time machine. We're going to take this one piece at a time and learn several important modeling techniques along the way. Let's start with the chair, and we'll tackle the rest in the next chapter.

Box modeling the main section of the chair

The main section of the chair is a fairly simple shape, so it's the perfect place to practice box modeling. As mentioned before, we start this style of modeling with a primitive shape (in this case, we'll use a cube). and then we use extrusions, edge loops, and other simple modeling tools to block out the major forms of the model.

First, let's create a cube. When we create new objects in Blender, they will spawn at the location of the 3D Cursor. It's best to reset the position of the cursor before adding new objects so that they spawn at the center of the grid:

1. Press the *Shift + S* hotkey to bring up the **Snap** pie menu.
2. Choose **Cursor to World Origin**:

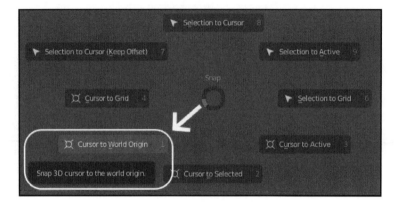

The Snap pie menu, with the Cursor to World Origin option in the bottom-left corner

Excellent, the **3D Cursor** has been reset to the center position. Later in this chapter, we will place the 3D Cursor in custom locations so that it can help us in our modeling workflow, but for now, we need it right here in the center, as shown here:

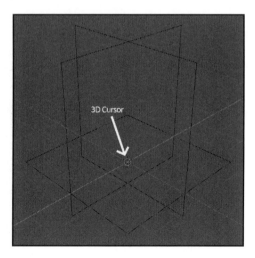

The 3D Cursor centered at the origin of the 3D scene

Next, let's add in a cube to begin our model:

1. Find the **Add** menu at the top of the 3D Viewport or press the *Shift + A* hotkey.
2. Choose **Mesh | Cube**.
3. Rename the cube object `Chair_Main`.

Perfect. Now, let's turn on x-ray mode so that we can see the reference images through the surface of the cube:

1. Press the Tilde (~) hotkey and then choose **Right** from the pie menu.
2. Find and click the **Toggle X-Ray** button in the top-right corner of the 3D Viewport:

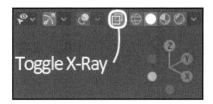

The Toggle X-Ray button is in the top-right corner of the 3D Viewport

Once the x-ray button has been enabled, your Viewport should look like this:

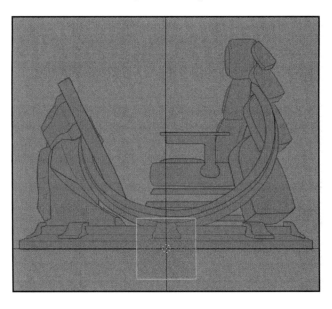

The reference image is visible through the cube

There we go! Now that we can see what we're doing, we can align the cube to the seat of the chair.

Feel free to toggle x-ray on and off as often as you need to during the modeling process.

Let's move the new cube into place:

1. Press the *Tab* hotkey to enter **Edit Mode**.
2. Press the *A* hotkey to select all of the components of the cube (if they aren't selected already).
3. Press *G* to grab the components and drag them upward to the seat of the chair.
4. Left-click to confirm the translation:

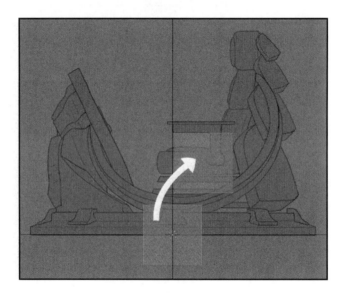

Moving the components of the cube up to the seat

5. Press *S* to scale the cube down so that it matches the vertical thickness of the seat of the chair.
6. Left-click to confirm the scale:

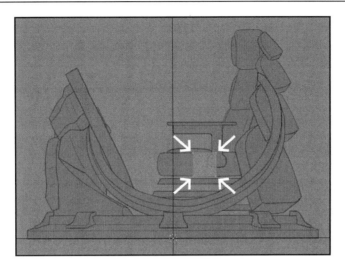

Scaling the cube components down

7. Press the *S* hotkey again to begin scaling again.
8. Press the *Y* hotkey to lock the scale to the *y*-axis.
9. Drag the mouse outward to scale the cube to match the size of the chair along the *y*-axis.
10. Left-click to confirm the scale:

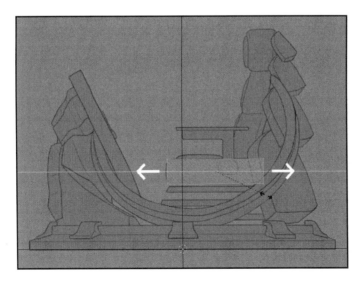

Scale the cube components along the y-axis

So far so good, but now we need to adjust the size so that it lines up with the chair from the Top view:

1. Press the Tilde (~) hotkey to open the **View** pie menu.
2. Choose **Top** from the menu.
3. Press *A* to make sure the components of the cube are still selected.
4. Press *S* to scale.
5. Press the *X* hotkey to lock the scale to the *x*-axis.
6. Move the mouse to resize the cube's width to match the width of the seat:

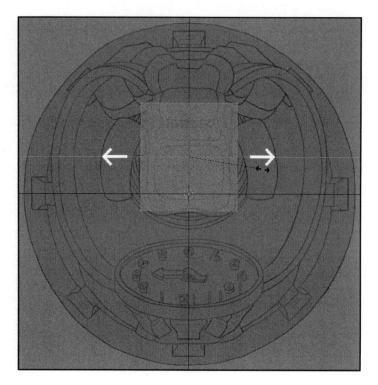

Scale the cube components along the x-axis

Good. Now we need to add some extra geometry so that we can build the back of the chair:

1. Go to the right side view (the ~ hotkey | **Right**.)
2. Select the **Loop Cut** tool from the Toolbar.
3. Hover the mouse over one of the horizontal edges, and a vertical highlight will appear.

4. Click to insert a new edge loop.
5. Select the **Edge Slide** tool from the Toolbar.
6. Click and drag to slide the edge to the spot where the back of the chair meets the seat of the chair (right behind the armrest, as seen in the following screenshot):

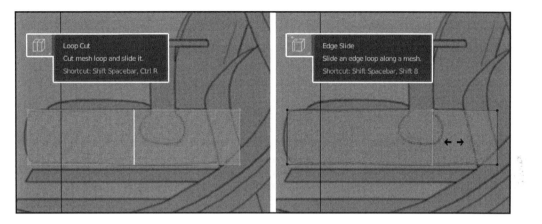

Using the Loop Cut tool, and then the Edge Slide tool, to add a new edge loop to the cube

If you're ready to learn some more hotkeys, you can use the *Ctrl + R* hotkey to bring up the Loop Cut operator, and you can press the G hotkey to grab, and then press the *G* hotkey a second time to enter Edge Slide mode.

Inserting edge loops like this is a very common way to add detail to a model. This method works very well for defining a region to extrude more polygons out of, which is exactly what we'll be doing next:

1. Press the 3 hotkey on the home row of the keyboard to switch to **Face Select** mode.
2. Select the face in the top-right of the mesh (it might be hard to see from this angle but it can still be selected).
3. Select the **Extrude Region** tool from the Toolbar.
4. Click and drag the extrude widget to pull out some extra geometry from the selected region.
5. Pull up until the extrusion aligns with the crease in the side of the chair.
6. Press the G hotkey to grab the extruded face.
7. Press the Y hotkey to lock the translation to the *y*-axis.
8. Move the face backward to align with the reference image of the chair.

9. Left-click to confirm the translation:

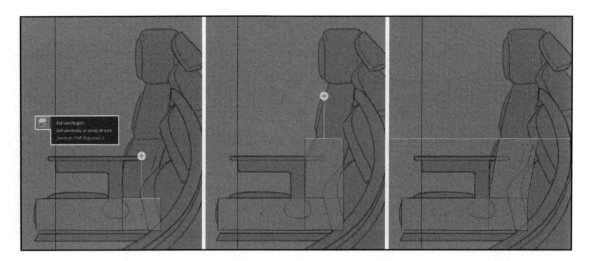

Extruding and moving the first piece of the back of the chair

Perfect! This is a very common modeling process: **Loop Cut, Edge Slide, Extrude,** and **Move**. We will be using this often. Extrude and move the back of the chair two more times to form the upper section and the headrest, as seen in the following screenshot:

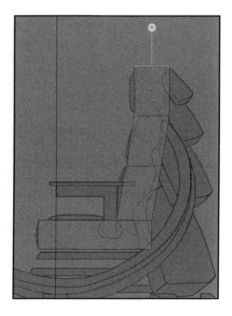

Extruding a new region for each section of the back of the chair

Extruding is another feature that we use all of the time; instead of grabbing the tool from the Toolbar, you can use the *E* hotkey to perform the extrude operation.

Excellent. Now we need to have a look at the front of the chair so we can adjust the width of each section:

1. Go to the Front View (the ~ hotkey | **Front**.)
2. Use the **Loop Cut** tool to add two new vertical edge loops.
3. Use the **Edge Slide** tool to slide the two new edge loops to align with the features of the chair in the following screenshot:

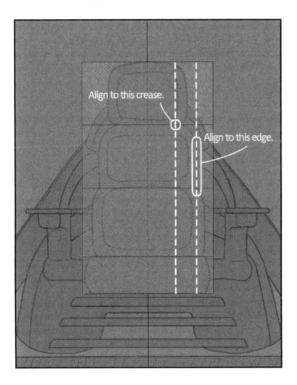

Inserting two new edge loops aligned to the details of the chair

Remember, if you need to select an edge loop, hold down the *Alt* key before clicking on an edge to select the whole loop.

Perfect! These new edge loops will let us carve away the unneeded sections of the chair while retaining the detail where needed. Up next, we can create a "Bridge" from the front to the back of the chair, which in this case will carve away the unneeded polygons:

1. Press the 3 hotkey on the home row of the keyboard to switch to **Face Select** mode.
2. Click and drag to box select the four faces in the front as well as the four faces in the back (refer to the following screenshot). Don't select the perimeter faces along the right side or the top, otherwise, the "bridge edge loops" operation won't work:

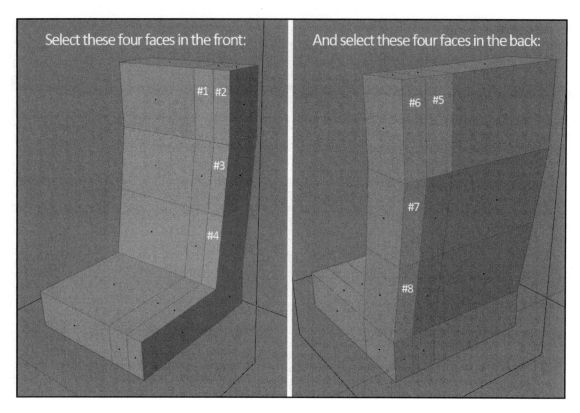

Box select the four polygons in the front and back of the chair, but NOT the perimeter polygons

3. Go to the **Edge** menu at the top of the 3D Viewport.

4. Choose **Bridge Edge Loops**:

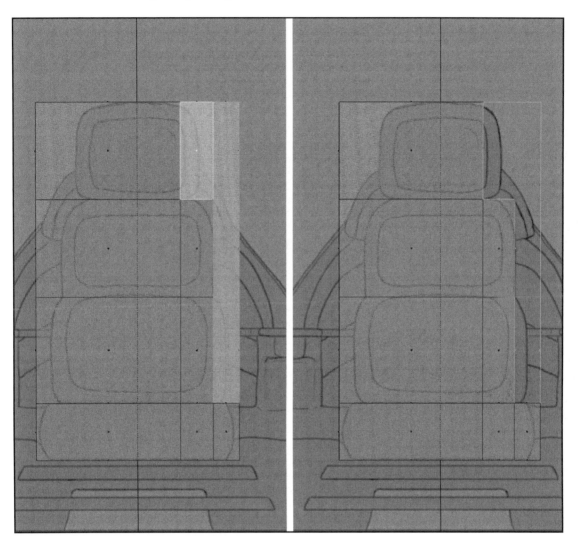

Bridging these faces has carved a hole in the chair

There. Now the polygons on the front of the chair have been bridged to the back of the chair, which has carved away the selected section. If we had just deleted these polygons, there would be a hole in the side of the mesh that we would have had to patch up. This method of bridging did, however, leave behind some unneeded faces around the perimeter, so let's delete those now:

1. Select the five faces around the perimeter.
2. Go to the **Mesh** menu.
3. Choose **Delete | Faces**:

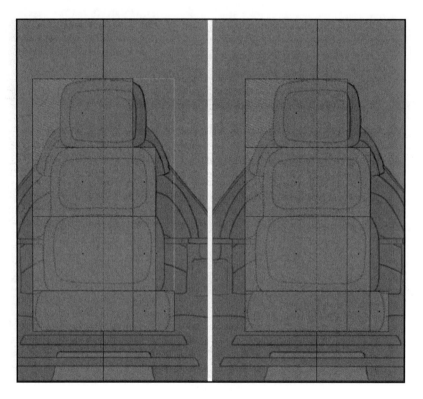

Selecting and deleting the leftover perimeter polygons

That's a good start! Now, we need to make a few more extrusions to round out the edges:

1. Switch to **Face Select** mode.
2. Select the face on the right side of the headrest.
3. Use either the **Extrude Region** tool from the Toolbar or the *E* hotkey to extrude the side of the headrest about halfway to the edge of the reference image.

4. Press the *S* hotkey to begin scaling.
5. Press the *Z* hotkey to lock the scale to the *z*-axis.
6. Scale the selected face down to more closely align with the reference image.
7. Left-click to confirm the scale.
8. Extrude again, this time all of the way to the edge of the reference image.
9. Scale down the extruded face to finish rounding out the headrest:

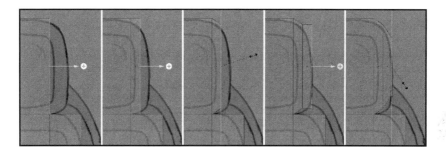

Making several extrusions to round out the geometry around the edge of the headrest

Very nice. Repeat this process for the lower section of the chair to round it out, as seen in the following screenshot:

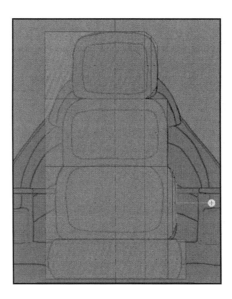

Extruding and scaling two small sections for the lower part of the chair the same way we did with the headrest

Good. Now let's round out that hard corner of the midsection. This time, we'll use a slightly different method—a bevel:

1. Click and drag with the middle mouse button to rotate the Viewport so you can see the corner of the chair's midsection (refer to the following screenshot).
2. Press the 2 hotkey on the home row of the keyboard to switch to Edge Select mode.
3. Select the corner edge.
4. Return to the Front View so that we can see the reference image again:

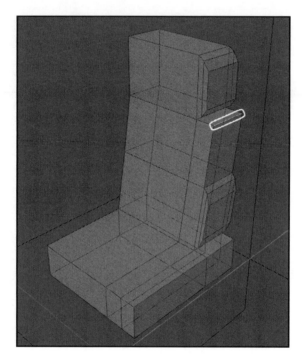

Selecting this corner

5. Go to the **Edge** menu at the top of the Viewport.
6. Choose **Bevel Edges** or use the *Ctrl + B* hotkey to begin the bevel operation.
7. Scroll up on the mouse wheel to increase the segments to two.

8. Drag your mouse outward to increase the width of the bevel to match the roundness of the corner in the reference image; in this case, about `0.125 m` works well (refer to the following screenshot).

9. Left-click to confirm the bevel operation:

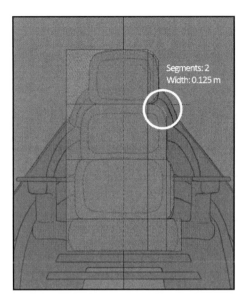

Beveling the corner

 You can see the details of the bevel operation on the status bar at the bottom of the UI.

Good. Now let's round out the edge of the seat:

1. Use either the **Loop Cut** tool from the Toolbar or the *Ctrl + R* hotkey to cut an extra vertical edge loop into the side of the seat.

2. Switch to **Face Select** mode.

3. Box select over the far right side of the edge of the seat to grab both faces along the side.

4. Press the *G* hotkey to grab the faces.

5. Press the *X* hotkey to lock the translation to the *x*-axis.

6. Move the faces to better align with the reference image (refer to the following screenshot).
7. Left-click to confirm the translation.
8. Press the *S* hotkey to begin scaling.
9. Press the *Z* hotkey to lock the scale to the *z*-axis.
10. Scale the selected face down to more closely align with the reference image.
11. Left-click to confirm the scale:

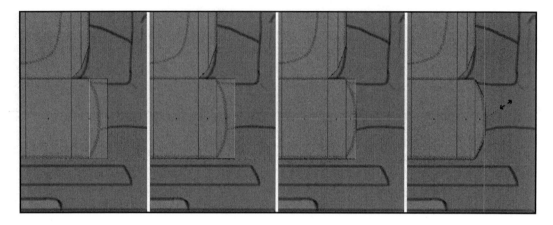

Inserting an edge loop, translating, and scaling the edge of the seat to round it out

Let's do one more bit of refinement to the seat before we move on:

1. Go to the Top view.
2. Switch to **Face Select** mode.
3. Select the two middle-most faces on the front of the seat (refer to the following screenshot).
4. Press the *G* hotkey to grab the faces.
5. Press the *Y* hotkey to lock the translation to the *y*-axis.
6. Drag the faces downward until the right-most edge of the selection aligns with the reference image (refer to the following screenshot).
7. Left-click to confirm the translation.
8. Deselect the right-most face, leaving just one face selected.
9. Press the *G* hotkey again to grab the face.
10. Press the *Y* hotkey to lock the translation to the *y*-axis.

11. Drag the face downward until it aligns with the reference image (refer to the following screenshot).

12. Left-click to confirm the translation:

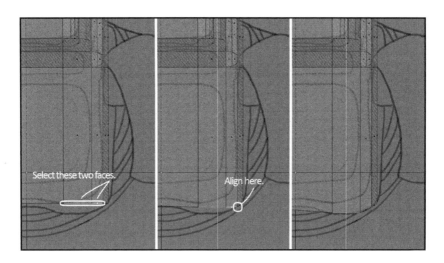

Rounding out the front of the seat by moving the faces downward

Perfect! Chairs with rounded corners are much more comfortable than ones with sharp corners! Now, we just have to make it symmetrical, and we have a super-easy way to do just that:

1. Press the *A* hotkey to select the entire chair.
2. Go to the **Mesh** menu at the top of the 3D Viewport.
3. Choose **Symmetrize**.
4. Click on the word **Symmetrize** that appears in the bottom-left to expand the **Adjust Last Operation** panel.
5. Change the **Direction** to **+X to -X** so that the correct side of the object is mirrored over.

6. Tab back into **Object** mode—we're done with the main piece of the chair:

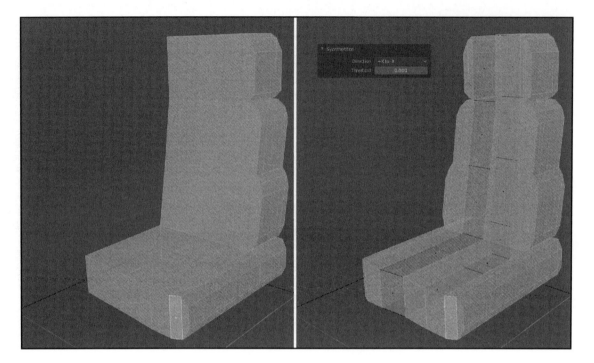

Using the Symmetrize feature for a more comfy chair

Wow! There were a lot of steps behind creating the chair, but we've powered through them and we've learned several important parts of the box modeling workflow along the way, well done!

We've learned how to do the following:

- Change between the Top view, Right side view, and Front View.
- Use the *G*, *R*, and *S* hotkeys to grab, rotate, and scale objects.
- Use the *X*, *Y*, and *Z* hotkeys to lock transformations to a specific axis.
- Use the **Extrude** tool to pull new geometry out of a selected region of the mesh.
- Use the **Loop Cut** tool to insert edge loops into a mesh.
- Use the **Edge Slide** tool to reposition our new edge loops.

From this point forward in this chapter, we are going to provide more streamlined instructions for the parts of the workflow that you've already learned. We will, of course, continue to introduce new tools and operators in detail, but we won't bore you by repeating the step-by-step instructions for things you've already learned. Many of these operations should be starting to feel familiar to you already.

If you do find yourself struggling to remember how to perform any of these operations, you can always refer back to this early part of this chapter for detailed instructions.

Now, let's move on and talk about two methodologies for modeling that will both come in handy.

Destructive editing versus non-destructive editing

Unlike some 3D software, Blender doesn't keep any construction history for objects or operations. This has the upside that our objects are always ready for the next operation to be performed, but it also has the downside that previous operations will be final as soon as we move on to the next operation. This is known as destructive editing.

Even performing small adjustments, such as transforming or deselecting, will apply the previous operation. All of the settings will be committed to the object and can no longer be adjusted. When working with destructive operators, you must set the settings correctly in-the-moment since you will be unable to change them after-the-fact.

Up to this point, we have modeled the chair with destructive editing methods, but in the next step, we can use some non-destructive editing methods for a parametric workflow—you're going to love it!

Modeling the cushions of the chair

Let's model the cushions:

1. Go to the Top view.
2. Choose the **Cursor** tool from the Toolbar.
3. Click on the center of the cushion in the reference image.
4. Choose the **Select Box** tool from the Toolbar to go back to the tool we were using before.
5. Press the *Shift + A* hotkey to bring up the **Add** menu.
6. Choose **Mesh | Cube**.
7. Set the **Size** to 0.9 m.
8. Set the **Location X** to 0 m.
9. Rename the cube object Chair_Cushion.
10. Scale down the cube along the *y*-axis to match the size of the cushion in the reference image (refer to the following screenshot):

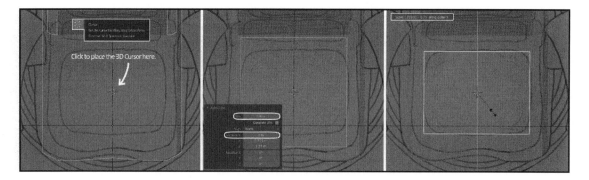

Placing the 3D Cursor, making a cube, and scaling it to match the reference

You can see the precise transformation values while you are performing the operation in the top-left corner of the 3D Viewport. In this case, you should see Scale: 0.7550 along global Y.

Excellent! Now that the cushion aligns nicely to the x and y axes, we just need to adjust the z-axis scale:

1. Go to the right-side view.
2. Scale the cube down along the z-axis to match the height of the cushion in the reference image (approximately **Scale: [.15|] = 0.15 along global Z**):

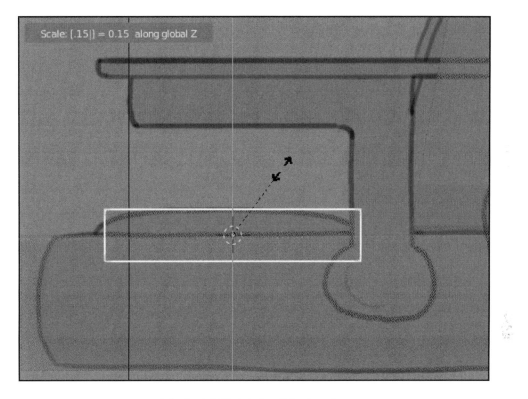

Scaling the cube height-wise to align with the reference image

Now, the cube is the correct size, but we have a slight problem: the object now has a non-uniform scale. All 3D software expects meshes to be a scale of 1 on the x-axis, 1 on the y-axis, and 1 on the z-axis. This is how the software understands what an object's default size is. If these values have been changed, we will get awkward results when we go to use our other modeling tools, so let's fix it!

Go to the **Object Properties** tab in the **Properties** panel. Here, we can see the **Transform** values for our selected object:

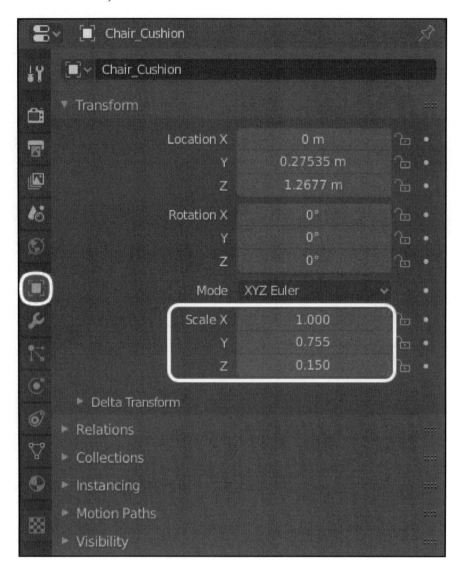

The Scale is non-uniform and needs to be "applied"

As you can see, the **Scale** values aren't set to 1, 1, and 1. Instead, they are: **1.000, 0.755**, and **0.150**. We cannot fix this by typing 1, 1, 1 in the scale values—all that would do is put the object back to its old size and it won't line up to our reference image anymore. Instead, we need to "apply" this scale information so that Blender understands that this is the *new* default size for the object:

1. Go to the **Object** menu at the top of the 3D Viewport.
2. Choose **Apply | Scale**.

Applying the scale means that the object's dimensions didn't change, but the scale has been reset to 1, 1, 1—perfect! All finished models should have a scale of 1, 1, 1. Now that the scale has been applied to the cushion, we can do one more bit of clean up. Only the top face and the four side faces of the cushion will be visible in the model. The bottom face is a wasted polygon, and it's going to cause some issues with the next step in modeling the cushion, so let's delete it:

1. *Tab* into **Edit Mode**.
2. Switch to **Face Select** mode.
3. Select and delete the bottom face of the cube that's inside the seat.
4. *Tab* back into **Object Mode**.

All of the edits we've done so far have been destructive edits—they are permanent. If we ever wanted to change something in that process, our only option would be to undo all of the changes, and then start over with new parameters. That's not really a problem in this case, but at this point, we can finish the cushion using a non-destructive method.

Now that that's taken care of, let's round out the corners of the cushion. To do this, we are going to use our first modifier, the Bevel modifier:

1. Go to the **Properties** panel and click on the **Modifiers** tab (it's the one that looks like a little blue wrench).
2. Click **Add Modifier**.
3. Choose **Bevel** from the **Generate** column.
4. Set the **Width** to 0.15 m.

5. Set the **Segments** to 4:

The Bevel modifier can be added from the modifiers tab

The **Bevel** modifier has added a bevel to all of the edges, which gives the cube nice rounded corners, as you can see in the following screenshot:

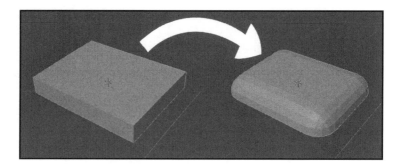

The cube (left side) has been given a Bevel modifier (right side)

That looks nice and comfy! Lastly, we need a few more cushions for the back of the chair:

1. Go to the right view.
2. Make sure the cushion is still selected.
3. Go to the **Object** menu at the top of the 3D Viewport.
4. Choose **Duplicate Objects**.
5. Drag your mouse to move the cushion up and over to the back of the chair.
6. Left-click to confirm the translation.
7. Press the *R* hotkey to rotate the cushion.
8. Rotate the cushion so that it aligns with the back of the chair.
9. Left-click to confirm the rotation:

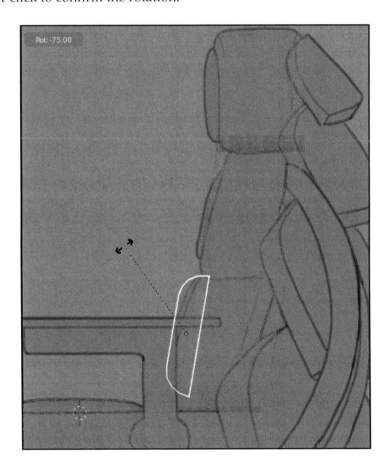

Moving and rotating the cushion into place

You can see the precise transformation values while you are performing the operation in the top-left corner of the 3D Viewport. In this case, you should see **Rot: -75**.

Repeat these steps for the other two cushions on the chair. Once you have all three back cushions in place, we need to resize them to better align with the reference image:

1. Go to the Front View.
2. Select the lowest of the three back cushions.
3. Scale the cushion's width and height as needed. Don't forget to lock the scale to the appropriate axes.

Repeat these steps for the middle and top cushions. If you need to adjust the positions and rotations, feel free to do so. Make sure that the **Location X** of each cushion is still set to 0 m, otherwise, they will be off-center.

Cool! Now we've got some padding on the chair, but our chair looks a little out of place without some rounded corners of its own. Now that we know how to add a Bevel modifier, let's add one to the chair with a few specific settings to make it look good:

1. Select the `Chair_Main` object.
2. Go to the **Modifiers** tab and add a **Bevel** modifier.
3. Set the **Limit Method:** to **Angle**.
4. Set the **Angle** to 18.

Without a limit method, all edges would be beveled, which would add way more polygons than we need. In this case, setting the angle to 18 means only the edges above an 18-degree angle will be beveled, which gives us a little more control over the bevel's results.

And there we have it; a seat with some rounded corners and comfy padding:

An astonishingly comfy chair

Aren't modifiers cool? Up next, we will model the Sci-Fi rings that levitate underneath the chair.

Modeling the sci-fi rings with modifiers

Let's dive in deeper with modifiers. These fictional levitation rings can be made entirely with modifiers (after we add the initial primitive shape); we won't even have to enter Edit Mode! First off, let's create a cylinder:

1. Press the *Shift + A* hotkey to bring up the **Add** menu.
2. Choose **Mesh | Cylinder**.
3. Click the little arrow to expand the **Adjust Last Operation** panel.
4. Set **Radius** to 0.97 m.
5. Set **Depth** to 0.09 m.
6. Set **Cap Fill Type** to **Nothing**.
7. Set **Location X** to 0.0 m.
8. Set **Location Y** to 0.54 m.
9. Set **Location Z** to 0.45 m.
10. Rename the cylinder Chair_Rings.

These settings will create and align a new cylinder perfectly to the bottom ring below the chair.

 Remember, creating a primitive object is a destructive operation. You will not be able to adjust these **Add Cylinder** settings later. Once we move on, they are final.

Now that we have the cylinder, let's use modifiers to finish the shape:

1. Go to the **Modifiers** tab in the **Properties** panel.
2. Click **Add Modifier**.
3. Choose **Solidify** from the **Generate** column.
4. Set **Thickness** to 0.05 m.

The solidify modifier has given the ring some dimension; this is supposed to be a 3D model after all! We can see the results in the perspective view if we rotate the Viewport. Next, let's use a modifier to create the second and third rings:

1. Click **Add Modifier**.
2. Choose an **Array** from the **Generate** column.
3. Set **Count** to 3.
4. Set **Relative Offset** to 0.0 in the first row, 0.0 in the second row, and 2.200 in the third row.

The array modifier generates copies of a mesh and offsets them, so it's perfect for making repeating patterns. Lastly, let's taper the rings so that they match the reference:

1. Click **Add Modifier**.
2. Choose **Simple Deform** from the **Deform** column.
3. Click the button labeled **Taper** to change the deformation type.
4. Set **Axis** to Z.
5. Set **Factor** to −0.275.

 Modifiers are a type of non-destructive editing; these settings will stay editable until you decide the edits are final and you choose to apply the modifiers.

The modifier stack works from top to bottom, so the order in which we add them does affect the end result.

And that's all there is to it for modeling the rings! Isn't modeling with modifiers great? Let's take a look at the result:

A strange science fiction levitation device holds up the time machine's chair

Our chair just needs one last thing before we finish up the chapter: armrests!

Modeling the armrests

The last pieces of the chair we need to make are the armrests. We're mostly going to use box modeling, but we'll introduce one more very useful modifier before we're done.

We're going to start with a plane, and cut in the details we need to match the curvature of the armrests:

1. Go to the Top view.
2. Press the *Shift + S* hotkey to bring up the **Snap** pie menu.
3. Choose **Cursor to World Origin**.
4. Find the **Add** menu at the top of the 3D Viewport or press the *Shift + A* hotkey.
5. Choose **Mesh | Plane**.
6. Rename the plane `Chair_Armrests`.
7. *Tab* into **Edit Mode**.
8. Press the *1* key on the home row to switch to vertex select mode.
9. Grab the top-right corner vertex of the plane and move it up to the top-right corner of the armrest in the reference image.

10. Move the other three vertices into their respective corners as well:

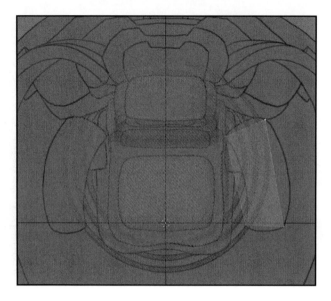

Placing the four verts on the armrest's corners

Now, we've got the major form in place. It doesn't look like much right now, but up next, we will add more edge loops and refine the shape:

1. Select the **Loop Cut** tool from the Toolbar.
2. Hover over the midsection of the armrest to highlight a horizontal line.
3. Click to cut a new edge loop into the plane. The two new vertices that resulted from the Loop Cut will automatically be selected.
4. Move the two vertices to the right to align them to the midsection of the armrest in the reference image.
5. If needed, scale the two vertices outward to increase the distance between them so they align with the edge of the armrest in the reference image:

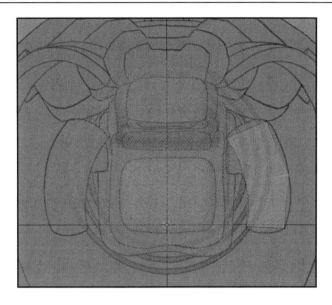

Aligning the new edge loop to match the inside of the armrest reference

There we go! Already, we're seeing a huge improvement; the Loop Cut tool is still active, so we can easily repeat these steps to add more detail to the armrest model. Add one new horizontal cut to the upper and lower sections, and then move those Loop Cuts into position:

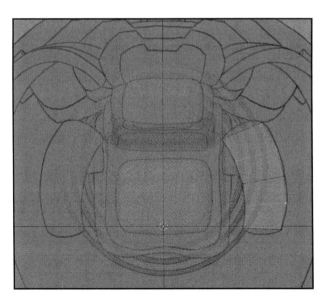

Two additional edge loops cut into the armrest and moved into place

Great! As you can see, adding more edge loops allows us to represent a more rounded form. Repeat this once more to add in an extra loop between each of the existing loops for a total of four new loops. Once that's done, let's add two vertical cuts to the armrest to round out the top and bottom as well:

1. Go to the tool settings at the top of the screen.
2. Set **Number of Cuts** to 2.
3. Hover over one of the horizontal edges of the armrest to highlight a vertical cut.
4. Click to insert two new vertical edge loops.
5. All of the new vertices will be selected; scale them up along the *y*-axis to round out the shape.
6. Click the **Select Box** tool from the Toolbar:

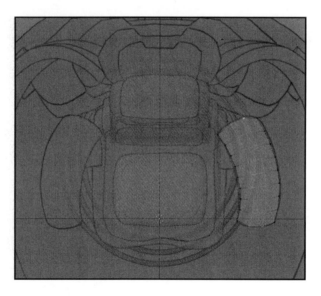

The two new vertical edge loops contribute a lot to the rounded shape of the armrest

Excellent. Now that we have the shape from the Top view, we need to check the alignment from the side view, and then give it some thickness:

1. Go to the right-side view.
2. Press the *A* hotkey to select all of the vertices.
3. Grab them and move them along the *z*-axis up to the topmost edge of the armrest in the reference image.

4. Either use the **Extrude Region** tool from the Toolbar or press the *E* hotkey to extrude the selection.

5. Move the extrusion downward to align with the underside of the armrest:

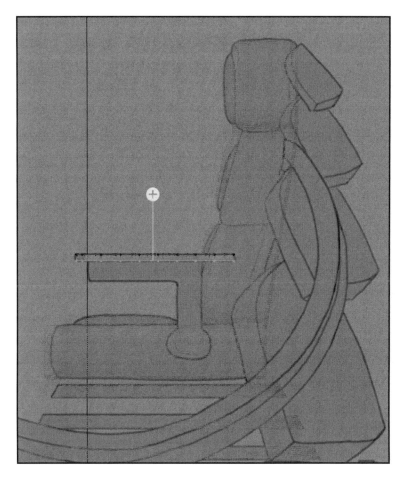

The armrest's verts aligned along the z-axis

Good. The upper part is finished, so now let's make the support bar underneath:

1. Rotate the Viewport to a perspective view.

2. Switch to **Face Select** mode.

3. Select the middlemost faces on the underside of the armrest (refer to the following screenshot):

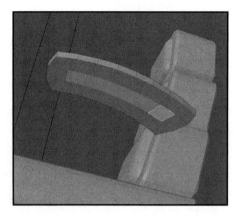

Selecting the underside faces of the armrest

Now that we have our selection, we can extrude it to form the support bar of the armrest:

1. Return to the side view.
2. Extrude the selected faces down to match the reference image.
3. Go to the **Select** menu at the top of the 3D Viewport.
4. Choose **Select More/Less | More**.
5. Grab and move the faces to the left along the y-axis so that the front most edge aligns with the reference image:

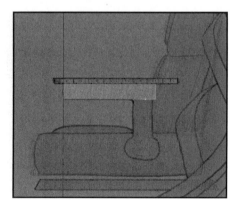

The extruded support bar

Good. Now let's make the vertical part of the support bar:

1. Select the right-most face on the underside of the extruded region.
2. Extrude the face down to meet the bulbous part of the support bar in the reference image.
3. Extrude once more down to the bottom of the bulbous part of the support bar.
4. Insert an edge loop in the middle of the bulbous part of the support bar.
5. Scale up the new edge loop to approximately match the width of the bulbous part of the support bar.
6. Insert one new edge loop above and one new edge loop below the edge loop that we just finished scaling.
7. Select just the two new edge loops.
8. Scale the two new edge loops up to round out this section of the support bar (refer to the following screenshot):

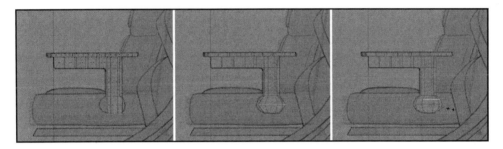

The step-by-step process for making the bulbous part of the armrest's support bar

Excellent! We're almost done! We just need the bar that connects the bulbous section to the main part of the chair:

1. Rotate the Viewport so that we can see the inside faces of the bulbous section of the support bar.
2. Switch to **Face Select** mode.

3. Select the four faces closest to the main section of the chair (refer to the following screenshot):

Selecting the four faces of the armrest

Now, we just need to extrude them. We are going to pull them inside the main part of the chair so they look like they are attached to it:

1. Press the *E* hotkey to extrude the selected faces.
2. Press the *X* hotkey to override the default axis lock and switch to being locked to the global *x*-axis.
3. Pull the extrusion inward until it completely clips through the main section of the chair.
4. Left-click to confirm the extrusion.
5. Press the *Delete* key to bring up the **Delete** menu.
6. Choose **Faces** to get rid of the unneeded internal faces.

Wonderful! We're done with the arm! Now, we just need one for the other side. We could use the destructive "Symmetrize" operation that we used earlier in this chapter, but let's use a non-destructive modifier instead:

1. *Tab* back into **Object Mode**.
2. Go to the **Modifiers** tab in the **Properties** panel.
3. Click **Add Modifier**.
4. Choose **Mirror** from the **Generate** section.

The mirror modifier is perhaps the most popular modifier in Blender; it's useful for doing anything symmetrical, which is most things!

If the armrest didn't mirror along with the appropriate center point, then the origin of the armrest object might not be centered on the grid. You need to apply the object's location: **Object | Apply | Location**.

Excellent, we're done! Now, we have a super cozy-looking sci-fi chair:

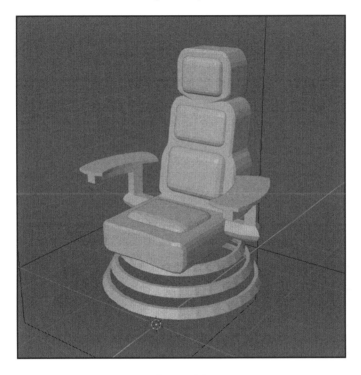

One snazzy chair

It looks great. If you had trouble with any part of this chapter, you can have a look at the TimeMachine_FinishedChair.blend file provided to compare your work. When you're confident with the quality of your chair, then you're ready to move on to the next chapter.

Summary

That was a lot to take in just to build a chair, but we've covered a lot of useful things for modeling just about any object. We learned how to set up reference images in our 3D scene. We went over some of the most important hotkeys for the transformation of objects and components. We got a lot of practice with box modeling using extrusions and inserting edge loops. We also learned some of the benefits of destructive versus non-destructive modeling. We took our first steps with Blender's powerful modifier system. And we used all of these new techniques to get a good start on the time machine model—how exciting!

In the next chapter, we will continue practicing these modeling techniques, introduce a few new modeling methods, and finish the rest of the time machine!

Questions

1. What are the differences between destructive and non-destructive modeling?
2. What is the hotkey for grabbing/translating/moving an object?
3. What is the hotkey for rotating an object?
4. What is the hotkey for scaling an object?
5. How can you make a blocky model look more round?
6. What are primitives?
7. How does box modeling work?
8. What is Blender's most popular modifier?
9. Can you use more than one modifier on a single object?
10. How do you enable the quad-view feature?

Modeling a Time Machine - Part 2

4

Welcome back! Time flies when you're having fun. In this chapter, we'll finish modeling our time machine. Then, we'll have all the time in the world!

In the previous chapter, we tackled some of the core concepts behind the modeling process. In this chapter, we will take a look at a few more modeling tools and modifiers that we can use to finish off the model. We will be using much more streamlined instructions this time around. The repetition we provided regarding the main modeling tools should have been enough that you now feel comfortable moving objects around, changing camera angles, and using the extrusion tool.

When you're ready to follow along with this chapter, you can start with the chair you created in the previous chapter, or you can start with the provided `TimeMachine_FinishedChair.blend` example file.

The following topics will be covered in this chapter:

- Modeling the base of the time machine
- Modeling the clock
- Modeling the side rails
- Modeling the rear assembly
- Modeling the front housing
- Adding smooth shading to the model

Modeling the base of the time machine

The base of the time machine is quite simple: it's a circle with a few extrusions in the middle and some clamps around the rim. Let's get started:

1. Reset the 3D Cursor to the center of the grid *(Shift + S* hotkey | **Cursor to World Origin**).
2. Go to the top view.
3. Bring up the **Add** menu (from the top of the 3D View or with the *Shift + A* hotkey).
4. Choose **Mesh | Circle**.
5. Set **Vertices** to 64.
6. Set **Radius** to 2.22 m.
7. Set **Fill Type** to Ngon.
8. Rename the circle Base.

Having more vertices in a circle will make it look more round and avoid us having a jagged edge look. Since this circle is so large, we need a lot of vertices to make it look nice. 64 is a good choice because it is a power of 2 (**2 -> 4 -> 8 -> 16 -> 32 -> 64**). Generally, we will get good results when working with nice, even numbers like this. Now, let's give it some thickness:

1. Go to the side view.
2. *Tab* into **Edit Mode**.
3. Select the entire mesh.
4. Extrude the selection upward to meet the first ridge.
5. Extrude again to meet the second ridge.
6. Scale down to match the thickness of the inner circle.
7. Extrude up one more time to meet the topmost edge of the base.

Our base piece should look as follows:

The main piece of the base of the time machine

Good – now, we just need the clamps. We'll start with a cube; however, the clamps are part of the base, so it will work nicely if all of their polygons are included inside of the same object that the circular part of the base that we just created is a part of.

If we use the **Add** menu to add a cube while we are still in **Edit Mode**, we won't see a new object appear in the Outliner. Instead, new polygons will be added inside of the Base object which we are currently editing:

1. Go to the top view.
2. Remain in **Edit Mode**, bring up the **Add** menu, and choose **Cube**.
3. Set **Size** to 0.43 m.
4. Set **Location X** to -1.89 m.
5. Set **Location Z** to 0.32 m.

That's a good start. Now, let's align it to the front view:

1. Go to the front view.
2. Switch to **Face Select** mode.
3. Grab the rightmost face and drag it to the left until it aligns with the edge of the clamp shown in the following screenshot.
4. Grab the topmost face and drag it down until it aligns with the edge of the little corner shown in the following screenshot:

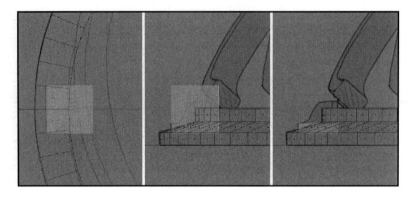

The new cube from the top view (left image), from the front view (middle image), and after adjusting the right-hand side and top (right image)

The next bit of this process should feel familiar since it's the same process we used to model the bulbous part of the armrest in the previous chapter:

1. Extrude the top face up to the bend in the clamp (see the following screenshot).
2. Scale down along the x-axis to match the reference.
3. Extrude up again to meet the height of the circular piece of the base.
4. Scale down along the x-axis to match the reference.
5. Extrude up one more time to meet up with the top of the clamp.
6. Select the right-hand side face of this latest extrusion and extrude it out to the right until it meets up with the edge of the clamp in the reference.
7. Switch to Edge Mode and select the top-left corner edge (it's hard to see it from this angle, so rotate the view if you need to and then return to the front view once it's selected).
8. Move the corner along the x-axis so that it matches the corner in the reference:

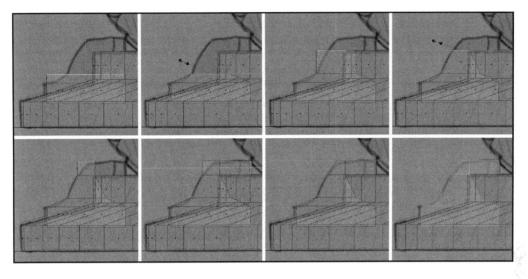

The extrusions required to make the clamp

Don't forget to lock to the appropriate axes during these steps; otherwise, you'll shrink the cube along the other two axes as well. If we look at it from the perspective view, our clamp should look like the following:

Locking the appropriate axes

Now, we just need to adjust the width at each of the extruded sections and we'll be done:

1. Switch to **Face Select** mode.
2. Select the two faces at the very top of the clamp piece.
3. Go to the **Select** menu and choose **Select More/Less | More**:

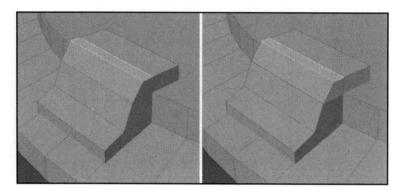

Selecting the top two faces and expanding the selection

4. Go to the top view.
5. Scale down along the *y*-axis to match the reference.
6. Go to the **Select** menu and choose **Select More/Less | More** again.
7. Go to the **Select** menu and choose **Select Loops | Select Boundary Loop**.
8. Scale along the *y*-axis so that it matches what we can see in the following screenshot:

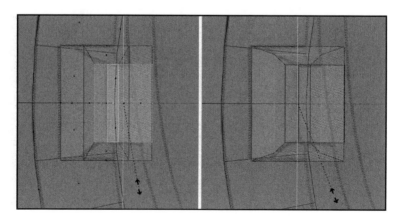

Scaling down the selected faces, then scaling down the boundary loop

Good – the first clamp is finished. Now, we just need to place copies of it around the rim of the base to make the other seven clamps. We have a special tool in the Toolbar that can help us with this:

1. Select any component on the clamp piece.
2. Go to the **Select** menu and choose **Select Linked | Linked**.
3. Activate the **Spin** tool from the Toolbar.
4. Click and drag one of the blue widgets to begin the spin.
5. Let go of the widget (precision doesn't matter here; we'll type in specific parameters in a moment).
6. Open the **Adjust Last Operator** panel.
7. Set **Steps** to 8.
8. Set **Angle** to 360.
9. *Tab* back into **Object Mode**:

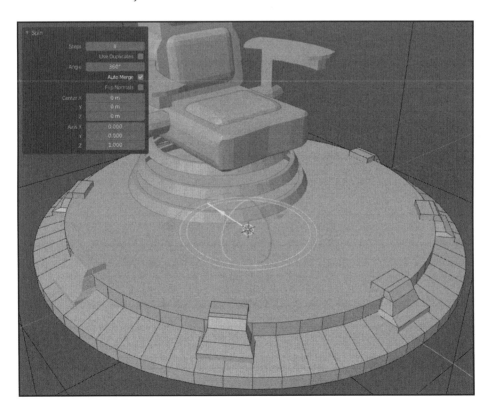

The Spin tool lets us duplicate the clamp around the center point

Excellent! The base is finished. Now, as long as we still have our internal reference images set up, we can go ahead and model the remaining internal piece: the clock.

Modeling the clock

The face of the clock can be made out of a cylinder. As for making the numbers, this will be a perfect opportunity to incorporate text into our modeling workflow. We will also look at one of the most important tools when it comes to precision: snapping. We'll begin by hiding the chair objects so that we can see what we're doing. Then, we will create a cylinder for the clock:

1. Go to the back view.
2. Click on the eyeball icon next to all of the chair objects in the Outliner to hide them. This will give us a clear view of the clock (see the following screenshot).
3. Use the **Cursor** tool from the Toolbar to place the 3D Cursor right in the center of the clock:

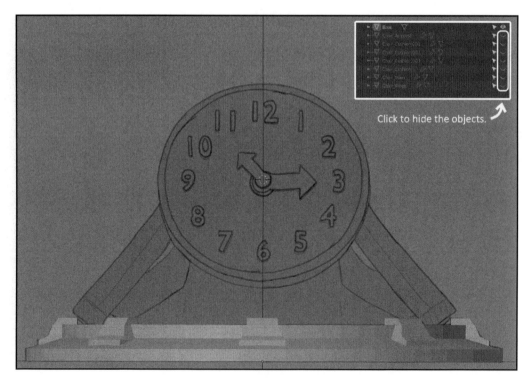

Click and drag on the column of eyeball icons to make the clock reference visible from the back view

4. Press the *Shift + A* hotkey to bring up the **Add** menu.

5. Choose **Mesh | Cylinder**.

6. Set **Vertices** to 32.

7. Set **Radius** to 1 m.

8. Set **Depth** to 0.2 m.

9. Set **Location X** to 0 m.

10. Set **Location Y** to -1.1 m.

11. Set **Location Z** to 1.58 m.

12. Set **Rotation X** to -64.

13. Set **Rotation Y** to 0.

14. Set **Rotation Z** to 0.

15. Rename the cylinder Clock_Main:

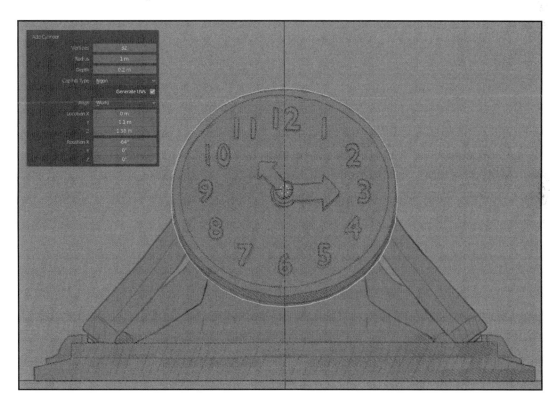

Modeling the clock with a cylinder

Good – now, we have the base piece of the clock. Using the 3D Cursor helped us get started, but typing in the location and rotation settings let us place the cylinder precisely in alignment with the reference image. Check the cylinder from the side view; you should see that the alignment is well centered.

Now, let's make the numbers for the clock. We're going to use a new type of object: `text`. Each number will be its own text object. But first, we're going to use a trick to create 12 snapping points for the text objects. As we noticed in the previous step, trying to place the 3D Cursor by hand is a little sloppy, but we can use our **Snap** pie menu to place it in a precise location instead of using the **Cursor** tool from the Toolbar:

1. *Tab* into **Edit Mode** for the `Clock_Main` object.
2. Switch to **Face Select** mode.
3. Select the large face on the near side of the cylinder.
4. Bring up the **Snap** pie menu with the *Shift + S* hotkey.
5. Choose **Cursor to Selected**:

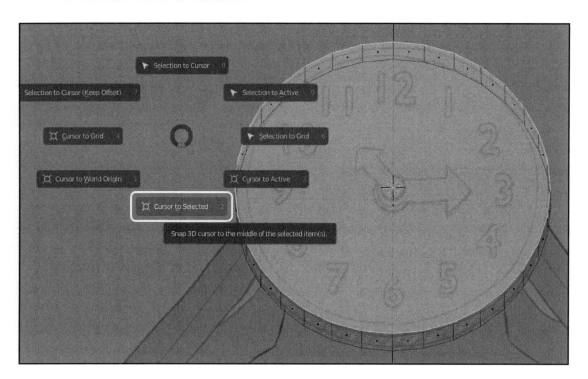

Snapping the 3D Cursor to the center of the clock face

Good – the **Snap** pie menu is a precise way of positioning the 3D Cursor. You will find the 3D Cursor to be a very useful tool once you take control over it like this. Next, we're going to make our 12 snapping points for the text by temporarily making a circle. Remember that new objects are created at the location of the 3D Cursor, so we're already off to a good start:

1. *Tab* back into **Object Mode**.
2. Add a new circle mesh object from the **Add** menu.
3. Set **Vertices** to 12 (one vertex for each hour on the clock).
4. Set **Radius** to 0.7 m.
5. Set **Rotation X** to −64 (to match the rotation of the clock):

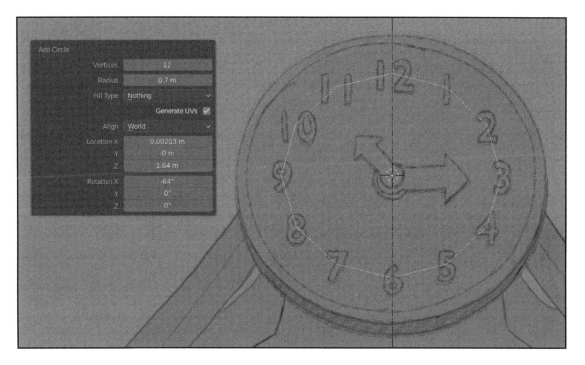

Creating a circle with 12 vertices to be used as snapping points

Excellent – we won't need this object for long. It's just here to serve as a set of snapping points for the numbers. Let's move on:

1. Bring up the **Add** menu again and choose **Text**.
2. Set **Rotation X** to 64 (to match the angle of the clock face).
3. Set **Rotation Z** to 180 (so that the text isn't backward).
4. Rename the text object Clock_Number:

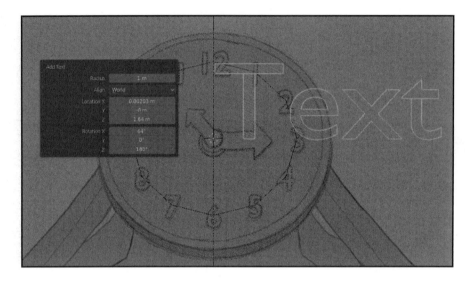

Creating the first text object

Text objects have their own version of **Edit Mode**. Instead of editing vertices, edges, and faces, text objects let you type in custom text. This will be perfect for creating the numbers on the clock:

1. *Tab* into **Edit Mode**.
2. *Backspace* four times to clear away the default letters.
3. Type 12 to get the number 12 for our clock.
4. *Tab* back into **Object Mode**.

Good. Now, let's give the text some thickness and center it. Text objects have a special set of options that will let us do both of these things in the **Properties** panel:

1. Go to the green **Object Data Properties** tab in the **Properties** panel.
2. Go to the **Geometry** subsection.
3. Set **Extrude** to 0.03 m.

4. Go to the **Transform** subsection within the **Font** subsection.

5. Set **Size** to 0.3.

6. Go to the **Alignment** subsection.

7. Set **Horizontal** to **Center**.

8. Set **Vertical** to **Center**:

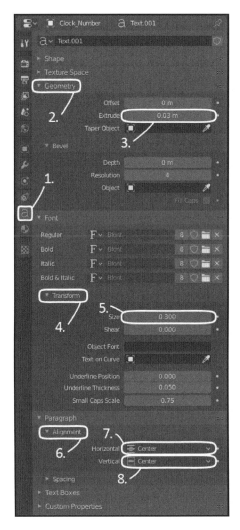

Use these settings to better align the new text object

The available fonts are different for each operating system. This example was created using Windows 10, so your text may look slightly different if you're using macOS or Linux.

Good – we've got our first number. Now, we just need to snap it in place:

1. Turn on snapping by clicking on the magnet icon at the top of the 3D View.
2. Open the snap settings pop-up menu to the right of the magnet icon.
3. Change the **Snap to** mode to **Vertex**:

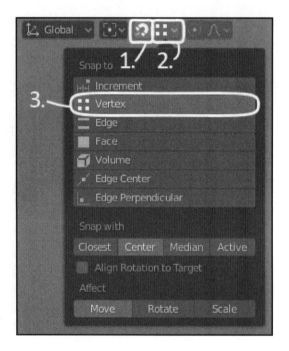

Enabling vertex snapping

Remember that circle with 12 vertices that we made a moment ago? Now, we're going to snap our text object to the top vertex of that circle:

1. Select the text object.
2. Grab it and move it upward, toward the number 12, as shown in the following reference image.

3. Confirm the transformation once it's snapped into place:

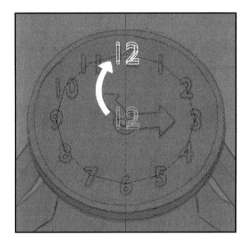

Snapping the number 12 into place

Excellent! Now, all we need to do is duplicate the text object 11 times and snap it around to the rest of the clock positions. Once we have our duplicates, we can edit the text to display the appropriate numbers:

1. Select the text object if it isn't selected already.
2. Press the *Shift + D* hotkey to duplicate the object.
3. Duplicating the object automatically puts us into grab mode.
4. Move the mouse over the number 1 shown in the reference image.
5. Confirm the transformation once it's snapped into place.
6. *Tab* into **Edit Mode**.
7. Press *Backspace* enough times to clear out the irrelevant text.
8. Type in the number that matches the position on the clock.
9. *Tab* back into **Object Mode**.
10. Repeat this until you have all 12 numbers.
11. Once all 12 numbers are in place, select the circle object (the one with 12 sides).
12. Delete the circle object by selecting it and pressing the *Delete* key.

Awesome – we've got numbers on a clock! Our result should look like this:

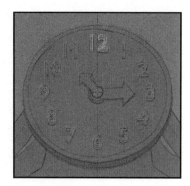

All 12 numbers in place!

Let's add a little more detail to the clock before we move on. We need to add the rim and the arrows. The rim is pretty easy:

1. Select the Clock_Main object.
2. *Tab* into **Edit Mode**.
3. Select the large face on the near side of the cylinder.
4. Either use the **Inset Faces** tool from the Toolbar or press the *I* hotkey.
5. Drag the mouse until the thickness is 0.08 and the face aligns with the inner circle of the reference image:

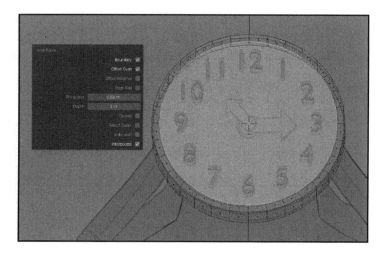

Insetting the clock face

There we go! Insetting is a lot like extruding, but instead of pulling outward, we pull inward. In this case, it has given us a loop of faces around the rim that we can now extrude to create the rim of the clock face:

1. Hold down the *Alt* key and click to select the face loop around the clock.
2. Use the **Extrude Region** tool or press the *E* hotkey to extrude.
3. Pull the extrusion out to 0.03 m so that it matches the thickness of the numbers.

 As with any operator, you can type in the precise number that you need. In this case, begin the extrusion and type 0.03. It will snap right into place.

Perfect! Now, let's add the clock hands:

1. Select the center face.
2. Bring up the **Snap** pie menu with the *Shift + S* hotkey.
3. Choose **Cursor to Selected**.
4. *Tab* back into Object Mode.
5. Add a new circle mesh object from the **Add** menu.
6. Set **Vertices** to 16.
7. Set **Radius** to 0.12 m.
8. Set **Rotation X** to −64 (to match the rotation of the clock).
9. Set **Fill Type** to **Triangle Fan**.
10. Name this new object Hand_Minute.

Perfect! Now that we have the circle, we can model the arrow:

1. *Tab* into **Edit Mode**.
2. Press 2 to switch to Edge Select mode.
3. Select the four edges on the right-hand side of the perimeter of the circle.
4. Extrude the edges and move them along the *x*-axis so that they align with the base of the arrow in the reference image (see the following screenshot).

5. Extrude and move again, this time out to the tip of the arrow:

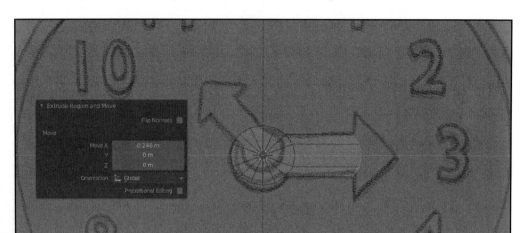

Extruding the edges along the *x*-axis to the base (do this a second time to extrude to the tip)

So far, so good. This next bit is going to get a tiny bit weird. Did you notice how the operation we just performed was called **Extrude Region and Move?** That's because pressing the *E* hotkey is actually a macro of operations; it begins by creating the extrusion, and then it takes us into grab mode to move the extrusion. What this means is we can extrude without moving if we right-click to cancel immediately after pressing the *E* hotkey. This isn't useful very often, but in this case, it will help us make the pointy sides of the arrow by following as few steps as possible:

1. Select the top and bottom edges between the base and tip of the arrow.
2. Press the *E* hotkey to extrude.
3. Right-click to cancel the movement but keep the extrusion.
4. Press the *S* hotkey to start scaling the extruded edges away from each other.
5. Press *Y* twice to lock the scale to the local *y*-axis.
6. Pull the mouse outward until the edges line up with the corners of the arrow.

7. Left-click to confirm:

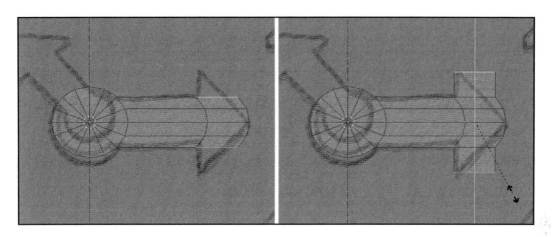

Scaling the edges away from each other effectively moves them into place

Good! Now, let's finish off the point of the arrow by merging all the vertices together:

1. Press *1* to switch to **Vertex Select** mode.
2. Select all seven vertices along the right-hand side. Remember to select the centermost vertex last.
3. Go to the **Vertex** menu at the top of the 3D View.
4. Choose **Merge Vertices | At Last**:

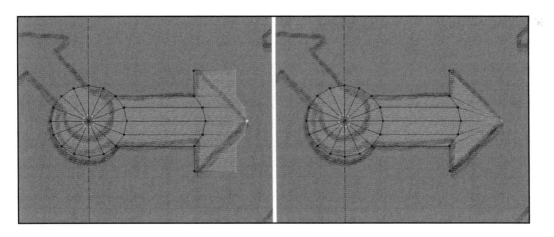

Merging the vertices to form the tip of the arrow

Awesome! The last thing we need is some thickness, and then we're done with the first arrow! And guess what? We already know how to add thickness – by extruding!

1. Press 3 to switch to **Face Select** mode.
2. Press the *A* hotkey to select all of the faces.
3. Press the *E* hotkey to extrude.
4. Type 0.015 to extrude to half the thickness of the numbers on the clock.

That wasn't so hard. The other clock hand is the same but smaller, so we can just duplicate the minute hand and transform it into place. Duplicating is another macro, so when we press the duplicate hotkey, it will create the duplicate, and then we will immediately be put into grab mode so that we can move the object into a more appropriate place. We will use that to snap the new arrow on top of the original arrow:

1. *Tab* into **Object Mode**.
2. Press the *Shift + D* hotkey to duplicate the arrow.
3. Move it up slightly to snap it on top of the minute hand.
4. Rename the new arrow Hand_Hour.
5. Rotate it by 130 degrees along its local *z*-axis (press *R, Z, Z*, type 130, and then press *Enter* or left-click to confirm).
6. Scale down along the local *x* and *y*-axes to 0.75 (press *S, Shift + Z, Shift + Z*, type .75, and then press *Enter* or left-click to confirm).
7. Click the magnet at the top of the 3D View to turn snapping back off:

The time machine, so far...

And there we have it – a clock for our time machine with a couple of beautiful arrows! Well done. Next, we will tackle a much simpler piece: the side rails.

Modeling the side rails

The side rails are a fun design piece that visually ties the time machine together. For this piece, we will use some more basic modeling tools and a couple of modifiers.

As obvious as it sounds, sometimes, it's helpful to think about how an object is constructed in real life when we're thinking about how to approach modeling it in 3D. As we can see from the reference images, the side rails are just two big circular parts with the upper section removed, so that's how we'll model them!

1. Go to the right-side view.
2. Place the 3D Cursor as close to the center of the circular side rail as you can (see the following screenshot).
3. Bring up the **Add** menu.
4. Choose **Mesh | Cylinder**.
5. Set **Vertices** to 64.
6. Set **Radius** to 1.35 m.
7. Set **Depth** to 0.3 m.
8. Set **Cap Fill Type** to **Nothing**.
9. Rename the circle SideRail.

That's a good start. Now, we can rotate and move it into position until it aligns with the reference images. Toggle between the front, back, and side views to check the alignment from all three angles. Rotate and move the side rail as needed:

Pressing *R* twice will enable "trackball" style rotation, which can be very helpful for arbitrarily rotating objects like this.

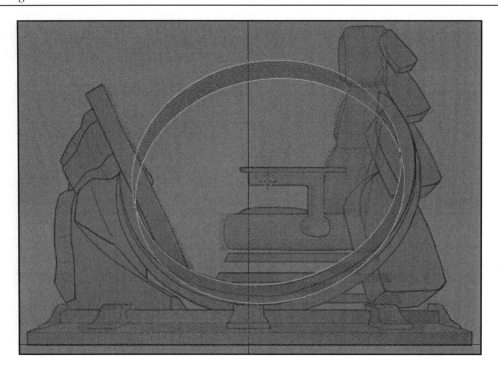

The 3D Cursor placed at the center of the side rail and the cylinder rotated into place

Your numbers may vary, but if you'd like to perfectly match our example, you can copy the following numbers into the object properties for the side rail object:

- **Location X**: 0.836 m
- **Location Y**: 0.195 m
- **Location Z**: 1.585 m
- **Rotation X**: -4
- **Rotation Y**: 54
- **Rotation Z**: -13

Remember that you can always toggle in and out of X-ray mode to make things easier to see. Just use the **Toggle X-Ray** button in the top-right corner of the 3D View.

Alright, that's looking good from all angles! Now, let's give it a little thickness:

1. *Tab* into **Edit Mode**.
2. Press *3* to switch to **Face Select** mode.
3. Press the *A* hotkey to select all of the faces.
4. Click and hold down the mouse button on the **Extrude Region** tool to expose the list of similar extrude tools.
5. Choose the **Extrude Along Normals** tool from the list.
6. Click and drag to extrude to about 0.13 m (type .13 while using the tool):

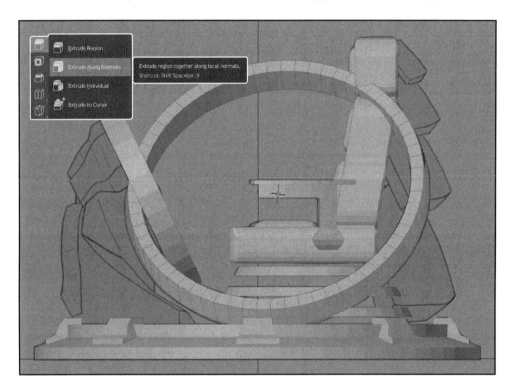

Using the Extrude Along Normals tool

Good. It may be hard to see, but the reference of the side rail has a little lip on the lower outer part of the rim. Let's add that now:

1. Use the **Loop Cut** tool or the *Ctrl + R* hotkey to cut a single new edge loop through the length of the cylinder.
2. Press *3* to switch back to **Face Select** mode.

3. Hold the *Alt* key and click to select the lower of the two face loops.
4. Use the **Extrude Along Normals** tool again to extrude out to about 0.05 m:

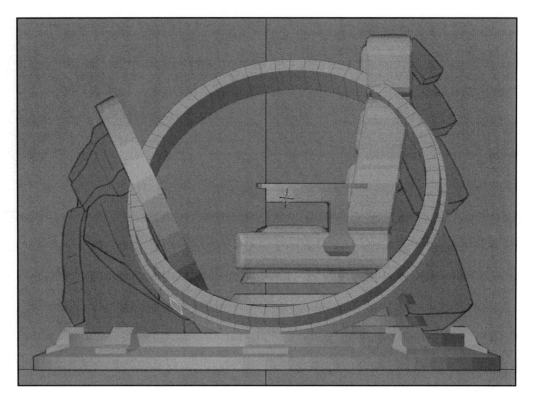

Extruding the lower of the two face loops to form the lip of the side rail

It's subtle, but little details like this will make the end result a bit flashier! Now, all that's left are the modifiers. When we made the armrests in the previous chapter, we used the mirror modifier. We're going to do that again, but this time, we will use a Mirror Object so that the side rail can mirror across the middle of the time machine instead of around its own center point:

1. *Tab* into **Object Mode**.
2. Go to the **Modifiers** tab in the **Properties** panel.
3. Click **Add Modifier** and add a mirror modifier.
4. Click on the eyedropper icon in the **Mirror Object** field.

5. Use the eyedropper to pick the **Base** object in the viewport:

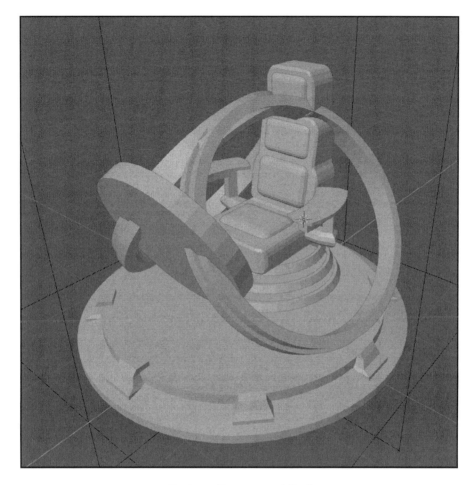

The mirror modifier gave us a second side rail

Bam! Now, we've got two rings. We just need to lop off the top of them and we'll be done. For that, we will use a new type of modifier: Boolean. The Boolean modifier will let us remove parts of an object where it intersects with another. So, first, let's add an object that we can use to subtract from the rails:

1. Go to the right-side view.
2. Bring up the **Add** menu.
3. Choose **Mesh | Cylinder.**
4. Set **Vertices** to 32.

5. Set **Radius** to 1.35 m.

6. Set **Depth** to 4 m.

7. Set **Cap Fill Type** to Ngon.

8. Set **Location X** to 0 m

9. Set **Location Y** to -0.05 m

10. Set **Location Z** to 2.4 m

11. Set **Rotation X** to 0.

12. Set **Rotation Y** to 90.

13. Set **Rotation Z** to 0.

14. Rename the circle SideRail_Boolean:

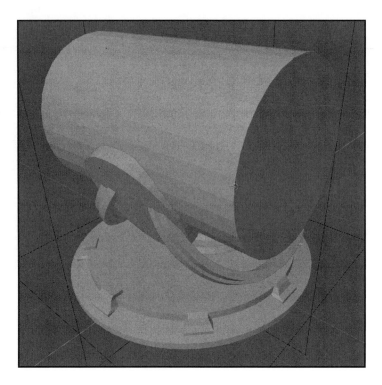

Our new cylinder will be used to cut a hole in the side rails

Good. Although it looks like we've got a big barrel blocking the view of our time machine, we can use a Boolean operation to carve away the intersecting geometry.

While Blender is a stable piece of software, using Booleans can be a bit finicky, and in some cases, they will cause our 3D software to crash. It's rare, but it's good to prepare for the worst: save your project before continuing.

Now, let's hide the cylinder and use the Boolean modifier to cut a hole in the side rail:

1. While the new cylinder is still selected, press the *H* hotkey to hide it.
2. Select the **SideRail** object.
3. Go to the **Modifiers** tab.
4. Click the **Add Modifier** button.
5. Choose **Boolean** from the **Generate** column.
6. The title will be red because we need to pick an object to perform the Boolean operation; click on the **Object** field.
7. Scroll through the list until you find the `SideRail_Boolean` object (you can also start typing in the name of the object and it will appear in the list):

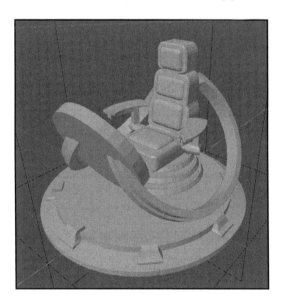

A nice finished pair of side rails

And we're done! Now, all we need is the front housing and the rear assembly. The rear assembly can be made with a familiar workflow: box modeling.

Modeling the rear assembly

We're finished with the interior pieces of the time machine. Before we get started on the last two pieces of the model, let's toggle the visibility of the interior and exterior reference images. Click on the eyeball icons for both of the "Interior" reference images in the Outliner to hide them. Next, click on the eyeball icons for both of the "Exterior" reference images in the Outliner to make them visible. Once that's done, we're ready to model the rear assembly.

The rear assembly isn't a terribly complicated piece. It requires a couple of simple extrusions, as well as some modifiers that will save us from having to model more than one of the repeated sections. We're going to start with the piece on the back of the headrest. Let's start by adding a plane:

1. Go to the back view.
2. Place the 3D Cursor near the middle of the headrest.
3. Bring up the **Add** menu and choose **Mesh | Plane**.
4. Open the **Adjust Last Operation** panel.
5. Set **Size** to `0.22` m.
6. Set **Align** to **View**.
7. Set **Location X** to `0`.
8. Rename the new object `RearAssembly`.

Setting the **Align** option to **View** has rotated the object. This means that Blender thinks the object is not in its default rotation right now. This will cause a problem later, so we need to apply the rotation:

1. Go to the **Object** menu at the top of the 3D View.
2. Choose **Apply – Rotation & Scale**.

The object shouldn't look any different, but now, Blender recognizes its current orientation as its default, which is good! Next, let's get some symmetry and thickness going with modifiers:

1. Go to the **Modifiers** tab.
2. Add a mirror modifier to the **RearAssembly** object.
3. Inside of the modifier's options, check the box that says **clipping**.
4. Add a **Solidify** modifier.
5. Set **Thickness** to `0.1` m.

The **clipping** option in the mirror modifier means that parts of the mesh that touch the symmetry line will "stick" to the symmetry line, which is very useful for making the object mirror seamlessly. You will see this in action now:

1. *Tab* into **Edit Mode**.
2. Press the *A* hotkey to select all of the components.
3. Grab the components and move them to the left along the *x*-axis until the leftmost edge aligns with the edge of the reference image (see the following screenshot).
4. Insert a vertical edge loop and slide it so that it aligns with the corner of the underside of the reference image (see the following screenshot).
5. Extrude the bottom-most edge on the left side down so that it meets the bottom edge shown in the reference image.
6. Cut one more vertical edge loop through the left half, as shown in the following screenshot:

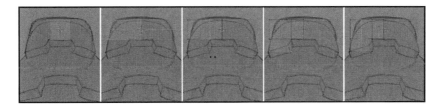

Step by step, we're adding the extrusions and edge loops needed to make the rear assembly

Now that we have the geometry we need, we need to move the vertices into place. Use the following image as a reference:

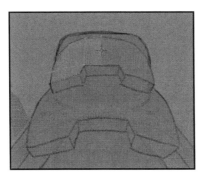

Moving the vertices into place

Now, we need to do the same thing from the side view. This will probably take some back and forth. Use the following image reference to do so and take it one vertex at a time:

Moving the vertices so that they align with the side view as well

When you're finished, *Tab* back into **Object Mode** and see what it looks like in 3D. You should have a piece that looks like this:

The upper piece of the rear assembly should look like this once all the vertices are in place

Take as much time as you need to get the vertices massaged into place. When you're ready, we can use a new modifier trick to finish.

The other three parts of the rear assembly are all identical, just in slightly different locations, rotations, and scales. If you remember, when we made the Sci-Fi rings under the chair, we used a super-cool modifier called the array modifier. At the time, we only used a basic type of offset. This time, let's create an advanced "object offset." To do this, we need to create an `Empty` object that we can resize, rotate, and reposition as needed for our offset:

1. Snap the 3D Cursor to the rear assembly piece (as seen in the preceding screenshot).
2. Open the **Add** menu.
3. Choose **Empty** | **Plain Axes**.

Excellent! Now, let's add the array modifier:

1. Select the rear assembly object again.
2. Go to the **Modifiers** tab.
3. Add an array modifier.
4. Uncheck the **Relative Offset** option.
5. Check the box for **Object Offset**.
6. Click the eyedropper in the **Object Offset** field.
7. Click on the **Empty** object in the 3D View to choose it.

Now that that is set up, we can transform the **Empty** object. After, the array modifier will create a copy of the rear assembly based on that transformation. And we're not even at the cool part yet – just you wait!

1. Go to the side view.
2. Select the **Empty** object.
3. Grab, rotate, and scale the **Empty** object until the copy of the rear assembly aligns with the reference images.

Avoid moving the **Empty** object along the *x*-axis; otherwise, it won't be centered anymore. Once you've got it in place, you should have something like this:

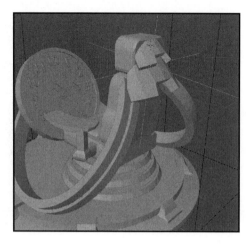

The Empty object is provides an offset for the rear assembly array

Once you're ready, select the rear assembly object again and take a look at the **Modifiers** tab. Go to the array modifier and increase the "Count" from 2 to 4. And just like that, bam! We've got a rear assembly:

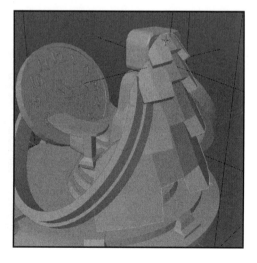

The rear assembly is complete!

Check the pieces against the reference images again and make adjustments to the **Empty** object if you need to. Once you're done, select the **Empty** object and press the *H* hotkey to hide it.

That's it; there's just one last piece we need to create before we're ready for time travel! Let's finish with the front housing.

Modeling the front housing

At this point, you've learned all the 3D modeling techniques that you'll need to create the front housing. We'll leave this part open-ended for you to practice your new skills. If you'd like, you can have a look at the finished project in the provided files so you can see one way of making it:

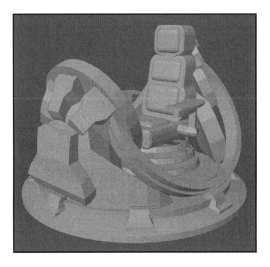

This is how our example front housing turned out

However you approach this final section, there's one last piece of cleanup we need to do for the model that will make it look a lot nicer. When you're ready, move on to the next section.

Adding smooth shading to the model

You probably noticed that the model has a faceted look to it. Most of the polygons catch the light and pop out. Polygons can either have "smooth shading" or "flat shading." Can you guess which one most of our polygons have right now? That's right, flat shading.

Flat shading is great for hard edges, but not so great for smooth surfaces. Luckily, we can do a bit of both.

These types of shading actually change the mesh data, so save your project before moving on.

First, we are going to apply smooth shading to all of the objects as a base:

1. Press the *A* hotkey to select all the objects.
2. Go to the **Object** menu at the top of the 3D View.
3. Choose the **Shade Smooth** option:

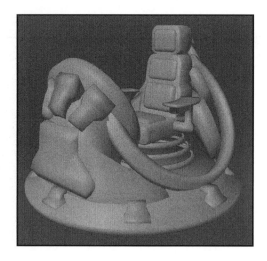

The time machine with smooth shading applied

The faceted look is gone, but now the time machine looks like a big nasty blob – yuck! As it turns out, some flat shading is a good thing, particularly around hard corners. Luckily, Blender gives us a way to adjust our shading automatically, based on the angle of the edges:

1. Select the **Base** object and go to the green **Object Data Properties** tab in the **Properties** panel.
2. Open the **Normals** section.
3. Check the box that says **Auto Smooth**.

4. Adjust the angle until only the edges we want have flat shading (45 works well for the base):

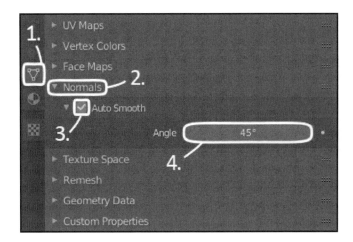

Settings for the auto smooth feature

That's looking better already. Now, we just need to do the same thing for all the other pieces. You'll have to set each **Angle** number individually since each object has different angles. When you're finished, you'll have a much better-looking time machine, similar to the one shown in the following screenshot:

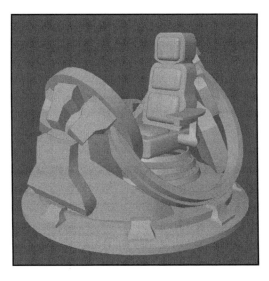

The final time machine, with cleaned up shading

And there we have it! There are more precise ways to mark specific edges as sharp, but that's a bit overkill for this project. Since it's looking so good, we've got to check it out from another angle:

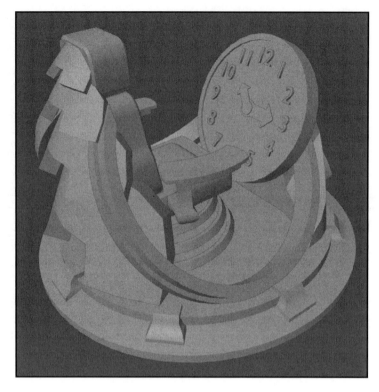

Alternative angle of the finished time machine

Oh yeah, that's the stuff. If I were you, I would totally time travel all around town in that thing! Give yourself a round of applause – we're done!

Summary

Wow, that was a lot to take in! We certainly learned a lot about 3D modeling: We learned about several new tools: **Spin** lets us create radial duplicates around the base of the time machine, while **Loop Cut** allows us to create new edge loops that support the extrusions we needed for new details throughout the model.

We also learned a new way to use vertex snapping to our advantage when we attached the numbers to the face of the clock. Snapping features are very useful when we need precision in our projects. Then, we learned how to use text objects, which let us add high-quality 3D text to the scene. We also learned about **Empty** objects, which don't contribute to the final render, but they can give us extra control over things such as the Array modifier's **Object Offset** parameter. We took a closer look at some of the most common modifiers in Blender, such as the Mirror modifier, the Array modifier, and the Boolean modifier. We learned what these modifiers' extra features do, such as Clipping, Mirror Object, and Object Offset. Getting to know the advanced features in these modifiers opens up a wide range of new possibilities, which is especially versatile when we wish to use several modifiers on a single object. Finally, we added a layer of polish to our model by fixing the shading. Applying a proper mix of flat and smooth shading can really improve the visual quality of a model. Most, if not all, of these techniques will come in handy over and over again when you work on your future Blender projects.

In the next project, we'll learn how to create a complex environment scene. We'll learn how to create lots of assets efficiently and have those assets work together in the most economic way.

Questions

1. What's the difference between inset and extrude?
2. How can we access similar stacked tools in the Toolbar?
3. How do we type custom text into text objects?
4. What can we do with the Boolean modifier?
5. How can we set specific rotation values for an object when we create it?
6. How can we create object-based offsets when using the Array modifier?
7. What's an easy way to add thickness to a model?
8. What are the two types of polygon shading?
9. How can we automatically apply flat shading to edges based on their angles?
10. How do we travel through time?

5
Modern Kitchen - Part 1: Kitbashing

Now that we've learned how to use Blender's core modeling tools to create a single model, we'll look at a variety of clever ways to put together a collection of models to make a whole scene. Blender 2.8's Collections feature allows us to organize lots of objects into a flexible hierarchy. In this project, we will use this to our advantage as we kitbash a sleek kitchen out of several preexisting assets.

Kitbashing is a common practice for rapidly prototyping a design out of assorted existing "kits." You might build a custom robot out of model airplane parts or develop a library of three-dimensional assets to throw a video game environment together. Embracing the kitbash mentality can be very freeing to your workflow because it means there's no single correct way to solve a problem.

In this chapter, we'll kitbash a kitchen with several strategies. First, we'll plan our layout using **previsualization** (**previz**), where the kitchen is modeled in full with basic placeholder shapes so that composition and scale are solved right away. We'll expand our modeling skills by seeing how modifiers can make generated models, such as tables and chairs. We'll use a variety of add-ons to expand Blender's capabilities, rapidly generating things such as cupboards, doors, and windows. Boolean modeling, where shapes are added and subtracted in a nondestructive modifier stack, will show a new approach to modeling. Lastly, we'll finish the kitchen with a library of pre-made assets—a vital shortcut when trying to hit a deadline.

We will cover the following topics in this chapter:

- Setting up the source files
- Previsualizing the kitchen layout
- Creating tables with box modeling
- Creating chairs with modifiers and curves
- Creating cabinets, islands, and a stove with add-ons
- Linking in canned assets

Setting up the source files

Because this project will focus on creating a final scene out of preexisting assets, we have provided several assets for you to work with. The asset files for this chapter can be downloaded at `https://github.com/PacktPublishing/Blender-3D-By-Example-Second-Edition/tree/master/Blender3DByExample_ch05`.

We've also included some examples of our scene layout, which you can reference at any time if you get stuck.

Now, let's begin by previsualizing the kitchen.

Previsualizing the kitchen layout

We'll start our sleek modern kitchen project with a process called **previz**. Previz is a handy starting point for three-dimensional production, similar to concept art for complex scenes. In this stage, we will block out the floor plan and layout elements of the scene using placeholders to test composition and get a sense of scale. When we're finished creating our composition, we can replace the placeholders with the finished assets. Let's get started with the floor plan.

Creating a floor plan

The best place to start a project is always referencing. What look do you want? Can you pin it down to certain styles, eras, or layouts? Scour the internet for images of modern kitchens that inspire you. Blueprints are often helpful, too, and even if you don't stick to them, they can help you get an initial idea for the real-world scale of objects and layouts.

Getting our scale correct is crucial for composition. There's no point in doing a bunch of detailed modeling work in our scene only to find out that our kitchen is only big enough for ants! We'll start off by creating a simple floor plan so that we know how large everything should be:

1. Start a new Blender scene.
2. Go to the **Top** view.
3. Add a mesh **Plane** object.
4. Rename the plane to `floor`.
5. Tab to **Edit Mode**.
6. Press 2 to switch to **Edge Select** mode.

There is a viewport overlay feature that we can use to help us visualize the scale while we create the floor plan. Let's turn it on now:

1. Find the viewport overlays icon at the top-right corner of the 3D View.
2. Click the drop-down arrow to open the pop-over menu.
3. Check the box for **Edge Length** under the **Measurement** section.

Good, now we can see the length of our selected edges in meters and we're ready to create our floor plan:

1. Click on the magnet at the top of the 3D Viewport to enable snapping.
2. Select an edge.
3. Grab, move, and snap the edge to the grid.
4. Use the **Loop Cut** and **Extrude** tools, which are required to create hallways and recesses in the floor plan.
5. Switch back to **Object Mode** when you're done.
6. Click on the magnet at the top of the 3D Viewport to disable snapping.

In addition to grid snapping, you can always type in exact units while moving edges around—for example, type `y` `.5` to move an edge exactly `0.5` m along the *y*-axis.

A floor plan does not have to be complicated; our example turned out like this:

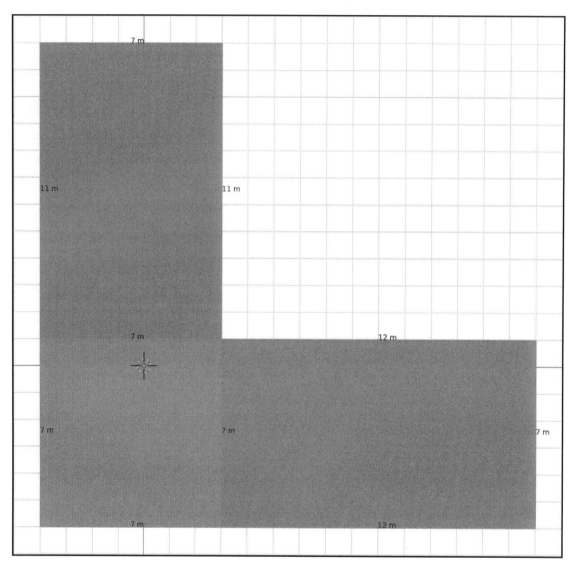

An example floor plan

Don't get too caught up in having the right layout. The joy of 3D is that alternative versions can be rapidly put together. If something isn't working, you can always come back and try out a new layout during this previsualization stage.

We've gone for a fancy, sleek modern kitchen for our example, so it is very large and includes space for a hallway, an outdoor area, a dining area, a sitting area, and a kitchen counter. Yours may be considerably smaller, depending on the type of kitchen you want to create. We won't know for sure whether it's a good size until we start to get some previz objects in there, so we'll take care of that next.

Creating previz objects

Now that we have a floor plan, we need to make some previz models to represent where our finished kitchen assets will go.

We want the models in our scene to match the dimensions of the real world. We don't have to get bogged down with the details, but as often as possible, we need to model our scene with accurate measurements. You can even go around your house with a tape measure to get measurements. Meters are the default unit in Blender, so we'll measure in m. Here are some approximate measurements for objects in the real world:

Object	Width	Depth	Height
Human	0.5 m	Varies with diet	1.8 m
Table	1 m	2.5 m	0.8 m
Coffee table	1 m	1 m	0.5 m
Island	1.5 m	6 m	1 m
Counters	Varies	1 m	1 m
Chair	0.6 m	0.6 m	1 m
Door	1 m		2.3 m
Window sill	Varies		1 m
Window top			2.3 m
Barstools	0.6 m	0.6 m	1.5 m
Sink	0.8 m	0.6 m	0.6 m
Refrigerator	1 m	1 m	2 m

When we previz these objects in our scene, we don't need to model in any of the details. Instead, we can simply create cubes that have the correct proportions for the objects they represent. Let's create a previz table according to the preceding measurements:

1. Add a cube.
2. Rename the cube to `table_p` (*p* stands for previz).
3. Move the cube 1 m upward so that it resets on the grid.
4. Open the sidebar by pressing the *n* hotkey.
5. Switch to the **Item** tab in the sidebar if it's not already active.

As we know, an object's transforms give us information about where that object is in the scene. The **Item** tab in the sidebar gives us a quick display of this information. If we look at the location data, we'll notice a problem with our new cube—it reads 0 m, 0 m, 1 m. This is because we moved the cube up 1 m in **Object Mode**. The orange dot in the center of the object, which represents the object's origin, also floats 1 m above the grid. When a model is centered in the scene, these numbers should read 0 m, 0 m, 0 m—that way, Blender knows that the object is in its resting position. When we move the object away from the center, these numbers will accurately represent how far away the object is from its resting position in each direction. But right now, Blender thinks that the object is not in its resting position; it thinks it's floating 1 m above the ground. Let's fix this by applying the location while the cube is centered above the grid:

1. Press the *Ctrl + A* hotkeys to open the **Apply** menu.
2. Choose **Location** from the menu.

Good, now we have a cube with an origin point that rests on the center of the grid. The cube's origin has returned to the center of the grid while leaving the cube's geometry sitting on top of the grid. As we can see in the sidebar, **Location** reads 0 m, 0 m, 0 m. In the later stages of this project, each object will be placed in a specific location in the scene and the **Location** numbers will perfectly correspond to its alignment in the scene.

 We only apply the location of the objects while they are centered above the grid. We will not apply the locations of the objects after placing them in the scene later on in the project, as that would defeat the purpose of applying their location at this early stage.

Lastly, we can use the sidebar to set the dimensions of the cube to match the table from our previous measurements:

1. Find the **Dimensions** numbers at the bottom of the sidebar.
2. Type 1 m in **X** for the width.
3. Type 2.5 m in **Y** for the depth.
4. Type 0.8 m in **Z** for the height.

Now, it's the correct size, but setting the dimensions has distorted the scale of our object. Right now, it reads 0.5, 1.25, 0.4, which is all sorts of wrong. All finished models should read 1, 1, 1 for scale, so we need to apply scale to fix it:

1. Press the *Ctrl + A* hotkeys to open the **Apply** menu.
2. Choose **Scale** from the menu.

It may just be an elongated cube, but it's a good enough representation of our table that we can use it to previsualize the layout and composition of our kitchen. Let's enable a **Viewport Display** option that will help us remember what this object is supposed to be:

1. Select the `table_p` object.
2. Open the **Object Properties** tab in the **Properties** panel.
3. Open the **Viewport Display** subsection.
4. Check the box for **Name**.

Good, now we can see the name of the object in the viewport. Make additional previz cubes for each of the objects that you want to use in your kitchen scene. Use the preceding chart for size references or get out a tape measure and gather some references of your own. Next, we'll use these previz objects to test out the composition of the final scene.

Laying out the kitchen composition

Now that we have a collection of previz objects, we can lay them out on the floor plan—there's not much to it. We're just moving objects around and seeing how they look:

1. Make sure you're in **Object Mode**.
2. Move each previz object to a spot you like.
3. Press the *Shift + D* hotkeys to duplicate the selected object if you need additional tables, chairs, and so on.

 Make sure you move objects in **Object Mode**, not in **Edit Mode**, since we are placing objects in the scene, not editing the objects.

Play around with several layouts for the kitchen; don't forget about the counters, the fridge, and the kitchen island. If you need to, you can always adjust the floor plan. Keep trying layouts until you're happy with the composition.

 You can use the **Viewport Shading** menu to change the color to **Random** to better visualize the objects' placement.

Our composition looks like this:

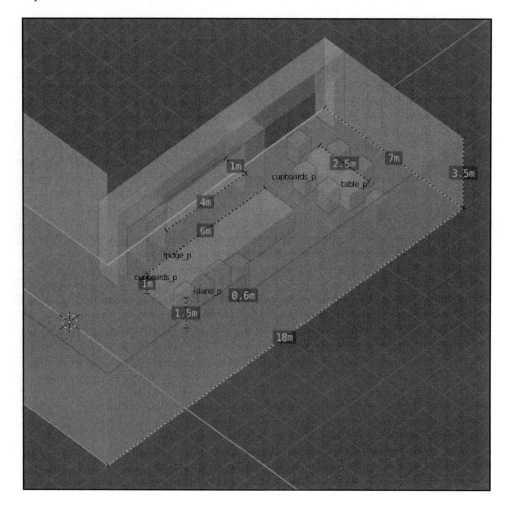

The composition of our kitchen layout

To add walls to your kitchen, we can extrude the perimeter edges of the floor upwards:

1. Select the floor.
2. Tab to **Edit Mode**.
3. Select the edges around the floor.
4. Extrude them up 3 meters.

5. Switch to the **Face Select** mode.
6. Select the walls.
7. Separate the walls out into their own mesh object with the *P* hotkey.
8. Tab back to **Object Mode**.

Walls are good, but how about a ceiling? Well, that's easy—we can just duplicate the floor:

1. Select the floor.
2. Press the *Shift + D* hotkeys to duplicate it.
3. Move the wall up 3 m to match the height of the walls.
4. Find the **Mesh** menu from the top of the 3D Viewport.
5. Use the **Mesh | Normals | Flip Normals** option to invert the mesh so that the normals point inward toward the room.

Normals describe the direction a polygon is facing. A cube object has its normals point outward, but in our kitchen's case, we're inside the cube. Visualizing the normal direction helps determine how to fix normals. To check whether they point inward, open the **Viewport Overlays** menu and turn on **Face Normals**. You should see little lines pointing inward, as shown:

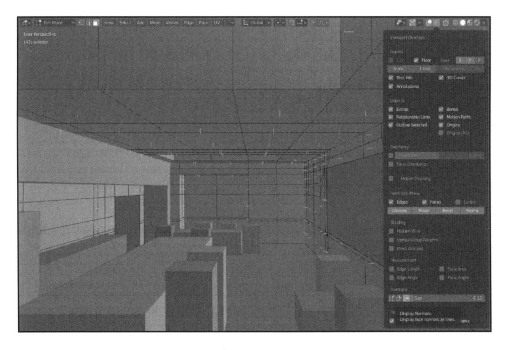

The face normals overlay

Awesome, we've got our layout. If you would like to compare your layout to our example, open the `ch05_kitchenBlueprint.blend` file.

This assembling process lets us think through the space early on and also provides us with a checklist for assets to create or polish for the final scene. Now, we need to take this kitchen layout out of the previz stage and replace some of these cubes with proper assets.

Save this Blender scene as `kitchen.blend`; we will be creating the final assets in a different scene before linking them back to this scene. We'll start with box modeling the tables.

Creating tables with box modeling

Now, we're ready to move on to the modeling stage to create a kitchen table and coffee table with familiar modeling workflows. When we're finished, we'll bring the table and other assets into the kitchen scene via linking, which allows us to assemble a complex scene from assets that come from separate scenes.

The kitchen and coffee tables will use old fashioned box modeling, plus a few modifiers to help. Let's get started by making a new Blender scene and making the tabletop shape:

1. Start a new Blender scene and immediately save it as `ch05_table.blend`.
2. Switch to the **Top** view.
3. Add a plane, then set its size to `1` m, as in the following screenshot:

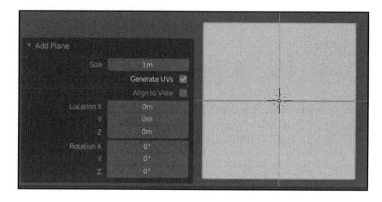

The settings for adding the new plane object

4. Tab to **Edit Mode**.
5. Open the context menu by right-clicking and choose **Subdivide**.

If you're using a right-click to **Select**, the context menu is available through the *W* hotkey.

Subdividing has given us an additional edge loop through the vertical and horizontal sections of the plane, which also means there is an additional vertex in the middle of each side. We can use this to spin a rounded section for our tabletop:

1. Switch to the **Vertex Select** mode.
2. Select the middle vertex along the right side (this will be the center of the half-circle on this side).
3. Open the **Snap pie** menu (*Shift + S*) and choose **Cursor to Selected**.
4. Switch to the **Edge Select** mode.
5. Select the following edge with the 3D Cursor.
6. Activate the **Spin** tool from the toolbar.
7. While still in the Top view, pull one of the + widgets to rotate edges out from the three-dimensional cursor.
8. In the tool's dialog, you can also set precision amounts—use 12 steps and a 180-degree angle, with **Auto Merge** turned on, as in the following screenshot:

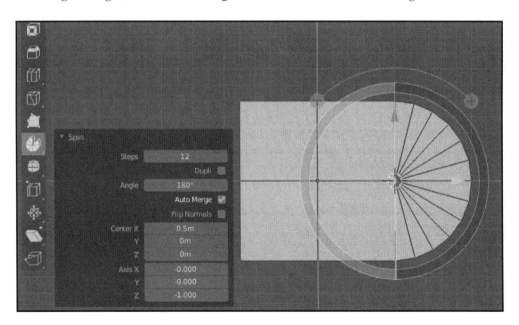

The settings for the Spin tool

Good, we've got some nice roundness to our table. Now, let's raise it up to the table height and extrude it downward to add some thickness:

1. Switch to the **Face Select** mode.
2. Select all the faces.
3. Move them up to the table height that we measured earlier with our previz table by pressing *G*, *Z*, and *.8*.
4. Extrude the faces downward with *E*, *Z*, and *-.1* to add thickness to the table.
5. Delete the faces on the non-rounded side.
6. Add a **Mirror** modifier.

Good, now we can create a metal border around the table as a separate object:

1. Select the face loop around the table's border edge and duplicate it with *Shift + D*.
2. Separate the selection into a new object by pressing *P*.
3. Tab to **Object Mode** and select the rim object.
4. Tab to **Edit Mode** for the rim object.
5. Scale all the faces on the *Z*-axis slightly to make the rim noticeable.
6. Tab back to **Object Mode** again.
7. Add a **Solidify** modifier to the rim object with a thickness of `.1`.

Our metal rim would look better with some smooth shading, just like we did for the time machine in the previous chapter:

1. Select the rim object, open the context menu with a right-click, and choose **Shade smooth**.
2. Go to the **Object Data** tab in the **Properties** panel.
3. Activate **Auto Smooth** under the **Normals** section.

Great—now, let's make the four table legs. They will be curved wooden planks that taper toward the bottom:

1. Create a plane.
2. Tab to **Edit Mode**.
3. Move an edge up to the table's height and scale it so that it tapers toward the floor. Insert an edge loop for where it curves direction, move it up for the turning point, and bevel it with *Ctrl + B*, using the middle of the mouse wheel for extra divisions.
4. Add a **Mirror** modifier and activate both the *X* and *Y* axes.

5. Add a **Solidify** modifier with a `0.03 m` thickness.

6. Rotate all the faces by $45°$ on the Z axis and place it to form the four corners of the table, as in the following screenshot:

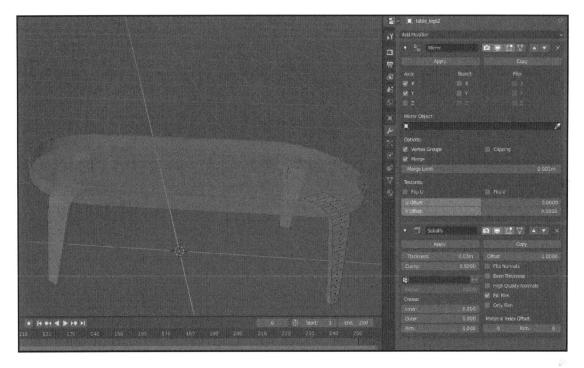

The finished table with a Mirror and Solidify modifier on its legs

Now, that's a good-looking table! Let's make a coffee table to go along with it using a similar workflow:

1. Start with a plane, then in **Edit Mode**, move it up to `0.5m`, then extrude down `0.05m` for the tabletop. Duplicate and scale these in **Edit Mode** for the coffee table's body.

2. Bevel the corner edges of the tabletop with *Ctrl + B*.

3. Inset the left and right faces for the drawers with the *I* hotkey and scale them to fit.

4. Finish them by extruding inward, duplicating the faces, and extruding them outward.

5. Create a new cube, resize it to a starting leg, and add a mirror modifier for the four legs.

6. Select the outer face of your drawer, set the 3D Cursor to selected with *Shift + S*, and add a cylinder. Taper the cylinder inward and outward for the drawer handles.

7. For added visual interest, turn a new plane into a quick chessboard on top of the coffee table.

Our example coffee table turned out like this:

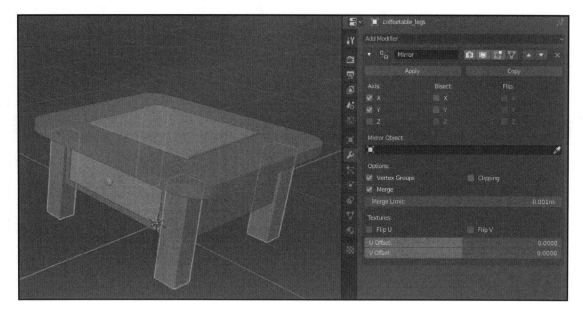

The finished coffee table

Nearly every Blender project will have something that is made with these polygonal modeling workflows, such as window sills, picture frames, and other furniture.

Now that we've made a couple of tables, let's link them back to our kitchen scene.

Appending or linking the tables to the scene

Appending and linking lets you peek into a Blender file, dig through its data, and pull that data into another Blender file. Meshes, objects, materials, and other data types can all be linked or appended. We'll use this to link collections from the ch05_table.blend file that we just created to the kitchen.blend file that we made earlier in this chapter.

When you link data (objects, materials, so on) from one file to another, a dynamic link stays between the source and target files. This means that once a table is in place in the kitchen, we could go back to the table file, change the table, and the link would update to the chairs in the kitchen.

When you append data from one scene to another, the information from the source file is directly brought into the target file as a local copy. Choosing whether to append or link is a matter of complexity and personal choice. If you're working by yourself and a project isn't too complex, appending reduces the number of files you need to maintain. If you're working as a team or need to simplify the setup, use linking. For instance, when animating a character in an environment, it's better to have the character file separate and link a character collection into the environment.

We've previously used Blender's collections to organize objects for improved visibility. Collections are also a way of organizing Blender objects for instancing. When you instance a collection, it creates a single object that represents all the objects inside it. After linking or appending table collections to the kitchen, we'll add a collection instance.

To do this, follow the steps given here:

1. In the table file, select all your mesh objects and hit *M* to move them to a new View Layer collection.
2. Rename the collection to `table` and hit *Enter*.
3. Repeat this for your coffee table, putting it in a collection called `coffee_table`.
4. Objects can be in multiple collections at once. Hit *Shift + M* and put the coffee table in the default `Collections` collection. Now, it's in both collections at the same time.
5. Use the number line on your keyboard to switch between View Layer collections. These are also visible in the outliner.
6. Use *Shift + A*, then go to **Add | Collection Instance** and select your table collection. An empty instance appears, representing all the table objects as a single object.

Now, to link the table collection to our kitchen scene, do the following:

1. Save the `ch05_table.blend` file.
2. Open the `kitchen.blend` file again.
3. Go to the **File** menu and choose **Link**.
4. Navigate to your `ch05_table.blend` file.

Because we are using the Link feature, the `ch05_table.blend` file will open in the file browser to reveal its data. All of the various data types in this file can be seen as a list of folders—objects, meshes, collections, and so on—as you can see in the following screenshot:

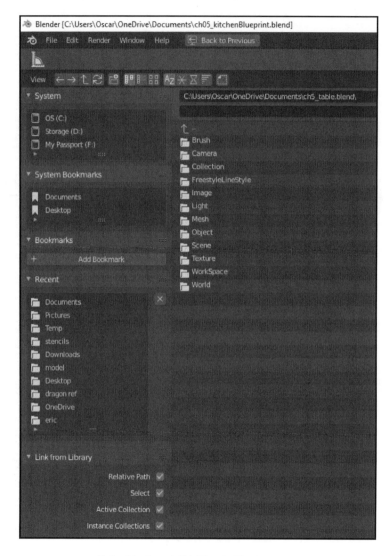

The list of data that can be linked from the ch05_table.blend file

Now, we need to tell Blender what data we are trying to link to the kitchen scene:

1. Open the folder labeled `Collection`.
2. Select the `Table` collection.

The "Table" collection has been linked into the `kitchen.blend` scene. The collection is represented by a special type of object called an **Empty**. Empty objects can be used for several different purposes. In this context the empty object's transforms (location, rotation, and scale) are used to create an instance of the "Table" collection from the `ch05_table.blend` file so that we can place the table in the kitchen scene. Because this is a linked collection, we can't select the individual objects within the collection, but we can transform the empty object to manipulate the table. We can now use this instance of our table to replace the previz table:

1. Select the linked empty object.
2. Move it to match the previz table.
3. Select the previz table.
4. Press *H* to hide the previz table.

Repeat these steps to link the coffee table into the kitchen scene as well.

Up next, we'll create some replacements for our previz chairs.

Creating chairs with modifiers and curves

Modifiers in Blender can be layered together in complex stacks to accomplish some fascinating modeling results. With just a few basic modeling techniques, modifiers can make impressive results and the puzzle of getting the stack just right is fun. Blender's curve objects also expand your modeling toolbox, allowing quick tubing or the arraying of meshes along a curve. We'll look at three methods for putting chair models together with increasing complexity.

For examples of the chairs made in this section, examine the `ch05_chair.blend` file.

Let's take a look at our first type of chair.

Chair 1 – a wooden slat deck chair

Curves are a major additional building block for this chair. They can represent tubing and also guide models with modifiers that allow lots of flexibility.

Here's how we'll make the first chair. Follow these steps:

1. We'll make a previz chair cube as a guide so that we know how large to model our chairs. Append or remodel the `.6 x .6 x 1` previz cube. In the **Properties** panel's **Viewport Display**, set **Display** to **Wireframe** for better visibility. Lastly, move it to a new collection called `Guides` and lock it in the outliner.

2. First is the metal chassis for this chair. Add a curve and in its object data, set the **Fill** mode to **Full** and its **Geometry Extrude** to `0.01` so that we can visualize its thickness.

3. In **Edit Mode**, curves have two components that can be selected—points and bezier handles. With a point selected, the major flow of the curve can be controlled and with the bezier handles selected, the curve can be adjusted. The handles have a specific relationship to their point; hit *V* for the **Handle Type** menu and they can be set to automatic for less control or turned into sharp angles with **Vector**. With a bezier point selected, you can extrude out curve extensions with *E*. Instead of using extruded geometry, these curves can serve as a helpful part of modifiers:

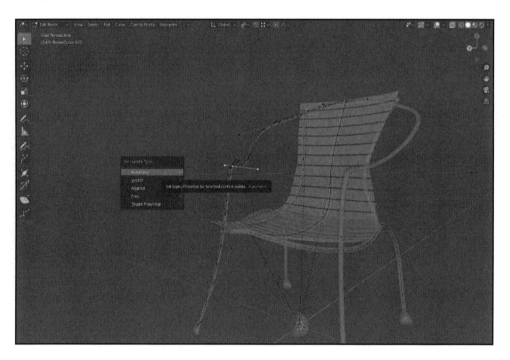

The handle type settings for the curves

4. Create a cylinder with a .02 radius and no end caps, then shade it smooth.

5. Give it an **Array** modifier, then change the modifier settings to **Fit Type: Fit Curve** and activate **Merge**.

6. Next, we parent the curve. Select your cylinder and then the curve and parent by pressing *Ctrl + P*, then go to **Curve Deform**. In addition to parenting, this adds a **Curve Deform** modifier with the curve selected.

7. Finally, add a **Mirror** modifier.

8. For the slats, I started with a single plane, then moved the left vertices to the center-line and added a **Mirror** modifier. The slats use a similar setup of **Mirror**, **Array**, **Curve**, but with the array's relative offset at 1.4 to put gaps in the slats.

9. Select a curve bezier, then use *Alt + S* to grow and shrink the slats' width to flow along with the chassis.

10. Lastly, I add a **Solidify** modifier and activate auto smooth, as on our first chair.

11. For the rubber feet, create a cylinder and taper one end.

12. In the **Array** modifiers for your metal tubes, select this object for your start cap and end cap.

13. Scale and rotate the foot mesh in **Edit Mode** to fit and orient to the end of the curves the right way.

14. Repeat on the other tubes until you've capped all the chair's feet:

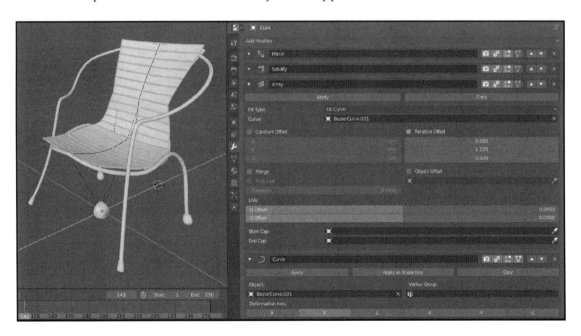

Our finished deck chair

This deck chair ends up outside the windows and sliding door of the kitchen, but can be used inside as well.

Now, let's make our second type of chair.

Chair 2 – a perforated plastic bar stool

The second chair starts with a tube chassis made from curves, as with the second chair, but we will use a different method for the feet and tube thickness.

Here is how we will go about this process:

1. Using the same techniques as we used for chair 1, create the starting beziers for a barstool's legs. Instead of a bezier curve, I use a bezier circle for a support ring.
2. In the curve's object data properties, set the **Fill** mode to **Full** and set **Bevel Depth** to .005.
3. Add a plane mesh, add a **Mirror** modifier, and create simple planes to represent the seat and back of this chair. With only four polygons, a modifier stack can make detailed plastic seating.
4. Add a subdivision modifier, then a **Wireframe** modifier with a thickness of .015. This removes the faces and changes the geometry edges into rigid tubing. The next few modifiers provide a flexible parametric interface for smoothing, plumping, and adjusting the plastic.
5. Add another Subdivision Surface modifier with all its subdivisions set to 1.
6. Add a **Smooth** modifier with a factor of 1 and a repeat of 20. This modifier performs the equivalent of smoothing in **Edit Mode**, but nondestructively.
7. Add a **Displace** modifier with its strength set to .005. Smoothing thinned out our plastic seats and this plumps it back up.
8. Then, add a third Subdivision Surface modifier and set it to 1. Within this stack, many different variables can be adjusted for any number of looks. By increasing or decreasing our first subdivision surface modifier, we can have a chair with a sparse or dense weave and it can be plumped or thinned with the Displace modifier.
9. For the foot caps on this chair, we'll use face instancing. This method instances a child object on each face of its parent. First, model a simple cylinder cap (the child).

10. Create a mesh object with four faces snapped to the bottoms of the chair legs, which is what we'll instance from. For perfectly aligned faces, make them from the chair's existing geometry. Duplicate the chair legs, convert them into a mesh, fill the holes of the feet with faces, and delete all the faces except the feet faces.

11. In **Object Mode**, set this mesh as the parent for your foot cap. Next, in the parent's object properties, set the instancing to **Faces**. An instance of the foot cap appears on each of these faces. Vertex instancing would instead put the instances on each vertex, but the benefit of face instancing is that the face normal directs the orientation of the instance.

The bar stools will go near the kitchen island. Our example turned out like this:

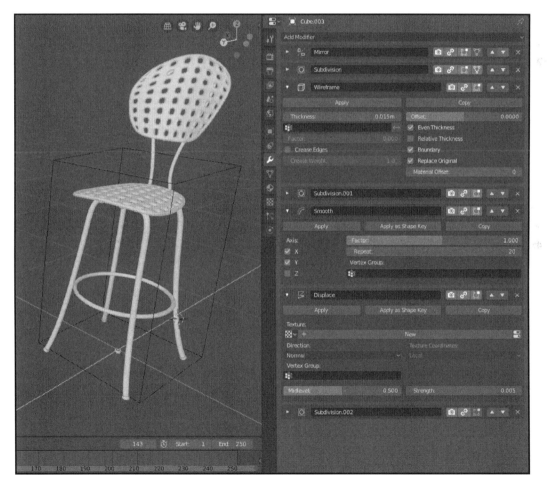

The finished bar stool

We're starting to get some good chair varieties now, but we need a cushioned chair to go with our coffee table next.

Chair 3 – cushioned coffee table chairs

This chair uses curves for the legs, as we've previously used. The cushions will be an object with three mesh chunks for the seat, back, and arms:

1. Using the curve methods previously used, create an *n*-shaped curve. Use beziers to give it a rounded square look.
2. Add another curve by going to **Add** | **Curve** | **Circle**. In the **Properties** window, set its **Resolution** and **Render U** values to 1, making it a square. Go to **Edit Mode** and rotate the bezier points by 45 degrees.
3. Return to the chair leg curve. In the **Properties** window's **Bevel** tab, choose the bezier circle you selected and the squared circle you added. Scale the square's scale until you like the chair leg thickness.
4. Add a cube. In **Edit Mode**, modify it to the size of a chair seat. Duplicate all the faces upward and adjust them for the chair's back.
5. Add an edge loop to the center of both cushions. Delete the left half of the cushions and add a **Mirror** modifier.
6. Model a 7-shaped simple chair arm. Like the seat and back, it now duplicates to the left.
7. Add a **Subdivision Surface** modifier by pressing *Ctrl + 2*, which sets the modifier's subdivisions to 2. The cube smoothes out from the new geometry.
8. Insert edge loops near the extremities of the cushions and armrests, positioning them to stiffen the **Subsurface** modifier. These can be adjusted to make different parts of the cushions softer or harder.

Now that's a chair you can drink coffee in! This chair will end up by the window, with one on each side of the coffee table. Ours turned out like this:

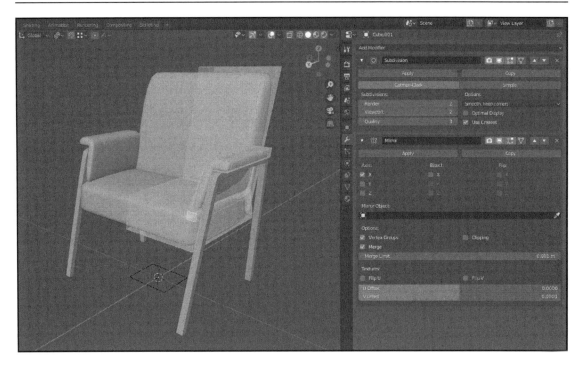

The finished cushioned chair

For the fourth chair, we'll make a plastic chair for the dining area.

Chair 4 – a plastic chair with air slits

This chair will also have metal tubing, but will use mesh edges combined with a **Skin** modifier. The plastic covering will use a **Solidify** modifier for instant thickness and a **Boolean** modifier to subtract the holes with a second object. Let's get started:

1. Add a cube mesh object and give it the following modifiers: **Subdivision**, **Skin**, and another **Subdivision** modifier. The **Skin** modifier's effect can be instantly seen – it ignores face data and adds thickness to edges.
2. Select all the vertices, then adjust the scale of the **Skin** modifier with *Ctrl + A*.

3. Edit this mesh object to fit a chair's chassis. Very few vertices are needed, due to the **Subdivision** modifiers, as you can see in the following screenshot:

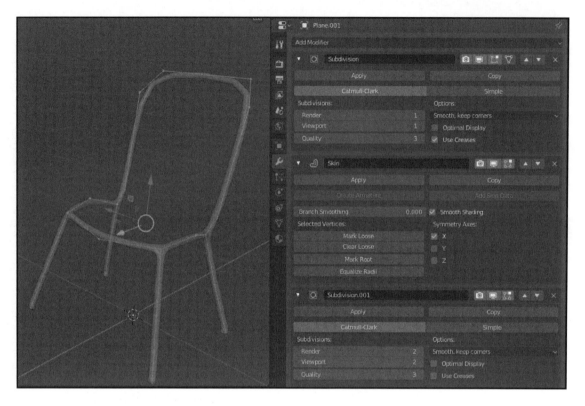

The metal tubing for the plastic chair made from Subdivision modifiers and a Skin modifier

Next, we'll make the plastic covering for the chair—nobody wants to sit on bare wires:

1. Add a plane mesh object, then give it a **Subdivision** modifier and a **Solidify** modifier. Set the **Solidify** modifier's thickness to .01.

2. Use **Edit Mode** to position this plane for the seat, extrude an edge up for the chair's back, and extrude the outer edges for an overlapping rim around the chair.

3. Select the side edges and then use *Shift + E* to change the edge crease, which affects how smooth or hard subsurface modifiers will appear.

4. Add a new cube mesh object and name it holes.

5. Give it an **Array** modifier with a relative offset of -3.4 on the y-axis and a count of 10. Edit the cube's scale in **Edit Mode**, as well as the array's relative offset so that it cuts 10 perforations in the chair seat.

6. Give it a **Simple Deform** modifier, set to **Bend**, and a 45-degree angle. Add a new **Empty** object and choose this in the **Simple Deform Axis** field. The empty object can be moved and scaled to affect the **Simple Deform** modifier.

7. Select your chair's plastic again and add a **Boolean** modifier. Change its operation to **Difference**, and for the **Object** field, select your holes object. This operation cuts slats into the chair.

8. Repeat this process for an arrayed set of holes on the chair's back. Also, repeat the process from previous chairs to put end caps on the chair feet.

9. In the outliner, disable rendering for your Boolean hole objects.

10. In the **Properties** window's **Object Viewport Display** panel, set the display as pulldown for your Boolean hole objects. That way, they won't impede the view of how they cut into the chair.

Excellent—being able to see through our Boolean objects really helps. Our example chair turned out like this:

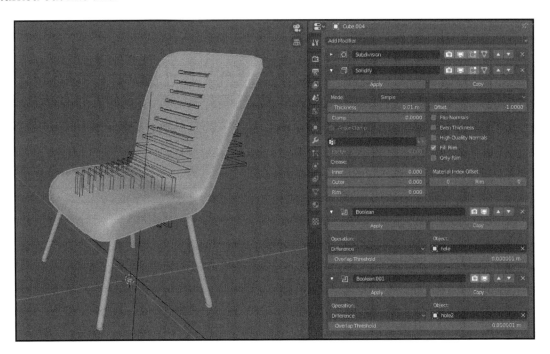

The finished chair plastic chair with slits made from the Boolean modifier

We'll put this chair type near the dining room table. Next, we'll go really crazy and make a chair out of wooden layers.

Chair 5 – wooden layers with Booleans

This geometric chair is manufactured out of sequential layers of cut wooden panels, which are then bound together. We'll make this in Blender by combining two objects with Boolean modifiers. We'll use one object for the overall chair shape, another object for the repeating wooden layers, and Boolean modifiers to cut the chair from the wood.

We will perform the following steps:

1. The initial "cage" of our chair will provide the overall shape that cuts out the wooden slats. Add a **Plane** object and scale it on the floor to the length and width of a chair. Extrude a front edge up, then back, then up again for a curving, spring-based chair back.

2. Add a **Mirror** modifier, then with the three-dimensional cursor set to the world origin, scale the left verts to 0 for the line of symmetry. Extrude an arm up as well.

3. Add a **Solidify** modifier and set the **Solidify** modifier's thickness to −.1. Add a **Subdivision** surface modifier set to 3 subdivisions and soften the overall mesh with a **Smooth** modifier set to a factor of 1 and a repeat of 5. Add edge loops and organic modeling choices and adjust the subsurface's edge crease on individual edges with *Ctrl + E*.

4. This "cage" will only be used to slice our chair, so in its object properties, go to **Viewport Display** and set **Display As** to **Wire**. Despite only using eight polygons, the modifier stack gives this chair an appealing form, as you can see here:

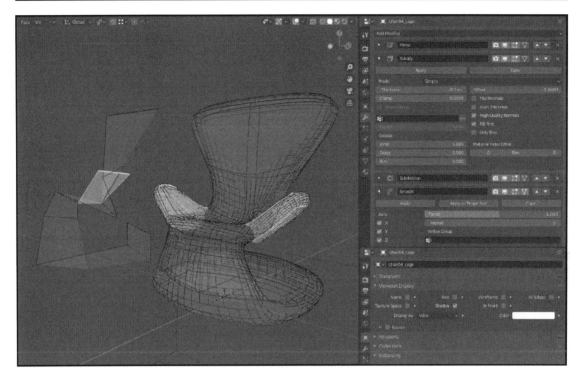

Our cage set to Display As Wire

5. Next, we'll create our wooden slats. Create a plane mesh, then add an **Array** modifier with a count of 50 and a constant offset of **Z** = .02.

6. Add a **Boolean** modifier, change its operation to **Intersect**, and choose your chair cage as the object. This modifier stack effectively creates a cube of planes, then cuts them into a chair shape.

7. Add a **Solidify** modifier with a thickness of .019, just slightly less than the array distance.

8. Finally, in the object's properties, turn on auto smooth. This "cube" can now be moved and rotated for a variety of cut looks. An angle of 90 degrees on the y-axis makes straight planes against each other, but a more organic diagonal rotation has a dynamic appeal.

9. As a final adjustment, use a second Boolean object to make the bottom of our chair flat. Add a cube, then on your arrayed plane object, add another **Boolean** modifier, set to **Subtract**, and set the new cube as the object. Move its top plane down to the z-axis, slicing away to make our chair flush to the ground.

That should do it! Our example turned out like this:

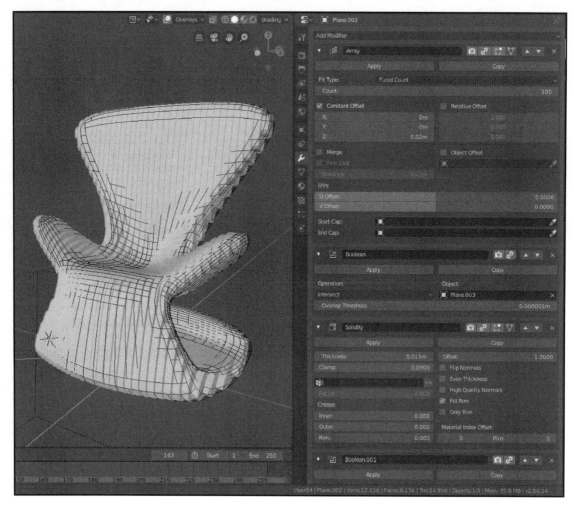

A beautiful final chair for our kitchen scene

Just like we did with the tables, we need to place each chair in its own collection, called `chair01`, `chair02`, `chair03`, and so on. Good organization is vital for the important parts of complex scenes. Once you've got each chair in a collection, we can link them back to the kitchen scene.

Appending, linking, and instancing the chairs

Now, we're going to link the chairs to the kitchen scene using the same techniques we used when linking in the table and coffee table. This time, we'll make several copies of the chairs using collection instancing.

To link your chair to your kitchen file, do the following:

1. Return to your kitchen file and append or link in your chair collection using **File | Link**.
2. Navigate to `ch05_chair.blend`, where you can then choose the data type you want to append or link.
3. Choose **Collection** and select your `chair01` collection to create a linked collection instance of your `chair01` collection.
4. Position the `chair01` collection instance in the kitchen scene.
5. Use *Shift + D* to make duplicate collection instances and position them around the scene.
6. Repeat this process with the barstools at the kitchen counter, the cushioned chairs at the coffee table, and the plastic chairs at the kitchen table.

The tables and chairs for the kitchen are now in place. Next, we'll look at some add-ons that can be added to Blender's tools and make it easier to add cabinets, islands, and a stove.

Creating cabinets, islands, and a stove with add-ons

Add-ons can greatly extend the power of Blender, often providing new tool suites that become practically separate programs in their complexity. With many of them shipping with the Blender factory settings, it would be crazy to let them gather dust when they could speed up our architecture workflow.

We'll use the **Archimesh** add-on to generate a variety of cabinets and cupboards quickly. Then, we'll use the **Bool Tool** add-on to speed up the **Boolean** modifier workflow that we used earlier. The **Archipack** add-on provides other architectural creation tools, which we'll use for quick windows and doors. Lastly, the **Extra Objects** add-on will give us additional mesh primitives.

Before we can use these add-ons, we—of course—have to enable them.

Enabling our add-ons

To enable the add-ons that we'll cover in this section, do the following:

1. Go to **Edit | Preferences** and switch to the **Add-ons** tab.

2. Enable the following **Add-ons** by clicking their checkmarks:
   - **Archimesh**
   - **Archipack**
   - **Extra Objects**
   - **Bool Tool**

3. For each of these add-ons, expand their tabs to see additional documentation. For instance, **Bool Tool** has some custom hotkeys that we'll rely on when using it, as you can see in the following screenshot:

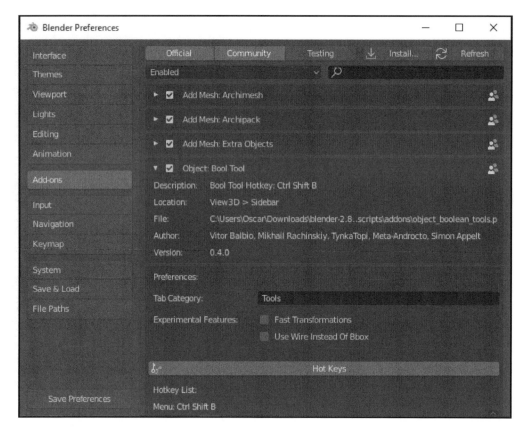

Enable these four Add-ons

4. On the **Archipack** add-on's tab, click the **Render** preset thumbs to generate thumbnails. This will create a set of thumbnails so that when you're using **Archipack**, you can select your choices with an idea of what it will look like. This might take a while to finish up.

5. While you're in **Preferences**, go to **Keymap | Preferences** and enable **Extra Shading Pie Menus**. Now the Z hotkey will let you toggle overlays more quickly, temporarily hiding your Boolean objects to see the composite model.

6. Hit **Save Preferences** so these changes stick around next time you open Blender.

Whenever a new version of Blender is released, it is good to look through the add-ons to see whether anything new was added to the ones that ship with Blender by default. Many other add-ons are available as independent projects, on sites such as `https://blenderartists.org/`, or available for purchase on sites such as `https://blenderartists.org/`.

Now that we have our add-ons enabled, we can create the remaining pieces of our kitchen. We'll make the kitchen island with **Archimesh**, the kitchen sink with **Bool Tool**, the doors and windows with **Archipack**, and other decorations with **Extra Objects**.

Let's begin with the kitchen island.

An Archimesh kitchen island

The **Archimesh** add-on creates an additional menu for a variety of architectural presets, with parameters that can be adjusted at creation. Create a new scene for our kitchen island. This island will include cabinets and drawers on the side facing the stove, seating space on the other side, and a marble counter with a recessed sink.

Here is how we will create the Archimesh island:

1. Add a cabinet by going to **Add | Mesh | Archimesh | Cabinet** or on the **N Properties Archimesh** panel. As with other new objects, a creation panel lets you change settings when the cabinets are added.

2. Change the number of cabinets to 2 and note that each cabinet gets its own settings you can play with.

3. Change the door of a cabinet to L so that the two meet in the center, set the cabinet width to .5, and turn off **Countertop Fill**.

4. An Archimesh cabinet comes with some basic rigging and materials and after creation, you can right-click on the parent mesh in the outliner and select **Hierarchy**, allowing you to edit the various meshes at once:

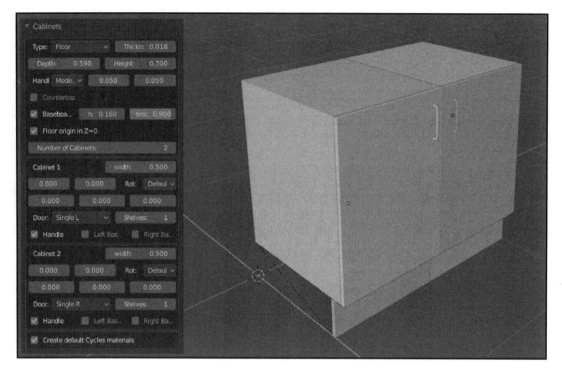

The settings for our Archimesh cabinets

5. Create additional cabinets for the drawers, an open cabinet for the end cap of the island, and a clear mesh for fine china. Move and snap them around in the Top view to fit the island's 1.5 x 6 rough dimensions.

6. **Archimesh** creates individual baseboards for each individual cabinet. Select these, join them into one object with *Ctrl + J*, and simplify unnecessary divisions in **Edit Mode**.

7. In this iterative workflow, space is left for a future dishwasher mesh, the hole for the sink can be added later, and any number of future set dressings (such as flowers, a bowl of fruit, and so on) await this kitchen island. I quickly modeled a cube into a .1m rim above the cabinets and created a single countertop that spans the whole island, using a **Bevel** modifier on the edges.

8. Finally, put everything in a collection called Island, save the scene, and link it to the kitchen scene, as before.

Our example island turned out like this:

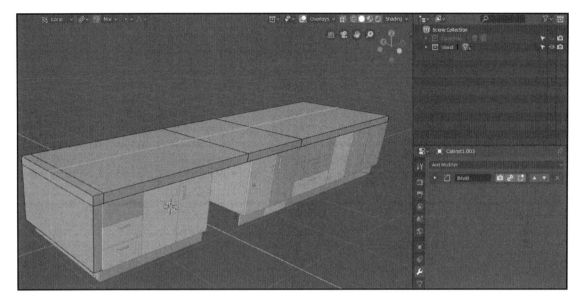

The finished cabinets

Archimesh is a fantastic add-on for creating cabinets and cupboards quickly. Explore some of the other set dressings it can add to the kitchen; then, let's move on to creating the kitchen sink.

Boolean modeling a sink with Bool Tool

We've used the **Boolean** modifier a couple of times in earlier parts of this book. Dynamically cutting holes for our chair earlier in this project was neat, but it involved many tedious steps, such as choosing the right Boolean operation, deactivating the Boolean object's rendering in the outliner, and setting the bounding box's draw mode. The **Bool Tool** add-on reduces those steps to a much faster workflow. **Bool Tool** has two methods—**Auto Boolean** and **Brush Boolean**. Using **Auto Boolean** will instantly apply the Boolean operation and discard the Boolean object. Using **Brush Boolean** will set up the necessary modifiers and change the display of the Boolean object.

To start, let's use **Bool Tool** to carve a hole in the counters for a sink:

1. In your kitchen island scene, create a cube and adjust it in **Edit Mode** to fit over two cupboard doors.
2. Select the cube in **Object Mode**, then select your kitchen counter.
3. Use the *Ctrl + Shift + B* hotkey and choose **Brush Difference**.
4. You can see the next layer of the kitchen through the hole you created; once again, select the **Brush** cube, then the next layer, and choose **Brush Difference**, repeating until it goes all the way down, as in the following screenshot:

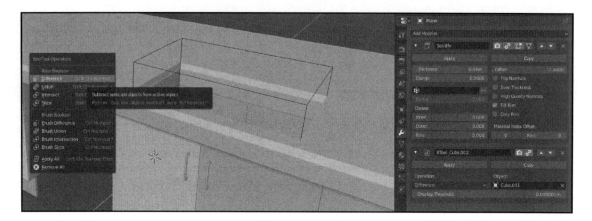

Use BoolTool to cut a hole for the sink

Now that we have a hole cut, we can model the sink:

1. Add another cube to fit inside this hole or create it from a duplicate of your previous Boolean object. This will be the start of our sink.
2. Duplicate this cube for a different object that will carve the sinks in. Move it up, scale it down, and leave more space on the backside to add our faucet later. Add your sink object to the selection, then **Brush Difference Boolean**.
3. For the divider between the two sinks, duplicate the previous sinkhole brush, scale it to a thin divider, and move it down. Boolean modifiers often require a nearby plane to make clear-cut decisions, so make sure the faces overlap, rather than sitting right on top of each other.

4. Boolean setups are most likely to break for a few reasons. If the incorrectly facing normals on the main or brush meshes are at fault, select the faces in **Edit Mode** and recalculate normals with *Ctrl + Shift + N*. Errors might also occur based on mesh proximity, as the **Boolean** modifier tries to find geometric neighbors. Try slight adjustments to the position and scale and note when a Boolean brush "pops" into a correct operation.

So far, our sink looks like this:

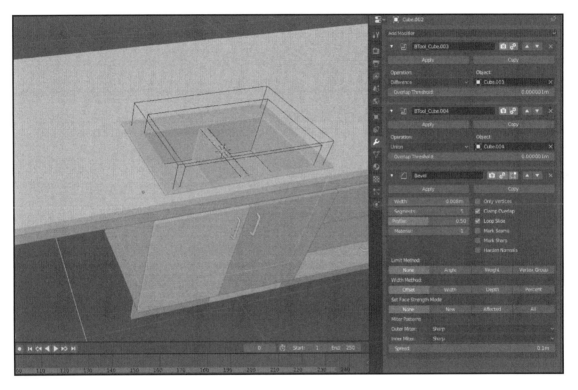

Several Booleans are used to form the base piece of the sink

So far, so good—but no sink is complete without drains. Let's make those now:

1. Set the three-dimensional cursor to the divider objects, add a cylinder, and put a **Mirror** modifier on it. In **Edit Mode**, move all its vertices to one side (now mirrored on both sink sides).

2. In **Object Mode**, add your sink to the selection, then do a brush difference, cutting circles into the bottom of the sink.

3. For the sink drain, I duplicated the brush and changed its draw mode back to textured and reactivated its rendering in the outliner. Quickly model some insets and extrudes and finish by deleting the planes for the drainage holes.

Now, our drains should look like this:

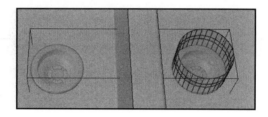

The drains for our sink

Very good—but we are, of course, missing a faucet. We can't pour water without a faucet, so let's make one now:

1. Create a cylinder for the faucet, then Boolean out several union cylinders to form a handle, with a thin cube as a difference Boolean to put a seam in the handle.

2. On the sink, use **Brush Union Boolean** on a scaled torus to add an inset for the faucet. You can model the neck and spigot from an extruded cylinder or with a curve with **Fill Mode** set to **Full** and some minor bevel depth, which you then convert into a mesh. Simple insets, extrusions, and scalings create the spigot head. Then, for the tiny detail of a switch on the faucet, I once again used **Brush Union Boolean**—a rectangular union Boolean—for the switch chassis, a duplicated and edited difference Boolean for the switch hole, and a diverted box for the switch:

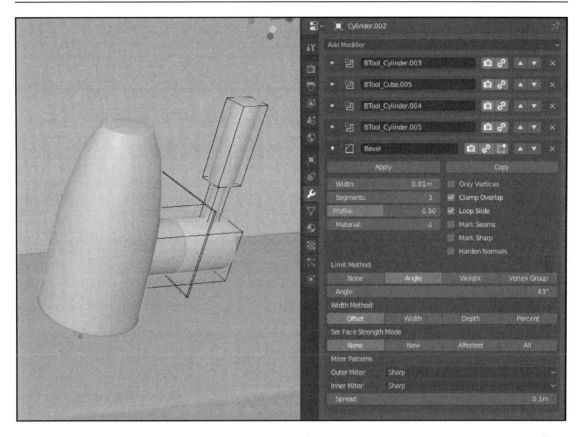

Get creative with Boolean unions to form the base of the faucet

3. Add a **Bevel** modifier to your sink object, set **Segments** to 4, set **Limit method** to an angle of 30 degrees, and right-click to set **Shade Smooth**. The **Bevel** modifiers are the last touch for our beautiful Boolean modeling, but we have to watch out for problems in the mesh, the modifier stack, and the Bevel settings.

4. Adjust the **Bevel** modifier's width until it's just right—in my case, .01. When it's done right, the bevel will soften the edges, but if adjacent faces are at similar angles, they'll be ignored. If you change one of your Boolean brush modifiers to be lower in the stack, the order of operations instead leaves a sharp seam.

5. Throw a similar **Bevel** modifier on your faucet and other objects, including your brush objects. I added one to the sink difference with much larger settings—0.1m width and 7 segments, with no limit method. The cut is sharp when it enters the sink, but creates a rounded interior. I softened some of the other difference brushes as well, such as the faucet handle and sink divider.

There we have it! Lots and lots of Booleans, but we've got ourselves a sink that should look like this:

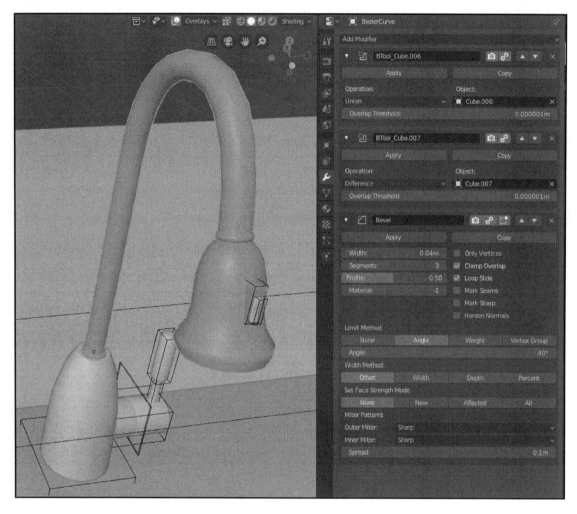

Many Booleans were used to create the faucet for the sink

The **Bool Tool** workflow is great for hard surfaces and leaves a lot of secondary freedom by adjusting your brush objects. Practice will help you with small adjustments to both the object placement and modifier settings whenever artifacts appear. For instance, I sometimes toss in an extra edge loop so that the jump the modifier makes when cutting isn't so far.

Up next, we'll take a look at adding doors and windows to let some air into our kitchen.

Doors and windows with Archipack

The **Archipack** add-on creates additional options for adding doors, windows, and stairs. Let's use it to line our walls and openings with windows, doors, and trim:

1. Open the **Add** menu and choose **Archipack | Door**, then select the **160x200** dual preset.
2. Rotate the door so that it's oriented with a wall.
3. For a taller or wider door, use the **Archipack** widgets to move them or click the **Archipack** numbers to type in specific values.
4. Using the same system, add an **Archipack** window, choosing the **180x110** flat 3 preset. Move it to the right wall.
5. With more details entering the picture, we can adjust the previz wall layout. Cut a hole out for where the **Archipack** window sits and also model a quick recessed wall.

Our kitchen is looking roomier already. Our example looks like this so far:

The example kitchen scene with doors and windows

Experiment with the other architecture options provided by **Archipack** and **Archimesh**. You can build entire scenes from their tools, which makes bashing a scene together a lot of fun!

Finally, let's add some extra decorations to our scene to liven it up.

Adding other decorations with Extra Objects

Let's finish our look at add-ons with **Extra Objects**. This add-on fills out the **Add Mesh** menu with a multitude of options beyond the basic primitives. We'll use it to create some kitchen props, such as a wine rack, fruit plate, and teapot:

1. On the end of the kitchen island, add a cabinet and remove the door and handle so that it's just an empty box. We'll put the wine rack there. Go to **Add** | **Mesh** | **Extras** and choose **Honeycomb**.

2. Modify its object creation parameters to 9 rows, 5 columns, a cell diameter of .09, and an edge width of .01. Switch to a side view, so that you're looking right at where the wine rack should go, and set **Align** to **View**. Edit the honeycomb's scale and position to fit inside the cabinet. Lastly, extrude the faces back to fit.

3. Play around with some of the other extra objects. Teapot+ is an homage to one of the first classic three-dimensional models and conveniently fits in a kitchen. The **Math** function > Z Math, plus a **Solidify** modifier and some scaling, makes a quick fruit bowl. Next, put a rounded cube in the fruit bowl, then instance it with *Alt + D* a few times:

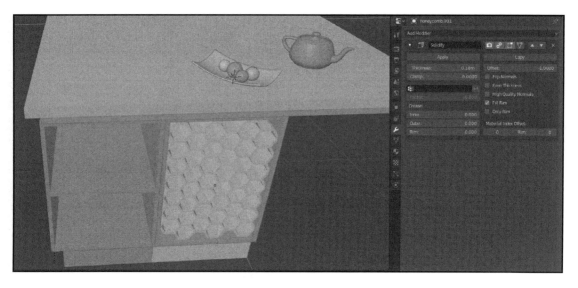

Some extra objects make the scene more interesting

Explore the other objects available in the **Extra Objects** add-on; there are a number of useful primitives to start with. When you're done, we can take a look at adding some pre-made "canned" assets to our kitchen scene to polish it off.

Linking in canned assets

We'll finish the kitchen by linking or appending from a library of canned assets. When deadlines strike, seasoned artists throw three-dimensional scenes together from other resources that can be found or purchased on other websites. You'll also find that curiosity about other peoples' models can teach you about their workflows. We'll round out the last elements of the kitchen by looking at some pre-made assets and appending or linking them to the kitchen, as well.

Let's start by touring the pre-made assets file and see what we can learn from some of the example models. Open up ch05_cannedAssets.blend to get started. Here are some general explanations for the canned assets provided:

- The scene is organized into collections. Some of these collections (fridge, dishwasher, stove, mirror, sideTable, and stoveCounters) hold a single complex thing made of many objects.
- Inside the fridge collection is a hidden collection called fridge junk. This contains Boolean brush meshes, which can be moved around to see how they create the final fridge model. There are similar junk collections in the stove and dishwasher collections. Individual beziers on the curve can be thickened or thinned by pressing *Alt* + *S* and rotated by pressing *Ctrl* + *T*.
- The mirror was made with curve objects. In the **Properties** window's **Geometry** tab, these curves were assigned with custom bevel objects. The bevel objects can be found in the junk_mirror layer, as in the following screenshot.

- Some collections include many separate objects, such as the dishes, food, and lights layers:

A beautiful pre-made mirror asset made up of many BezierCurve objects

At this point, you have all the skills required to append or link these files to your kitchen scene. How you choose to use them for decorating is up to you. Here are some tips we recommend while appending them:

- Use the **Array** modifiers on these models frequently. The **Array** modifiers can stack plates high, repeat light fixtures every 6 feet, and lights can be repeated.
- While you might append the whole collection for something such as the fridge, in other cases, such as the wine bottle, you might append just a single model.
- When first bringing assets over, double-check the scale. For instance, the mirror is too big.
- Complex hierarchies such as the fridge can be difficult to position without breaking the Boolean placement and work best at the origin. If you're appending, I recommend appending the collection, then adding a collection instance while hiding the original collection. The instance can then be moved, scaled, and rotated without breaking.
- When placing things such as goblets on a shelf, use vertex snapping and grid snapping.

Don't forget to add some food to the kitchen. Look around the canned assets for things such as these:

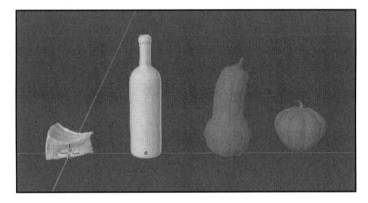

Some food assets that can be added to the kitchen

Wonderful—placing in a bunch of pre-made assets can really bring the scene to life. Don't feel guilty about using pre-made models; if the project is focused on composition, then nobody will criticize you for borrowing assets.

That concludes the modeling phase of our kitchen project. There's more to do before the scene is complete, but we've made it past the composition phase.

Summary

While kitbashing a kitchen together, we've explored a number of new methods to reach your project's goals. Modifiers and curves expanded our modeling toolkit, providing flexible ways to create assets. Add-ons gave access to both new workflows and quick asset generation, and by appending and linking across files, multiple Blender projects can be combined. Next, we'll create materials for our kitchen objects while looking at Blender's node editor.

Our kitchen is lacking two major components right now, which are materials and textures. Everything has the default gray material, so it doesn't look as pretty as it should for a final result. Materials will make wood look like wood, metal look like metal, and all of the other objects look the way they are supposed to. In the next chapter, we'll construct the materials that we'll use for our kitchen.

Questions

1. What is the purpose of pre-visualization for a three-dimensional project?
2. Why is a correct sense of scale important at the beginning of a project?
3. What are the differences between linking and appending and between duplicating and instancing?
4. What are the benefits of using modifiers to complete your models?
5. Go through the add-ons in Blender's preferences. Activate one that is not covered in this chapter and read its documentation. How might it assist your future workflows?
6. How can a Boolean workflow help in comparison to modeling only in **Edit Mode**?
7. When would you choose to use canned assets instead of modeling them yourself?
8. What are the benefits of organizing assets in view collections?

Further reading

There are lots of corners of the internet where you can find additional canned assets to get started with a project. Even if it's just research, opening up other files and poking around is a great way to pick up workflows from other artists. As part of Blender's open source goodwill, many of these have Creative Commons options that you can use even for commercial purposes. If you want additional bells and whistles for your kitchen, model them yourself to your heart's content or look on sites such as `blendswap.com`, `blendermarket.com`, and `blenderartists.com`.

6
Modern Kitchen - Part 2: Materials and Textures

We've finished the modeling stage of our kitchen scene, but all of the objects are gray and boring to look at. A real kitchen is full of colors and materials such as metal, marble, and wood. This is the perfect opportunity to explore one of the finest additions to Blender 2.8: the Eevee renderer.

As we learned earlier in this book, rendering lets us turn our boring gray scene into a beautiful final result. We have several renderers available to us, but Eevee is a fantastic choice because it can render in real time by using techniques employed in modern game pipelines. The lights, settings, materials, and textures we'll add in this chapter will directly translate to modern game engines such as Unity and Unreal.

Eevee uses **Physically-Based Rendering (PBR)**, which simplifies materials and lighting down to a handful of variables in the real world. We'll modify these settings with nodes, which give us powerful mathematical control over textures to control these variables, and determine how these textures interact with our geometry. Lastly, we'll use these tools to approach problems of aesthetics, trusting our eyes and our gut as we compare results to reference and patterns in nature.

First, we'll learn to navigate the complexities of Blender's node interface with some testing shaders and textures. We'll use these skills to create a variety of complex materials, which we'll then add to our kitchen scene. Last, we'll set up Eevee for real-time goodness, and try out a variety of custom lighting setups. The project files for this chapter , which should be examined in depth for the more complex node trees, can be found in `https://github.com/PacktPublishing/Blender-3D-By-Example-Second-Edition/tree/master/Blender3DByExample_ch06`.

For more information on getting your real-time Blender assets into the Unity game engine, check out *Hands-On Unity 2018.x Game Development for Mobile* (Packt), by Raymundo Barrera.

The following topics will be covered in this chapter:

- Simple materials and the nodal workflow
- The Eevee renderer and physically-based materials
- Navigating Blender's node interface
- Manipulating procedural textures
- Creating procedural and texture-based materials

Simple materials and the nodal workflow

The kitchen has several objects whose materials are simple to set up and will serve as a good introduction to the basics of PBR. Eevee's real-time rendering is based around controlling a limited set of variables that have the potential to replicate all of the physically possible materials in the entire world. Take any dirt, meteor, banana, or liquid in the universe, and you can map its properties from a value of 0 (0%) to a value of 1 (100%):

- Black to white colors (distributed over Red, Green, and Blue (RGB) pixels)
- Transparent to opaque
- Rough to smooth
- Dielectric to metallic

Nodes are a way to map those values. A value of 0 Roughness means not rough at all. A value of 1 Roughness means very rough. A value of 0 Transparency is completely opaque. A value of 1 Transparency is completely transparent. If you took a photograph, it has pixels, which have values ranging from black to white. A node could simply use the input (a picture) to drive an output (such as transparency), and the light pixels will be transparent, black pixels opaque, and grayscale pixels somewhere in between.

The coordinates for your materials can *also* be represented in this way, usually through a vector input. The bounding box for an object could map the bottom of the object (0, 0%, black) to top (1, 100%, white), and the same for its transition from left to right or front to back, like colored syrup at the top of a snow cone, dispersing down. Instead of a pixel's location in the bounding box, you could instead map the direction each face's normal is pointing, like cliffs where snow only lands and sticks to the faces pointed upward. The Fresnel effect causes many materials to change properties depending on whether a plane faces you (black) or is turned away from you, eventually being on the hidden backside (white). Distant lake water is a mirror, reflecting the sunset (fresnel 1, white), but when you look down it's instead transparent, where a carp is swimming around your ankle (fresnel 0, black).

Nodes are a form of visual programming and a little scary to newcomers. Although it *sounds* like a lot of math and logic, the payout is tremendous, and the concepts extend into other areas of Blender as well. When nodes become overwhelming, try to reconstruct the node trees of others verbatim, and the results often reveal how nodes work. Use existing node materials, and see what happens when you break or modify the node tree. Test out your hunches, and don't be afraid to experiment. Let's have a look at how to control these properties with shader nodes.

Navigating nodes with a test material

Before designing good materials, we need to get comfy with the basic syntax of how nodes work on an exploratory play material that will eventually turn into wood. Open up `Ch06_nodes_start.blend`. This file contains an array of dragon models that we can use to view our materials side by side. It also comes with an interface set up to view our materials: a sun object for casting shadows, Viewport shading set to Material Preview mode, and the default shading interface. The Material Preview mode has placeholder settings for reflections, making it ideal for doing material studies without needing all of the scene's lighting in place. As you work, compare your results to `Ch06_nodes.blend`, which has the completed materials. The **Properties** panel has a tab for material settings and a tab for texture settings, but the real power in creating materials comes from nodes in the **Shader** editor.

We will spend 99% of our time in the **Shader** editor when making materials, so let's have a look at it now and learn about the nodes:

1. Select the first dragon in the 3D Viewport.
2. Look in the **Shader** editor to see its material nodes.

There are just two nodes: a **Principled BSDF** (input) and a **Material Output**, which can be seen in the following screenshot:

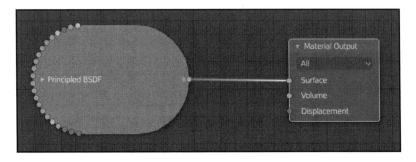

The Principled BSDF input and the Material Output

Nodes will generally read from left to right; the input nodes work together and develop into the final output node on the right. Many of the hotkeys from the 3D Viewport are also used in Blender's node interface, with individual nodes functioning like vertices, noodles (the lines connecting inputs and outputs) functioning like edges, node groups functioning like objects full of other data, and so forth. Let's try out some of our familiar hotkeys:

1. Select the **Principled BSDF** node inside the **Shader** editor.
2. Move it with *G*.
3. Pan around the nodes with the middle mouse button.
4. Zoom into the nodes with *Shift* + the middle mouse button.

The noodle connecting the **Principled BSDF** to **Material Output** can be connected or disconnected in multiple ways:

1. Click and drag on the green dot of the **Material Output**'s **Surface** output to disconnect it.
2. Reconnect it by clicking and dragging the **BSDF** output back to the Surface output.
3. Disconnect it again by slicing the noodle with *Ctrl* + right-click, and then clicking and dragging across it.
4. Reconnect them by selecting both nodes and hitting *F* to make links. This is how we'll generally connect our nodes.

To supercharge our node workflow, we need to enable the **Node Wrangler** add-on:

1. Go to **Edit | Preferences.**
2. Go to the **Add-Ons** tab.
3. Search node to quickly find the add-on, as seen here:

The Node Wrangler add-on can be found in the Add-Ons tab

4. Click the checkbox next to the **Node Wrangler** add-on to enable it.
5. Click **Show Hotkey List**, and you'll find a massive amount of additional hotkeys to speed up your node interface.

The **Node Wrangler** is a fan favorite among Blender users who spend a lot of time working with materials, and you'll come to love many of the hotkeys that it provides. Now, let's try hooking up a texture to our **Principled BSDF** node with a **Node Wrangler** hotkey:

1. Add a **Wave** node with *Shift + A* | **Texture** | **Wave**.
2. Press *Alt* + right-click and drag from the **Wave Texture** node to the **Principled BSDF** node.

Thanks to **Node Wrangler**, the connection is highlighted in red, as seen in the following screenshot, and then it automatically connects the wave to the BSDF's assumed default input, which is **Base Color**. You can also specify the inputs and outputs when connecting nodes with *Alt + Shift* + right-click. This quick connection is shown here:

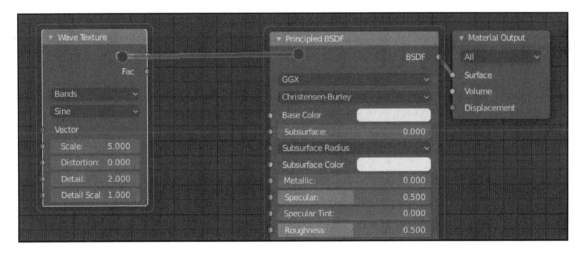

Node Wrangler Lazy Connect

Another powerful **Node Wrangler** hotkey that comes in handy all of the time lets us create a "viewer" node that allows us to preview the node's output. Let's try this now:

Press *Ctrl + Shift* + left-click on **Wave Texture**. With **Node Wrangler**, the node is now hooked up to a **Viewer** node.

As we can see in the following screenshot, the **Wave Texture** output can be viewed on the dragon thanks to the **Viewer** node:

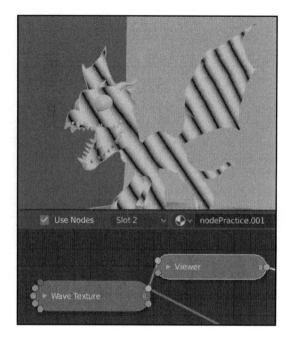

Automatic Viewer node setup

When we're ready to hook the **Principled BSDF** node back up to the material output node, we can use the same **Node Wrangler** hotkey but this time, we click on the **Principled BSDF** node:

Press *Ctrl* + *Shift* + left-click on the **Principled BSDF** node.

Now, let's add some color to that wave! We can add color with a **ColorRamp** node:

1. Press *Shift* + *A* to open the add menu.
2. Choose **Convertor | Color Ramp.**
3. Connect the **Wave output** to the **ColorRamp Factor** input.
4. Connect the **ColorRamp Color** output to the base color of the **Principled BSDF** node.

ColorRamp remaps the input to colors, distributed by stops along a ramp. We can adjust the colors by editing these stops:

1. Click on a stop, then move it around to change its position. New stops can be added by pressing *Ctrl* + clicking on the ramp, and their color modified by clicking the swatch at the bottom of the node. Give it three stops with varying colors.

2. Add a **Texture Coordinate** setup to your Wave node by selecting it, and then pressing *Shift* + *T*. This **Node Wrangler** shortcut adds a **Texture Coordinate** node and **Mapping** node quicker than the **Add** menu. Change the values in the **Mapping** node around to see the color move around on the dragon.

If you've been following along, your node setup should look like this:

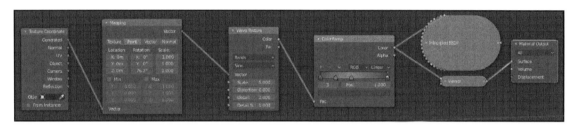

Node setup

Now, let's try mixing it up a bit with some more nodes:

1. Box select the **Mapping, Wave Texture**, and **ColorRamp** nodes, and then duplicate them while maintaining connections by pressing *Ctrl* + *Shift* + *D*. Type in new mapping coordinates and check the results with **Viewer Node**. Next, select the **ColorRamp**, then change its node type by pressing *Shift* + *S*, and choosing **Color | Hue Saturation Value**. Connect the **Wave Texture Color** output to **Hue**, and change the HSV node's color to red. The red's hue now shifts based on the black and white waves.

2. The **ColorRamp** and **Hue Saturation Value** nodes can be combined with a **MixRGB** node, found in **Add | Color | MixRGB**. **Node Wrangler** also lets you auto-mix nodes; press *Ctrl* + *Shift* + right-click and drag from the **ColorRamp** to the **HSV** node, and they're automatically hooked into the two color inputs. The factor adjusts how much **Color2** influences **Color1**. The **MixRGB** blend mode can be changed to other options such as **Multiply**, which darkens **Color1** based on **Color2**, or **Hue**, which replaces **Color1**'s hue with that of **Color2**. Scroll through all of the blend modes by hovering your cursor over the dropdown and pressing *Ctrl* + middle mouse button scrolling, and then setting it back at **Mix**.

3. Connect your first **Wave Texture** to the **MixRGB**'s factor. Using a texture as a factor masks the effect of the **Mix** node, interpreting black as 0 and white as 1.

4. Create a **Math** node with **Add | Vector | Math**. Drag and drop it onto the noodle connecting the **Wave Texture** to the **Mix** node's factor, and a connection is automatically established. Change the operation to **Less Than**. Adjusting the second value now determines where the Wave is clipped into black and white.

5. **Math** nodes are often faster than **MixRGB**, and perform the same functions, such as **Multiply**. **Node Wrangler** offers some hotkeys, such as *Ctrl*, *Shift*, +, -, *, and /, which hooks two selected nodes into a Math node with that operation.

As you can see in the following screenshot, node trees get complicated really quickly, but they let us create some very interesting materials:

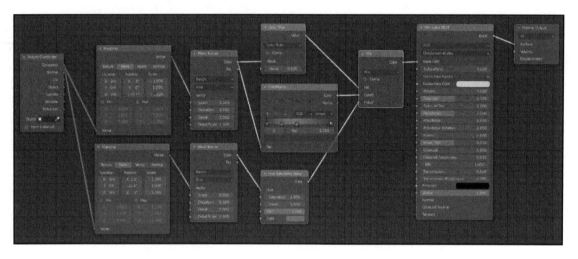

The Test material

This interface of connecting inputs and outputs is how we'll continue building materials throughout this chapter. Although you can get by without **Node Wrangler**, it adds tons of functionality to an interface that, when noodling, you'll spend hours inside. Hold on to this play material; later, we'll make some more adjustments to turn it into wood.

The end goal of creating these node trees is, of course, to make our materials fit our needs. However, you'll frequently need to understand why a node works the way it does. Use these kinds of play materials often to teach yourself how inputs, nodes, and textures work.

Any time we work with a node tree, the final node before the Material Output node is called a shader node. The shader node determines what the surface of the material will render like in the final result. The most versatile shader node is called the **Principled BSDF**. Up next, we will take a closer look at how this node works to replicate real-life materials.

The Principled BSDF material

Almost every item in the kitchen will use the **Principled BSDF** material, and to make successful materials, we need to understand the science and practice of physically-based materials. **BSDF** (short for **Bi-directional Scatter Distribution Falloff**). When an emission of light hits a surface, there's a limited number of plausible physical effects.

First, the light ray is an emission. That ray can reflect off the surface, bouncing back light's energy. The ray can *scatter* through the surface, partially getting absorbed, and partially bouncing that light back out as diffuse reflections, also called albedo. The part of this scattered ray that sends out the remaining light is characterized by the energy that *wasn't* absorbed, as seen in the base color. When the light can scatter deeper in and back out of a surface, like a candle flame visible through the wax, it's called subsurface scattering. But the light ray might never reflect, having transmission through a surface, going straight through, and continuing on the other side. This transmission through the shader can slow the light ray, changing its angle, known as *refraction*.

We can visualize many of these properties with the following screenshot:

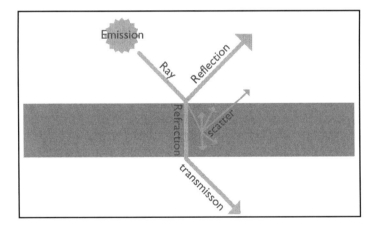

A light ray and the things it might do when hitting a surface

Roughness complicates this model. On a perfect mirror, the ray bounces directly off of the surface in one direction. Most surfaces have nooks and crannies that change the angle at which the light bounces based on a polygonal angle (called normals) or microscopic detail (called roughness). The result is an approximation of bounces, with more roughness spreading the reflection out. This softened averaging of rays at the surface level could also happen at the emission level, based on the surface area of the light. A tiny lightbulb filament means all of those rays coming from one point in space, but a cloudy day or photographer's softbox means many points in space averaging out together.

Here is a similar reference with roughness taken into account:

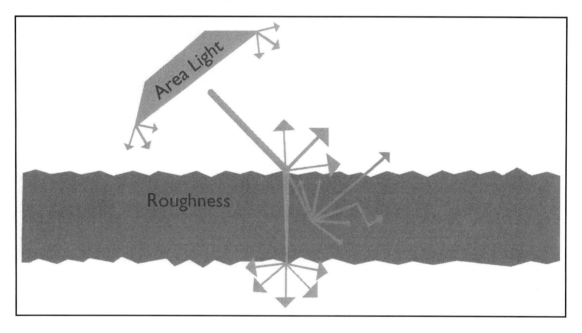

Light rays potentially scattered via the light source, normals, roughness, and scattering

Reflections can further be broken down into two types, Diffuse and Specular, which have an influence on two categories: metals and non-metals. Specular reflection directly bounces off the surface. Although roughness can distribute the rays, they bounce at a predictable angle of incidence. Diffuse rays will instead have a dispersed direction from scattering in and out of the surface and limit their color to the energy that wasn't absorbed in that scattering.

We can see these effects on metal surfaces versus non-metal surfaces in the following screenshot:

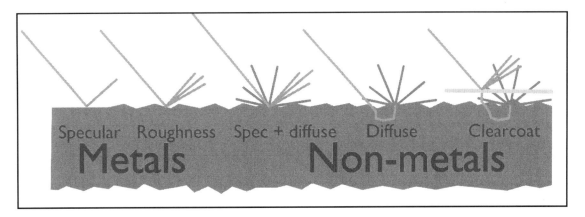

Ways that metals and nonmetals play with light

A material in Blender should be *explicitly* metal or non-metal. There are exceptions, such as superconductors or the anti-alias pixel between metals and non-metals in a texture map, but usually, there is no in-between. Metals should have their **Metallic** property set to 1. The **Base Color** property of the shader can combine with the metallic property to color a metal brilliant gold or dark iron.

Non-metals, also called **dielectrics**, show their diffuse reflection via the base color. They can *also* have specular reflections at the same time, and most materials will be a combination of the two. The physics can get much more complex than that, but Blender's **Principled BSDF** strikes a balance between physical accuracy, ease of use, and potential edge cases. For instance, clay tiles are rough and low on specular reflection. However, a glaze would make them shiny, while allowing the light to transmit to their base color below. This edge case is shown in the **Clearcoat** property.

Transmissive materials let light rays pass through them. Transmission should usually be set to either 0 or 1. The **Index of Refraction** (**IOR**) determines how much a light ray slows while transmitting through a substance, resulting in a warped look. The vacuum of space has an IOR of 1, and the air we breathe has such a low IOR that it, too, can just be 1. Water has an IOR of 1.325 and glass 1.5. You can find the IOR for exotic materials such as diamonds or emeralds online. Tint your transmissive materials with the **Base Color**, and "frost" them with **Roughness**. Transmissive materials also reflect specular light.

By messing with each of these properties on the **Principled BSDF** node, we can create all sorts of combinations, as seen in the following PBR chart:

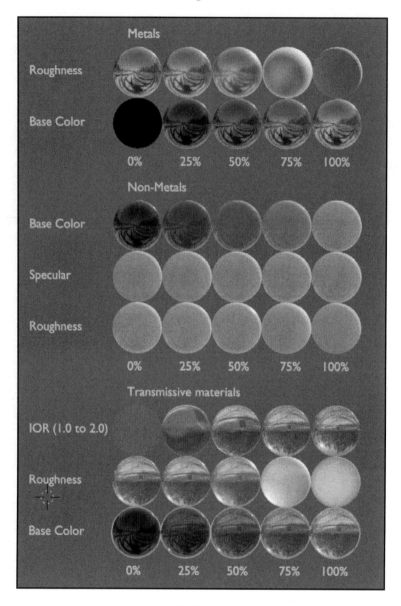

The PBR chart

The PBR chart is a fun example of node power itself. If you would like to see the node setup for the PBR chart, open up the ch06_bsdfChart.blend file from the source files. The **Principled BSDF** is doing most of the work, as you can see here:

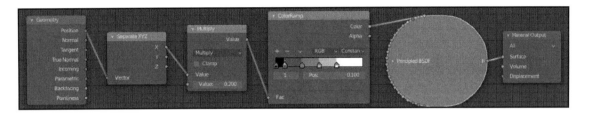

Automatic BSDF chart values controlled in a material

You can use the materials here to test other attributes in the BSDF from 0 to 100%. The shader starts with a **Geometry** node (**Add | Input | Geometry**) whose **Position** output is separated with **Add | Convertor | Separate XYZ**. Previewing the X output shows a black to white gradient based on its position in 3D. One meter from the world origin is seen as 100% (white) and anything further than 1 clips this value. The 1-meter spheres have array modifiers going out 5 meters, so multiplying this by 0.2 with a Math node stretches the gradient from 0 to 100% over 5 meters. Feed this into a **ColorRamp** set to **Constant**, and then add stops at positions of **0, 0.1, 0.3, 0.5,** and **0.7**, whose corresponding colors have a value set to 0, .25, .5, .75, and 1.

Most of that might sound really complicated, but you don't need a physics degree to make good materials. From here, material design is an artistic choice, mostly a matter of trusting your eye and comparing it to a real-world reference. In fact, lots of attributes on the **Principled BSDF** are hacks that break the laws of physics to achieve a look more artistically, such as sheen (which fakes the light-catching of some fuzzy fabrics) or Specular Tint (which colors the specular reflection with the **Base Color**, even though specular reflections are light rays that *didn't* scatter through the material.) And when you're struggling to make shaders for plastic cups or painted walls, start by looking at real-world examples around you. Many of the **BSDF** values for real-world materials can be found with an internet search.

Let's get out of science mode and back into kitchen creation mode! We'll start by making some metal materials for the kitchen.

Simple metals

We can make kitchen materials now that we know how nodes and the BSDF works. We'll start with simple metals for polished chrome, buffed steel, and cast iron. We'll use these on things such as the faucet and mirror in our kitchen.

First up, let's make the polished chrome:

1. Open the `Ch06_nodepractice_start.blend` file.
2. Add a new material to a new testing object. Name it `chrome_polished`.
3. Change the **Metallic** attribute to 1. Again, BSDF materials should almost always have a metallic value of either 1 or 0.
4. Change **Roughness** to 0.02. Even in laboratory settings, materials have tiny amounts of imperfection. Avoid putting the roughness at full 0 or 1.

That one was easy! Next, let's do the buff stainless steel:

1. Select a new tester object, and then in the **Shader** editor, create a new material and name it `steel_buffed`.
2. Change the diffuse color to an **RGB** of .3, 3, .25, and a roughness of .2 for a baseline. Metals rarely go beyond a roughness of .3.
3. Add a **Noise Texture** node, and plug it into the **Roughness** value. Press *Ctrl + Shift* + click on the noise texture, which hooks it into the **Viewer** node thanks to **Node Wrangler**. Press *Ctrl + Shift* + click again to cycle through the outputs and view its factor. Using **Viewer** nodes to preview different data in our shaders is crucial to the node workflow. Based on the **Viewer** node, I changed the **Noise Texture** node's scale to 30.
4. The Noise texture is overkill when plugged into the **Roughness** value; limit it to .3 with a **Math Node** via **Add | Vector | Math** or by using the search field. **Node Wrangler** also simplifies math node operations; type `Ctrl Shift *` to hook it up to a **Math node** set to **Multiply**. Type in .25 for the second value. For any given pixel (0 at black, white at 1), it multiplies it by .25. The result is that our noise pixels only range from black (0) to dark gray (.3). Hook the **Multiply Math** node into **Roughness**.

5. Add a **ColorRamp** node, which we'll use to increase the noise contrast. Move **ColorRamp** over the noodle between the **Noise Texture** and **Multiply** math nodes. It lights up with a new connection and execution inserts it into the node tree at that point. **ColorRamp** nodes remap an input to match the color stops along the way. New stops can be added by pressing *Ctrl* + clicking on the ramp. Delete selected stops by clicking on the minus button. For this ramp, I increased the noise's contrast by pulling the black and white stops to positions of .15 and .85.

6. These variations in roughness are accompanied by nooks and crannies, which can be faked via normals by using a bump map. We show these nooks and crannies by controlling the material's normal output. Add a **Bump** node. Connect the cloud texture's **Factor** output to the **Height** input of **Bump**. Set **Strength** and **Distance** to .05, and assign it to the **Normal** attribute of **Principled BSDF**.

This one was a touch more complicated, but our result should look like this:

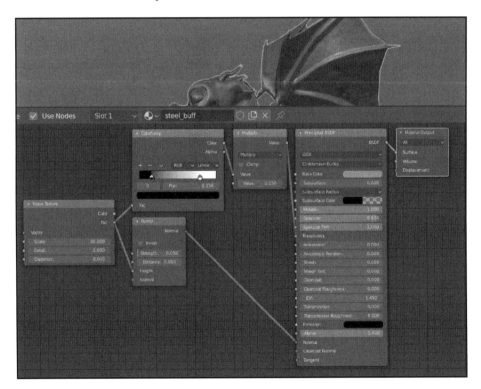

A rougher metal using a noise texture

To finish out our set of simple metals, let's make a cast iron material. Cast iron is about as rough as metal can get, and brings a strong dark base color. Don't forget to gather references! A pitfall that happens all of the time is to spend hours tinkering in confusion on a shader or model when a 30 second trip to the kitchen could solve a problem. For all of the materials in this chapter, we looked around at real-world sources to see what the materials should look like. For the cast iron, we can reference a cast iron skillet like the one in the following screenshot:

A cast-iron skillet to which materials can be compared

Now that we have our reference, we can get started:

1. Create a new material on your next testing dragon called `cast_iron`. Get a baseline that matches the reference using only the **Principled BSDF**. I landed on a dark gray base color, `.34` roughness, and `.4` specular.

2. For the texture of cast iron, create a noise texture and adjust its scale until it matches the scale of a cast iron pan. The dragon is 2 meters tall, so his eye is about the size of a pan. Duplicate your **Noise Texture** node, then combine it with a **MixRGB** node set to **Linear Light**, which both lightens using a texture's light values and darkens with the dark values. Adjust the scale of the new texture to even larger.

3. For the **Base Color**, multiply the **Linear Light** node's output by `.07` with a **Math** node.

4. For the **Roughness**, duplicate the **Multiply** math node while maintaining the connection by pressing *Ctrl + Shift + D*, and run this into the **Roughness**. Change it to `0.9`.

5. Add a **Bump** node. Run the **Linear Light**'s color output into its **Height**. Turn on **Invert**, set **Strength** to .15, and **Distance** to .5. Run its **Normal** output into the **Normal** input of **Principled BSDF**.

6. Too many nodes result in noodle soup, where you can't understand the flow of decisions that resulted in a material output. Rerouting nodes, found in **Add | Layout | Reroute**, is a handy way to clean these up. These vertex-like points can be dropped onto a noodle and allow for clean, readable flow. Via **Node Wrangler**, add reroutes easily by pressing *Shift* + right-click-dragging over a noodle.

And there we have it, a cast iron material. Our node tree ended up looking like this:

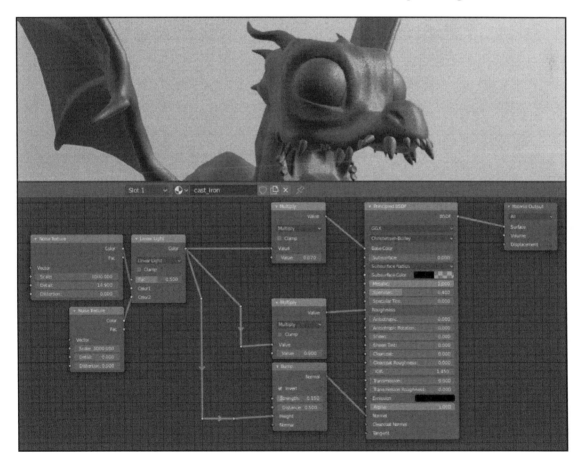

The finished cast iron skillet node tree

Not all objects in a kitchen are made of metal, but this is a good start. Up next, we'll create some of the non-metal materials for the kitchen.

Simple non-metals

The walls, dishes, chair seats, and other objects have materials that require minimal setup. We'll use their materials to study some additional ideas. First, let's add a ceramic material:

1. Add a new material called `Ceramic`. For the initial **Principled BSDF**, let's use a nice blue for its **Base Color**; **Specular** is `.9`, and **Roughness** of `.01`.

2. Add a **Layer Weight** node, and assign a preview to its Fresnel output.

   The Fresnel effect makes light affect a material differently depending on the angle of a given plane: weaker when face normals orient toward the viewer, and stronger when oriented away from the viewer. When you look across a lake, it mirrors the sunset because the distant water is almost perpendicular to your line of sight, making the water appear reflective. But when you look down at your feet, the angle is parallel, and the water is instead transparent. Many materials benefit from even a mild influence of layer weight. The **Layer Weight** node's strength is controlled with the blend. The facing output gives a similar black-and-white map for meshes facing toward or away from you, as you can see in the following screenshot:

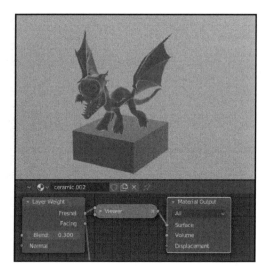

The Fresnel effect

3. Assign the **Layer Weight** node's Fresnel output to the **Specular** input of **Principled BSDF**. Set the **Layer Weight** blend to 0.3; this will give us a nice result that you can see in the following screenshot:

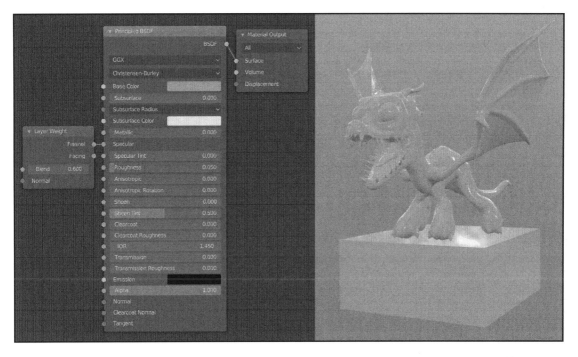

The ceramic material nodes

Our ceramic is looking nice and shiny with an appropriate amount of Fresnel effect.

For the wall paint material, let's take a different approach:

1. On a new tester object, add a material called housepaint. Recreate the node tree from the following screenshot:

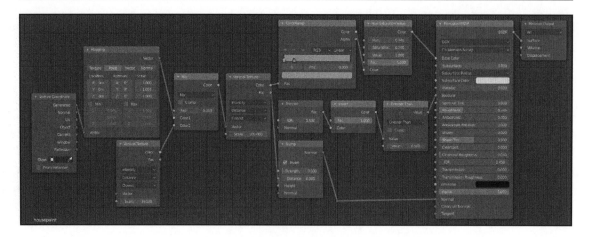

The wall paint's starting nodes

The problem with this setup is clarity. It all works, but figuring out which nodes are doing what is a pain! The **Frame** node cleans up your layout, with labels and colors to help clarify further:

1. Add a **Frame** node with **Add | Layout | Frame**.

2. Select the **Texture Coordinate**, **Mapping**, and **Voronoi** textures and **Mix** node. Grab them with *G*, and hover them over the **Frame** node. **Frame** encompasses them in a box, and after clicking in **Frame**, they can be moved en masse.

3. Select **Frame**, and then hit *F2* and rename its label **Vectors**. Hit *N* for the **Sidebar** panel, and on the **Items** tab, this node can be further customized. Turn on **Color**, and choose a purple color reminiscent of the **Vector Output** dots.

4. Repeat this process with a frame for the **Base Color** nodes and **Specular** nodes, naming those frames **Color** and **Specular**. If you accidentally drop a node into **Frame**, moving it will just resize the frame. Instead, remove it from the frame with *Alt + P*.

There, that's much clearer! Your Vectors, Color, and Specular frames should look something like this:

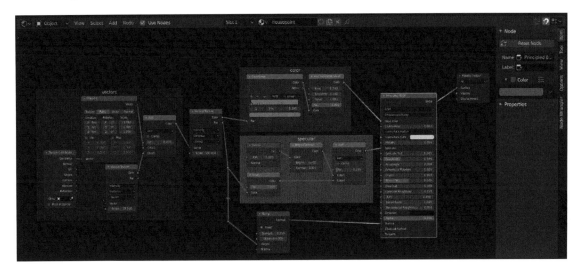

Frame nodes, used to organize and label a node tree

The generated vector is distorted by adding a tiny bit from a starting **Voronoi Texture**. This controls the **Vector** of the **Voronoi** at the heart of the material, whose nooks and crannies are colored with a **ColorRamp** and **Hue Saturation Value**. The **Specular** mixes a **Fresnel** pass with the inverted **Voronoi**, making it shiny on the bumps and matte in the nooks and crannies. Lastly, more detail is added via a **Bump**. If you handed this off to another Blender user, they would have a much easier time understanding your node logic now.

Now, let's make some glass, using the following steps:

1. Create a new material, add a `GlassBSDF` node to **Add | Shader | GlassBSDF**, and assign it to the **Material Output**. This is similar to using the **Principled BSDF** node with **Transmission** at `1`, but is much simpler.

2. The window glass can ignore shadows to simplify rendering and allow sunlight passing through them. Open the **Sidebar** panel with *N*, go to the **Options** tab, and change the **Shadow Mode** to **None**.

3. Rays going through glass will eventually run out of bounces, resulting in black artifacts. We'll solve this with a Math node set to **Greater Than 10**.

4. Combine your **Glass BSDF** and a **Transparent BSDF** with a **Mix Shader** node, and use the **Greater Than** node as the factor.

5. Add a **Light Path** node with **Add | Input**, and use **Ray Depth** as the first value in your Math node.

The result: when rays are still bouncing about, Blender will use the **Glass BSDF**. When it runs out of rays, it will use the **Transparent BSDF** node and let whatever's behind the material instantly pass through your glass. The glass nodes should look like this:

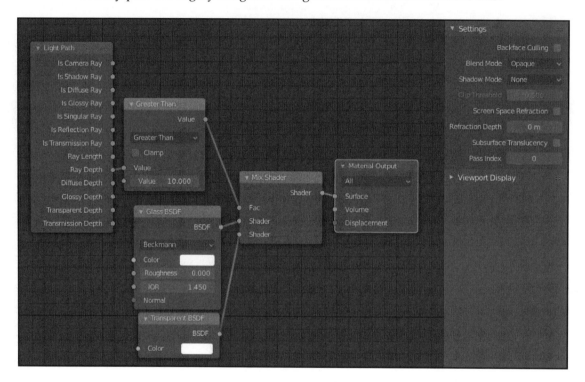

The glass material

Up next, we need some rough plastic, so recreate the following node tree:

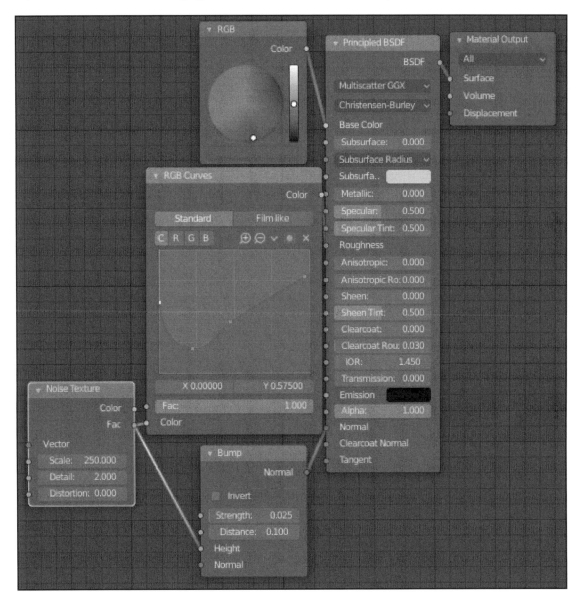

Rough plastic

Remember, you can always use the search function from the **Add** menu to find nodes by name.

For fabric, the addition of displacement adds even rougher texture. You can create this material be recreating the node tree you see here:

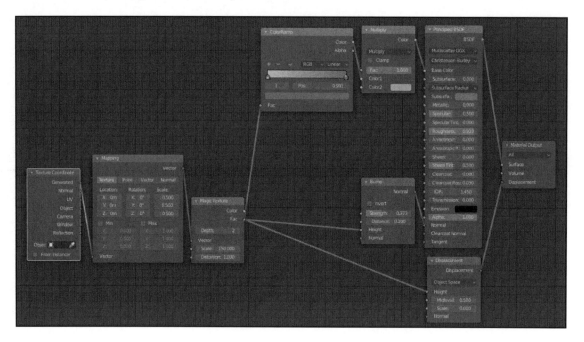

Couch fabric material

When adding materials to the kitchen scene, use these materials as a baseline for similar objects. For instance, you can duplicate the glass material to make a wine bottle's glass material with the addition of some roughness and red color.

Next up, we're going to make some slightly more complicated procedural materials, starting with wood.

Wood

Kitchen materials from this point require more complex procedural solutions. Wood is one such example. The advanced shader setup will require us to break things down into smaller chunks and think through how a material actually looks. For the complex shaders remaining in this chapter, it is highly recommended that you examine the final results in ch06_nodes.blend as you work, found in the wood and wood_boards materials. When in doubt, the exact replication of another user's shaders is a great start to understanding their node logic.

A close examination of wood can break its patterns down into separate problems:

- The swirling grain usually splits into two sections, one darker than the other.
- Within those two sections, the wood grain often has separate directions and sizes.
- Knots gather in certain locations, even darker in color.
- The grooved artifacts from cutting the wood can leave behind trace artifacts that can affect normals, roughness, specular, and base color, even with the most perfect polish and lacquer.
- A larger mosaic of staining breaks up the wood's color.
- For the wood floor, the seams between the floorboards add grooves, and no two floorboards will flow into each other.

Breaking this down into individual problems, let's tackle them in a more logical, easy digest manner:

1. Start with the core of the wood shader: two sections that have different levels of grain. This is reminiscent of our first mess-around material, with a **Wave Texture** for the first grain, a **Voronoi Texture** for the stretched flecks in the second grain, and a **Greater Than** node from the first **Wave Texture** driving their separation. **Mapping** nodes change the scaling of the wood, and **Reroute** nodes let us use a single coordinate to drive all of their coordinates. The flowing grain and dispersed flecks are both modified with **ColorRamps**:

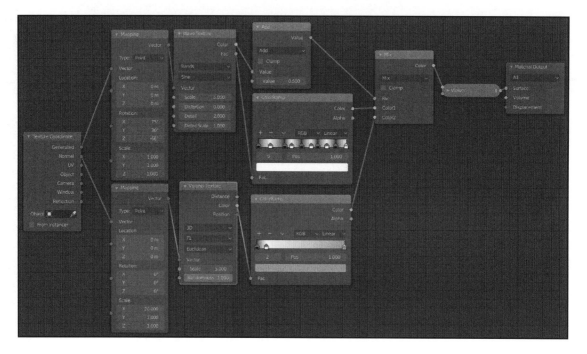

Wood grain starting patterns

2. Use **ColorRamps** and **Mix** nodes to tweak and transform your two wood patterns.
3. Replicate the flecks three times with varied mapping, and combine them with **Multiply** Math nodes.
4. Use a starting **Mapping** node to drive all three **Voronoi** flecks' individual mapping, allowing for rotation offset. Then, avoid noodle soup with some frames.

The colored wood grain and flecks have expanded the node tree, as shown here:

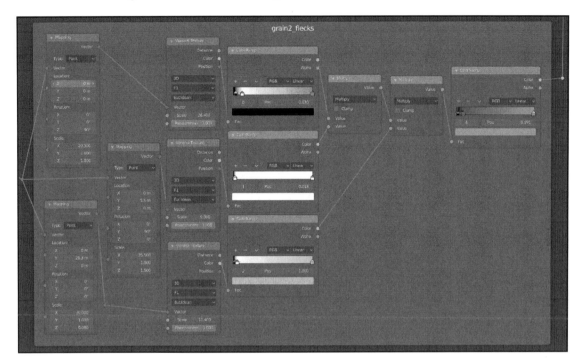

Separate frames for separate wood grain operations

5. The knots start by adding the wave texture to a new vector. Visualizing this is hard, as any value *above 1* will just look white, but the added waves will "push" the coordinates using the new vector.

6. Apply this to a **Magic** texture for a series of knots, and because there are *too many* knots, use a noise texture to add white, thereby erasing them. Note that, on the **Add math node**, **Clamp** is checked. When unclamped, new totaled values will visually output from 0 to 1, and when clamped, they'll clip the light values. This is then recolored and multiplied on top of our previous node tree.

The knots are shown here:

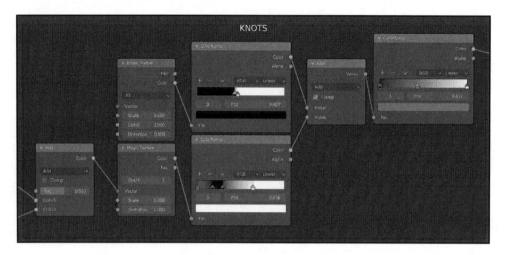

Adding a Wave Texture to a vector for distortion

7. We can break the wood's monotony up even more with a larger discoloration. Add a noise texture set to 2D with a **Mapping** node, and then modify the scale. Duplicate the noise texture, and use the previous noise as its vector input for eddies of color.

8. Combine this with your previous wood's rightmost node using a **Mix** node set to **Multiply**. I also used a second **MixRGB** node to tone the overall wood toward a specific color.

9. Organize these in a new frame. Assign this to the wood's **Principled BSDF** color.

Here, the wood discoloration is multiplied by the off-screen previous wood steps:

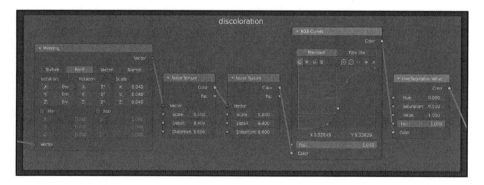

Discoloring the wood

Specular, **Roughness**, and **Normal** come along easily after that.

10. Add an **RGB** to **BW** node, and then use the node where you combined the discoloration and grain as its input.

11. Use **Color Ramps** for **Roughness** and **Specular**; since the wood is polished, the roughness should be dark with low contrast, while the specularity should be lighter and low contrast.

As you can see in the final wood results, all of those nodes payoff:

Wood, with a complex material setup

The completed wood gives us a baseline for wooden floors. We'll start with a duplicated material, and modify the vector and color with floorboards and then add grooves:

1. Assign a duplicate of the wood material to a new tester, and rename it `wood_boards`. Tweak the colors to a different wood shade.

2. At the start of our node tree, add a **Brick Texture** with a **Mapping** node to orient the bricks with the wood grain.

3. Use a **MixRGB** node set to **Add** to combine this with the texture coordinate that drives the whole material.

The multicolored bricks push the vectors in random amounts, making it so the wood floorboards look cut from different tree sections. This vector shift is shown here:

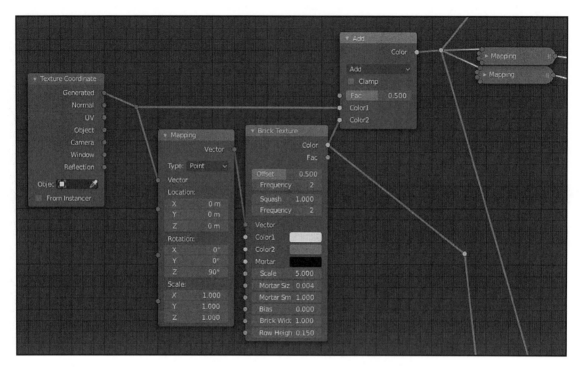

Adding the Generated Texture Coordinates to a Brick Texture that represents floorboards

4. Use reroute nodes to get the brick nodes all of the way to the end of our tree, and put it in a **Frame** node called **Brick** so you don't lose track. Combine it with a **Mix** node set to **Overlay** as the last step for the **Base Color**, which makes the floorboards lighter and darker for more randomness and adds dark grooves between them.

5. **Specular** and **Roughness** require the grooves as well. Run the **Brick** output into a color ramp that remaps it to *just* the black mortar. For the **Specular**, use a **Math** node to multiply the mortar over the final input, as the cracks would be *less* shiny (or black).

6. For the **Roughness**, the cracks should be rougher (or white). Invert the mortar with an **Invert** node, and then use a **Math** node to add these white lines to the final **Roughness** input.

In the following, the **Brick Texture** from the start of the node tree has traveled via reroute nodes all of the way to the end, where it's been stored on a **Frame** node to affect the color, **Specular**, **Roughness**, and **Normal**:

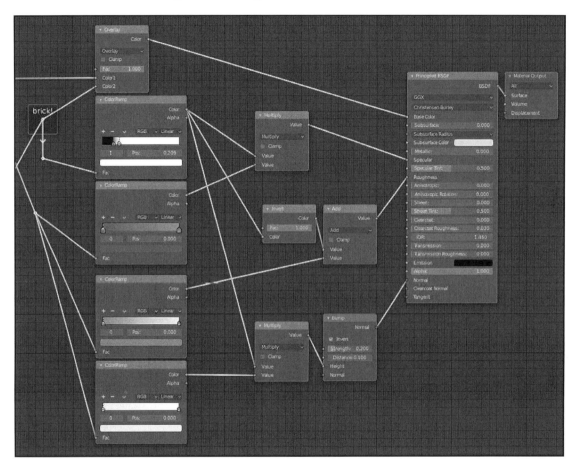

The Brick texture affecting multiple BSDF properties

7. For the **Bump** node, use a color ramp to lighten the wood grain and lower its contrast. Next, use a Math node to multiply the mortar on top. Use a Bump node set to .2 strength and .1 distance. Previously, we reduced the wood grain's strength with the Bump node, but since we have to combine it with the mortar, **ColorRamp** instead reduces it.

The final wood floorboards are very complex, but thanks to good organization, another artist could delve into your shader and make sense of things. This tidiness will pay out later when you might choose a different wood color or use that initial reroute node to map the floor with UVs:

The final wood floorboards material

The wood was a lot more complicated than the previous materials, but it has given us a chance to dive into the power of nodes. Up next, we have material for some tiles.

Tiled backsplash

For the kitchen's tiled backsplash, we can use node groups to simplify our shader even more and build a modular setup that allows for reuse on multiple tile variations. This material uses a basic UV layout. For more information on UVs, refer the *UV Unwrapping* section in Chapter 13, *Baby Dragon – Part 3*. To view the complete node tree, see the tiles material in the final project file Ch06_nodes.blend.

1. Before creating the nodes, we need UVs, as this shader uses procedural UVs, so on a new dragon tester, switch to the top view and unwrap it in **Edit Mode** using *U* | project from view.
2. Start with a tile pattern, using two multiplied **Wave Texture**'s, with **Mapping** nodes to rotate them horizontally and vertically. An **RGB Curves** node will allow us to later determine the cutoff point for grout versus tile. Scale all of the UVs on X or Y until they're square. Next, create grout texture with a **Noise Texture** node and **ColorRamp**.

In the following screenshot, the initial tile shape is seen from the starting nodes:

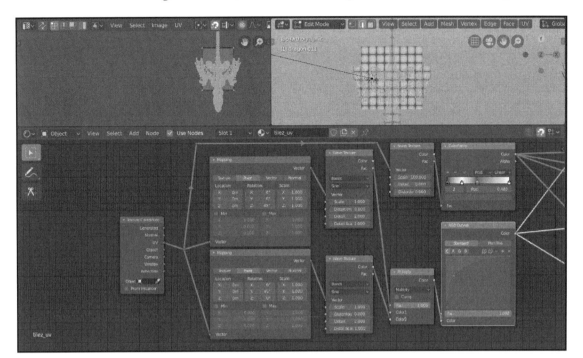

Tiles mapped over UVs

3. Select the **Mapping** nodes, **Wave Texture** nodes, and **Multiply** node, and then group them by pressing *Ctrl* + *G*.

   Group nodes are vital to keep your shaders clean and provide reusable chunks of nodes with customizable parameters. Hitting *Tab* expands and collapses the Group. When tabbed into the Group, an Input node and Output node encompass what we grouped. A Group can be ungrouped by pressing *Ctrl* + *Alt* + *G*. Also, now, when you add a new node with *Shift* + *A*, this group appears as an option to the instance via **Add** | **Group**. Create a group for **Noise** and **ColorRamp** too, named Grout.

4. For the base color, use a **Mix** node with the grout as Color 1, and your tile color as Color 2. Use the **Tile** as the **Factor**, with a **Math** node set to **Greater Than** to cut them off right where the tile turns to grout. The **RGB Curves** node can now increase or decrease the grout width.

Notice how much tidier the material is thanks to Groups:

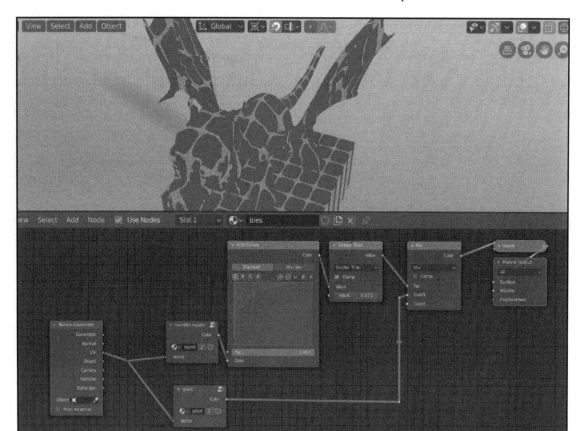

Tidier material

5. As regards **Specular** and **Roughness**, we'll create a reusable group that can control the **grout** and tiles individually. Run the **Greater Than** node into a **Math** node set to **Add**, and do the same with another **Math** node for the **grout**.

6. Group them by pressing *Ctrl + G*.

7. When tabbed into the Group, hit *N* for the sidebar panel. On the **Items** tab, rename the inputs Mask and **grout**.

8. Add two new inputs called **mask spec** and **Grout Spec**. Modify these two values to have a minimum of −1 and a maximum of 1. Use them as the second inputs on the **Add** nodes.

9. Lastly, combine these with a **Mix** node set to **Mix**, with **Mask** as the factor.

An example of customizing a group node's interface can be seen here:

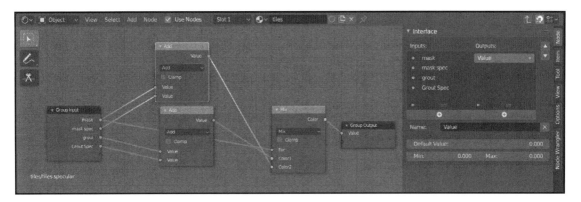

Group node inputs and outputs

We'll create a similar group for normal and displacement, once more with a focus on flexibility and cleanliness.

10. Group a **Bump** node and **Displacement** node together, and name the group Tile Displace.

11. Add inputs to this group for **Mask**, **Grout Texture**, and **Tile Shape**, and plug in their corresponding outputs. Add more two more inputs for **Grout Strength**, **Normal Size**, and **Displacement Scale**, with **Min** and **Max** values of −1 and 1.

12. Multiply the **Grout Texture** and **Grout Strength** together.

13. Mix this with the **Tile Shape**, using **Mask** as the factor.

14. Finally, use this as the **Height** for the **Bump** node and **Displacement** node, and plug these into the **Principled BSDF**'s **Normal** input and Displacement input on the final **Material Output** node.

The expanded group for the tiling normal and bump are shown here:

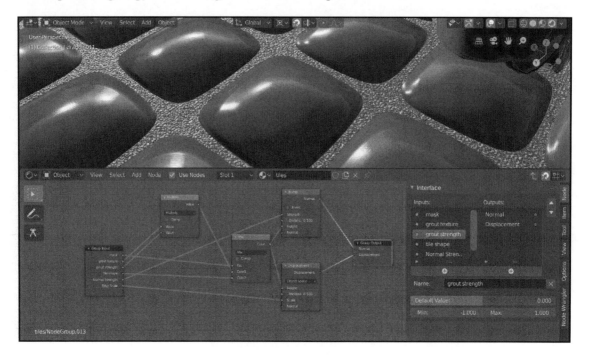

A group node to manage bump and displacement

The Tile shader ends up with much less clutter than our wood material because the groups keep things so tidy. The flexibility provided with groups is also useful. For instance, instead of the rounded Tiles group as our start point, use a **Voronoi** with its third variable set to **Crackle**, and instead of neat tiles, you have mosaic tiles!

Now, let's look at making some granite countertops.

Granite counters

The granite counters are the centerpiece of the kitchen island. Settings such as its specular, roughness, and normal will be pleasantly easy, as it's polished to a fine finish. However, its **Base Color** will be very complex, with swirling layers stacking one on top of the other, and flecks of assorted minerals. To view the complete nodetree, see the granite_polished material in the final project file `Ch06_nodes.blend`.

1. Begin by building the following tree, which is similar to our starting Wood shaders, with a series of Wave textures that differ in settings, color, and mappings, and mixed together using masks for the factor. Once they're combined, the look is further tweaked with an **RGB Curves** node and **HSV** node.

   Although many nodes were cleaned up and organized at the end, the process of getting the right blend of nodes is usually a stream of consciousness. In the following, the first pass at various ingredients for our marble material is shown:

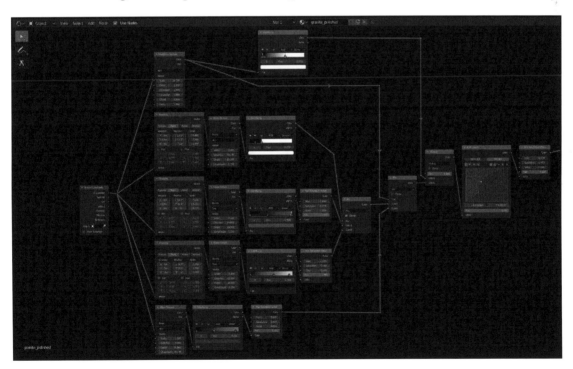

Initial setup for marble

2. Scroll over to a new area, and set up nodes for a first pass at granite flecks. **Voronoi** textures set to Cells can be used for future masking factors and random colors, while **Voronoi** textures set to Intensity give shading variation. A **MixRGB** node at the end offers a final recoloring **Color2** and **Factor** for the flecks:

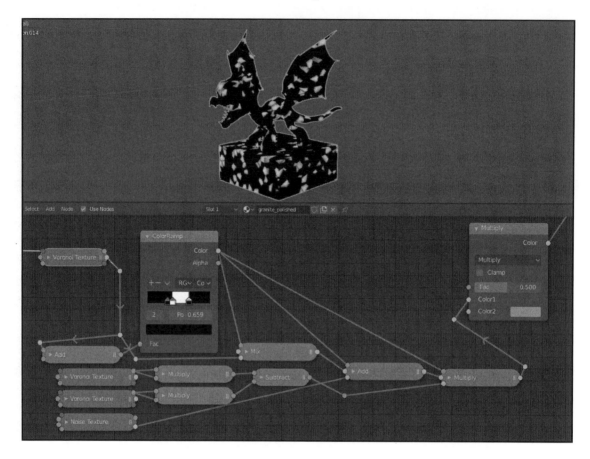

Granite flecks; another marble ingredient

3. Group these into a new Group node, and rename it `Granite Flecks`. Add attributes to the **Group Input**, so that this node setup can be reused with different settings. **Group Input**'s also allow for reusing values, such as controlling the scale of the Intensity and Cell **Voronoi** at the same time. The final fleck tint color and strength also add the last adjustment. For the outputs, we'll create a mask from the **Crackle Voronoi**.

Here are the inputs and outputs of the granite flecks for the organized group:

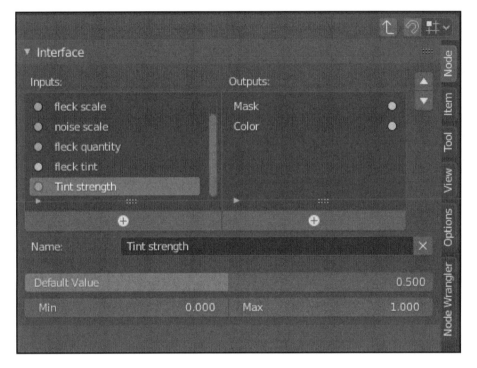

Granite flecks in a group for cleanliness

4. The reusable group means we can make three different variations on flecks, modifying their individual group parameters. Combine their colors with **MixRGB** nodes, and combine their masks with Math nodes. Next, combine the flecks with the starting marble swirls using a **MixRGB** node, with the fleck masks as the factor.

This organization now pays off; many parameters can be isolated and tweaked in our node tree, and the noodle soup is kept in check. Three granite flecks are joined together here:

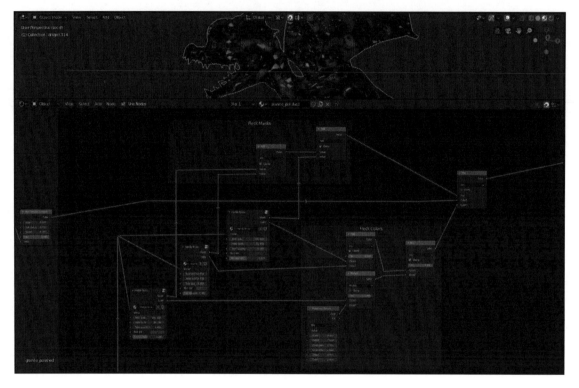

Putting the granite flecks to work

The marble's layering of materials with different levels of transmission can be shown with subsurface scattering. While the **Base Color** on non-metals approximates diffuse reflections back out after some light is absorbed, subsurface scattering describes a more complex approximation of a light ray's journey. When it can penetrate further than the initial molecules, it refracts and disperses before exiting out. The result is a softer, luminescent look, sometimes even transmitting out the other side, like a batwing membrane. Use the Swirls as the Subsurface Color, excluding the flecks as if they'd dissipated a few millimeters deep. The default Subsurface value of .05 looks good, and we can replicate that with an invert of the **Fleck Masks,** lowering the brightness to .05 with a Math node:

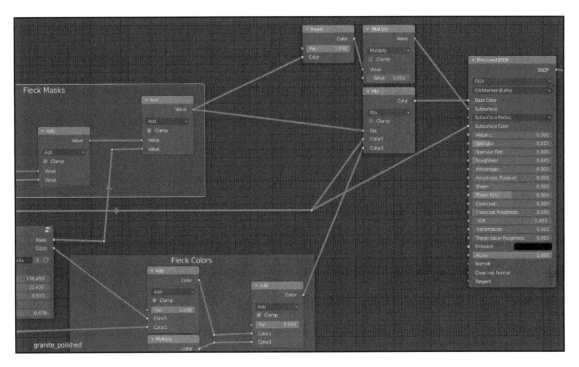

Bringing subsurface scattering into the equation

With some slight adjustments to the **Specular** and **Roughness**, the marble is done! Now for a change of pace. Let's create some materials for plants that will bring a nice organic touch to our kitchen.

Plant alpha cards

Using image textures to create materials is a very common workflow. The benefits of images are that they are immediately from real life and so can convey believable results quickly. If the wood, tile, and marble's node trees made your head hurt, image textures are a gentler alternative. Image textures can also be reprocessed with nodes or image editors, turning a single photo into roughness, metal, specular, and normal maps. In the later *Baby Dragon* chapters, you'll also use images to store custom textures for a character. Plant alpha cards are one example of using image textures and encapsulate all of the problems that image textures might bring up: alpha transparency, normal maps, and bit depth.

The detailed silhouettes that occur in nature for plants, fences, and hair can make modeling that detail unfeasible. Instead, those silhouettes can be controlled with image planes known as alpha cards; alpha refers to their transparency, and they're moved, scaled, and rotated as cards to give an organic distribution. If you're shooting your own photographs, you'll need to edit them in Krita, Photoshop, or other image editors. We'll make some using Krita, a free, open source, industry-standard image editor.

To make textures for our plant materials, perform the following steps:

1. Take some photos of plants. Shoot them on a solid background of black or white, with soft lighting, and then compile them together in a **4096 x 4096** document in Krita, Gimp, or Photoshop.

2. Use selection tools such as **Select Color Range** to create a starting layer mask, so that the background is entirely removed. As a baseline mask, you can also use your highest contrast channel to start, and then adjust it with levels. When the selection is good, apply it as a transparency mask in Krita or as a layer mask in Photoshop:

A transparency mask made with selection tools in Krita

3. Duplicate your masked plant layer, and then, in Photoshop, right-click on the layer and choose **Apply Layer Mask**, or in Krita, right-click on the layer and choose **Flatten Layer**. Move it to a lower layer.

4. We need to extend the plant's color from end to end. In Krita, use **Filter | Use G'Mic | Repair | Solidify**. If using Photoshop, use **Filter | Other | Minimum** set to 1, and then repeat multiple times with on duplicate layers by pressing *Ctrl + Alt + F*.

5. Save this as a flattened image, with the plant selection saved as an alpha channel in the Channels dialog. In Photoshop, do this by pressing *Ctrl* + clicking on the mask thumbnail to load the selection, and then, in Channels, create a new channel. In Krita, do this by right-clicking on the transparency mask, and then choose **Split Alpha | Alpha into Mask.** Do this again, this time choosing **Split Alpha | Write as Alpha.** Save this as `archtitecture_plant.tga`.

6. Image textures can also be used to make normal maps. First, change your image to a higher bit depth with **Image | Mode | 32 Bits** in Photoshop, or **Image | Properties | Image Color Space | Depth | 32 bit** in Krita. Next, use **Filter | 3D | Generate Normal Map** in Photoshop, or **Filter | Edge Detection | Height to Normal Map** in Krita. Save the normal map as `architecture_plant_n.exr`.

Of course, you can also just use the textures provided. Jump back over to Blender for our alpha card plants:

1. Add a plane object, and name it `plant_cards`. Give it a new material with the same name.

2. In **Node Editor**, add an **Image Texture** node, and open `architecture_plant_c.tga`. Connect this node for the **Base Color** and its alpha to the Alpha channel.

3. With the **Image Texture** node selected, hit *Ctrl + Shift + S*, which will add an automatic texture setup via **Node Wrangler**.

4. Use another **Image Texture** node for the normal `.exr` file, and change its **Color Space** to **Non-Color**. Hook this into a **Normal Map** node (**Add | Vector | Normal Map**) and hook it into the **Principled BSDF's** normal input.

5. In the **Shader** editor, open up the **Settings** panel with *N*. In the **Options** tab, change its **Blend** mode and its **Shadow** mode to **Alpha Clip**. This cuts the texture off to make the leaf silhouette and cast shadows from the texture. The Clip Threshold determines its intensity. For fuzzier plants that would blend together, **Blend** mode can use Alpha Blend, with **Show Backface** turned on.

6. Open up the **UV Editor**, and scale the plane's UVs down to cover a single plant. It can then be subdivided and organically modeled.

7. Duplicate this process for multiple stems. Careful UV placement along a plant stem makes positioning easier:

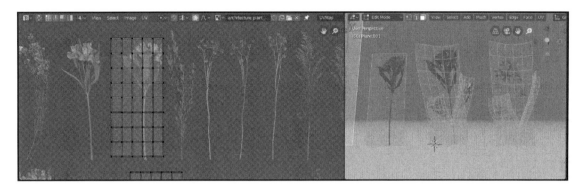

Alpha card plants, controlled via UVs

In the example file, this plant texture has four evolutions of planar models for these alpha cards. Using multiple images in one as a texture atlas can be used for things such as fridge magnets, paper documents, or wall decorations. Up next, we'll take a look at using this technique to make textures for wall art.

Wall art texture atlas

Take a walk around any given room, from a kid's bedroom to a grungy subway, and the sheer quantity of decorations you'll come across is astounding. We'll use another texture atlas for picture frames, and some simple vertex painting to differentiate between matte wood or plastic frames and the shiny glass protecting some art.

Look at `kitchen_pictures_c.tga` in the files folder. This texture atlas was taken from pictures around my house, including family photos, old artwork of mine, and art created by various family members (credits: Phil, Travis, Felix, and Susan Baechler.) Gather pictures from around your house or the internet to decorate your kitchen and, using an image editor, assemble your photos into a single **2048 x 2048** pixel file. Save it as a `.tga` file. Then, we can get mapped as an atlas in Blender:

1. In Blender's preferences, enable the add-on **Import Image** as **Planes**.

2. In the 3D Viewport, add a plane with this texture using **Add** | **Image** | **Images as Planes**. The planes appear with a material setup already created, which will prevent distortions from manually placing UVs.

3. Enter **Edit Mode**, and then use *Ctrl + R* to **Loop Cut** and **Slide** an edge to one picture's vertical border and again for a horizontal border.

4. Delete blank faces between two pictures, and dissolve any leftover cuts by pressing *Ctrl + X*, until each picture is one plane.

5. For pictures with frames, inset with *I*, and then extrude the frame out a little.

6. The pictures in frames should have reflective glass over them, which we'll use through vertex painting. To see this, in the settings for Viewport Shading, switch to Solid draw mode, set **Lighting** to **Flat**, and **Color** to **Vertex**.

7. Switch to Vertex Paint mode. In the **Properties** window's **Vertex Color** tab, a Vertex Color group was created just by switching modes, with white for the colors. Use **Paint** | **Set Vertex Colors** to set your selected faces to the black color, chosen by the swatch in the Header. Next, invert the colors with **Paint** | **Invert**, so that the glass is white.

In the following screenshot, the vertex colors are visible in one window via Vertex Paint mode, and the reflective effect is seen via glass over some of the photos:

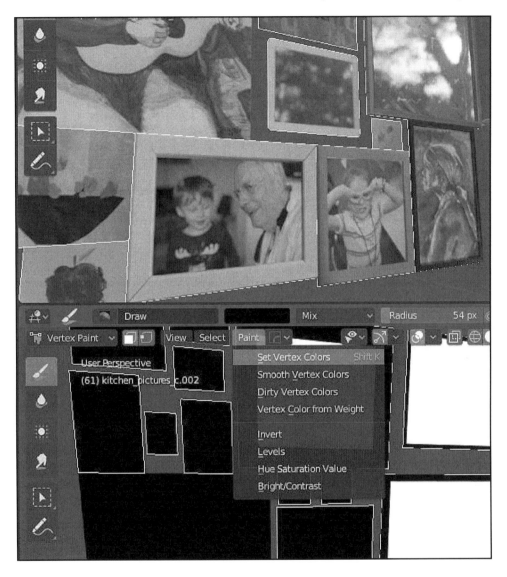

A Vertex Color attribute driving the specularity

8. Add an **Attribute** node in the Kitchen pictures material. Type in `Col`, the same namespace as our Vertex Color. Plug the **Attribute** node's **Color** into the **Specular** input on the **Principled BSDF**. Connect the **Attribute's Color** to an **Invert** node, and use this for the **Roughness** attribute. Change your viewport shading back to **Material Preview**, and the glass is shiny while the picture frames are matte.

9. Separate your pictures into individual picture objects by going to **Edit** mode, selecting all, and pressing *P* to **Separate by Loose Parts**. With all of the pictures selected, center them with **Object | Origin | Set Origin to Geometry.**

These pictures can now be appended or linked as one final aspect of modeling additions to the kitchen scene.

And now we're done with material creation! How did you do? If you struggled with any of these steps, don't worry. All of our examples are available in `ch06_nodes.blend` from the source files.

Summary

In truth, materials and lighting are rarely separate. Procedural textures happen alongside the lighting conditions they'll be viewed in and can dramatically change in their coordinate mapping once they're wrapping around a specific mesh. You might find areas where UVs, Box, and other setups work best. There are many aspects to the final kitchen where you'll tinker in areas that might benefit from a new material or a quickly modeled addition.

In the next chapter, you'll put these materials into their final arena as we light our kitchen with Eevee's real-time rendering tools.

Questions

1. What are node inputs and outputs?
2. What purpose does the Vector input have on a texture node?
3. What is the goal of the **Principled BSDF** node?
4. Why should your metalness value be 0% or 100%?

5. What are the benefits of frame, group, and reroute nodes?

6. What nodes could you use to mix two procedural textures together?

7. When do you need to modify a material's Blend Mode and Shadow mode options?

8. Why would you choose to use bitmap textures instead of procedural textures?

Further reading

Whenever your Blender project dictates that you'll be in the node editor all day, be sure to enable the **Node Wrangler** add-on and keep the hotkeys listed in its description handy. To learn more about node setups, a good way to learn is to deconstruct other node trees that you can find on www.blendswap.com.

7
Modern Kitchen - Part 3: Lighting and Rendering

We've come a long way with our sleek, modern kitchen project. We've got a composition, models, materials, and textures. There's just one final ingredient before we can render: lighting. Up to this point, we have seen what our materials look like in an isolated material preview mode used for look development. But that is not representative of what a final render can look like when the scene is properly lit. In this chapter, we will add lighting to our kitchen scene so that the Eevee renderer can create a realistic result.

When we're finished, we'll have a beautifully rendered image of our sleek, modern kitchen.

The following topics will be covered in this chapter:

- Preparing the scene
- Daylight rendering
- Indirect lighting
- Using filters and postprocessing

Preparing the scene

Lighting our modern kitchen begins with a combination of the models and materials that we created in the previous two chapters. Work off your progress from those chapters or use the `Ch07_start.blend` example file if you prefer to use our example. This file has the models and materials all in place and ready for lights to be added. Names were cleaned up and collections were organized for clarity. Duplicate meshes were turned into instances so that one change to a cupboard would affect all cupboards. Linked libraries have been reworked for cleaner structure and immediate modification. Many additional models and decorations have been scattered in the scene—too many to explain individually. You can endlessly build additional set dressings for your kitchen. Whether you are modeling it all yourself, pulling ideas from the demo files, or jumping right into lighting your kitchen is up to you.

Assigning the materials that we created to the models can require some unique changes and also highlights some new organizational tools. Let's cover how to append these materials to the kitchen scene and make sure they map correctly to our models:

1. Begin appending materials from the blend files you made in `Chapter 6`, *Modern Kitchen Part 2 – Materials and Textures*. Apply them to objects as a starting pass and hide objects once they've got their materials checked off. You can select all objects with the same material by using *Shift + L*.

2. A good library of procedural materials is great to have in your arsenal. However, as you add the materials, you'll discover that some need their mapping tweaked. It might be a matter of scale, where the material displays far too large or too small when placed on the model. It can also be a matter of mapping, with UVs or object mapping working better with the final meshes. The consolidated mapping nodes at the start of our node trees will assist in these edits.

3. As an example of this, select your floor object, which can be mapped with UVs for more intuitive tiling. In the node editor, change its materials' mapping to UVs.

4. Select all the floor faces and from the top view, unwrap by going to **U** | **Project from View**. In the **UV** editor, select all these UVs and scale them on **X** or **Y** individually. The dimensions of the boards can be remapped in a more intuitive way using this procedural UV approach.

Many meshes only work when their modeling and materials are approached at the same time. Take a moment to refine your models, such as redistributing plant alpha cards in vases or planters. In the following screenshot, you can see how the finished material and the scale of UVs *both* contribute to the final look of the wooden floorboards:

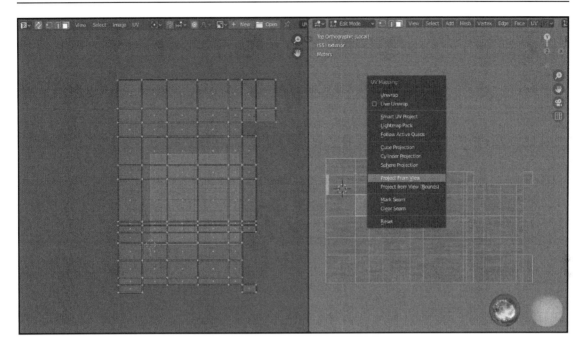

Scaling UVs horizontally and vertically to place wooden floorboards

You can always add more details later, such as food on the shelves, dishes in the cupboards, and people sitting in the chairs. Hit pause on this polish for now while we tackle the big missing element—lighting. Once lighting elements are in place, future assets will have something more tangible to be considered when placing them.

Daylight rendering

The immediate feedback for lighting in Eevee is truly a joy. We'll start by getting the basics of natural light—a sun and a sky. Next, we'll extend their realism by baking our light with irradiance volumes. Daylight can be deceptively simple; although we only need a single light for the sun, we'll need to massage Eevee's lighting tools to avoid artifacts and enhance realism.

Preliminary lighting with a sun object

If the sun is out, it's probably the most defining light source. So, that's a good place to start our look development:

1. Set your **Display mode** to **Material Preview**, with **Scene Lights** and **Scene World** off. The **Material Preview** mode provides a combination of fake environment lighting and your own scene lights. This has two benefits. First, we can get a sense of how light and materials interact even when we haven't finished our lighting. Second, when your lights and settings get too complex, we can use **Material Preview** to work with quicker real-time feedback.

2. Click on the **Material Preview Shading** options and click on the thumbnail of the **High Dynamic Range Image (HDRI)** sphere. Choose from among the premade HDRIs that come built into Blender. HDRI is an advanced form of a photograph that combines a spherical panorama with full lighting information from multiple exposures. Put simply, it makes reflections look really cool and is key to photorealism.

3. With the **Render Stuff** layer selected, add a sun by going to **Add | Lights | Sun**. To see this light, turn **Scene Lights** back on. Move it outside the bounds of the kitchen.

4. In the **Properties** window, select the sun's context panel, 🔘. Set the strength to 100.

5. Switch to your camera view. Then, with your sun selected, rotate it around until it casts appealing shadows through the window. Raking shadows from blinds, fences, and window panes are something photographers hunt for. Note the hack on the **Glass** material, which has **Shadows** disabled in its options, thus not letting light in.

6. Activate **Shadows**, then adjust **Clip Start** and **End**. This determines the distance of objects affected by the sun. Objects outside of **Start** and **End** won't be affected, but the smaller the range, the less Blender needs to compute. To encompass all my objects, I landed at a start of .001m and an end of 20m.

7. Activate **Contact Shadows**. Set the distance to 1.5m so that neighboring polygons interact more.

8. In both the **Shadow** and **Contact Shadow** settings, set the softness to .1, as our sun is strong, sharp daylight. This will increase objects affecting each other and compensate for thin meshes.

From this top angle, you can see how the sun's angle and settings create the raking shadows on the ground:

Shadows cast by the sun through the window

If you're having trouble nailing the sun's parameters, inspect `ch07_kitchen_end.blend` to see how our example is set up.

Up next, we'll have a look at world lighting, which will make the surroundings of our kitchen scene feel like a real place instead of floating in a gray, empty world.

World lighting

World lighting is the next puzzle piece for our lighting. In real life, we can see things for miles around us. We can account for all that detail with a single environment image. This also provides continuous realistic reflections and with the right environment map, it can even generate shadows in Blender's other renderer—**Cycles**.

In the **Viewport Shading** settings, turn **Scene World** back on. Since there's no world set up, we see pure black, plus the sun. As our main lighting source, this isolation helps position it for ideal shadows. As you work, you should frequently switch between different viewing options; isolating rendering tasks like this makes it easier to spot things to fix.

Let's go over how to set up an HDR image to light our world, now:

1. In **Shader Editor**, switch from **Object** to **World**.

2. Add an environment image by going to **Add | Image**. This is similar to an image texture but is mapped to infinite space in Blender. Plug this into the background's color input.

3. Open up `kitchen_environment_snow.hdr`. HDR is a 32-bit image format, which stores much more lighting information.

4. Add a **Texture Coordinate** node, then a **Mapping** node, and connect these to the environment texture. Use the **Z** rotation to change the position of the world coordinate. As a hack, you can also increase the **Z** scale to pull the tree line down, making it look further away.

5. Add a **Principled Volume** node with **Add | Shader**. Attach this to **World Output**'s **Volume** input. The kitchen fills with smoke. Reduce the **Density** value until there's only a slight haze in the kitchen, enough that it catches the rays of sunlight from the window.

Here's the final world node setup, allowing mapping adjustments, background strength, and volumetric lighting:

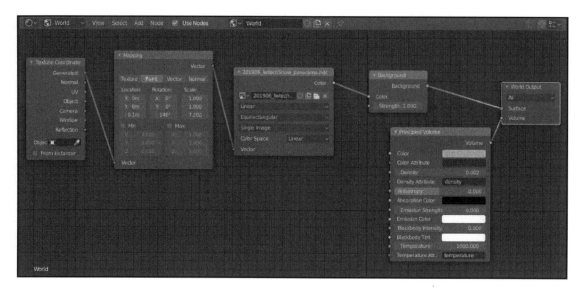

The world nodes

When balancing the strength of **Sun** versus **World**, reference is always helpful. If you added in man-made lights, reference will tell you that the ratio of the sun's light to man-made light is heavily weighted toward the sun. The core beauty of this scene is the strong raking window light and so the ratio of sun energy, world energy, and overall exposure has to serve that goal.

Now that we have a good start on daylighting with **Sun** and **World** set up, we can take a look at using indirect lighting to fill the environment with bouncing light.

Indirect lighting

Light in real life bounces around from one object to the next. In a properly lit and rendered scene, we would be able to see sublet bounces of color from one object casting onto another. Some renderers have the ability to calculate these light bounces for realistic results, but the Eevee renderer is a real-time renderer and it needs a little help to show bouncing light. Right now, light might pour through the corners of the room as if the walls weren't there. Reflections on shiny objects seem to show the environment map, even if a red chair is right next to them.

To fix these issues and give Eevee the help it needs, we can use **irradiance probes**. Irradiance probes store the lighting information with baked-in data. This means that the bouncing light can be calculated ahead of time and the models can access that information in real time and display realistic lighting without needing long render times. Let's learn how to set up irradiance volumes, now.

Irradiance volume

To make our kitchen lighting more realistic, we'll start by adding an irradiance volume. This object type has an inner boundary, outer boundary, and a matrix of light probes to approximate ambient light for a number of points in space. For the inner and outer boundaries, we simply move and scale them to the correct spot, then adjust the number of probes in the **Properties** window.

You can see an irradiance volume being used in the following figure:

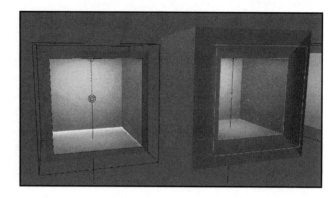

Irradiance volumes with various wall thicknesses, inner boundaries, and outer boundaries to show their effects

Take a moment to look at `ch07_irradianceTest.blend`. This file has example irradiance volumes scaled to different amounts, showing the problems that occur with incorrect placement. When the volume is too small, shadows can incorrectly bake around the corners. When the volume is too large, light leaks from the sun incorrectly bake into the corners, when they should be blocked by the wall. The biggest one shows the ideal placement, with the inner boundary aligning to the interior walls and the outer boundary inside the walls. We'll need to keep these targets in mind when adding irradiance volumes to the kitchen, which is what we'll do now:

1. Return to the kitchen scene. Add an irradiance volume with **Add | Light | Irradiance Volume**. Irradiance volumes create a field of samples, with each sample calculating the light and shadows for that point in space. The result is that nearby objects can use the nearest irradiance point to determine lighting.

2. The irradiance volume needs to be adjusted to encompass the whole of the interior. The inner boundary should line up to the walls; if it's too small, the shadowing changes in the cracks, but if it's too large, the volume will sample beyond the room. The outer boundary should be encapsulated in the walls to prevent lighting with the world that ought to be blocked outside. Use the top view with wireframe shading, then scale the irradiance volume until the inner box extends just beyond the borders of the room. Switch to the side view, then scale the irradiance volume once more to fit.

3. Select your kitchen exterior mesh. In the **Modifiers** panel, add a **Solidify** modifier. Set its thickness to `.2m`. Check **Even Thickness** to keep the outer walls parallel. This thickness will stop **Irradiance Volume** light leaks coming from the world.

4. We'll distribute the irradiance volume's samples evenly, which can take some guesswork. In the **Properties** window's **Object data** tab, change the irradiance volume's resolution **X**, **Y**, and **Z** values until the sample points look evenly spaced from the front, top, and side views. I landed on **X**, **Y**, and **Z** values of **16**, **7**, and **6**, respectively, but it differs from scene to scene. When positioning your irradiance volume, aim to have all the probes inside the volume of the house. You want them near the walls—but not touching, or they'll cause spotting.

The irradiance volume setup we ended up with looks like this:

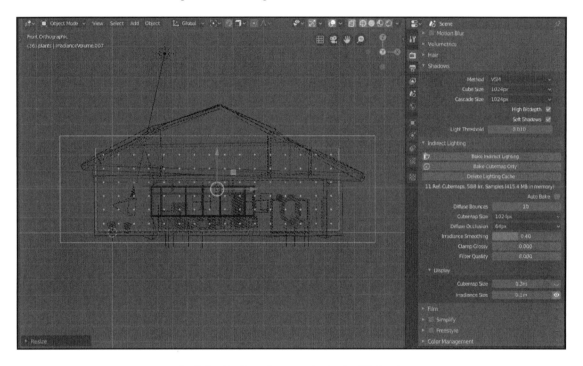

The distributed irradiance volume measured against the solidified exterior

Next, we'll bake the data for our irradiance volumes. By baking a more complex and realistic lighting representation, it can be accessed on the fly for real-time goodness. Use these settings for a finalized bake cache; if you're still testing things out or tweaking models, use a lower resolution:

1. In the **Render** settings' **Indirect Lighting** tab, turn off **Auto Bake**. This avoids the slowdown of rebaking and the approximation will give you acceptable lighting while getting everything in place.
2. Turn the **Cubemap** size to `2048px`.

3. In the **Shadows** panel, set **Cube Size** and **Cascade Size** to 2048px. Activate **High Bitdepth** and **Soft Shadows**, as well.

4. Click **Bake Indirect Lighting**. This bake might take a *very* long time, depending on your computer. Do some stretches, make yourself a snack, or go to bed and check the results in the morning. When you return, the scene's realism will have taken a jump forward.

5. If your computer couldn't handle the render load, lower the shadow and indirect lighting to a lower setting. Depending on your lighting scenario, you might not even need that resolution; I arrived at my settings by testing at lower resolutions and increasing them if artifacts still persisted. For bake times, assume your testing bakes will finish during a 1-hour lunch break and a final quality will finish overnight. Having a finished irradiance bake is handy for working without a lag while you continue to modify your scene. When testing changes, re-bake with low settings to save time, then up the resolution to bake while grabbing lunch. You can crank the resolutions up to 4096 for amazing results, at the cost of an enormous file size.

6. Check the render without the probes by toggling the overlays in the header. In the **Indirect Lighting** tab, the irradiance spheres can be scaled or hidden under **Display**.

You can see the baked probes in the following screenshot:

The visualized irradiance volume probes once baking is complete

File sizes will swell as the various lighting bakes are generated, compounded by the number of probes and their resolution. Turning off the **High Bitdepth** shadows will also dramatically reduce file sizes, but will limit their accuracy when adjusting the scene's exposure. The ch07_kitchen_end.blend project file used lower settings than the ones listed here on account of file size, but if you increase the settings and re-bake, they'll take a noticeable jump forward.

If you had trouble with your baked probes, there are several things we can try to address the artifacts. Let's take a look at some of these fixes, next.

Addressing artifacts

Lighting errors will persist, even with the irradiance volume, especially around corners and areas that touch the infinite exterior. This can be due to the meshes, light probes, or resolution. Here are some potential solutions:

- Some lighting problems are caused by wall thickness. Select your house exterior mesh and apply the **Solidify** modifier. Next, go to the **Edit** mode and hunt down any problems caused by extruding, such as polygons intersecting each other. You don't want your exterior thickness to be too visible in the window and you don't want it to block the sunlight. Outside of those concerns, the thicker you can make the walls, the better they'll block exterior light.
- Sometimes the light still spills over the mesh, especially around the all-important walls. As a hack, you can add another irradiance volume that's two probes thick and size it directly over the window, where problems tend to gather.
- When finding problems, don't waste time on re-baking at full resolution. Compare the problems with lower resolutions in **Cube Size** and **Cascade Size** of the **Shadows** tab and lower **Cubemap Size** and **Diffuse Occlusion** in the **Indirect Lighting** tab.

Alright, now that we've fixed our baking errors for the indirect light, we need to make a second type of probe for reflection data.

Reflection probes

The kitchen has a handful of extra reflective objects, such as the mirror and sink. Highly reflective areas will need a reflection probe for more accuracy. Focus your view on the mirror and you might notice that none of the kitchen appears in the mirror; it just shows the world. Reflection probes will fix that:

1. Set the 3D Cursor to the mirror (*Shift + S*) and go to **Add | Light Probe | Reflection Probe**. Scale it to fit over the whole of the mirror so that the sphere is slightly in front of the mirror.

2. In the **Render** settings, click **Bake Only Reflection Probes**. This deletes **Irradiance Volume**, but we don't need to worry about this while getting the reflection probes set up.

3. Go to the **Rendering** panel's **Indirect Lighting** tab, then click **Bake Cubemap Only**. Once the bake is done, examine the mirror again.

Now, the dining room table is reflected in the mirror properly, as you can see in the following screenshot:

The mirror's reflection after adding a reflection probe and baking

4. Add another reflection probe and in the **Object data** panel and change its data type to **Box**. Move it into position over the sink and scale the box to fit the rough area of the sink. Once again, use **Bake Cubemap Only** and the improved reflections will pop into place. When you're satisfied with all your baked probes, bake the indirect lighting. Make sure the smaller probe radius for probes is within the kitchen bounds. In the following screenshot, you can see how the reflection probe fixes the fridge to reflect the kitchen instead of the snow environment, but when it clips through the back wall, the environment map is incorrectly baked through the wall.

5. Add another reflection probe and in the **Object data** panel, change its data type to **Box**. Move it into position over the sink and scale the box to fit the rough area of the sink. Once again, use **Bake Cubemap Only** and the improved reflections will pop into place.

6. Add a larger reflection probe in the center of the room, another in the front of the room, and smaller ones near areas with intricate detail, such as over the stove, over the kitchen table, or near the fruit and decorations at the front of the room.

7. When you're satisfied with all your baked probes, bake the indirect lighting.

You can see our reflection probes are starting to bring some higher quality reflections into the scene, just like in the following screenshot:

Reflection probes restricting the shiny fridge's reflections to the inside the kitchen.

That's it for probes; they're a bit of a pain but they add a lot to the quality of the image. Another set of features that we can use to improve our render is called filters and postprocessing.

Using filters and postprocessing

The kitchen is ready for Eevee's final postprocessing effects, found in the **Render** panel of the **Properties** window. These can add the benefits of added realism, as well as more artistic control. The best part is that their effect is immediate, without the need for additional render times.

When figuring out a render, go for two approaches. The first method follows the order in this chapter, where render issues are isolated and cured, first. Only after these technical hurdles are out of the way do you turn to post effects, to avoid obfuscating where the pain points are. In the second approach, you go for a "look" right away, such as a foggy night or fireplace lighting, and then build your scene after. At other times, you can combine the two approaches simultaneously.

First up, we're going to have a look at screen space reflections.

Screen space reflections

Screen space reflections provide automatically computed reflections. They lack the accuracy of reflection probes, but the benefit is they catch many edge case scenarios, so you don't have to fill your whole scene with probes. They'll provide specific benefits to the marble counter, which is mildly reflective but too sprawling to use a reflection probe on. It's especially useful over long distances; an irradiance probe in the foreground might miss a white-hot reflection beyond its clipping end, but from the screen space, it's still visible. Let's enable this feature now:

1. Go to **Properties** | **Render** | **Screen Space Reflections**. Without any re-rendering, the reflections pop into place.
2. Some of the screen space reflections are inaccurate. The sliding back door's reflection appears on the floor, even though the kitchen island would block it. To solve this, up the thickness until it looks better (try about 3m).

You can see the settings we used for our example in the following screenshot:

Screen space reflections improve the marble countertop

That was a much easier effect to add than the probes and it added a lot to the scene. Now, let's add another postprocessing effect that will give our scene some glow.

Bloom

Bloom mimics the natural light spill that occurs when light is diffused by something such as grease on a lens or dust in the air. When combined with strong lighting, it adds a beautiful atmospheric effect. Let's try adding it now:

1. In the **Properties** window, go to the **Render** panel and then go to **Bloom**. The lit areas of the scene glow with a new luminous quality.

2. Adjust the settings to your liking. I changed **Threshold** to 1, **Radius** to 3, and **Intensity** to .8.

3. The **Bloom** settings should be adjusted in tandem with the **Principled Volume** settings in our world material. After the bloom is in place, I reduced the **Principled Volume** density to .004.

Ours turned out like this; notice the glow around the lights in the scene:

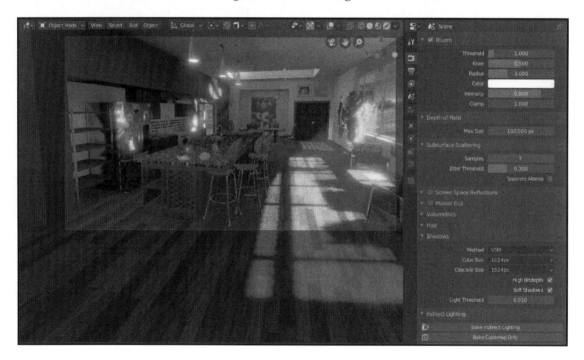

Bloom adding a diffused glow around light sources

Another effect we can add will give us back some dark shadow information. Right now, the objects in the scene aren't making any contact shadows and this next effect will help us out with that.

Ambient occlusion

Ambient occlusion simulates the nooks and crannies where, if we sampled endless light bounces, the inability of rays to reach them would cause extra shadowing. The default settings work for us. If your scene uses a distorted scale (for instance, bug characters rendered at a 100x scale), you might need to adjust **Distance** to fit. You can see our settings for **Ambient Occlusion** here:

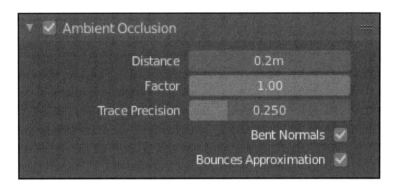

The Ambient Occlusion settings

Good—now, let's make some changes to how the color in the scene is managed to get a juicer and more colorful result.

Color management

The kitchen's overall balance can be adjusted in the **Color management** tab. This offers several overall controls for exposure and works in tandem when balancing the light in your scene:

1. Note that **View Transform** is set to **Filmic**. This mode is designed to preserve the color balance and more accurately resemble our eyes. Avoid changing **View Transform** or **Gamma**.

2. Change **Sun Strength** to 200. This is double our previous ratio of **Sun** to **World**. Although the ratio might be more accurate now, the scene becomes overexposed.

3. To compensate for this, change **Exposure** to -1. This returns the overall render to a balanced exposure. If your shadows had **High Bitdepth** turned off, they will respond less accurately to this. Adjust the settings further to your liking.

There are all kinds of styles you can create with good color management. Now, we need to adjust our camera settings so that we can get some artistic lens settings for our final image.

Camera settings

If we were photographing this kitchen with a real-world camera, it would offer many settings that extend your artistic license. A good lens is often defined by the range and extremities of zoom and aperture it offers. The physical effects that come from aperture (depth of field) can be controlled from our camera. Let's tweak a few of these settings, now:

1. Select your **Camera** object, then go to the **Camera** panel in the **Properties** window.
2. Activate **Depth of Field**. Everything turns blurry.
3. Drag the **Focus Distance** attribute until the depth is at a distance you like.
4. Alternatively, choose an object from your scene for **Focus** on the **Object** field. The camera auto-focuses on that target.
5. The **F-Stop** attribute works similarly to a real camera. A low f-stop in the real world is around 2.8, with a high f-stop around 35. At an extreme f-stop of .1, you can fake the feel of macro photography.
6. The focal length can also dramatically change your render. A low focal length creates a wider angle, while a higher focal length mimics a telephoto lens. I set the camera to 24mm to capture a wide angle. Note that because focal length in the real world is related to your zoom, you will need to position your camera after changing it.

These settings have made quite the difference, as you can see in the following screenshot:

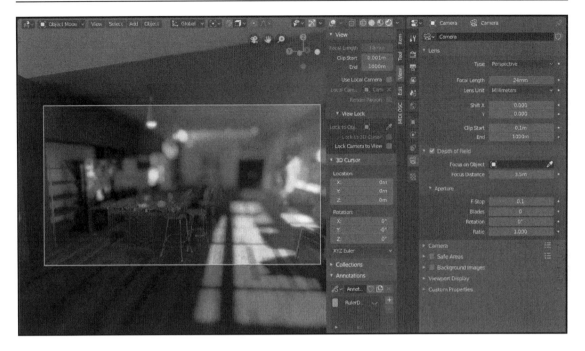

Extreme depth of field

We've chosen a focal length of 24mm, a focal length distance of 3.5, and a f-stop of 2.8. You can also right-click and animate these attributes to mimic zooming and focusing on a camera and create a little animation if you wanted to. For now, though, we need to add some indoor lighting that will take this render up to the highest quality possible.

Rendering with indoor lighting

At night, this kitchen would take on a different mood entirely. Instead of streaming sunlight from the windows, the kitchen lights will be bright for cooking, with more intimate lighting by the dinner table. We'll need to make use of Blender's three other light types (Point, Spot, and Area) for a kitchen with interior lighting.

You can see some examples of how different lights behave in the following screenshot:

Different lighting types shown placed against a wall

Open the `ch07_lightingTypes.blend` file. This reference shows the three basic lighting types, with comparisons between the default settings and a customized setting. Point lights emit evenly in every direction. Spot lights limit the light to a cone. Area lights mimic a spread surface, such as softboxes or computer monitors. The physical light spill and surface area of area lights make them my usual preferred light in Eevee. The modified versions have two major changes. First, **Custom Distance** is on and set to a nearby radius (2 to 4 meters). Their energy is also modified. The distance the light travels and the brightness of the light are the two main things to adjust artistically when designing lights.

Eevee's problems can also be seen with some of the light fixtures. Light objects don't include the physical lightbulbs that might spread the emission over a glass panel or frosted bulb. To account for this, use mesh objects with emissive materials. When the light is inside the mesh, such as on the point light, modify **Blend Mode** and **Shadow Mode** in the **Material** options so that the lightbulb is ignored. Meshes for light fixtures are also often too small to correctly create shadows. On the modified area light, **Clip Start** is reduced so the light's housing will affect the shape.

It's also important to contextualize the shape when light hits a surface versus when light passes through a medium. The lights by the wall look a certain way because of the wall receiving the light. The lights out in space take on a specific shape because of the **Principled Volume** node for the world settings, filling them with smoke. Note the much higher energy levels needed to get this effect. When attempting specific lighting shapes, such as the cone of a street light, having a volume for the light to affect is often needed.

Now, let's create some lights for the kitchen to finish off our render:

1. Return to your kitchen scene. On the **World** node setup, set **Strength** on the **Background** node to 0, the equivalent of night time outside.

2. Set your 3D Cursor to the hanging lights with *Shift + S*. Add an **Area** light. Move it down into the body of the light. The **Blend** mode on the light mesh's **Light** material is set to **Additive** in the options so that it won't block the light.

3. Instance the area light with *Alt + D* and move to the inside of the next light. Repeat until they all have a lamp. By instancing, we can change the values on one lamp and all the other lamps will change too.

4. Select all the lights, then move them to their own new collection, named lights_kitchen, with **M**.

5. Activate **Custom Distance** on one of these lights and set it to 5m. Next, set the power to 1000w. With this approximation, adjust **Strength** and **Distance** to control the light shape to your liking.

6. Set **Shape** to **Disk**, then adjust **Size** until the disk shape matches the light shape—around .15m.

7. Under the light's **Shadow** settings, change **Clip Start** to .001m so that the light fixture will occlude the light. The bottom ring of faces on the lampshade can be pulled up and down to modify the light's shape even more.

8. Set **Softness** to .2. Too much softness will add light to areas that ought to be shadowed.

9. Turn on **Contact Shadows** and adjust the thickness until you get good results. At 1m, the countertops accurately shadow the chairs and wine rack.

We'll use **Spot** lights for more directed shapes over the kitchen counter:

1. Select the light fixture over the kitchen table and set your 3D Cursor to this by pressing *Shift + S*. Add a **Spot** light by pressing *Shift + A*, then go to **Add | Light**, and instance it multiple times so that each recessed light has a spot with shared settings.

2. Turn on **Custom Distance**. Set it to 3.5m and change the power to 5000w. This strength will help illuminate the volume so that the light cone will be visible.

3. Under **Spot Shape**, change the size to 60° and the blend to 1.

4. Turn on **Shadow** and **Contact Shadows**. If there are lighting artifacts, adjust the **Bias** and **Thickness** values until they disappear.

Lastly, we can add some `Point` lights to fill in the foreground shadows. We can position these off-camera so that we see their effect but we don't have to add extra meshes to explain them:

1. Add a **Point** light. Position it off-screen near the wall so that it shines on the chairs.
2. Set **Power** to `100` and **Custom Distance** to `10m`. Choose an incandescent warm color. Turn on **Shadow** as well and leave the settings at their default.
3. Instance this light by pressing *Alt + D* and move it to the opposite wall. This adds some fill light near the shelves and wine rack so that they're not completely lost in cast shadows.

Here is our result with the lights in place:

Man-made lights illuminating the kitchen at night

The three lighting types each contribute to a kitchen render ready for a real estate listing. To further enhance it, you might add lights for the stove range, or perhaps street lights visible through the window. Reduce or remove the environment map in the **World** settings to simulate night time in a well-lit kitchen.

You can press the *F12* hotkey to render out this image and turn it into an image file that you can share online or in a portfolio. You've worked really hard on this project and we've come a long way—you should be proud of that kitchen!

Summary

The finished kitchen uses all the tricks of Eevee to get physically realistic lighting, with the added benefits of real-time feedback. If this scene was for a prospective client, you could fly through the scene and show them custom angles, without the burden of overnight renders. These concepts instantly translate to game engines, such as Unity and Unreal. Lastly, scenes such as these work in parallel with both Eevee and Cycles.

Your next step might be to render this in Cycles for the specific features it has that Eevee doesn't—IES lights, micro-displacement, denoising, compositing, and other advanced techniques. When you find yourself in a room with beautiful lighting, be sure to study it from both a physical and artistic standpoint. Different bulbs and equipment produce vastly different results, but the human element of how these are arranged is a major aspect of interior design.

Up next, we're going to take a break from the three-dimensional part of Blender and have a look at some two-dimensional production tools that were added in Blender 2.8, namely, one called **Grease Pencil**.

Questions

1. What settings do you activate on a Sun object for shadows?
2. What benefit does world lighting provide?
3. If your irradiance volumes include world lighting when walls would logically block it, what could be the issue?
4. When should you use a reflection probe to improve a render?

5. Can you name three Eevee postprocessing effects that you can activate in the render tab?

6. What benefit can the Volume attribute of the World Output node provide?

7. What are the differences between Point, Spot, and Area lights?

8. When should you modify a material's Blend mode or Shadow mode?

Further reading

For a bounty of CC0 HDRIs, head over to www.hdrihaven.com, where Greg Zaal has a number of options at height resolutions.

8
Illustrating an Alien Hero with Grease Pencil

Grease Pencil is a set of vector drawing tools, named for the easily erased pencils used in the days of animating on paper. Before diving into animation, we'll use these drawing tools to their maximum potential to illustrate an alien hero that will utilize all the layers, brushes, effects, and modifiers that Grease Pencil has to offer. This kind of avatar drawing is used as concept art for 3D models, or as an illustration for science fiction projects as a planetary representative. Creating concept art will let you master the brush and layer interfaces, and emulate the styles of rough pencil, clean ink, and color palettes:

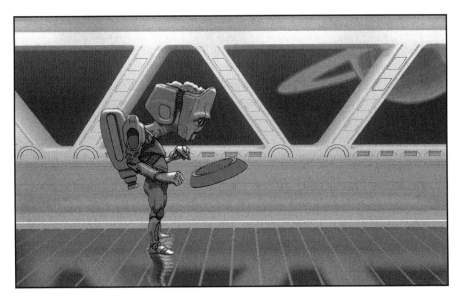

Our finished Alien Hero concept art

To draw and paint the character, the best process starts with broad idea, gathering reference images, and sketching lots of thumbnails. Once a direction is clear, we'll do a loose draft utilizing several drawing approaches, and then build up the design with inking and color. We can then use Grease Pencil's other tricks to get custom looks and painterly touches. Lastly, we'll place this alien adventurer in a spaceship corridor.

 To learn more about digital drawing and painting, check out *Krita Illustration by Example*, first edition, by Oscar Baechler (2021).

In this chapter, we will cover the following topics:

- Drawing with Grease Pencil's brushes
- Using Grease Pencil layers and objects to maximum effect
- Developing a character idea with thumbnails and references
- Thinking out a character with gesture, contour, construction, and value
- Layering illustrations with ink, color, and lighting
- Using effects and modifiers to complete the illustration's look.

Playing with Grease Pencil objects

To use Blender's 2D animation tool, **Grease Pencil (GP)**, we'll begin with a series of warm-ups to see how the tools work. GP has two modes: **Notation** and **Object**. For **Notation**, the annotate mode is used to draw on top of your scene, leaving notes, and marking up your blend files in a non-destructive fashion. The GP object has layers that store brush strokes that can have a variety of line styles and fills. These can store different strokes across multiple keyframes for animation, and are extensible with modifiers and effects. Annotation is useful for taking notes and sharing file instructions with others, while GP objects are where we'll create our alien hero and their environment. In fact, many of the figures in this book have arrows and labels drawn directly in Blender using the **Annotate** tool.

Setting up a tablet and stylus

Although GP drawings can be done with a mouse, these drawings are enhanced significantly with a stylus interface, and so it is strongly recommended that you get the right kind of hardware. Many 2-in-1 laptops include built-in stylus support. If you're on a laptop or desktop without pen support, there are a variety of graphics tablets that you can plug into a USB, as well as monitors with stylus support. If you only have a mouse, some GP handling in this chapter will be harder to emulate.

I will alternate between a 2-in-1 laptop and a PC with a USB graphics tablet. For the tablet, I modify the pen's side buttons to be right-click and middle-click for better integration with Blender. On most Windows 10 laptops, you can't modify the buttons to middle-click. If your stylus setup has this problem, go to **User Preferences | Input** and activate **Emulate 3 Button Mouse**, which lets *Alt + right-click* work like middle-click. Your pen's sensitivity and other settings can also be modified, as shown here:

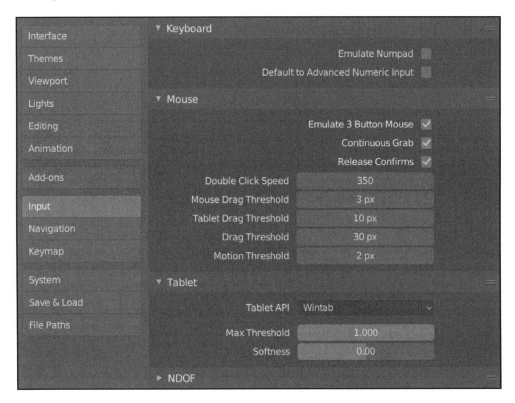

The Blender Preferences input settings

If you don't have a tablet, you'll usually rely more heavily on the **Curve** tool when drawing GP strokes. If your first use of GP doesn't have the right feel, a change of settings could be needed.

Lastly, if you are using other hardware, such as a Wacom tablet, your GP issues might be related to the hardware maker. Make sure to install all the drivers for that hardware, and investigate their driver software for other preferences to tweak.

When your hardware is ready to go, let's use the **Annotate** tool, which lets you draw on top of Blender's interface.

Annotating with Grease Pencil

We'll use the **Notation** functionality to annotate the very tools and menus we'll be relying on. **Notation** is a great way to write notes to yourself while working in Blender. It's especially useful in scenes you'll hand off to other people, who might get lost in your custom setups. The colored labels in the following screenshot were drawn on top of Blender's interface with the **Annotate** tool:

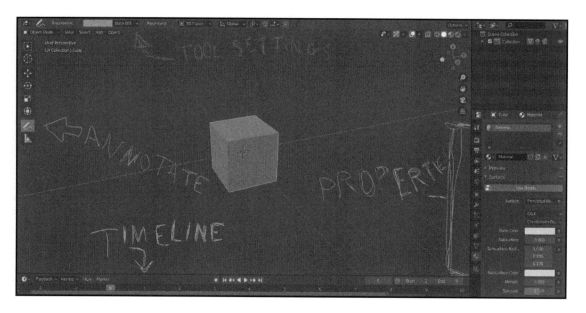

Using the Annotate tool to label interface components used by Grease Pencil

Let's get acquainted with Annotate by doing the same:

1. Start a new file using **General Preset**, and then select the **Annotate** tool from **Tool Shelf** (*t*).

2. Draw an arrow in the 3D view, pointing at the **Annotate** tool. Write `Annotate` next to it.

3. Turn **Tool Settings** on via **View | Tool Settings**.

   Tool settings lets you create multiple notes in different colors, and layers control stroke thickness. Click the pulldown to add new notes on individually colored layers.

4. Add a new red layer, draw an arrow at the tool settings, and write `TOOL SETTINGS`.

5. Create a yellow annotation layer. At the bottom of the interface, by the timeline, write the letter `T`.

6. Go forward one frame with the → key, and then write the letter `I`.

7. Repeat this for all the letters in `TIMELINE`.

   Animation occurs whenever a new frame has a new drawing. These are called keyframes, which we'll use frequently in this chapter. Hit the *Space bar* to play the animation, and the word is spelled out. Be careful with the *Space bar* and arrow keys; going to a new frame by accident can often leave you wondering why your GP strokes disappeared. That drawing you're looking for is probably stored on a different frame.

8. Create a green layer, and go back to frame 1.

9. Draw a bracket encompassing the **Properties** window. We'll use these settings later on with the GP object type.

10. Press and hold on the **Annotate** tool icon to view other options, and then select the **Annotate_Polygon** tool. Draw a zigzag with several mouse clicks, and hit *Enter* when finished.

11. Press and hold on the **Annotate** tool icon to view other options, and choose the **Eraser** tool. Erase your zigzag.

12. In **Tool Shelf**, change **Placement** to **Surface**, and draw over the default cube with the default **Annotate** tool. The strokes are drawn directly on the surface of the cube in 3D.

Drawing on the surface is a handy way to think through edge loops. This covers the extent of annotation; the rest of our art will be done with the help of the GP object.

Testing in the default Grease Pencil scene

The **Annotate** tool uses GP to mark up your scene with notes, but the real animation power lies in the **Grease Pencil** object. We'll use the GP preset file to explore the basics of how brushes work. Before creating a finished project, let's explore how the tools feel, and emulate real-world materials and rendering styles such as pencil, ink, marker, and stipling.

Let's start with the **Draw** tool. Create a new scene, and choose the 2D animation preset. This scene layout contains the following: An empty **Grease Pencil** object, toolbar, tool settings, **Outliner**, **Properties** window, and **Dope Sheet** window set to `Grease Pencil`. The toolbar holds brushes to draw freehand strokes, Bezier strokes, and some basic shapes. The **Draw** tool is the default start. The other tools create strokes with either a drawing interface or Bezier interface, destroy strokes with erasers, or create flood fills with the bucket. The GP **Dope Sheet** window stores animation keyframes, which can be selected and re-timed. The **Properties** window's **Object Data** panel has layers for organization, and the **Material**, **Effects**, and **Modifier** panels will also be used. We'll cover these all in depth, but for now, let's test out the basics of the **Draw** tool:

1. In the **Tool Settings** header, click on the icon next to **Pencil**, and select the **Marker** preset, one of several real-world material equivalents.
2. Change the size of your brush's radius by pressing *F*, or using the slider in **Tool Settings**. Draw a number of test strokes.
3. Change the size of your brush's radius by pressing *Shift + F* or using the sliders, and then test again.
4. If you have a stylus, toggle the stylus pressure sensitivity in the tool settings. Test again.
5. Use each preset to spell out the preset name.

When doodling with brushes like this, my preferred way to get a clean slate is to draw on a new keyframe. Just go forward a frame and start drawing again. This will create a new keyframe in the GP **Dope Sheet** window, storing an entirely new drawing on a new keyframe. To get rid of a keyframe permanently, select it in the **Dope Sheet** window and delete it with **X**.

As you can see in my doodles here, we're still using the same interface areas, and each drawing preset has a unique look:

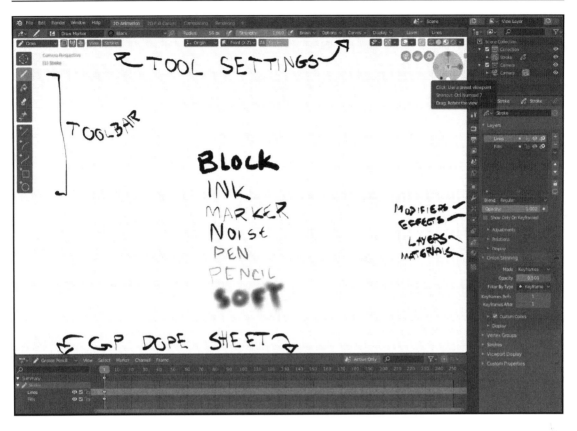

Different draw presets, plus the major UI areas for GP

The next tool we'll look at is the **Curve** tool. If you don't have a stylus, the **Curve** tool is where you'll do almost all your GP strokes. This uses a Bezier interface with precise control. The **Curve** tool can draw straight lines, Beziers, and arcs all at once. In fact, I rarely use the **Line** or **Arc** tools on the toolbar, as their functionality can be entirely replicated with the **Curve** tool. By toggling curves, you draw with C, the curve will switch from **Curve** to **Arc** mode. As for straight lines, leaving the Bezier handles untouched will leave curves as straight lines:

1. Activate the **Curve** tool on the toolbar. Click and drag to draw out a curve.
2. Click the two blue Bezier handles, and move them with the mouse to change the curve shape.

3. Click and drag on the two yellow end points at the start and end of the curve to move them.

4. Press **Enter** to finish the curve.

5. In the **Toolbar**, activate **Thickness Profile**, and draw a new curve, which is now tapered from the start to the end.

6. Hit *F* to adjust the taper thickness of the live curve, modified before completing the curve by pressing *F*, which resizes the curve using the mouse.

7. Draw another curve, and then hit *E* to extrude a new curve. Do this multiple times.

8. During an extrude, hit *C* to toggle between **Bezier** mode and **Arc** mode, which instead has a single handle. Adjust the handle to change the arc.

As demonstrated in the following diagram, the **Curve** tool offers lots of variation in a single tool:

Curve tool with varying thicknesses used for straight, arcing, and curved lines, including mixing them all at once

The **Curve** and **Draw** tools will be our primary weapons for most GP tasks. Now that you can throw down some strokes, let's look at the **Edit** and **Sculpt** modes, which offer additional ways to adjust strokes once they've been drawn.

The Edit and Sculpt modes

Switch to **Edit** mode and GP strokes can be controlled by their components, just like with mesh objects. **Edit** mode has three component types: *Points*, which function like vertices; *Strokes*, which are all connected points; and *All Stroke Points between Different Strokes*, whose selection stops upon intersecting another stroke. We'll try each of these options out on some test strokes, and look at **Edit** mode tools that will be familiar from **Edit** mode on mesh objects:

1. Use the **Draw** or **Curve** tools to make two loop-de-loop strokes.
2. Switch to **Edit** mode with *Tab*, and then set your **Select** mode to **Point** with the hotkey *1*. Select a point by *left-clicking*.
3. Turn on **Proportional Edit Falloff** in the header, or by pressing the hotkey *O*. In its settings, activate **Connected Only**, as shown here:

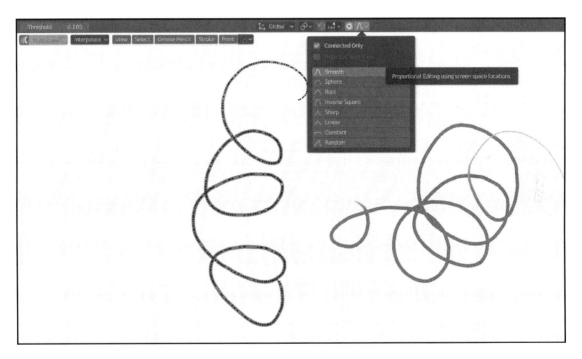

Proportional Edit Falloff with Connected Only

4. Move the vertex by pressing *G*. Use your scroll wheel to adjust the **Proportional Edit Falloff** distance.
5. Press *L* over a point to select all linked points, the equivalent of a stroke.

---

[295]

6. Switch to **Stroke** mode by pressing 2. Click between your strokes to select them.

7. Adjust a selected stroke's weight by pressing *Shift + S*.

8. Switch to the third mode, **All Stroke Points between Different Strokes**, by pressing *3*.

9. Click on a tail end of your loop-de-loop. The selection will stop at an intersection.

10. Delete these points by pressing *X*.

11. Select another line segment, and then separate its selected points into their own stroke by pressing *P*.

Edit mode comes in handy for minor adjustments. For instance, if you over-draw a stroke, the third mode can select just the tail end and delete it. If you under-draw a stroke, you can move the end point over to close with a neighboring stroke.

Sculpt mode instead uses a brush interface to deform aspects of existing strokes. Use **Sculpt** mode to deform the placement of strokes, paint a stroke's opacity up or down, or affect a stroke's thickness. The sculpting brush hotkeys of *F* and *Shift + F* change the size and strength of the brush, just like with **Draw** mode, and pressing *Ctrl* will reverse a brush's direction.

Switch to **Sculpt** mode and test the brushes in the tool shelf with the following steps:

1. Select the **Push** brush. Use *F* to set a large falloff, and push your loop-de-loop strokes around.

2. Switch to **Edit** mode, and select half the points. Return to **Sculpt** mode, and then activate **First Selection Mask** in **Tool Settings** as follows, prior to testing the difference:

The Point, Stroke, and Points between Strokes selection masks

This limits your sculpting to just points that are selected in **Edit** mode.

3. Switch to the **Thickness** brush. Paint over the selected strokes to thicken strokes, and paint while pressing *Ctrl* to thin them.

4. Switch to the **Smooth** brush, and paint over your strokes to reduce jittery points.

5. Switch to the **Strength** brush. Paint over the selected strokes to increase their opacity, and paint while pressing *Ctrl* to reduce it, much like erasing.

Sculpting strokes is a great way to modify a whole drawing, and many of the **Draw** mode settings work similarly in **Sculpt** mode, such as enabling pen pressure or stabilization. With the combined power of the **Draw**, **Edit**, and **Sculpt** modes, let's practice our brush control with some calligraphy.

Adjusting the brush tool for calligraphy

Let's practice our penmanship using the **Draw** and **Curve** tools, which will highlight additional brush settings. The finished calligraphy can be seen in `ch08_calligraphy.blend` in the project files:

1. Switch to the **Front** view.
2. In **Outliner**, turn off visibility for the camera.
3. In **Viewport Overlays**, turn the **Grid** on.
4. Select the **Draw Ink** preset, and set the radius to 1 pixel.

With this viewing setup, we'll draw four guidelines using four different methods.

1. Use the **Draw** tool, and hold *Alt* while drawing to draw while locked to the *x*-axis.
2. For the next line, turn on **Guides** and, in the pulldown, choose **Grid**. Draw a line, and it automatically snaps to **X** and **Y**.
3. For the third line, use the **Curve** tool, and hold the *Shift* key to draw in straight lines. Leave the Beziers alone to keep it straight.
4. For the fourth line, use the **Draw** tool again, but attempt to draw the line by hand.
5. The human errors can be corrected in **Edit** mode, where GP strokes function a lot like mesh data. Hit *Tab* to enter **Edit** mode, select a vertex on your wonky stroke, and then press *L* to select **linked**.
6. Scale the stroke on the *z*-axis to 0, and then move it to the correct place on the grid by pressing *G* and *Z*.

Layers are a major organizational tool for GP. They can be modified and selected in the **Properties** window, or in the **Layer** pulldown on the tool settings. When we tweak our penmanship, keeping the guidelines on a separate layer will keep them from getting moved. The default GP object has **Lines** and **Fills** layers. We'll add a third layer for letters, and use the layer locks to protect our straight lines:

1. In the **Properties** window's **Layers** panel, click the + symbol to add a new layer.
2. Double-click the layer's name, and rename it `letters`.

3. Hit the lock on the **Lines** layer to protect it.
4. Using the layer pulldown in the **Tool Settings** header, choose the **letters** layer.

Moving layers up and down in the stack changes which one displays on top. **Blend** mode can be changed to mix a layer situated above differently to a layer situated below. An example of modifying the **Opacity** and **Blend** modes is to set a layer to **Multiply**, which effects darkening, and lowering its opacity to control the effect. This is all the layer setup we need for now, as seen here:

The Layers panel

Now to practice penmanship over these lines. Getting strokes to handle in a calligraphic way requires a number of modifications. Each one of the following options can be added to increase smoothing when using a stylus. We'll use **Active Smooth** to automatically even out jittery penmanship. **Stabilizer** can also fix this, by making your stroke follow a few pixels behind, and **Post-Processing** averages out a stroke once it's completed. The tools in **Edit** mode allow us to clean strokes just like a model, especially when averaged using **Proportional Editing Falloff**. Lastly, GP's **Sculpt** tools let us shape and smooth strokes with a brush interface:

1. Select the **Draw Ink** preset. In the **Options** menu under **Tool Settings**, turn **Active Smooth** to 1.
2. To stabilize a stroke, draw while holding *Shift*, and your stroke follows a few pixels behind the cursor, allowing for careful directional changes.

3. In the **Stroke** menu, turn the stabilizer on by default, and change the **Radius** (how far it drags behind) and **Factor** (which affects speeding up to the cursor.) I like a setting of 20px **Radius** and .6 **Factor**, which cleans lots of handling artifacts while barely disrupting stroke direction.

4. Activate **Post-Processing** in the **Options** tab. This performs a stroke-wide smoothing at the completion of strokes. Keep the settings low or off entirely, as these can dramatically change a stroke from how it looked originally.

5. Draw out some letters on your grid, ignoring errors in pressure sensitivity errors and focusing on the lines being placed correctly.

6. Switch to **Edit** mode, and select a single vertex at the end of a stroke.

7. Turn on **Proportional Editing** by pressing *O*, and then use **Shrink/Fatten** by pressing *Alt* + *S*. Minor adjustments in **Edit** mode are frequent.

Switch to **Sculpt** mode to modify some of your calligraphy. **Sculpt** mode uses a brush interface, with the familiar hotkeys of *F* for brush size and *Shift* + *F* for brush strength:

Adjust your strokes with the **Grab** brush, shrink the thickness by means of the **Thickness** brush, and smooth out artifacts with the **Smooth** brush:

Examples of calligraphy

It takes practice to get the effortless hand for good calligraphy. Not every quill or brush can be mimicked in GP (such as chisel tips), and you might be limited by the quality of stylus hardware. Next, we'll use materials to affect the look of your strokes.

Customizing Grease Pencil materials

Let's examine the settings of GP materials. The two main components of a GP material are the stroke and fill. Each one has a color swatch to change its color and alpha. It's important to note that the final strength of a stroke is a mix of the material alpha, the layer opacity, *and* the stroke's individual alpha, which is often affected by pen pressure. Changing the style allows for images or gradients to go across the stroke. My usual preference is to use materials that are *only* stroke, or *only* fill, which we'll also want when using the **Fill** tool:

1. Start a new GP scene. Draw both a closed circle and an almost-closed circle with the help of the **Inks** preset on the **Lines** layer.
2. Select the **Fills** layer. Move to the **Materials** tab, and select the **Grey** preset material, which has **Fill** activated but not **Stroke**.
3. Select the **Fill** tool from the tool shelf. Click in your closed circle, and it fills the circle.
4. Instances such as your almost-closed circle mean the **Fill** tool will leak out, but the **Fill** tool can temporarily be switched to the draw brush with *Ctrl*. Hold this down, and draw a line closing your circle. Next, fill the rest of the circle, as shown here:

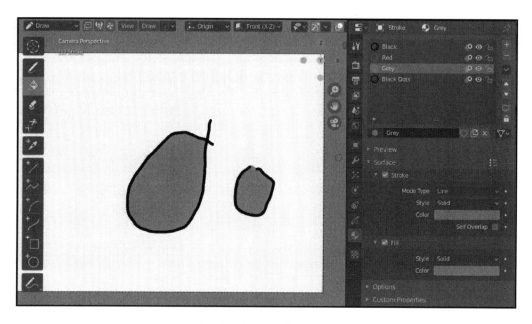

The circles can be filled in with the Fill tool.

We'll use **Fills** later on in this chapter. Toggling **Stroke** can thicken the fill, but this means keeping their colors identical and preventing alpha from working, so I usually leave **Stroke** off. Next, we'll create a new material called `chalk`, and give it the following settings:

1. Have **Stroke** activated on the new Chalk material, but not **Fill**.
2. Change the **Style** to **Texture**, and load `ch08_stencil.png` (`https://github. com/PacktPublishing/Blender-3D-By-Example-Second-Edition/blob/master/ Blender3DByExample_ch08/textures/ch08_stencil.png`) from the `Textures` project folder. Draw a test stroke, and the chalky stencil draws along the stroke.
3. Scrub the **UV Factor** attribute to change the charcoal's stretching along the stroke.
4. Activate **Use as Stencil Mask**, and then click the **Color** swatch. Pick a color, and the stroke will use the color while the stencil only affects the alpha.

As shown in the following screenshot, a stencil can help mimic the texture of real chalk and charcoal:

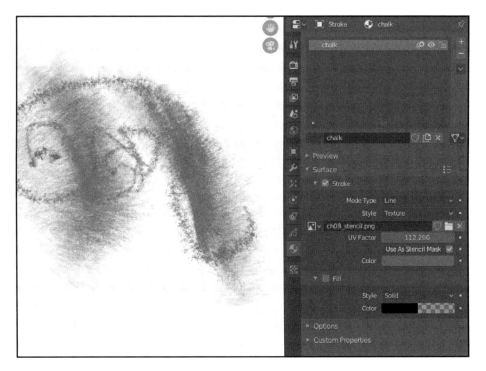

Chalk material using a stencil

Use different brush sizes for broader chalky strokes. This material can also be softened via the brush's strength and pen pressure activation for slow build-ups. Now, let's try one more material with a more fully realized warm up: stippling.

Stippling over a photo with a dots material

For our last warm-up, we'll emulate stippling to copy a photo portrait, using a custom stroke material to make dots from lines. Stippling is a process that builds up values with endless pen dots. In high school, I *hated* stippling, and in adulthood as an art professor, I realized stippling wasted a student's whole day on busywork. In GP, however, a mix of materials and brush settings makes for the stippling look with a rapid drawing speed. We'll stipple over a reference image; use a favorite photo of your own, or the one provided. The completed stippling project can be seen in `ch08_stippling.blend` in the project files:

1. Create a new GP scene. Switch to **Object** mode, and then add a reference image with **Add | Image | Reference**. Select an image that you'd like to stipple.

2. In the **Properties** window ![icon], change its **Depth** to **Back**, so that our strokes will always show in front of the reference.

3. Select the **Stroke** object. In the **Properties** window, go to the **Materials** tab and turn the stroke's **Mode** type to **Dots**.

4. Switch to **Draw** mode, and choose the **Draw Ink** preset. Disable pen pressure for both **Radius** and **Strength**, and set your **Radius** to 5px.

5. Start tracing your image. The faster you draw, the more distributed your stippling dots will be. Draw the overall image first, and then build up dots in darker areas.

6. For long strands or clean edges like hair, go to the **Options** pane and turn on **Stabilize**. The dots will flow out closer together.

7. To build up the larger, tedious dark values, turn on both **Stabilizer** and **Jitter**. The dots are more frequent, but dispersed over an area.

8. As you work, occasionally switch to **Object** mode, and then select your reference image and lower the transparency. By the time your stippling is finished, it should be completely hidden.

9. For a shortcut to building up value, draw a "patch" of stippling dots. Next, in **Edit** mode, select them and duplicate them around your drawing in areas with extra darkness, such as the hair or shadows. In the **Viewport Overlays** window, disable **Edit Lines** to view just the stippling.

10. To see your drawing come to life, go to the **Modifiers** tab and add a **Build** modifier, with **Mode** set to **Concurrent**. The drawing appears over multiple frames when you hit play.

As you can see in the final result, the stippling builds up until the reference is copied faithfully:

The final stippling, with a Build modifier to animate it.

Now that you're warmed up with basic brush feel and style options, let's put these tools to use with a complete character illustration.

Roughing in a character

Now that you're familiar with Grease Pencil, we'll illustrate an alien denizen of the stars, starting with a solid rough draft. Don't sit down and expect a good drawing to instantly flow out of your stylus. Instead, we'll begin by researching and experimenting with a design, drawing things to see whether we like it, and refining the rough character.

In movies, a cool alien design is often the best part of the film, and variety makes for a dangerous and interesting cosmos. Is your character a muscular warlord, or sophisticated ambassador? What real creatures and organic forms do they reference? Biped or quadruped, mammalian or reptilian, or perhaps floating through the air with an unseen energy? Design elements such as weaponry, biology, and fashion can give it a dynamic silhouette, and imbue them with a sense of history and culture.

Drawing techniques such as thumbnails, skeleton wire frames, gestures, contour drawing, polygonal construction, and value studies can all help you take your idea to the next level. See the separate layers for these rough draft techniques listed here: `https://github.com/PacktPublishing/Blender-3D-By-Example-Second-Edition/blob/master/Blender3DByExample_ch08/c08_alien_rough.blend`.

Thumbnailing with layers and keyframes

The alien hero starts with rapid drawings called thumbnails. Try to draw at least 10 for any new idea, and aim for a pace of *2 minutes, 30 seconds, or even 10 seconds* each. We'll draw while adjusting the timeline with 1 frame per thumbnail, and use a brush with limited options to focus on speed instead of settings. When I thumbnail on paper, I draw with only 2 or 3 inches per drawing, and a fat-tipped Sharpie to keep me focused on the silhouette.

Jump between drawing approaches with every thumbnail. Some aliens come to life with pure scribbles. For others, my thumbnails are a first impression of the silhouette. Constructing a skeleton with one quick line per major bone or limb can help posture, with egg or box shapes to place things. Use gesture lines, where a single stroke captures the emotion of an arm, leg, or even the head-to-toe character:

1. Start a new scene with the GP default.
2. Rename the **Fills** layer to `Grid`, and rename the **Lines** layer to `Thumbnails`.
3. Similar to the calligraphy warm-up, draw a grid of 11 straight lines.

   When thinking of characters, you can measure them in "heads." Humans are between *6* and *8* lengths of our head tall, but can be drawn with different amounts for effect; babies can be *2* heads tall, and fashion models *12* heads tall. Many human features land close to an amount of "heads".

4. Use the following brush settings to emulate a marker or pigment liner: 8 **Radius**, 1 **Strength**, turn off **Pressure Sensitivity** for both, no **Post-Processing**, no active **Smooth**, **Stabilize** on, **Stabilize Radius** set to 20px, and **Factor** at .75. Test how it handles. Aim for a brush that follows fast and turns well when you're scribbling, but smoothed enough to avoid jittery artifacts.

5. Draw a basic human figure that corresponds to the grid.

   Use this to familiarize yourself with some good reference points. If a human male is 8 heads tall, you can go down head by head and find an approximate landmark at each next head distance: chin, nipples, belly button, groin, tips of fingers at rest, knees, and 2 heads down for the feet, as seen in the following drawing:

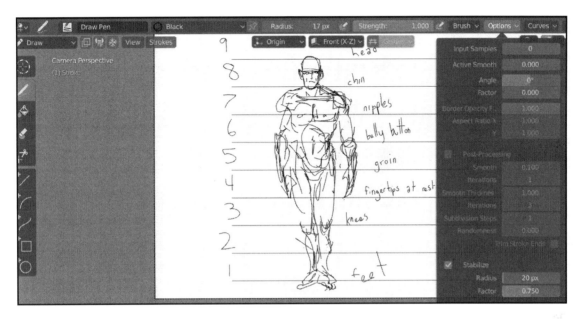

Simplified human proportions as measured by heads

6. Go forward a frame with the arrow key, and draw out a quick character idea. Limit yourself to 30 seconds max!

   The instant the new strokes are down, a keyframe is added in the GP **Dope Sheet** window. It corresponds to the active layer (Thumbnails), leaving the grid layer unchanged. By jumping forward after every thumbnail, we can work on a clean start every time.

7. The **Layers** panel has four optional toggles for each layer: **Mask**, **Lock**, **Visibility**, and **Onion Skin**. Set your grid layer to **Locked** to avoid drawing on it, and turn **Onion Skin** off for both layers. As you work, the grid layer's **Visibility** option can be toggled to view your thumbnails.

Test out 10 or more thumbnails for a sci-fi hero, using some wildly disparate ideas: a reptilian assassin, a cybernetic fighter pilot, a hulking insectile brute, and a cunning ambassador. Since I spend a maximum of 2 minutes per thumbnail, I try to push these themes in new and interesting directions, never settling for the first idea. After you bang out a few, scrub the timeline to see which one you like the best, or use a thumbnail on the thumbnail layer from the `C08_alien_rough.blend` project file as a starting point. Here are some of my thumbnail examples:

Rapid gestures of alien proportions

Dope Sheet navigation hotkeys:

With one thumbnail per frame, you'll want to scrub the dope sheet efficiently. When dealing with keyframes in the **Dope Sheet** window, use these hotkeys to speed up your workflow.

Left-click: Select keyframes.
Right-click: Scrub the timeline.
Left and right arrows: Move one frame.
Up and down arrows: Move to the next keyframe.
Space bar: Toggle play/pause.
Ctrl + Shift + Space bar: Toggle play/pause backward.

Thumbnails are an excellent way to stretch ideas to their boundaries. Pick one or two of your favorites to work on. The first thumbnail is rarely the best one, and just like toys in a toy store, a plethora of choices makes the winners pop out. Next, we'll refine the rough draft with several different approaches to drawing that can help you think through the finished character.

Sketching rounded forms in Pencil

When drawing an organic creature like our alien, a simple pencil can generate endless variety. Hold a pencil almost flat to the paper, and soft, broad strokes can gently layer shadows. Hold a pencil near the tip like for handwriting, and dark, sharp lines can be made. This slow, transparent buildup is also emulated in real life with low-opacity copic or prismacolor markers, or lighter or dried-out markers, before committing with pen later. The rounded forms of organic living creatures are built up slowly, turning ovals into heads and muscles. We'll flesh out our drawing with the creature's actual flesh by emulating a real-world pencil in GP. In doing so, we'll briefly cover some typical drawing approaches:

1. Go to the frame with the thumbnail you like.
2. In the **Layers** panel, change the **Thumbnail** layer opacity to .2, which is traceable but not distracting.
3. Switch to the **Draw Pencil** brush preset. Change the **Radius** to 90px and **Strength** to .2. I also turn on **Stabilize**, with a **Radius** of 20px and a **Factor** of .75.
4. Create a new layer called **Pencil**, and lock the other layers. Draw out some loose bubbles for the major masses: head, chest, and pelvis. Continue adding soft bubbles for the joints and limbs, and connecting them together.

 Look up references for *everything* whenever you feel like you're struggling with hands, arm muscles, facial features, or how a skeleton would work. If you have the internet or a library, there's no good excuse to forego references!

As a rounded form emerges, the borders can be solidified and shadows drawn in. Use *F* and *Shift* + *F* to go between two extremes: a large brush radius (as much as 150px) with a weak strength (.1), and a small brush radius (30px) and a moderate strength (.5). These represent drawing with the broad side of a pencil lead versus drawing sharply with the point. Use the first extreme for big shadows and toning. Use the second mode for features, contract shadows, and outlines.

Control the opacity from three different places:

- The first one is your brush strength. Don't rush it, and build up values with five repeat strokes, rather than one perfect stroke.
- Second, in the **Materials** tab, you can reduce the **Alpha** of the **Stroke** color, which reduces it across the board.
- Third, you can reduce the overall layer opacity, and simply create a new layer on top of it for an extra layer of shading. As your drawing is built up, reduce the opacity of the **Thumbnails** layer until it eventually is turned off entirely.

Use the **Eraser** tools to clean up your drawing. The **Eraser Point** preset erases entire GP points, and the eraser soft brush can gently lighten over-rendered areas. **Eraser Soft** with a large radius and low strength is especially nice.

 To watch your drawing build up as an animation, go to the **Modifiers** tab and add a **Build** modifier. Set the layer to your **Drafting** layer, and turn off **Visibility** for your **Thumbnails** layer. Press the play button and each stroke appears in the order it was drawn.

As shown here, I take my time to build the drawing up, rarely getting darker than middle gray until the very end:

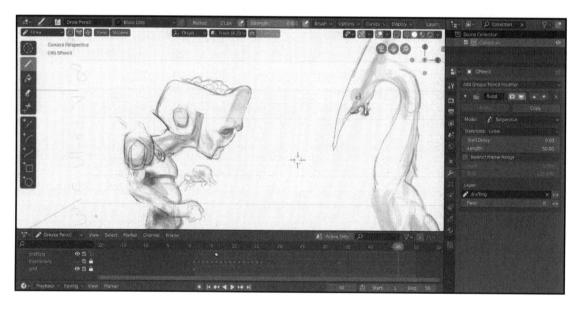

Sketching with the Draw Pencil preset

Drawing in real life with physical materials will improve your GP drawings, and provide you with experience for what you should try to emulate when drawing in Blender. If you're familiar with another medium, such as watercolor, ink, markers, or dry brush, perform some experiments to see whether you can emulate the same experience with GP. However, when I can't immediately figure out a drawing problem, I use construction drawing.

Construction drawing

Pulling a fully realized organic form from your imagination is a frustrating experience. Roadblocks occur when placing feet on the ground, following the cylinders of the body, and making the face symmetrical when it turns in space. Approaching the illustration from the point of view of some construction techniques can greatly improve these technical issues.

Construction drawing simplifies forms into geometric shapes such as cubes, cylinders, and spheres. For extreme angles, I'll even draw a person entirely encased in a box to understand how the front and back distort. We'll differentiate between these shapes with a new layer, and bypass the need for a new material by using a layer tint, which will override materials with a new color specific to individual layers:

1. Create a new layer called `Shapes`. In the **Adjustments** panel, change the **Tint** color to red, and set the **Factor** to `1`.
2. Use the **Draw Pencil** preset with a **Radius** of `20` and a **Strength** of `.7` to draw loose egg shapes for the skull and chest. Add a box for the jaw and pelvis, whose planes show the angle that it's turning.
3. Use smaller bubbles for the joints and draw skeleton connectors between these masses.

Cylinders, spheres, and squares all have unique flair. If you have the inclination, you could work through a construction drawing with only cubes, only cylinders, or only eggs. These simple shapes don't just help with perspective, but also with shading. In the following screenshot, I put shadows on the underside of shapes to test out lighting:

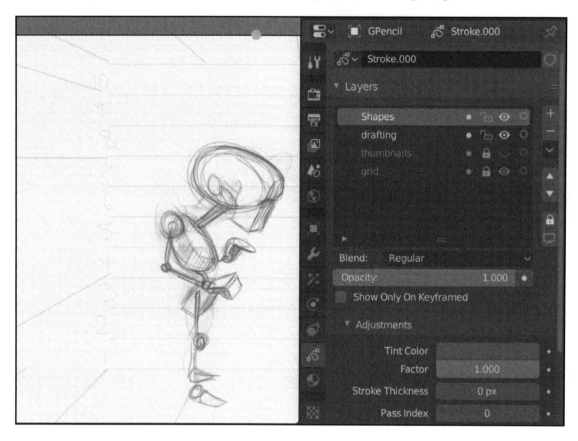

Construction drawing out of simple shapes

These ideas can be expanded with contour construction. With this technique, draw as if you were looking for good edge flow on a 3D model. Fashion often adds the same benefit as contours, with the cylindrical shape of cuffs and the flowing lines of fabric seams helping us to understand the curvature of form:

1. Create another layer called Construction.
2. Lower the opacity of your other layers to make tracing over them easier, and give the **Construction** layer a red 1.0 tint.

3. Set your brush to a **Radius** of 5px, a **Strength** of 1, no **Pressure Sensitivity**, and turn **Stabilize** on, so as to emulate a sharp pen.

4. Draw lines of symmetry contouring around the body. Follow this with major cylinder curves, such as the wrists, to show turning in space.

Keep drawing edges as if they were the edge flow on a polygonal model. These contours can get very detailed, such as going inward with the eye socket, out and in with the eyelid, rounding over the eyeball, out with the bottom lid, and continuing with the cheek. Just like a 3D model, more edges will gather as the form turns from the viewer.

Change the **Outliner** window to another 3D view and, in the **Gizmo** panel , turn off the **Navigate** gizmo for extra screen real estate. With two views, you can work zoomed in on details while still seeing the big picture.

This construction guide will be especially invaluable for incorporating planar shadows. It also helps with many design ideas, such as where seams in armor or clothing go as they follow along the body parts, as shown in this close-up:

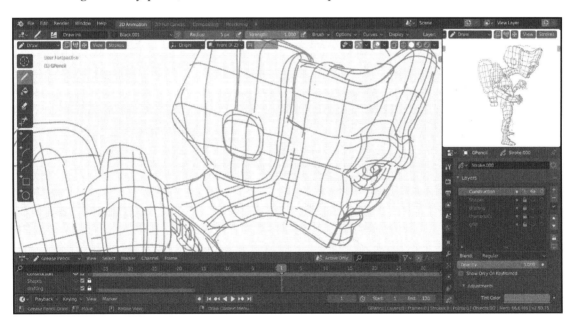

Construction drawing with contour lines

Whenever I feel as though I can't understand a drawing, I use construction to solve the problem. When it's an extreme perspective, like a fist coming toward you, these contour lines explain the way a form like an arm is turning in space. This composite of rough draft drawing techniques should tell you everything you need to know for inking the final design.

Inking the alien hero

A clean-inked hero illustration is a work of art in its own right. The high-contrast black and white of ink makes it ideal for comics and print for its strong impact, and in 2D animation, clean ink is a vital ingredient for coloring and separation. Ink lines can taper thin to thick like an old-fashioned quill, or use strict line weights such as pigment liners. Good ink uses placement and weight to create a drawing hierarchy, conveying shadows and crevices, and contours and sections. Through hatching and patterns, it can fully render the light and shadow of a scene all by itself.

First, we will ink the major lines of our alien, paying extra attention to sections that separate major colors, such as the head versus clothing. Then, we'll add smaller lines to aid the eye regarding details of light and form.

The starting ink

Our space traveler's first inks will segment him into major features with a medium line weight. Later, this will help with creating fills that separate him by major color areas. As it's part of the final render, you can see the results of all the following sections in `ch08_alien_final.blend`:

1. In **Object** mode, move your draft GP object away from the camera on the **Y axis** by `.01`.

2. Add a new blank **Grease Pencil** object, and rename it `Final`. Since the **Draft** object is behind it, the strokes on **Final** appear first.

 The order used when stacking GP strokes is first determined by the distance from the view of strokes on an object level (called the Z depth), followed by the layer stack inside individual GP objects, followed by the Z depth of strokes within a single layer. Putting the ink on a separate object, and closer to the camera, lets us guarantee they're in front.

3. Select the **Draw Ink** preset, set your **Radius** to 10px, and turn **Active Smooth** to 1. Turn off **Stabilize**, but set its **Radius** to 70px and a **Factor** of .9. Rename the GP layer to line_main.

4. Ink the character freehand when drawing organic forms such as the face and clothes.

5. When drawing clean lines, such as on the jet pack, temporarily activate **Stabilize** while drawing by holding *Shift*. **Stabilize** lets you pause, change angles, and work carefully when tracing the rough draft.

6. For straight lines and long, careful contours, use the **Curve** tool. Enjoy the challenge of finding long contours where one stroke encapsulates an entire limb.

7. Closure between lines helps later when using the paint bucket to fill areas. If there's a gap in the strokes, draw the closure freehand.

These starting lines have a thicker weight to emphasize importance. In the following drawing, you can see how major sections get priority:

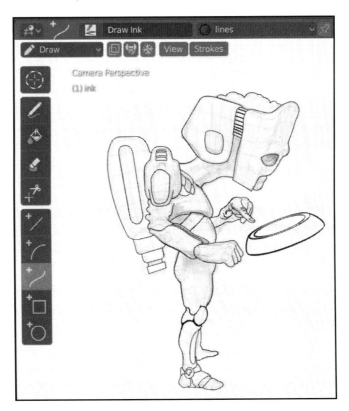

Main ink lines

Hand-drawn strokes might fail to connect with an intersection, or overdo it. If this happens, it's often better to tweak minor errors like this in **Edit** or **Sculpt** mode, rather than undoing, redrawing, or erasing. Here are some workflows for cleaning up lines:

- In **Edit** mode, change your select mode to **All Points between Different Strokes**, and then select and delete straggling stroke ends.
- Select an end point that is either too far or not far enough. Turn on **Proportional Edit Falloff** and, in **Settings**, turn on **Connected** only. Select the end of your stroke, and move it by pressing *G* until it lines up.
- In **Sculpt** mode, the **Pinch** brush can pull a stroke into closing with a neighboring stroke, and the **Grab** brush will only affect points inside the initial brush click.

We'll use a thinner line weight to draw details such as clothing seams, pimples, cloth wrinkles, and form accents, sometimes called greebles. Greebles are fine detail lines of industrial grooves and patterns that follow the contours of your construction guides to show the alien's form. With greebles, avoid using lines to shade, and instead use it to show 3D form. For organic areas, breaking the lines up into a Morse code of dots and dashes can show form details without overpowering the main ink:

1. Create a new layer called `line_detail`.
2. If you have detail lines left over on your `line_main` layer, select them in **Edit** mode using Stroke Points, and moving them to the `line_detail` layer by pressing *m*.
3. Draw secondary inks for the character on this layer.

Note the detail lines drawn here:

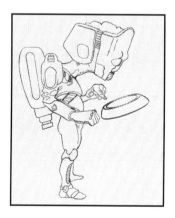

Detail ink

Once the whole character is inked, use the **Sculpt** and **Edit** modes to finalize your line weights. For instance, I do a final pass with the **Thickness** brush over lines where contact shadows would appear, such as armor seams.

The character's finished line art is ready for color. There are many styles of ink: minimalist, heavy shading with cross hatching, aggressive thick lines, or efficiently unified line weights with *no* lightweight tapering. I avoid over-drawing it with hatching or shading as we'll add that lighting information when coloring. This setup will provide an ideal basis for the next stage of the pipeline, where flat areas of color can be filled in quickly.

Adding color with the fills pipeline

To give this character color, we'll use a pipeline based around fills, also called flats. Fills are a coloring technique that cuts out the silhouette of the character, or individual parts of the character. In essence, it's a layer with flat color. These serve as a mask for other layers of local color, texture, light, and shadow. In 2D animation, the efficiency of fills is also vital in replicating an image over many frames, which is much harder to do with a painterly approach. We will create an overall character flat, followed by additional layers for individual components of our alien.

Silhouette and local color

The first fill is a silhouette of the whole character. This will be followed by multiple sections for clothing, details, and separate parts:

1. Make a material that has a fill but no stroke. Switch to the **Fill** tool, , and select a layer called **Fills**.

2. We can get a silhouette of the whole character much easier using the outside of the character, rather than the inside. Zoom so that the character fills the screen, and then click outside of him. The crop of the 3D viewport will determine where this outside fill is placed.

3. Repeat this at different camera pans, and continue filling around the character. Use *Ctrl* to temporarily draw, and cover any unclosed strokes if they're interfering with the **Fill** tool.

4. Once the background is blocked out, turn off visibility for every layer except fills. Use the **Fill** tool inside the cut-out. Then, switch to **Edit** mode, click on strokes from the outer temporary border, select **linked** (*L*), and press *Delete*. As shown in the following screenshot, the initial outside fills can be thrown away while we use the fill created inside them:

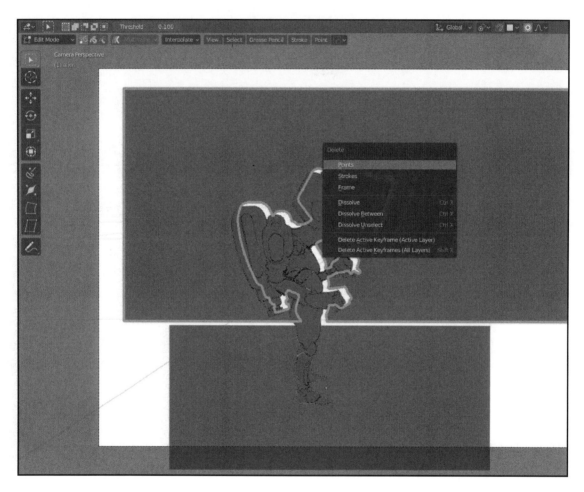

The fill tool's exterior start and interior finish

5. Add a new layer called `skin`, and turn on its **Mask Layer** button. This will clip any strokes on the layer using the lower fill's layer, thereby preventing us from coloring outside the lines.

6. Add a new material called `skin` as well, with no stroke and a green alien skin fill.

7. Turn off the `line_detail` layer, so it won't contribute to borders when using the **Fill** tool. Use a combination of the **Fill** and **Draw Brush** tool to fill in all the character's skin areas.

8. Add a new material called `tech`, and a new layer called `tech1` as well, also with **Mask** turned on. Fill in the major tech areas.

9. The mask, which has a hole for the eye, will struggle with the **Fill** tool. In these instances, position the eye halfway off screen to crop with the 3D view, and fill the cropped top mask. The area in the bottom mask can now be filled.

10. Add another new layer called `tech2`. In the **Adjustments** panel, set the **tint** to `.5`, which will mix our material colors in even amounts with the tint color.

11. Fill in the minor tech areas.

    By using tints, a single material can represent a main color, with tints adding lighter, darker, or more saturated variance. If you decide to change the material color, they will stay unified.

12. Repeat this technique with a new layer called `skin2`, the skin material, and a yellow layer tint. Turn on **Clipping**, and use the **Draw** tool for a mottled yellow underbelly.

As shown here, managing your layers and materials in tandem takes patience:

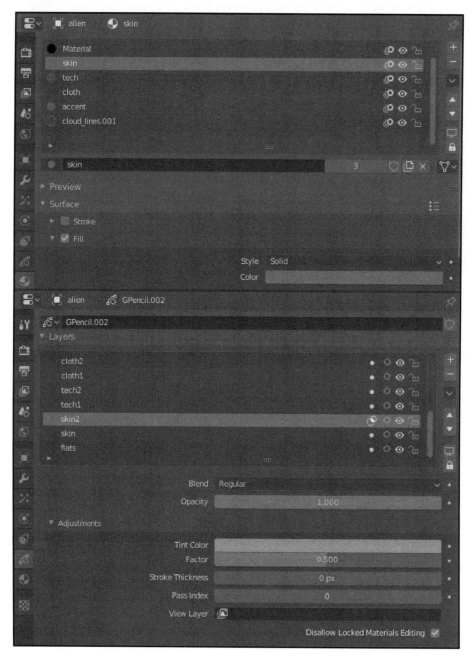

Materials and layers

13. Add a layer called `accent`, plus a new material with no stroke and a brightly colored fill. Use this on areas of fine detail, such as LED lights and decorative stripes. Add as many of these layers as your design requires.

The character tells a much better story with the fills for his alien skin, worn clothes, and factional accents. We'll use similar techniques for the line art and fills of a background, plus additional 3D elements for instant perspective. Your completed fills should look something like this:

Fills for the alien

These fills come together easily thanks to the **Fills** layer. Play around with color options for your fills via their tint colors and find your spacefarer's signature color scheme. Next, we'll give him a background to exist in.

The background

An alien hero doesn't exist in a vacuum, unless he was perhaps floating in the vacuum of space. But even then, the distant stars and planets would tell the story of his predicament. Is your character in a starship hangar? A backwater crime haven? A bustling metropolis? On the deck of a starship? The focus of our art is the character, but a pass at a background will complete the scene. GP strokes can be combined with the native 3D for dynamic results. We'll model a starship corridor with windows out into space, give it stylized lighting, and add the details and ornamentation by drawing GP strokes on top of it.

Start by modeling a simple sci-fi corridor with a mirror modifier, turned off so that it doesn't block the view. Don't focus too much on good modeling or detail. Use repeating shapes of rectangles and trapezoids for the windows, panels, floor, and lighting. Give them some diffuse principled BSDF materials, an emission material for various light paneling, and a world background of a purple gradient texture. An example model can be found in `ch08_alien_final.blend`. Next, we'll paint on this object:

1. Add a GP object called `Space`, and position it outside your corridor windows.
2. Set your **Stroke Placement** to **Origin**, and give it a starting material with no stroke and a martian pink fill. Draw a simple circle for a distant planet.
3. Add another GP layer called `Shadow`, with **Mask** turned on. Set its **Blend** mode to **Overlay**. Switch to a **Stroke** material, and with a large soft pencil, sketch in some loose pencil strokes to shade the interior of the planet.

   The **Overlay blend** mode keeps the shadows and both darkens and lightens the layer below, making a built-up gradient for a soft planet shadow.

4. Add another layer called `rings`. Use the fill's material to draw out a ring silhouette.
5. In the **Effects** panel, add a **Glow** effect, with a color close to the planet's surface. Turn on **Use Alpha Mode**. Adjust the radius until there's a small atmospheric glow to the planet.

Now, the windows have some proper outer space vibes, as shown here:

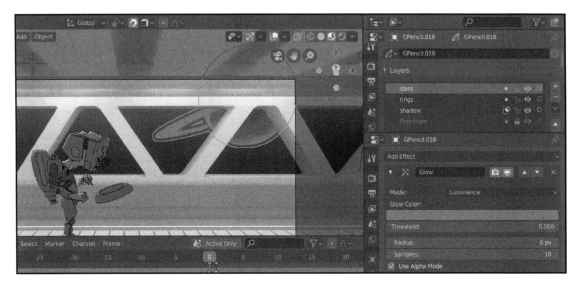

A planetary background

Next, we'll add greebles, which are contouring technological details that highlight form, and do so on top of our corridor mesh:

1. Add a new GP object called `greebles`.

2. In **Tool Settings**, change **Stroke Placement** to **Surface** (Surface) with an offset of `.0001`.

3. Set your camera to an orthographic view, with the corridor's **Mirror** modifier turned off.

4. Use the **Rectangle** drawing tool to place a rectangular greeble on your wall.

5. In **Edit** mode, select the stroke you drew, duplicate it to the left or right, and then repeat this with *Shift + R* several times. This repetition technique is useful for duplicating patterns as you draw them.

6. Draw some additional greebles with the **Draw** tool, with **Guides** set to **Grid**, or use the **Draw** and **Curve** tools while holding down the *Shift* key to draw at 90 and 45 degree angles. Also do this from the top view with the ceiling hidden.

The greebles are all placed in 3D space along the corridor, as shown here:

Greebles drawn onto a 3D surface

Using 3D elements to set up staging for 2D elements is a good way to get instantly correct perspective, and mixing them together can yield a number of styles. Next, we will expand on layers for lights and shadows and we will use effects and modifiers on our alien.

Lighting and texture

A space-faring alien needs lighting to set the drama of the scene and highlight his form. Unlike in 3D, 2D illustration often means explicitly drawing in lighting changes. Brush textures will add organic detail to the character, and lighting can be built up over several layers:

1. Select your alien, and create a new layer called Shadow.
2. Change its **Blend** mode to **Multiply**, and change the layer's **Tint** factor to 1 with a neutral gray color. The **Multiply** blend mode will use a layer's strokes to darken the underlying layers.

3. Use one of your fill materials to circle the shadow shapes that would occur on any downward-facing planes, including under the chin, and the arm's cast shadow. The adjusted tint color and **Multiply** blend mode clamp the effects to a maximum darkness.

Here, you can see the shadow darkening colors it passes over:

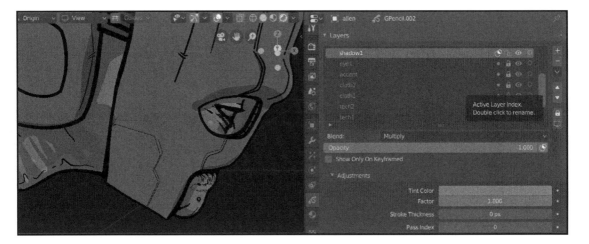

The shadow1 layer multiplying over flats

Now, we'll repeat the process, but with highlights:

1. Add a layer called `highlights`, with a **Tint** factor of 1 and a light blue color.
2. Use the **Draw Pencil** tool with a large size and low opacity to mark out planes of highlight.
3. Repeat step 3 on a new layer, set to `pure white`. Build up the strokes gradually. Emphasize the corners of metallic planes where light would catch.
4. In the **Effects** panel, add a rim modifier. Set the **Offset** to −1 and −5, with **Blend** mode set to **Add**, and a pinkish rim color.

The metallic floor material doesn't reflect the GP object, but we can fake reflections with effects and modifiers. Modifiers are generally concerned with changing the settings and placement of your GP objects, while effects instead affect the draw method of GP. Add a reflection and rim light with the help of the following steps:

1. Duplicate your character and then, in **Edit** mode, scale all the stroke points to −1 z.
2. Move the objects around in space until the character is in front of the reflection, but both are visible.
3. Go to the **Effects** tab. Give the alien and his reflection a **Blur** effect set to 0 and 5.
4. On the reflection, also distort it with a **Wave** effect.
5. In the **Modifiers** tab, add a **Hue/Saturation** modifier, and lower the overall value, so the reflection is darker on the floor.

The result adds a rim light along his back, and shows him on the floor:

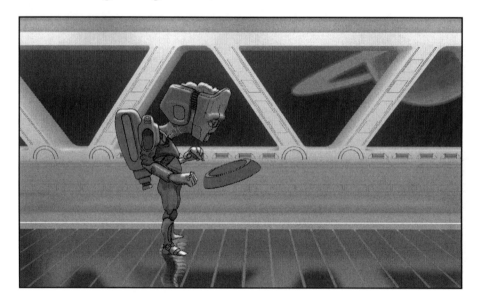

Modifiers and effects adding the final flair to the character's look

A shadow layer tells us the direction of a main light source. If you're drawing on the clock, I always try to at least budget for a shadow pass. You can keep adding as many layers as you like to keep building up the shadows and highlights. There are many additional modifiers and effects worth playing with as well.

Summary

With the core of Grease Pencil's strokes, layers, materials, and tricks, we've taken this alien from thumbnails to completion. The alien hero can be used as concept art for a 3D model or an illustration for a Sci-Fi novel. Furthermore, the fills-based GP layering can be replicated from frame to frame for animation. In the chapters to come, we'll expand on the animation tools to add movement and life to future projects.

Questions

1. What is the difference between the annotate GP tools and the GP object?
2. What GP tool is best if you don't have a tablet and stylus to draw on?
3. Name some of the methods that are used to draw straight lines with GP.
4. Name some of the methods that are used to draw graceful curved lines.
5. The time constraints we used with thumbnailing are a great way to develop confident strokes in your art. Use GP to warm up, using figure drawing to test yourself with poses at 30-second, 2-minute, and 5-minute timers.
6. Pick your second favorite character thumbnail. Use the drafting, shapes, construction, ink, fills, and lighting layers to render it as a fellow denizen of the cosmos.
7. How do you activate clipping on a layer, and what are some examples where it is beneficial?
8. Model a simplistic floating computer for the alien, and then use the techniques for placing strokes on a surface that we used for the hallway to cover it with greebles.
9. Experiment with three other effects on your alien to create new looks.
10. Experiment with three other modifiers on your alien to create new looks as well.

Further reading

New features are getting added to Grease Pencil all the time. Follow its development at `https://www.blender.org/features/grease-pencil/`.

9
Animating an Exquisite Corpse in Grease Pencil

A great advantage of animating in 2D is the audacity of what it's capable of conveying. Through a series of drawings, you can draw a person melting into an eyeball, which explodes into a flock of birds, which congregate into a hand, which has its fingers cut off, then morphs into a young girl. In 3D, that many assets would take forever, but in 2D, it's simply a few keyframes of drawing away. We'll explore these possibilities with an exquisite corpse animation. In the process, we'll also examine the traditional principles of 2D animation, and also get comfortable with the animating tools and conventions of Blender.

Exquisite corpses are a perfect game to follow this philosophy. The term "exquisite corpse" comes from poetry, in which cut-up sentences and words are put together at random to form ideas you could never land on deliberately. Versions of this exist in many mediums, including music, drawing, and video, among others. In animation, an exquisite corpse simply requires that one animation chunk's final frame is the same as the next animation's start frame. Then when you combine two unrelated animations, they flow together seamlessly. Animation sections can then be completely independent, and when you put them together the results can be psychedelic and unpredictable. While reading, follow along with the project files for `Chapter 9`, *Animating an Exquisite Corpse in Grease Pencil.*

In this chapter, you'll learn how to do the following:

- Plan your animation out with storyboards
- Employ straight-ahead animation for mind-bending transitions
- Use pose to pose animation for strong keyframes
- Animate classic animation challenges, like a bouncing ball
- Use 2D animation techniques like smears, multiples, and exaggeration
- Harness the power of 3D tools for planning and transitions
- Quickly duplicate and adjust keyframes
- Manage multiple animated variables with layers, the Dope Sheet, keyframes, and modifiers
- Combine your animations with video editing

Animating a bouncing ball

The bouncing ball is our first, simplest animation, and a classic beginner's exercise. We'll utilize some of the core principles of animation with this simple subject:

- **Pose to pose**: This is where we get the bedrock extremes keyed in first to nail the timing, then create in-between frames after.
- **Arcs**: A bouncing ball doesn't travel in a straight line from the high to the low poses. Instead, it will flow along a guiding arc.
- **Ease in, Ease out**: A bouncing ball should slow at the top of each arc for a bit, and attain quicker velocities as it slams into the ground and ricochets back up.
- **Squash and Stretch**: The ball will stretch out, arrow-like, as it approaches and leaves the ground. When it hits the ground, it will squash down into the ground.
- **Timing**: Each bounce will get shorter as the ball loses momentum. Also, we'll give the animation time to breathe at the beginning and end.

In the following diagram, the plan for our bouncing ball is laid out, including what frames poses will be on, and how the bounce will use these animation principles:

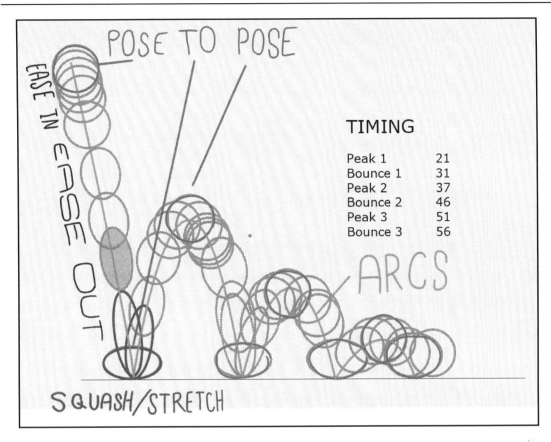

Animation ideas with a bouncing ball's timing

As part of the exquisite corpse, we'll start with a simple circle in the middle of the screen, which will zoom up to our start point on frame 21. After the bouncing is over, it will zoom back to the exquisite corpse default frame. See the finished results in
ch09_bouncingball.blend.

Pose to pose beginnings

Pose to pose is an ideal way to animate. We'll create only the most important frames to begin with; six to eight key poses will let us figure out the motion as a kind of preview. When these key poses look good, we'll fill in the keyframes between them with in-between poses, or **tweens**. One benefit of pose to pose is that, when budgeting your time for an entire animation, pose to pose lets you get a semblance of the finished animation early on, and the tweens can be cut to meet the deadline if needs be.

Start with the file ch09_circleStart.blend. This has keyframes on frames 1 and 100, with our start and end circle. All of our modules on exquisite corpse animation will start from this file. As long as we transition from frame 1 to frame 100, these separate modules can sync together. If we want a longer or shorter animation, we can adjust the timeline length. Start the bouncing ball animation as follows:

1. Create a layer called Floor. Switch to **Draw Mode**, then use the **Curve** tool to draw a straight line along the ground, holding *Shift* to constrain your stroke to the **X axis**. Lock the layer.
2. Create a new layer called Guide. Switch to **Draw Mode**, then use the **Curve** tool to draw a bounce path from the top left to the bottom right. Use *E* to extrude out each bounce, and switch to **Arc** mode (*C*) to get quick arcs. Lock this layer.

The ball will start on frame 1 in the middle, move to the top of our arc and rest at frame 21, then will hit the peaks and impacts along our arcs following the timing in *Figure 1*. Adding or changing strokes in **Draw**, **Edit**, or **Sculpt** modes will either modify the existing keyframe in the timeline, or generate a new one.

Each layer stores its own keyframes. A layer can be locked or hidden in the **Grease Pencil** Dope Sheet, just like in the **Properties**. Add markers at key pose points with *M*. These don't affect the keyframes; they just mark where important ones are, as shown here:

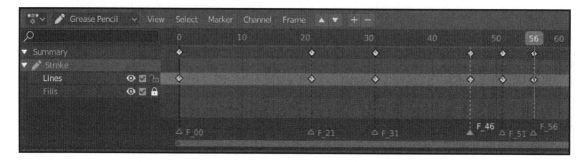

The Grease Pencil Dope Sheet

Grease Pencil keyframes in the Dope Sheet can be selected and moved just like vertices. You can box-select multiple frames, and move or scale them with *G* and *S*. Play the animation with the *Space bar*, and use your eye to judge the timing while moving keys around. Jump from one keyframe of a selected layer to the next with the ↑ and ↓ arrows.

3. On frame **21**, switch to **Edit Mode** and move the ball to the upper-left corner. Note the new keyframe.
4. Move to frame **31**. In **Edit Mode**, move the ball to the bottom of the first bounce.
5. Go forward in the timeline, and add new keyframes via **Edit Mode** at the top and bottom of every bounce. The bounces should get closer together in time as the ball loses momentum.

I have the ball hit the ground at **31**, **46**, **56**, and **62**, and the ball is at the zenith of each bounce at frames **21**, **37**, **51**, and **59**, as shown here:

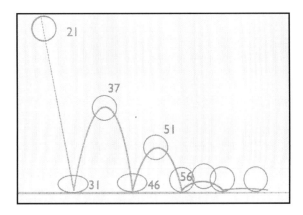

Bouncing ball timing

Blocking in animation with pose to pose is usually my favorite way to start a 2D animation. We can now start adding more frames, and distort the ball with squash and stretch.

Arcs, timing, and squash and stretch

We'll get more cartoon out of the bounces with squash and stretch: squashing the ball when it impacts the floor, and stretching it out before and after the impact. Timing will also come into play; the ground hits will happen rapidly, with more frames used during the ball's flight in the air:

1. Go to frame **29**, two frames before the ball hits. In **Edit Mode**, move your ball to the midpoint between the top and bottom of the bounce, so that it follows the guide arc. Scale it to stretch toward its impact.
2. Go to frame **33**, two frames after the ball hits. Once again, move the ball in **Edit Mode** to the midpoint between the top and bottom of the arc, and follow your arc guide.

3. Go back to frame **29**. In **Edit** mode, scale the ball up bigger on the **Z axis**, and smaller on the **X axis**. Rotate it so that it orients along the arc. Do the same on frame **33**, after the bounce.

4. On frame **31**, scale the ball's "squashed" form to be shorter on the **Z axis**, and wider on the **X axis**. To maintain contact with the ground, I set my 3D cursor to where the ball and floor make contact, and set my pivot point to the 3D cursor.

5. Repeat this squash and stretch process for the other keyframes on and surrounding the impact points.

You might be tempted to put the middle pose at the exact middle keyframe. Don't! By putting the midpoint of the ball drop closer to the impact, it will feel like it's gaining velocity. With 10 frames till its first impact, 8 were used just to reach the halfway point. Repeat this process between the other bounces. Even now, we're utilizing pose to pose, creating midpoints between our existing keyframes, as shown here:

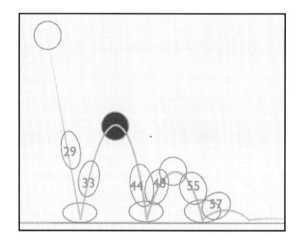

Squashed and stretched midpoint frames

 Turn on onion skinning for the ball layer, which let you see the keyframes before and after your position on the timeline. This can help to locate a midpoint along the arc.

A huge benefit of pose to pose is that you can move the timing of those poses around, hit play, and see how you like your animation in rough draft form. Does the animation *feel* right? At this early stage, you could even put the timeline cursor at frame **1**, select all the keyframes, and scale them as a group to see what longer bounces feel like. Try to get the pose to pose flow correct before you move to the tweens.

The space you leave from one key to the next is called ones, twos, threes, and so on, in reference to how many frames a drawing lasts until a new frame. Usually, I aim for twos to attain acceptable smoothness. For slower movements, threes can often get you what you need, and for faster movements I'll do the extra work for animating on ones. When your ball has good pose timing and good squash and stretch, it's time to go through and add a keyframe at least every 2 frames.

 Check your animation when it's on twos, and hunt for motion that's too fast or too slow. The best solution is to re-time by deleting a keyframe, and moving its neighboring keyframe around to get better movement. Afterward, you can re-do the tween.

Animating on ones is useful for fast transitions like the impact on the ground. Sometimes, the approaching key has a better start point than the preceding key; frame **12** will be more similar to the stretching key on **13** than the squashing key on frame **11**. You can save time by harvesting existing keys for a good start point. Here, you can see the totality of keyframes, positioned a little at a time:

Bouncing ball keyframes

Following the pose to pose animation with tweens helps to flesh out the ball bounce. Make sure you don't settle for tweens that are direct midpoints of the keyframes in front and behind it. Keep in mind animation principles such as arcs, timing, and squash and stretch when tweening. Next, we'll add some color to our ball.

Adding a visual style

The motion looks good, so the next step is to get our line style unified. I want all animations to be unified with a simple line style: 1px thickness, full opacity. Too bad I already animated the whole bounce with a ball stroke that goes from thin to thick and varies in opacity! We can modify *all* our keyframes with the **Multiframe** tool, though. **Multiframe** lets you move things in the Sculpt and Edit Modes on *all* selected keyframes, overlayed on top of each other. Let's give it a try:

1. Select all your keyframes in the Grease Pencil Dope Sheet.
2. In **Edit Mode**, turn on **Multiframe**. Select the strokes for every keyframe.
3. Switch to **Sculpt Mode**. Using the Strength brush, brush over everything until the strokes are at full opacity.
4. Use the **Thickness** brush, then hold *Ctrl* to instead reduce thickness, and brush over everything. This resets everything back to the default 1px stroke. Alternately, you could do this in **Edit Mode** by selecting all the strokes on all the keyframes, then use Shrink/Fatten with *Alt + S* to remove any thickness. The ball, now at full strength and identical thickness for all frames, is shown here:

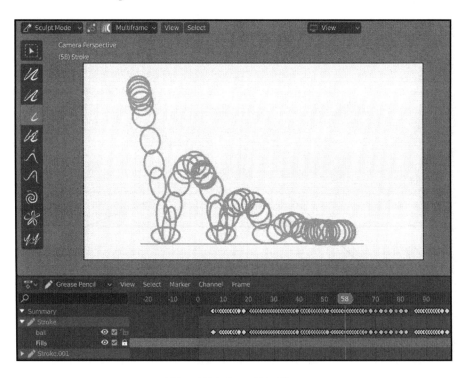

Editing multiple keyframes with Multiframe

Next, we'll give some animated colors to both the bouncing ball and the background. This will highlight the difference between the Dope Sheet Grease Pencil keys and regular Dope Sheet keys. A **GP** (short for **Grease Pencil**) object with strokes and keys can combine this with key affecting properties associated with the rest of Blender's interface. Do the following:

1. Remove all but one material on your ball object. Turn on **Fill**, choose the color green, and set its **alpha** to 1.

2. Go to frame **30**, the key right before the squash pose. Right-click on your material's **Fill** color, and select **Insert Keyframe**.

3. Go to frame **31**, and change your fill to red. This time, simply hover your cursor over the color swatch, and hit *I* to insert a keyframe. Blender can use this hover context trick to key all kinds of values!

    Now to edit the material keyframes. Grease Pencil keys are stored differently than object keyframes. In the Dope Sheet, click on the **Grease Pencil** pulldown and switch to the **Dope Sheet**. The material's keys can now be seen. Although Grease Pencil keys hold a pose until the next one shows up, most things in Blender will change values from frame to frame, rather than holding a frame until the next one appears.

4. Go to the next bounce, change the color to blue, and key the value. Notice how instead of a sharp color change, it transitions from red to blue.

5. We'll fix this with holding keyframes, where two identical frames keep things static over a frame range. Select your key in the dope sheet from frame **31**, when it first turned red. Duplicate it with *Shift + D*, and move it to the frame right before your blue key. Now the red can be maintained over that stretch of frames.

6. Repeat this color change for all your bounce arcs.

7. In the **Properties** window, switch to the **World** tab. Choose yellow for the background color.

8. Keyframe the background color on frame **30**, and on frame **31**, change it to a new color just like we did with the ball's fill. Repeat this once more on every impact, so both the ball and the world switch colors on every bounce.

In the following screenshot, you can see the material keyframes, as well as the onion skins on the GP layers, hinting at the frames to come:

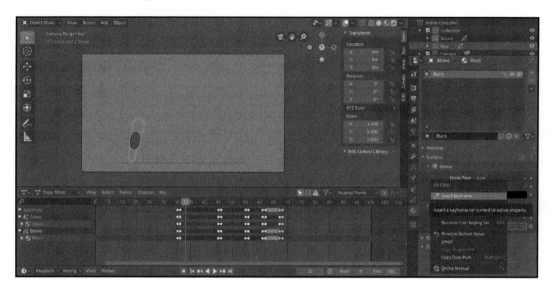

Material keyframes in the Dope Sheet

You'll find things all over Blender that can be animated with keyframes. Color changes like this are especially appealing when synced to music. Now we'll add an animation take at the start and end.

Adding an ease-in, ease-out anticipation starting take

Remember the starting key, which we hid for later on frame **0**? A simple take, where the ball zooms from the middle to the corner, can preempt the bounce. The ease-in, ease-out animation principle will be seen in the slow pause before the bounce begins. The take will also utilize anticipation, the principle that preparing for an action (such as bouncing) with an opposite action makes the action land better visually:

1. Go back to frame **1**, when the circle starts in the middle. In the Grease Pencil Dope Sheet, move that key to frame **6** to start with the ball holding still for **6** frames.
2. Go to frame **21**, when our bounce begins and our ball is at its apex. Duplicate it with *Shift* + *D*, and move it to frame **18** for a similar held pause.

3. Go to frame **12**. In **Edit Mode**, move the ball to create a tween. Grab, scale, and rotate it so that it's closer to the upcoming pose at frame **18** than it is to the preceding frame **6**, and is elongated as it "zooms" toward frame **18**.

Sometimes when tweening, I go to the middle keyframe and make it more like the start than the end or vice versa, to get an ease-in-ease-out. Other times, I go to a frame that's closer to the before or after pose, and use onion skins to position the new frame in the center, but favoring one pose via timing.

4. Add tween keys, then continue breaking the animation down until the start is animated consistently on twos from frames **6** to **18**.

5. Duplicate this process at the end of the animation, so that the ball zips back to the starting point on frame **100**:

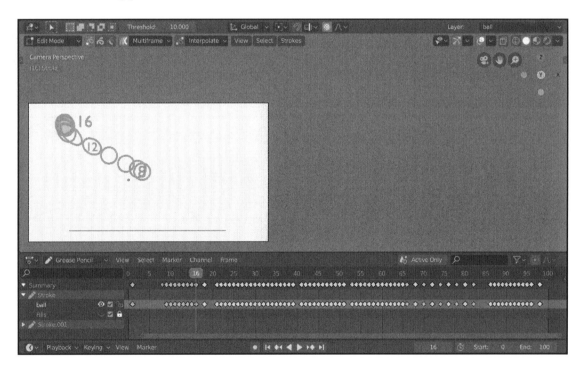

Ball zips back to the starting point

The exquisite corpse starting circle on frame **1** now animates up to the corner, to begin our bouncing ball, and at the end, returns to the exquisite corpse starting circle, so that it will align with future animations. Let's finish the bouncing ball by deforming its arcs to cartoon extremes with Multiframe.

Reusing and reworking frames with Multiframe

The ball's animation is complete, but with **Multiframe**, we can see the whole of the animation arcs, and push them to even more exaggerated motion in **Sculpt** and **Edit** modes. By using **Multiframe** and **Proportional Edit Falloff**, a bouncy arc can quickly be made bouncier:

1. Select all the keyframes from **31** to **46**, which comprise the first bounce arc.
2. Switch to **Edit Mode**, and turn on **Multiframe**.
3. Select a point on the circle at the zenith of the bounce, then hit *L* to select **Linked**.
4. Turn on **Proportional Edit Falloff** by pressing *O*. Next, hit *G* to move the selected points. Use your middle mouse wheel to adjust the **Proportional Edit Falloff** size. Pull the ball upward, stretching its neighboring frames proportionately, and play the animation to see the difference.
5. Select frames **46** through **56** in the Grease Pencil Dope Sheet, comprising the second bounce.
6. Switch to **Sculpt Mode**. Use the **Grab** brush to pull the second bounce arc up. Modify your brush size and strength with *F* and *Shift + F* so that you don't affect where the ball touches the ground.

Look for other areas where you can smear or exaggerate your animation with **Edit** and **Sculpt** mode via **Multiframe**. You can see its dramatic impact in the following screenshot:

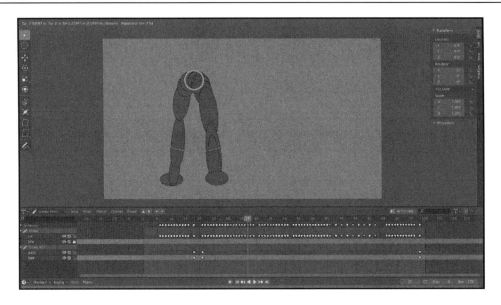

Multiframe squashing and stretching

Our planned keyframes already used motion, timing, squash, stretch, and arcs to emphasize the cartoon motion of the ball. Multiframe's ability to modify multiple frames at once, while showing us the overall animation effect on the arcs, lets us push those animation ideals even further, by creating a field of Blender eyeballs.

Blinking Blender eyes

For our next exquisite corpse transition, we'll use our starting circle as the blue dot in a Blender logo, then turn the logo into a blinking eye. By duplicating and modifying it slightly, we can then turn one eye into a sea of eyeballs, blinking before disappearing. In the following diagram, you can see the plan for the animation:

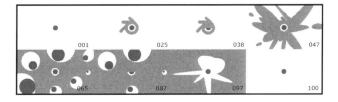

Blinking eyes from frames 1 to 100

See the finished project file, `ch09_eyeblinks.blend`, to dig through the results.

Reusing frames for the Blender blinking animation

This blinking eye animation will emphasize reusing your animation assets for maximum impact, and will capture a psychedelic sensibility that works great in an exquisite corpse. It also pays homage to our favorite software, Blender! This animation begins once again with the file `ch09_circleStart.blend`:

1. Start with Blender's colors. Create a new material called `blender_blue` with no stroke. Change its fill to full alpha. For the color swatch, switch to **Hex** mode and type in `265787`.

2. Create another material called `blender_orange_stroke` with no fill, and a stroke with the hex color `E87D0D`. These are the official colors of the Blender logo. You can find more info on Blender's logo at `https://www.blender.org/about/logo/`.

3. Assign the blue color to the starting circle. Rename the layer `Blue`.

4. Create a new layer called `lines`. Switch to **Draw Mode**, and select the ink preset. Make sure the thickness profile is disabled, as well as disabling pen pressure for radius and strength. Draw the main swooping line with curves and arcs, modifying its size with *F*.

Here's what we have so far:

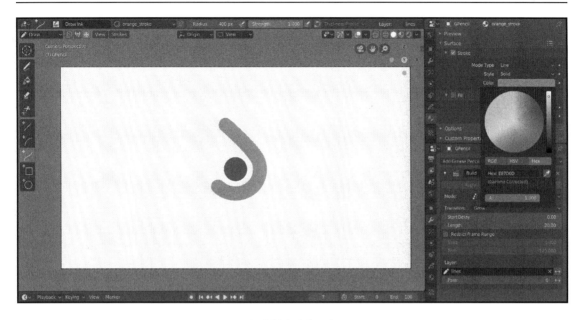

The official Blender logo colors

5. Repeat this for the other two arms of the Blender logo.

6. In the **Properties** window, switch to the **Modifiers** panel. Add a **Build** modifier with a length of `20` and the **Layer** set to **Lines**.

   Instead of needing multiple keyframes, this modifier simply builds the strokes of the target layer to match the length. Now when you play the animation, it starts at nothing and builds the strokes out. Be careful—depending on what mode you're in, on frame 1 this can look like you deleted your strokes when they just haven't been built yet.

7. Go to frame **30**, create a new layer named `eyelid`, then create a new material named `orange_fill`. In **Draw Mode**, use the **Circle** tool to draw a circle shape that covers the eye of the Blender logo. This is the ending pose for the blink.

8. Go forward to frame **32** to keyframe in the opened eyelid pose. I use the **Isolate Layer** button to work only on the eyelid, then use the 3D cursor set to the middle to scale the bottom half of the eyelid up.

9. On frame **31**, I select the eyelid circle and use **Interpolate** to get a midpoint blink.

The `Interpolate` command is a great way to get middle keys quickly. It assumes that the under-the-hood stuff stays the same, so it works best on strokes that were modified in **Sculpt** or **Edit Mode**, but *not* added to or deleted from. The eyelid's interpolation can be seen in the following screenshot:

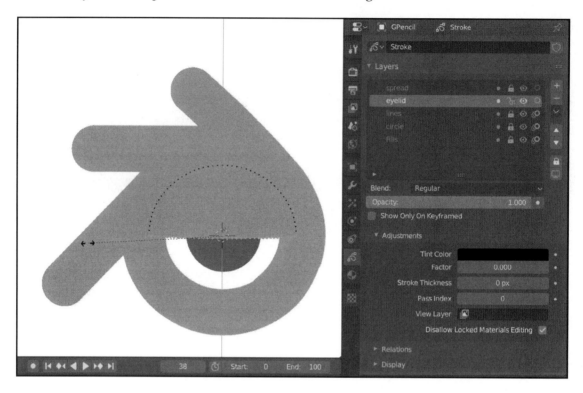

Creating a middle key with Interpolation

10. Select the keys on frames **30**, **31**, and **32**, and duplicate them to frame **35**. With the timeline on **31**, hit S -1 to scale them into reverse, opening the eye. After testing the motion, I delete the middle frame to make the blink even more rapid: closed on **34**, open on **35**.

11. Select all the blink keys, then duplicate them out to frame **37** for a second blink. I increase the pause, so the eye is closed until frame **45** and opens on frame **46**.

The eyeball blink is done. But what about the rest of the eyeballs?

A field of eyeballs

As the eye opens on the second blink, the orange will spread across the entire scene, and many other eyeballs will suddenly pop into place. With clever use of layers, key adjustments, and Multiframe, we can reuse one eye over and over with organic differences:

1. Create a new layer called `Spread`. On frame **45** in **Draw Mode**, insert an empty keyframe with **Strokes | Animation | Insert blank keyframe.**

2. On frame **46**, use a combination of the **Draw** tool and **Curve** tool to create tendrils of orange emanating from the Blender logo's orange, right after the eye opens.

3. In the **Draw Mode** header, turn on **Additive Drawing** 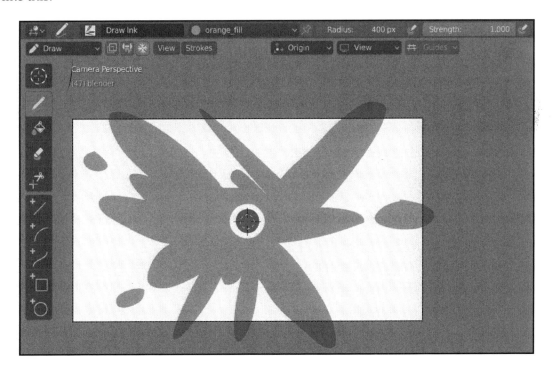, and on frame **47** draw the orange spreading out even more. Additive drawing will keep our existing strokes as a start point.

Repeat this additive drawing on **48** and **49**, so that on **49** the orange has spread beyond the borders of the camera view. The middle of the exploding spread should look something like this:

The expanding eye of Blender

For our additional eyeballs, we'll create a single eyeball blink first, then duplicate and offset it for quick organic blinks:

1. In **Object Mode**, add a new Grease Pencil object with *Shift + A* | **Grease Pencil** | **Blank**. This new eye will open out of our new field of orange.
2. Rename the starting layer `Whites`. Add a new material called `white_fill`, with no stroke and a white fill.
3. In **Draw Mode**, on frame **49**, use the **Circle** tool and constrain axes with *Shift* to draw out a circle somewhere in your field of orange.
4. Create a new layer called `Blue`, add the previous blue material as a material slot, and draw an iris circle on top of your eye's white.
5. Turn on **Mask** for this layer, clipping it to the boundaries of the white layer. This makes it so that we can just animate eyes looking sideways, and the pupil will disappear behind the eyelid.
6. Go to frame **47**, when this eye would be closed. In **Edit Mode**, hit *L* while mousing over the whites stroke to select the whole eye, then scale it closed with *S*, *Z*, 0.
7. Duplicate the key on **49** to **48** as a start point, and modify it to be half-closed. From **47** (closed) to **49** (open), this new eye blinks into existence.
8. The eye will remain open for a bit, looking around, then blink once more, then close permanently so we can return to the exquisite corpse start frame. Select keys **47**, **48**, and **49** and duplicate them with *Shift + D* to land on **55**, **56**, and **57**.
9. Put the timeline at **56**, then scale the keys into reverse with *S* and −1, so the eye closes instead of opening.

Your cursor should be over the Dope Sheet so you scale keys, as that will determine where they scale from. In the following screenshot, you can see frames for blinking the eye shut, then open again:

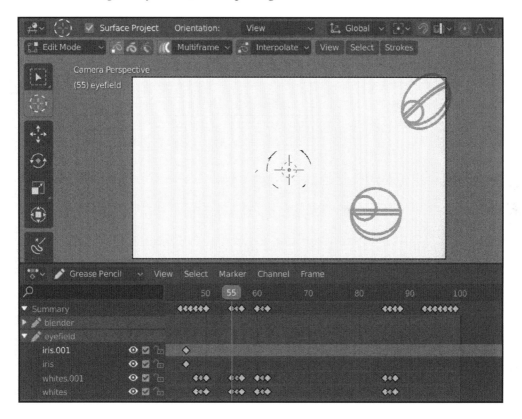

Eye-blink keyframes

10. Once more, duplicate **47**, **48**, and **49** out to frame **60**, **61**, and **62**. The eye opens.
11. Now to close the eye for the animation's end. Duplicate the close frames from **55**, **56**, and **57** to **85**, **86**, and **87**.

So, we've got a second blinky eye. Now let's make multiple by reusing those layers, editing a whole duplicate blink at once with Multiframe:

1. Use the **Layer** pulldown to duplicate the **whites** layer and the **iris** layer. They get renamed `whites.001` and `iris.001`.
2. Lock layers so you're only working on the `.001` layers. Switch to **Edit Mode**, activate **Multiframe**, and select all the keyframes for the `.001` layers.

3. In the viewport, select all the strokes; if the strokes are on a keyframe selected in the Dope Sheet, they can be selected in the viewport. Use *G* and *S* to move them to a new location, such as the upper-left corner. Test the animation, and it retains the previously keyed blink.

4. Select a single point in the 3D view, and turn on **Proportional Edit Falloff** with *O*. Move it to deform the whole eye into a less uniform shape across multiple frames.

5. In the Dope Sheet, move all the keyframes on the .001 layers forward by one frame. This gives an organic overlapping action, so that the blink doesn't time exactly with the previous eye.

6. Repeat! Do the same process of duplicating layers, editing their placement with Multiframe, and deforming the eyes multiple times. A sea of big eyes, little eyes, narrow eyes, and dilated eyes, until the field of orange is filled up.

The eyes now blink with slight offsets from one another, both in time and space. This process leaves your Dope Sheet cascading with keyframes, as shown here:

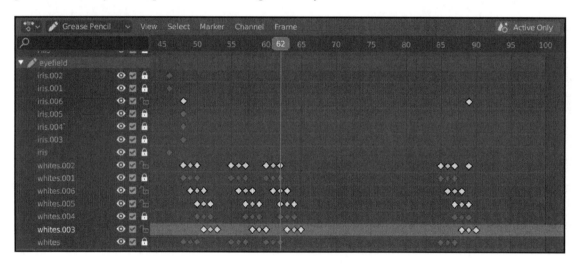

The Dope Sheet with offset blink keyframes

The amount of frames needed to create an animation means you should always be on the lookout for ways to recycle your existing work. A little keyframe nudging makes that reuse look fresh.

Returning to the start frame

The last transition is returning to the default frame. We'll add a final blink to the center eye, and when it opens, the white color will expand outward to clear the scene:

1. Select the Grease Pencil object with your original eye. Duplicate its blink keyframes out to the ending, so they line up with the last blink of the eyeball field. In my case, the final eye goes from closed to open on frames **93**, **94**, and **95**.

2. Create a new blank Grease Pencil object called `finalWhite`. It will be much easier to simply draw white on top of all the other junk we've created, rather than mess with moving all that orange out of the way. Switch its material to a white fill.

3. On frame **95**, when the eye once again opens, draw a tendril of white extending out from the white of the eye.

4. Turn on **Additive Drawing**. Then on frame **96**, add more tendrils and waves extending out.

5. Continue expanding the eye white on frames **96** and **97**. By frame **98**, the camera view should be back to a white field with a blue circle.

The finished animation turns our start circle into a Blender logo, then an eye, then a bunch of eyes, before returning to our default. What will this circle transition to next? Something more hand-drawn in focus: a fight scene.

Building a zooming fight scene

A green circle. It's an island in the middle of the ocean. You zoom in to see two warriors, ready to fight, standing on opposite ends of the grass. One of them launches an energy blast, but the other deflects it with his spinning staff.

This dynamically shifting fight is the sort of thing you see in anime introductions and fight scenes. We can do straight-ahead animation to flow through their battles with extreme angles. A thin, contouring line style and a loose, edge-breaking color style lets us focus on the motion.

This workflow assumes you're drawing with a stylus. If you don't have stylus capabilities on your computer, use the **Curve** tool. As seen at https://github.com/PacktPublishing/Blender-3D-By-Example-Second-Edition/blob/master/Blender3DByExample_ch09/ch09_fight.blend, these steps get through the fight's motion block-in, which could be expanded with full ink and paint using the techniques of Chapter 8, *Illustrating an Alien Hero with Grease Pencil*.

The lines layer

In straight-ahead animation, all you need for figuring out the next frame is the previous frame, visible through Grease Pencil. We will use **Draw Mode** settings that have been purposefully simplified into a limited brush, forcing us to draw boldly and quickly move to the next frame. We'll draw the animation using a single brush and material, designed to mimic the feel of a thin pigment liner. We'll animate on twos; every time you feel a frame is done, just go forward two frames and start drawing again:

1. Start with the file at `https://github.com/PacktPublishing/Blender-3D-By-Example-Second-Edition/blob/master/Blender3DByExample_ch09/ch09_circle_start.blend`. We'll start on the lines layer using a black stroke-only material.

2. In **Draw Mode**, switch your brush to the **Draw Pen** tool. Set **Radius** to `1px`, **Strength** to `1`, and deactivate pen pressure for both.

   Test out the brush with some doodles. As you sketch the fight, focus on drawing confident, flowing lines. Depending on what I'm drawing, I also turn on **Active Smooth**, from `0.1` to `1` depending on how the line feels. Capture whole limbs, or even whole bodies, with a single human stroke. Contour drawing can help prevent hairy lines. With contour drawing, progress through the entire sketch without ever lifting the pen.

3. Go to frame **3**, and draw in a slightly bigger circle. Repeat this on frames **5**, **7**, and **9**, speeding up the enlargement. With straight-ahead animation, you'll constantly just move forward a few frames and dive into the next pose.

4. The point of view will transition to the side of the island. Draw the side view as a new frame, then use onion skinning to draw the frame in between, when the island is oval and going down in perspective.

Test the motion by playing it. If it seems too quick, move keyframes out further, then draw a tween pose to smooth out the animation. When straight-ahead animating, you'll frequently improve the movement by retiming the keyframes and tweens. The three-keyframe transition from the top to the side of the island is far too fast, so I add tweens to space it out to five frames.

The camera shift toward the island can be seen in the following diagram:

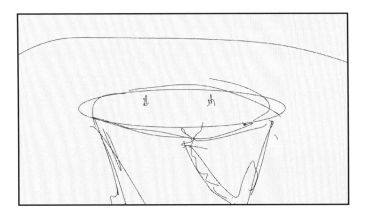

An example straight-ahead keyframe

I sometimes space out frames and add tween frames. These often recycle their neighboring frames; instead of drawing a new frame, use **Edit Mode** to shift vertices around to create a new frame. In the Dope Sheet, add space between frames as the camera zooms in. Recycle poses sparingly; it often turns out to take longer than simply drawing a new frame.

Blocking in frames should be loose and disposable, providing a finished rough draft before polishing the frames further. Next, we'll zoom to the action with the combatants.

The fighters

As we approach the fighters, we'll shift focus to drawing dynamic poses and emphasizing anatomy. Use these techniques to get accurate figures quickly when drawing.

Start with a rough line of action poses with a contour line. Your starting stroke should sketch in the *entire* figure from head to toe, then refine the pose with arms, legs, and details. See if you can limit yourself to 30 seconds per pose before jumping ahead 2 frames to the next pose. This will prevent over-rendering a single area. Nothing stings like working hard on the face, only to get the rest of the motion in and realize you have to redo the face. Get the motion *first*.

When refining poses, draw gesture drawings. These might emphasize flowing lines that encapsulate the whole character, or structure poses with the shapes approach discussed in Chapter 8, *Illustrating an Alien Hero with Grease Pencil*. Capture the whole of a pose with a single line of action, then build it up from there.

This shot shows just how loose the pencil test is before moving to another frame:

Loose pencil test drawings; the color fills were added later

When tying down a pose, center lines can show the orientation of the head, chest, and face. A simple *T* through the face can show you which way the eyes and nose are oriented. Use the contour construction techniques from `Chapter 8`, *Illustrating an Alien Hero with Grease Pencil*, to place anatomy.

Simplify! Drawing the feet 50 times over 100 frames means reducing them to their essential shape: a triangle. Hands can be drawn as a simple circle with just a thumb. Don't get lost in the details. The pigment liner line style means you should only retrace your lines when the whole pose is finished. At that point, you might have two or three attempts at tying down an arm position, and then retracing can emphasize the one you want viewers to focus on.

Solid drawing is essential to hand-drawn animation. The poses and camera angles I sketch in are informed by decades of weekly drawing workshops, daily doodling, drawing my dreams first thing in the morning, and keeping a sketchbook on my person at all times. If your attempts at drawing human figures are frustrating, good! That means you're doing the right thing: struggling with a discipline whose development is a lifetime endeavor. The only path to good drawing is the act of drawing.

The view zooms to a foreground/background shot, with the foreground fighter (a burly sumo type) shooting energy from his forearm. For this arm-centric sequence, rely on **Edit Mode** and **Sculpt Mode** to reuse frames:

1. Draw this close-up arm as separate lines, getting the whole arm in with one or two contour lines where you never lift the pen up.
2. Switch to **Edit Mode**. Select a point on the hand, and select **Linked** with *L*.
3. Go forward two frames, then move and scale the points in **Edit Mode** to create a new keyframe.
4. Switch to **Sculpt Mode** and activate the **Selection Mask** for stroke points in the **Tool Settings**.
5. Use **Sculpt Mode** on the arm for another anticipatory pose, which will now ignore points that aren't selected.

An example of these **Sculpt** and **Edit Mode** keyframes being made is shown here:

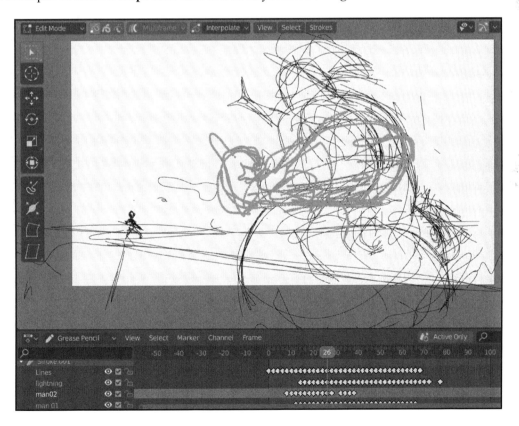

Selections in Edit Mode and selection masks in Sculpt Mode for making new keyframes

Draw poses for the arm's forward punch, the view's movement along the wrist, and rushing toward the opposite fighter. Start with the extremes of this motion, test the animation, and decide where it needs to be slowed down with additional tweens. As the energy blast approaches the other fighter, he spins his staff to deflect it.

The spinning staff is a great place to use **Guides**. Setting the 3D cursor at the center of the spin means we can automatically make radial and circular lines. Take the following steps:

1. Turn on **Guides**, and choose **Circular** in the pulldown.
2. Put the 3D cursor at the center of the spinning staff. In **Viewport Overlays**, turn on the 3D cursor so you can visualize its location.
3. Draw with the **Guides** for instant-but-organic spin lines. Draw the blurring rotation of the staff along the ends, plus inner motion lines.
4. Switch **Guides** to **Radial** and draw lines that converge on the 3D cursor.
5. Go forward two frames and redraw the pose.
6. In the Dope Sheet, select these two spinning staff frames, and duplicate them forward several times to alternate between the poses. The repeated back-and-fourth of these two poses creates the illusion of the staff spinning rapidly.

These are accompanied by the visual chaos of the energy getting ricocheted in every direction; for every pose, I have two to three zigzagging energy lines rushing toward the target. Using the **Guides** can be seen in the following screenshot:

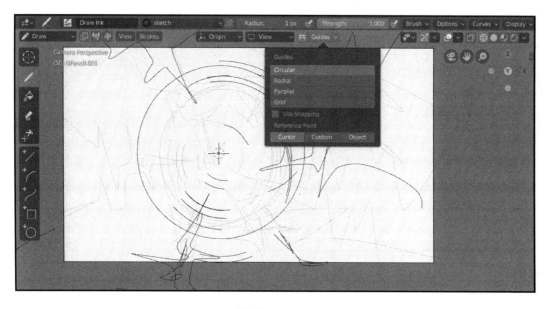

Guides for spinning lines

Finish with the camera zooming out as the last of the energy dissipates. Keep adding straight-ahead poses to return the circle of the spinning staff to the beginning circle, ready to transition to the next exquisite corpse animation. The fight animation's lines are complete. Next, we'll add some color.

Adding color

Our eight subjects – water, sky, cliffs, grass, path, fighter 1, fighter 2, and the energy blast – will all need colors. We'll use a different layer for each with custom layer tints so that they can all use single fill materials:

1. Return to the first frame. Select the **Fills** layer, and rename it Water, the furthest-back subject in our first frame.

2. In the **Adjustments** tab of the **Layers** panel, set the **Water** layer's **tint** to 1, and change its color to an ocean blue. Draw a big rectangle to encapsulate the whole view. The adjustment recolors this. Tints mean we can use a single fill material and set custom colors for each individual layer.

3. Add a new layer called Grass with a green **tint** set to 1. Draw in a shape roughly comprising the island. You can draw multiple shapes to comprise the whole, but avoid too much accuracy. Go forward every pose, adding keyframes to the grass for every keyframe.

4. Add a dirt layer underneath the **grass** layer, with a sand-colored tint in **Adjustments**. Go back to the start, and fill in the color for the cliffs on each keyframe.

5. Add a Sky layer, with a lighter blue adjustment tint than the water. On the last pose before the camera moves to a side view, insert a blank keyframe with **Strokes | Animation | Add Blank Keyframe**. On the next pose, draw in the distant sky, then transition it to encompass the whole view.

6. To emphasize the distance between the two fighters, I create another layer with an adjustment tint set to lighter green than the original grass. Add a path on poses with a strong foreground-background using three extrusions of the **Draw Curves** tool for an instant one-point perspective.

7. Repeat this frame-by-frame coloring on color layers for fighter 1, fighter 2, and the energy blast. These smaller, detail-oriented layers are good to use the **sketch** material on, and simply draw in their colors.

Most of the time, I just use the fill material for quick coverage. Other times, I use the **sketch** material, the **Draw Ink** preset with 500px size, and pressure sensitivity for the radius. This fat-tipped brush lets you scribble in color as in a coloring book, in combination with larger fills. An example of these loose fills can be seen here:

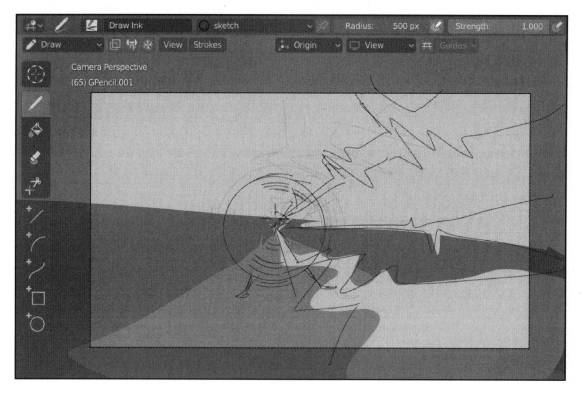

Loose fills with layer tints

Hand-drawn animation can be an intimidating endeavor. But with straight-ahead animation techniques, you can break it down into a smaller problem: what's the next frame? Set yourself a timer, get drawing, and zone out while flowing through an animation.

Bringing it all together

These three animations can click together front to back using our exquisite corpse start frame, not to mention infinite other possibilities. Now to edit them together and get them *out* of Blender as video files that can be displayed. You can edit videos together in Blender using the **Video Sequence Editor** (**VSE**).

Editing videos together can be accomplished in a number of ways. You might open your various exquisite corpse files, render them to videos, and combine the videos in the VSE. Production wisdom recommends rendering to image sequences rather than video files, and saving video output for the last step. That way, if your computer crashes on frame **99** out of **100**, you've still got **99** usable frames. Blender allows us to also combine *scenes* in the VSE. This will utilize linking like we used in `Chapter 5`, *Modern Kitchen – Part 1: Kitbashing*. We'll go through each of these options (image sequences, scene linking, and final video output) to complete the exquisite corpse.

Rendering to external files

We'll start with the Blender blinks file, and render it to an image sequence. This file presents a unique challenge because the Blender logo colors are a branded RGB value:

1. Go to the **Properties** window's **Render** panel, and scroll down to the **Color Management** tab. Change **View Transform** to **Standard**. Normally, **Filmic** is the preferred view transform for realistic exposure and appearance, but to get the Blender files to match their brand colors, this will directly emulate the RGB hexes.
2. Go to the **Output** panel, then in the **Output** tab choose a render destination folder and name.
3. For the file format, choose **openEXR** with **DWAA** for the codec.
4. Press *Ctrl + F12* to render your animation.

Instead of rendering out a full movie, it will render individual frames of the movie. That way, if your file unexpectedly quits mid-render, you'll have the earlier files available to salvage. OpenEXR will avoid compression issues when we render, and is usually the correct file format. Other file formats have their uses, as follows:

- **JPEGs** are the most common format available, but are *lossy*. To save memory, they compress information, which becomes noticeable when they get compressed again when rendering to video. If you're low on space and personal standards, JPEGs come in handy.
- **PNGs** are less lossy than JPEGs, and also render with alpha. However, their alpha method doesn't preserve color, and thus can cause problems when compositing pipelines.
- **OpenEXR Multilayer** is the best format available, and can store all kinds of data in any number of layers. On the **View Layer** tab, you can see inputs that multilayer EXRs can store, which are useful for compositing. It's more than we need for these animations, but usually my favorite format.

- **OpenEXRs** are ideal, but can be *very* large in size. To reduce the file size, change the codec to DWAA compression, and if you don't need 32-bit features, change **Color Depth** to **Float (Half)**.
- **FFMPEG** renders to a `.h264` video. Usually, I don't render directly to video straight from 3D, because it won't preserve quality when edited and re-rendered (and re-compressed) later, plus you risk losing your work if your computer crashes. But if your file is simple enough and you're not doing future postproduction, it's good for quick outputs.

Since these Grease Pencil files are pretty light, we can use scene linking for the other two animations, interpreting scenes as video files.

Editing the scenes together

Now that you've seen how to render frames to files, we'll combine that in Blender's VSE with another type of "video"—Blender files themselves! Lastly, we can render our animation to a final video output. Let's begin:

1. Open up your `fight.blend` file. In the header, rename the scene to `fight`:

2. Open up your bouncing ball file, then rename the scene to `ball`.
3. Create a new Blender file, then save it as `Ch09_videoEdits`. Choose the **Video Editing** preset. This layout has two **Sequence Editor** windows. In the **Preview** view, we can see our video edits, and in the **Sequencer** view, we'll move, trim, and adjust our clips.
4. Use *Shift + A* | **Add** | **Image/Sequence**. Navigate to the directory where you rendered the Blender eyeblinks. Select all the files, and hit **OK**. The VSE interprets the individual renders as an image sequence we can scrub through.
5. We'll bring the bouncing ball and fight animations in as Blender scenes, rather than renders, but first, we need to link them in. Go to **File** | **Link**, then choose your bouncing ball file. Navigate to **Scenes**, and choose **Ball**. This adds a clip and even previews the render in the VSE. Also, because we used linking, the file is dynamic; we can go back to the ball file, change the animation, and it will update in the video edits file.
6. The clip is added at the current frame. These clips share much of the functionality found elsewhere in Blender. Grab them with *G*, and hold *Ctrl* to add snapping in, making it easier to place at the end of the previous clip.
7. Repeat this with the `Fight` file, so that one clip enters into the next.

8. Change one of the windows to a **Properties** window. In the **Output** panel, set your file type to FFMPEG, and set your timeline to the frame at the end.

9. Render out your exquisite corpse.

As shown here, the scenes and render combine into a final video file:

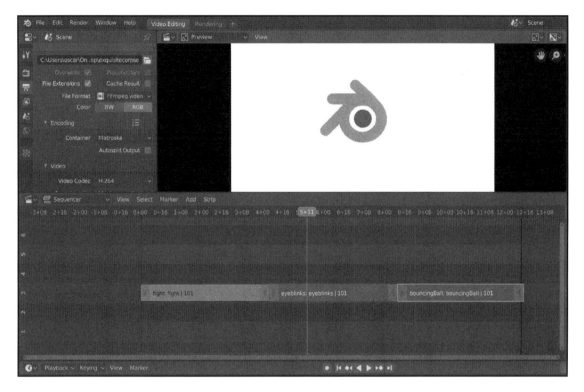

The VSE

In the final animation, the uniting circle frame at the beginning and end lets one idea flow into the next. Individually, the three clips are conventional animation ideas. But when combined, they have a surreal ebb and flow that allows for infinite expansion. What will your *next* exquisite corpse be?

Summary

These three animations have allowed us to explore different approaches to animation. The bouncing ball showed the pose to pose approach, plus many animation principles. Animating the Blender logo employed several tricks of Grease Pencil to reuse and control animations. The fight scene took us through a straight-ahead workflow, tackling each keyframe right after the next.

This is only the start of where Grease Pencil can take you. I've got three or four other files with exquisite corpse experiments that could be polished into the next sequence of the overall animation.

Questions

1. What is the difference between pose to pose animation and straight-ahead animation?
2. How does making Grease pencil keyframes differ when using **Draw**, **Edit**, and **Sculpt** Modes?
3. How can you modify multiple GP keyframes at the same time?
4. Using mask layers and a second layer, see if you can animate a shadow on your bouncing ball, and also a layer for a shadow cast on the floor.
5. What modifier can you add to a grease pencil object to automatically grow your strokes over time?
6. What are the benefits of moving keyframes in the Dope Sheet to change their timing?
7. Why should you limit how much time you spend on each frame when roughing in animation?
8. Where in Blender's video editing pipeline is it good to use image sequences, scenes, and video render outputs?
9. Make a new animation that relies on pose to pose to sync up with your other exquisite corpse animations.
10. Make a new animation that relies on straight-ahead drawing to sync up with your other exquisite corpse animations.

Further reading

Share your further exquisite corpse creations on Blender Artists. I've created a thread at `https://blenderartists.org/t/exquisite-corpse-animation` where your future exquisite corpse animations can join together with others.

10
Animating a Stylish Short with Grease Pencil

Animation is expensive. 2D animation can require characters, backgrounds, rough drafts, line art, coloring, and effects, and that's even before you get to frame 2. Since the dawn of the medium, savvy animators have leaned heavily on the power of style, simplicity, good design, and motion hacks to turn these limitations into timeless beauty. By embracing these principles in **Grease Pencil**, even a single animator can complete an animated short from start to finish.

In the 40s, 50s, and 60s, UPA and Hanna-Barbara made animations exemplifying this philosophy, and the stylish graphic focus of their work still feels fresh decades later. Their influence can be felt in animation today in both 2D and 3D animation, where clean graphic shapes can inspire much more than realistic anatomy, rendering samples, or intricate details.

In this chapter, you'll do the following:

- Go through the entire production cycle of a 2D animated short
- Animate a walk cycle and reuse it over multiple frames
- Animate a take, where a character reacts to something it notices
- Evolve your animation from rough pencil tests to finished color frames
- Use layers for flexible control of a character's individual body parts
- Create a looping background and stylize it with modifiers
- Animate with smears for appealing transitions
- Use the Type tool for the final credits

Getting started

Preproduction encompasses all of the work needed before we actually start animating, including story, mood boards, concept art, and storyboards. The preproduction files are done to get you started faster and can be perused in `ch10_storyboards.blend`.

Preproduction

The story is a simple riff on the animated shorts about the concessions stand that would prelude movies back in the day. A happy girl is out on the town to see a movie and gleefully buys her ticket. She walks right past the concessions stand, where an anthropomorphic bag of popcorn is crying. It's sad because it wants to see the film too. The kid buys the popcorn and takes it into the theater. The punchline: the bag of popcorn realizes its horrible mistake as the girl eats him alive. The credits for the short roll onscreen while the popcorn is consumed.

`ch10_storyboards.blend` has some quick storyboards, drawn in **Grease Pencil**, all from the front view so that they can all be viewed at once. The animated camera view goes through each one; if you render these out, you can load them as reference images to copy or trace. You can see them in their entirety here:

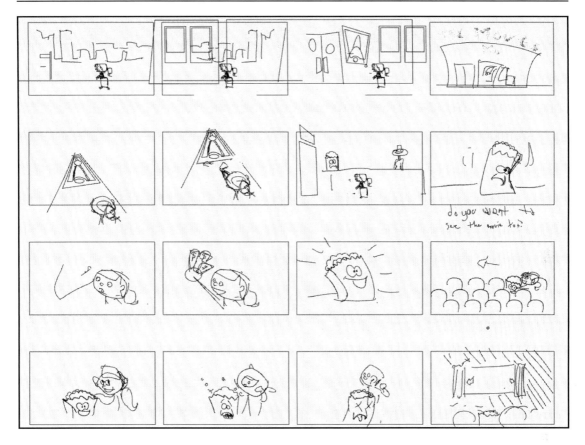

Storyboards for the animated short

Embrace the benefits that come with simple animation. Since the scope of our story can be done by one person, you control the whole pipeline. That means you can jump back, change designs or animations as you see fit, and follow your instincts without needing prior approval.

Navigating this chapter's files

The results of this chapter's efforts can be found in the file `https://github.com/PacktPublishing/Blender-3D-By-Example-Second-Edition/blob/master/Blender3DByExample_ch10/ch10_animatedshort.blend`. This file has two workspace presets: Video Editing and 2D animation. Every shot of animation was stored in its own scene in this file. By order of appearance in this chapter, the animation scenes are **walk**, **ticket**, **concessions**, **crying_buying**, **seats**, and **credits**. When examining these scenes to see how their animation was put together, use the 2D animation workspace. Use the Browse Scene pulldown in the Header to switch between the various scenes, as shown here:

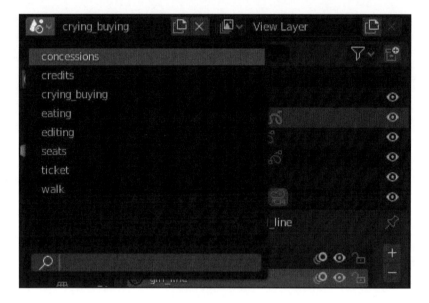

Switching between scenes

The one remaining scene, **editing**, combines these scenes in the **VSE (Video Sequence Editor)**, using techniques covered in `Chapter 9`, *Animating an Exquisite Corpse in Grease Pencil*. When combining your scenes for their final output, combine them together, similar to the editing scene, and use the Video Editing workspace.

The walk cycle

The walk cycle can fill up several seconds, even though we're just leaving it on repeat. We'll use a pipeline with three steps. First, we use expendable scribbles that make sure the animation will move correctly. If you try and get finished character rendering when the motion is wrong, you might have to throw away polished frames that wasted your time. Second, break the body down to its major masses on individual layers and get key poses. This will let us isolate problems, re-time keyframes or whole loops, and quickly fill the gaps with interpolation. Third, we'll polish the finished frames, loop the animation, and combine it with a background loop. See an example of this in `https://github.com/PacktPublishing/Blender-3D-By-Example-Second-Edition/blob/master/Blender3DByExample_ch10/ch10_animatedshort.blend`, using the walk scene.

The pencil test

A pencil test cuts detail in favor of lots of quick drawings. This lets us see the *motion* of the character, then add details later:

1. Start a new **Grease Pencil** scene. Rename the scene `walk`.
2. Rename the two starting layers `Ground` and `Draft`. Draw a straight line on the Ground layer to put our walk-in context, then lock it.
3. On the **Adjustments** tab for your pencil test layer, give it a **Tint Color** of light blue and a **Factor** of 1, turning your lines blue. Traditionally, pencil tests were drawn in blue pencil. When the drawings were inked, the blue would disappear after scanning.
4. On the Draft layer, draw with the **Draw Pencil** with **Active Smooth** of 1 and **Strength** of .3. Loosely sketch in the first walk pose.

   Reduce the character to simple shapes. Don't draw the nose, eyes, and mouth; just use a loose X/Y cross so we can see the head's direction rotation. Draw the legs and arms as flowing lines from start to finish before you refine them, as shown here:

Pencil test keyframes for the walk cycle

5. A keyframe was added on frame **1** in the **Dope Sheet** window's **Grease Pencil** panel. Select the new keyframe and duplicate it with *Shift + D,* then move it to frame **11**.

6. Duplicate it again, and move it to frame **21**.

7. Set your timeline end to **20**, when the walk ends and loops back to the beginning.

   The walk cycle will be 20 frames in total. On frame 1, the character's camera-side foot is forward; on frame **11**, her opposite foot is forward; and frame **21** will return us to the starting pose. Keyframes can be selected, moved, and scaled just like 3D Viewport components.

8. Go to frame **6**, drawing our first "up" pose, and note her feet placement. Here, her front foot has moved back until her center of gravity is a straight line from her head to her foot. Her back foot is up and centered as it moves forward.

9. Turn on onion skins in both the Layers panel and Viewport Overlays. This helps to visualize what came before and after.

10. On frames **3** and **8**, the onion skin shows where to draw her head so that it's between the poses of **1** and **6** and the poses of **6** and **11**. Draw the head in and test the motion by hitting play with the spacebar.

The major body masses, the center of gravity, the whole line of action, and contact points for footfalls and hand positions can be improved by seeing their movement in onion skins. In the following, you can see how the feet were positioned on arcs between their before and after feet:

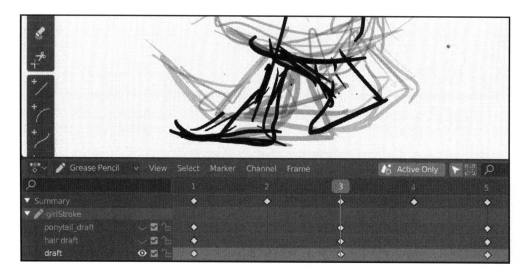

Onion skins helping with placement

If the motion looks wrong, delete! New animators can feel crushed at how often you draw something nice, only to throw it away when it doesn't animate well. Pencil test drawings should be light, loose, quick, and regularly erased or redrawn when they don't stick the landing. My first attempt at feet was too directly between the onion skins and didn't have a good "snap." I erased, tried again with better arcs and footfalls, and liked it better. In this pencil test stage, I'll often store a keyframe for later by duplicating it off to a distant frame, then use Sculpt to test out a more exaggerated or different revision. If it works, I can keep it, and if it doesn't, I don't fuss over tossing an idea that took 30 seconds to test. Try shifting frame **3** around. How does the motion feel if it's on **2**, **4**, or even **5**? Shifting the motion like this can sometimes find improved results or happy accidents.

Now, we'll add the second half of the walk cycle and the hair:

1. Do some minor redrawing on **11** to show the foot switch from **1**. On frame **1**, the foreground foot is forward and the foreground arm is backward. On frame **11**, I show the switch by having the foreground arm's shoulder more forward to imply the torso is rotated.

2. Frame **1**, **11**, and **21** mark the core of our walk cycle. Frame **6** and **16** mark the opposite extremes. Finish up frames **3**, **8**, **13**, and **18** as our in-between frames, or tweens.

3. Create a new layer called `hair_draft`. Draw the hair like the storyboards on frame **1**, flouncing up on **3**, and straight down on **5**.

4. The bouncing bangs and ponytail are overlapping animations, with motion driven by the head, which is driven by the feet. Using a second layer makes it easier to re-time by moving keyframes.

You don't need a pencil test frame for every frame, but I aim for **2**'s, a new frame drawn every other frame. For slower transitions, you don't need every frame to land. To finish up the pencil test from the foreground foot's journey front to back, I have a keyframe on **1**, **2**, **4**, **6**, **8**, and **10**. I then recycled frames **1** through **10** as a starting point for frames **11** through **20**. The final walk frames are shown here:

The girl's walk cycle

When you feel you have enough walk cycle structure to move on, we'll next draw clean layers for individual body parts. First, we'll do the head and pelvis.

The head and pelvis

Clean, finalized animation can now be completed on top of our pencil test. By relying on simple shapes and cloned keyframes, we can also maximize interpolation to get lots of frames done via tweens:

1. Create a new layer called `Head`, below your **Draft** layer.

2. Switch to **Draw Mode**, activate the **Thickness** profile, then use the **Curve** tool to trace the head on frame **1**, using *E* to extrude the four sides.

    I often hit *C* to switch between a single curve or two beziers, and I often leave the two beziers untouched for straight lines. I also adjust the line weight while drawing with *F* and re position while drawing with *G*. Lastly, add a nose.

3. Add a new material with black lines and a light purple fill. Then, on the **Layers** panel's **Adjustments** tab, add a skin color with a **Factor** of 1.

4. In **Edit Mode**, select all of the head shape's vertices and assign them.

    With this single material plus individual layer tints, the colors can vary from layer to layer while all using the same material, as shown here:

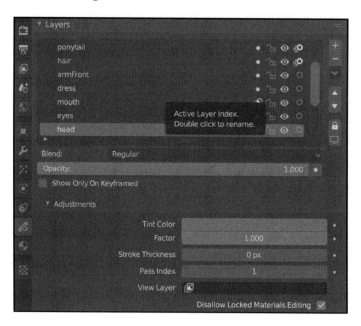

Layer tints to customize a single material on each layer

5. Go to frame **6**. Use a combination of **Edit Mode** with proportional edit falloff (*O*) and **Sculpt Mode** with the grab brush to reshape the head so it matches your pencil test. Do this on frames **3** and **8** as well.

6. Select your keyframe on frame **1**, then duplicate it with *Shift + D* and move it to frame **11**, for when the head returns to its low point. Set your timeline to end on frame **10**; the head bounces twice (once per foot), and we can polish the frames for the first pose before duplicating them later:

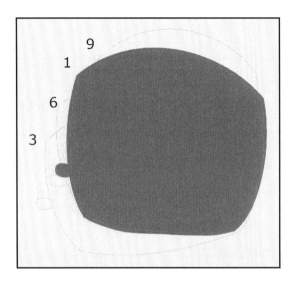

The head keyframes positions in relation to each other

7. Go to frame **2**, then use **Stroke | Interpolate | Sequence**. This generates in-between frames (tweens) automatically between frame **1** and frame **3**. By sculpting key poses instead of redrawing them, you can interpolate their tweens. Interpolate looks at each frame, then for each stroke on that frame, interpolates it to the same stroke index on the next frame.

Deleting and redoing keyframes is key to a good "snap" to the head bounce. If the energetic landing is too slow, delete the midpoint of a slow part, and move its neighboring frames around until it feels right. Edits made after interpolated tweens might no longer fit, so get comfortable with deleting and re-interpolating.

The simple dress shape represents the girl's center of gravity. We can draw it out just like with the head, with some added benefits. Repeat the process you used for the head but on a new layer called Dress. Give this layer a dark blue .5 tint, which mixes partially with the mother color of the purple material. Instead of the bob of the head, the dress has a secondary flutter, where it has a bell shape on frames **1** and **11**.

With your dress and head on separate layers, a savvy animator can test new things out in the dope sheet. Click and drag a selection over all of the dress keyframes and see how the animation looks if moved forward or backward **1** or **2** frames. Do either of these lands better than the defaults? The separated layers allow regular testing in this way and building up overlapping action. Notice the arcs they follow, shown here:

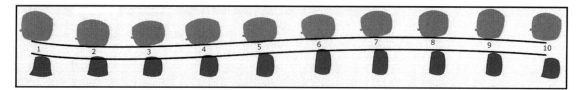

The Head and Dress layers

By using simple shapes and making alternate keyframes in **Edit Mode**, their shape and point order stay the same, allowing heavy use of **Grease Pencil**'s interpolate tools. Next, we'll add the feet.

Footfalls

The feet start stretched apart on frame **1**, planting early on the ground and carrying the body's weight. By frame **10**, they should move to the back extreme position. The background foot starts frame **1** all of the way back, but instead comes off of the ground, floating forward and switching to weight-bearing in frame **10**. Frames **11 to 20** repeat this, but on opposite feet. We'll differentiate the right foot with a darkening tint to imply shadow and moving a little further up in space to imply perspective:

1. Create a new layer called `Foot_front` beneath the dress layer.
2. Use the **Draw Curves** tool to extrude out a foot shape in frame **1**. Aim for as few curve extrusions as needed.
3. Go to frame **10** and draw the foot at the farthest back position.
4. In frame **5**, draw the midpoint of the foot, when the girl stands up the straightest. Make sure the layer has onion skin turned on, so finding the midpoint and maintaining the foot size is easier.
5. Frame **3**'s foot lands between **1** and **5**, but lands with a "snap." Draw this foot with full contact on the ground. Frame **8**'s foot also still has full contact.

You can see the snap of the foot here:

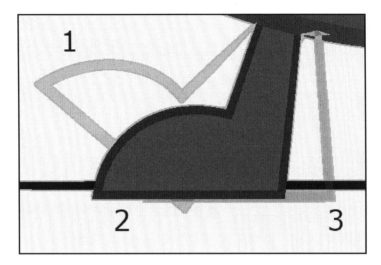

Footfalls connecting with the ground

6. Set your timeline to a start and end of **1** and **10**, and hit play to test this loop out.

For frames **11 to 20**, the foot comes off of the ground, then moves forward. In frame **15**, it's directly under the body, and by frame **20**, it's close to frame **1**. Test the animation with only three key poses (**11**, **15**, and **20**). Next, get important motion poses; on frame **16**, the foot tilts backward, and in **17**, it snaps forward, preparing to land. Test the animation. Key in-between every two frames, using **Edit Mode**, and **Sculpt** to reuse poses. Test the animation. Be willing to re-time, delete, and retry. Test the animation. Always test!

The back foot can mostly reuse the front foot, but offset by 10 frames:

1. In the **Layers** panel, select the **Foot_front** layer and use the **Layer** dialog to duplicate it. Lock everything but this layer.
2. Grab all the **foot_back** keyframes and move them 10 frames with G, **10**.
3. Select the keys from **11**-**20** and move them back with G, **-20**. The back leg now starts in the opposite pose.

This layer recycling is shown here:

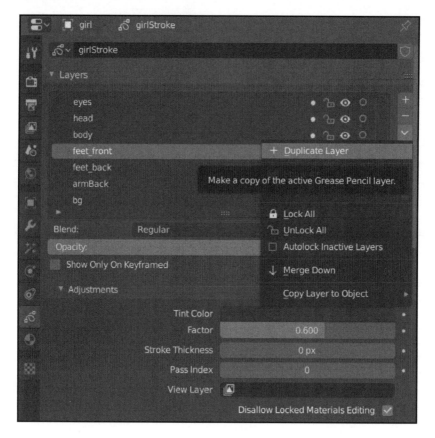

Layer recycling

4. Go to the **Adjustments** tab of the **feet_back**. Change its tint to slightly darker than the **foot_front** color, making it look more shadowed than the front leg. This prevents the legs from blending together on the overlap frames of **5** and **15**.
5. In **Edit Mode**, turn on **Multiframe**.
6. Select all of the keyframes, then, in the viewport, select all the stroke points. Move them up on the **z-axis** a little, so the back foot looks more in perspective.

The front and back feet are offset from one another, with the back foot darker, and the hair higher up to imply perspective. Now, let's move on for the rest of the walk cycle.

Finalizing the walk cycle with loop and pizzazz

The head, dress, and feet are the main anchors of the walk cycle. With these movements secure, the rest can be added—the secondary action of the arm, the shirt, and the facial features:

1. Animate the arms much like the legs: key poses first, then tween through them on twos, with ones around moments of quick action.
2. Animate the shirt on a new layer, with key poses on **1**, **5**, and **10**. I positioned it above the back arm and leg, but below the dress and head.
3. Create two new layers called `hair` and `ponytail`. Use the **Draw Curve** and **Draw Tools** to make her bangs with a stroke, her head hair (including ear silhouette) with a stroke, and her ponytail with a stroke. By separating the hair into separate layers, the secondary animation on the ponytail can be re-timed more easily.
4. Go through the first 10 frames, and keyframe the hair in **Edit Mode** with movements that follow the head. Save time by keyframing **1**, **5**, and **10**, then interpolating a sequence. Do the same with the ponytail, emphasizing the squash to stretch on frames **3** and **5** when the ponytail rushes down.

Next, we'll add her facial features:

1. Add a layer called `Features`.
2. Use a material with full stroke and no fill and de-activate the **Thickness** profile.
3. Use **Draw Curves** to make eyes out of a single thick line, resizing with *F* during drawing.
4. Like the hair, keyframe the eyes for the whole walk cycle to follow the correct orientation and position of the head.

    We'll make a cut-out smile with a subtraction layer.

5. Create a new layer called `Mouth`. Draw a triangle cutout for where a mouth would be in profile.
6. Set the layer adjustment's tint to white with full alpha.
7. Set the layer's blend mode to Subtract.

The white RBG 1/1/1 will be subtracted from any other layers' colors. The result is a profile where the mouth reads in the shape. Keyframe this triangle's stroke points in **Edit Mode** to follow the head as well. The mouth's subtract blend mode is shown here:

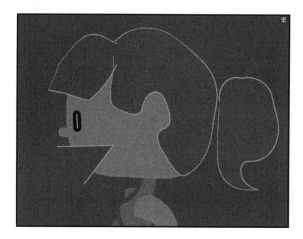

Hair, ponytail, eyes, and a subtracted mouth

Judging the walk cycle's loop is easy with only 20 frames looping. Now we need it to continue throughout the animation. With modifiers, we can set it to an infinite loop and add some extra oomph. The **Time Offset** modifier will let us repeat this walk cycle indefinitely. The **Time Offset** modifier will add transformations to individual layers, and by animating these transforms, we'll get nondestructive secondary animation. First, let's use the **Time Offset** modifier:

1. Set your timeline's End frame to **250**.
2. Go to the **Modifiers** panel of the properties window and add a **Time Offset** modifier. Set its start to 1 and end to 20. Now the animation loops the whole length of the timeline.

Now, let's use the Offset modifiers:

1. Add an **Offset** modifier called body. This adds a change to the three basic transforms, which we keyframe and loop.
2. On frame **1**, set this modifier's **Scale** Offset to 0, 0, and −.1, and right-click on the values to insert keyframes.
3. Re-keyframe these values on frame **11** so it returns to the starting pose.

4. On frame **6**, key them at `.05`, `0`, and `.05`.

5. Change your **Dope Sheet** pulldown from **Grease Pencil** to **Dope Sheet**. The modifier keyframes can be adjusted here. I re-timed the springing modifiers to `2`, `12`, and `22`, as shown here:

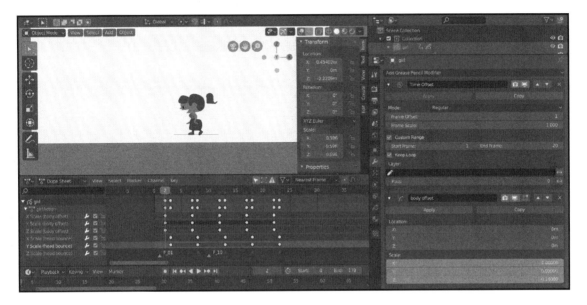

Modifier's keyframes in the Dope Sheet

Next, we'll make these modifier keyframes cyclical:

1. Open a **Graph Editor** window and select one of your keyed values, such as the **X** scale.

2. Hit *N* to bring up the **Properties** panel, and switch to the **Modifiers** tab.

3. Activate modifiers on the selected channel, and a **Cycles** modifier is added. This restarts the curve when it reaches the last keyframe.

4. Use the modifier copy and paste buttons in this **Modifier** tab to transfer this modifier from **X** scale to the **Y** scale.

5. The keyframes in the graph editor can be selected and moved up or down on the **y-axis**, making them more extreme or subtle.

Repeat this for the other modifiers' keyed channels, shown here:

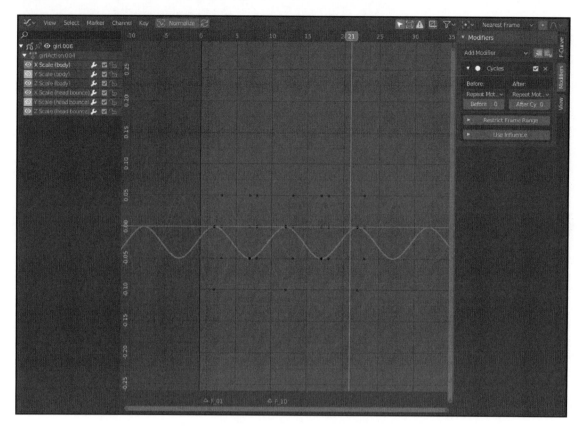

The cyclical channels as seen in the Graph Editor

The girl's walk is now exuberant, with an easily edited hierarchy and nondestructive modifiers. Now, we'll make a background for her to walk in front of.

The background

Our next goal is to take a metropolitan skyline and movie theater, then boil it down to its simplest elements. We'll move the city and theater at different paces than the moviegoer, creating parallax. Big graphic shapes and a limited color palette will stylishly sell the scene.

The city skyline

We'll use a handful of lines, fills, and subtracted elements to capture all of the windows and buildings of our city skyline, then use modifiers to repeat and move it:

1. In the **Properties** window, go to the **World** tab and change **World Color** to a dark purple for our evening metropolitan sky. Switch your **Viewport Shading** to **Rendered** to see the color.

2. Create a new **Grease Pencil** object and name it Skyline. Delete the **Fills** layer, and rename the line layer City.

3. Create two materials on the object. Name the first material city_lines and the second city_fills. Change the **city_lines Stroke** color to yellow and deactivate its fill color.

4. While your cursor is over the stroke's color swatch, hit *Ctrl + C* to copy it. On the **City_fills** material, activate **Fill** and deactivate **Stroke**. Hover over the **Fill** color swatch and hit *Ctrl + V* to paste in the copied RGB value.

The two materials are shown here:

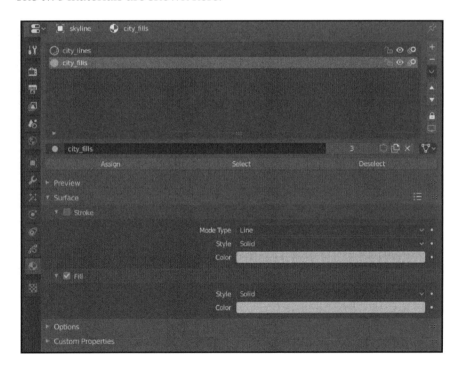

City materials

5. Switch to **Draw Mode**. Start with the Draw Pen preset, deactivate pen pressure for both strength and radius, and deactivate the **Thickness** profile. Set the **Radius** to 25px.

6. Using the **Draw Curves** tool with the **city_lines** material, draw out a city skyline, hitting *E* to extrude new lines.

7. Switch to the **city_fills** tool. Draw windows inside about half the buildings with **Draw Curves** again, extruding out the big silhouettes of the windows inside the building and ignoring the mortar between them for now.

8. In the other half of the buildings, draw in some wind abstractions using straight lines with the **Draw Curves** tool, either horizontal or vertical lines.

Mix up the building shapes and line angles. Build out the skyline until it's about twice as long as the camera view. Before you complete the stroke, hit *F* while drawing it to change its size to your liking. The line and shape elements of the beginnings of the city are shown here:

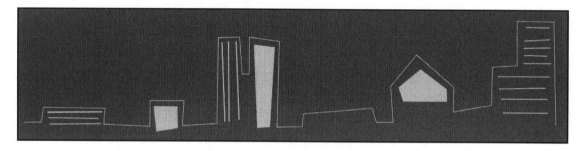

The beginnings of the city skyline

9. Create a new **Grease Pencil** layer named Subtract, and change its **Blend** mode to **Subtract**. Also, turn on the **Mask** Layer so that its transparency is dictated by the city layer.

10. Use the **city_lines** layer and the **Curve** tool to draw a mortar stroke through your big window shape, then adjust its thickness with *F* before finishing the stroke.

Continue to draw subtracting strokes throughout the windows, or use **Edit Mode** to duplicate existing strokes. Here are the resulting windows:

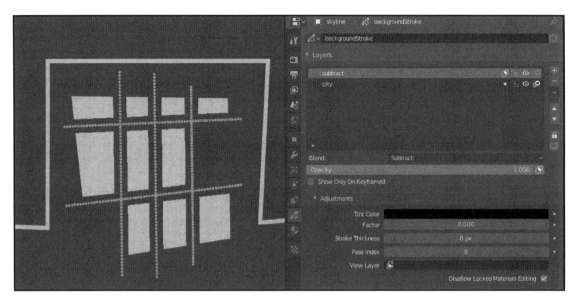

Windows cut using subtractive strokes

Now, we'll extend this skyline object using modifiers and animation. First, an **Array** modifier will repeat the skyline. Second, we'll animate its movement with an offset modifier and linear interpolation. Third, we'll give it a glow in the Effects panel:

1. In the **Modifiers** panel, add an **Array** modifier. Set the count to 3, then increase the **X** offset until there's just a small gap between each array duplicate.

2. Go back to your city layer, and in **Draw** mode, add a stroke to close the gap between the two with a connecting stroke, so the array repeats seamlessly.

3. Add an **Offset** modifier to the skyline object. In frame **1**, right-click on the offset modifier's **Location** values, and **Insert Keyframes**. Move to frame **200**, set the **X** value to 10m, and Insert Keyframe again.

4. In the **Dope Sheet**, switch from **Grease Pencil** to **Dope Sheet**. Instead of seeing our **Grease Pencil** keyframes, we see the keyframes we applied to the **Offset** modifier. Select them all, then right-click and choose **Interpolation Mode | Linear**. Now the city will move at the same speed the whole time, rather than easing in and out.

5. Storing the animation via Offset means we can move and scale the city with the regular transforms. In the Timeline, turn off Autokeying and move the skyline around as needed. You can also adjust the speed by moving the Offset modifier's end keyframe's position in the **Dope Sheet**.

6. In the **Properties** window, switch to the **Effects** panel. Add a **Glow** effect. Paste in the yellow color from the city materials.

The final setup of the animation, modifiers, and effects can be seen here:

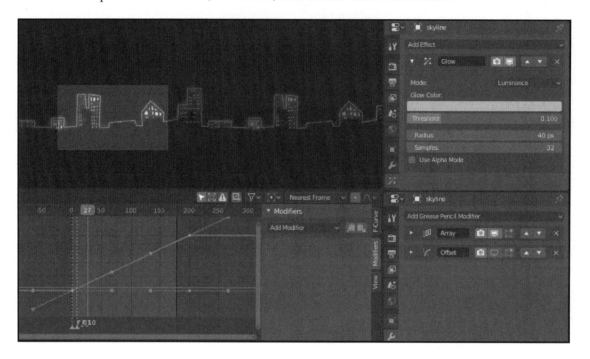

The completed skyline

The girl walks in the middle of the screen, while the city behind her passes by at a slower pace. Now, let's move on to her destination: the theater.

The theater and usher

The theater and usher will also rely on simple, readable shapes for the usher kiosk, movie posters, and reader board. We'll choose carefully when to use a new layer versus a new **Grease Pencil** object, hence allowing us to take advantage of layer masks:

1. Create a new **Grease Pencil** object and name it theater, with just the **city_fills** material. Give it two layers named Theater and Shadow.

2. In the **Layers** panel's adjustments tab, put both layers' Tint **Factor** at 1 and set a **Tint Color** of light purple.

3. On the **theater** layer, draw out a simple theater shape with the **Curve** tool, including a middle silhouette for the marquee roof.

4. On the **shadow** layer, draw in a shadow underneath the marquee roof, extending all of the way down. Turn on **Masking** 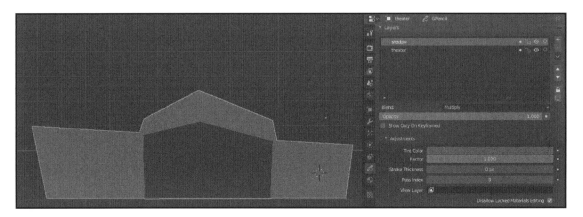 to clip this layer.

This starting layout is shown here:

The theater start

For the other theater set dressings, we'll use a new **Grease Pencil** object. This will allow us to use masking and stick with simple silhouettes:

1. Create a new **Grease Pencil** object and name it Posters, and just the **city_fills** material. Give it three layers called posters, lights, and window. By using a new **Grease Pencil** object, we can employ masks on the silhouettes of these building details.

2. On the posters layer's **Adjustments** tab, put the tint factor at 1, and choose a dark purple-brown for the color.

3. Switch to **Draw** mode, and use the **Draw Curves** tool to create some poster rectangles on the side of the building with quirky angles. I also drew in rectangles for the preceding marquees and the ticket booth.

4. On the **lights** layer, turn on masking, and use the **city_fills** material. Draw internal rectangles for the marquees and poster text. Next, use **Draw** mode to create a simplified abstraction of a movie poster illustration. A simple circle makes a sun, horizontal zigzags make a landscape, and some polygon's quick **Draw Curve** extrusions can imply distant buildings.

5. On the **text** layer, change the **Tint Factor** to 1, and for the **Tint Color**, use a color picker to sample the purple-brown of your posters. In Draw mode, use the **city_lines** material to draw some squiggly text lines in the marquee, and on the bottom of the posters.

Repeat this process on a new **Grease Pencil** object for the kiosk. I used the same technique—a separate layer for a new color, this time tinted dark brown for the kiosk shadow, as shown here:

The theater with posters, titles, and a kiosk

You can always add more layers and eschew new materials in favor of layer tints and order them via a layer stack. What determines the **Grease Pencil** draw order, from front to back? In order, they are the distance of separate GP objects from the view (also called **Z depth**), the order of layers in a single object, the Z depth of separate GP *strokes* on the *same layer* as one another, and lastly the order the strokes were drawn in. Use that order when trying to organize cartoon depths.

The usher, window, and speaking slot show this relationship. The window could serve as a layer mask for the usher's bottom half. However, the usher needs to serve as a mask for his own hat and lips, so I made him his own GP object. The speaking slot is most easily solved as another object as well, in front of everything else. This means using the closeness to the camera to determine Z order rather than a layer stack:

1. Create a new **Grease Pencil** object, and name it `slot`. In **Object** mode, make sure perspective-wise that it's slightly closer to the camera than the theater.
2. On the first layer, use a previous fill material with a **Tint Factor** of 1 and a **Tint Color** that samples the kiosk, making them identical in color.
3. Draw a simple circle for the speaking slot.
4. Add another layer with another tint (in my case, yellow) and draw another circle inside the first one. Repeat this for a darker circle.

Now, let's move on to the usher:

1. Create a new GP object, and name it `usher`. Give it the following layers: `features`, `hat`, `head`, and `body`, in that order, with the body layer as the bottom layer.
2. Set the features and hat layers to masked. I set the body and hat layers to a red tint layer and the head layer to a skin tone tint.
3. Select the body layer. Using the **Draw Curves** tool with a flat's material, create a simple arc to represent his whole body.
4. Select the **heads** layer. Draw a simplified shape for the head and hat. I drew separate strokes for his two ears; later, this will make animating easier, as the ears can be moved independently of the head by selecting strokes in **Edit Mode**.
5. On the **hat** layer, draw a shape around the top of his head. Because it's masked and red-tinted, the head silhouette determines its boundaries.
6. Switch to **Object mode**. From the perspective view, move the usher between the slot and theater objects.
7. On the **features** layer, with a stroke material, draw a simple line for the mouth, two lines for the eyebrows, and two vertical lines for the eyes. Adjust the line weight with *F* to style them to your preferences.

Putting the features on a separate layer does two things. First, it determines the Z depth as the top layer, which allows cartoon effects such as the eyebrows going above the hat. Second, since the features will animate the most, we can isolate the layer 🔒 grab strokes easily in **Edit Mode**. The finished usher is seen here:

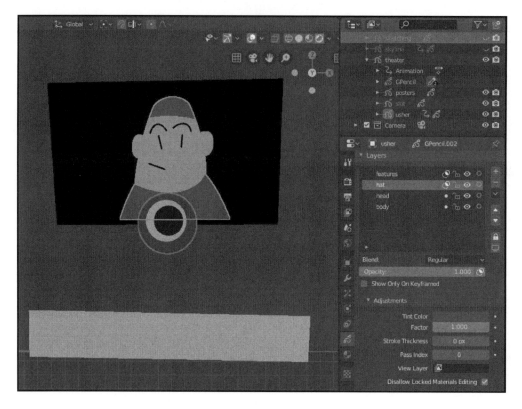

Usher, kiosk, and speaking slot

The scene is set. Before animating, I clean the file up to make things run smoothly:

- All of these **Grease Pencil** objects should only have one keyframe for all layers. Comb through the **Grease Pencil Dope Sheet**, and make sure the key where each layer's drawing is stored is on frame **1**. It's easy to make wrong, extraneous, or improperly placed keys when doing layouts.
- Parent the **usher**, **posters**, and **slot** objects to the theater object. You can do this in the outliner by shift-clicking and dragging the child objects (usher, posters, and slot) onto the parent object (the theater.) Alternatively, you can select all of these objects, then shift-click on the theater, making it the last object selected, and parent them with *Ctrl + P*.

- Check to make sure that your usher's origin is set to his stomach. If the GP object's origin is far from where the strokes were drawn, use the 3D cursor to click on where his origin should be, move all of the strokes in **Edit Mode** to be centered on the object origin (shown by an orange dot), then in Object mode, position his start point to the right spot.

With all of our theater objects in order, let's animate the usher's take as he responds to the girl's approach.

Animating the usher's take

The girl approaches the theater, which moves faster than the skyline, creating an illusion of depth. The usher does a take, noticing the customer, and turns to keep looking at her as she gets closer.

In animation, a take is when a character reacts to something. It requires a starting state, an anticipation, and a reaction. In our case, the usher is staring out the window, which is his starting state. He squints upon hearing something, which is his anticipation. He turns toward the sound – his reaction.

First, let's set the stage.

The theater approach

We'll handle the theater's movement as the girl walks toward it:

1. Go to frame **100**. Select the theater object, and move it on the **x-axis** to its end position, with the girl right by the kiosk. Because of parenting, the child GP objects follow along.
2. Insert a keyframe for the theater's position. You can do this by right-clicking on the location in the item panel, right-clicking in the **Dope Sheet** or timeline, hitting *I* in the 3D view, or just using auto-keyframing before you move the object.
3. Go back to frame **1**, and move the theater to the left, so it starts outside the camera view. Insert a keyframe for the location again.
4. In the **Dope Sheet**, select the theater object's **2** keyframes. Right-click to change its handle type to Vector, so her walk speed looks consistent.

You can re-time the animation by moving these two keyframes around. Make it faster or slower until the footfalls line up. I prefer to handle this in the **Dope Sheet**, shown here:

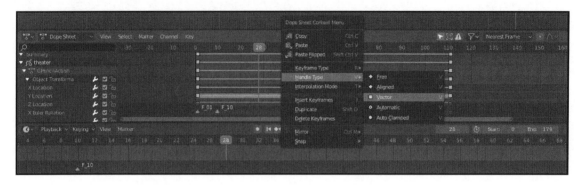

Setting keyframes and modifying their handle type

Next, let's work on the usher.

The first take

The usher is minding his own business. He perks up at the sight of a customer. He tracks her movement as she comes to buy a ticket:

1. Select your **usher**. Move through the timeline until the point when he might notice the girl's approach. Duplicate the keyframe on frame **1**, then move it out to this point in time for our start pose.
2. Go forward five frames, and animate on the usher's various layers to make an anticipation pose. Use **Sculpt Mode** to move the figure into scrunched down body language. I entirely re-drew the face, squinting and frowning to anticipate the surprise and joy of a new movie patron.
3. Go forward five more frames, then use sculpting, editing, and redrawing for the new pose, in which he turns to smile at the girl. Since his head is now turned, his nose comes into profile.
4. Go between these two five-frame jumps, then create tween keyframes. On layers where new strokes weren't created, you can interpolate a tween with **Strokes | Interpolate | Interpolate**.
5. Select the last two keys (a tween and the final reaction), and move them forward two frames. This holds the pose for an extra moment, easing in and out of the take. You can continue to smooth it with more interpolations, tweens, and re-times.

Repeat all of these steps for another take, as the usher switches from looking at the girl to looking out his window down at her. The take's progress is shown here:

The usher turns and looks

There's much more to character animation than cycles and takes. But the next time you watch some cartoons, you'll see them everywhere. The rest of the short is almost all takes and recycling the walk!

The money exchange

In the next scene, the girl reaches into a pocket and hands the usher some money, and he reacts positively. The change in angle means we'll redraw most of the scene, but we can recycle the materials and layer structure we've built to get things rolling quickly. See an example of this in `ch10_animatedshort.blend`, using the ticket scene.

Setting up the scene

The shot of the girl handing the usher money will be handled in an entirely new scene:

1. In the header's Scene pulldown, click the **New Scene** button, and choose **Full Copy**. This will make a new scene with duplicates of all of our objects. That way, we can start by deleting keyframes, then redrawing the scene from a new angle on frame **1** with the same materials and layers.

2. A full copy is needed for fresh **Grease Pencil** objects with their own data blocks, but other aspects work better linked from the other files. For instance, the duplicated materials are redundant. I replaced materials in the duplicate scenes with the original materials, to avoid a pile of materials with `.001`, `.002`, and `.003` suffixes.

3. On the theater object, redraw the poster layer to fill the whole camera view. Delete the other layers.

4. Select your posters GP object, where all of the layers and materials are set up for reuse. Draw out a worm's eye perspective for the kiosk, followed by a new window on the window layer.

5. Repeat this start pose refresh for the usher and the little girl, both with a worm's eye perspective. Things like the legs and poster text layers can be deleted or left empty.

In the example file, you might find remnants of these copied scenes from time to time, where leftovers from the walk cycle are just slightly off-camera.

Animating the characters

Start with the girl's take—from standing, she anticipates by hunching down to grab money, then reacts by thrusting it at the usher:

1. In frame **1**, I drew her simply from the back. The layers and shapes in place give me a starting point for how she looks from this lower angle.

2. In frame **21**, draw the hunched pose.

3. In frame **30**, draw the money-handing pose. Use a mix of **Edit Mode** for adjusting the head and body, plus draw mode for pose-specific things such as the arm.

   I also created a new layer with a green tint called **money**, and drew money in the girl's hand on frame **30**, with a blank frame **15**. The hand-off can be seen here:

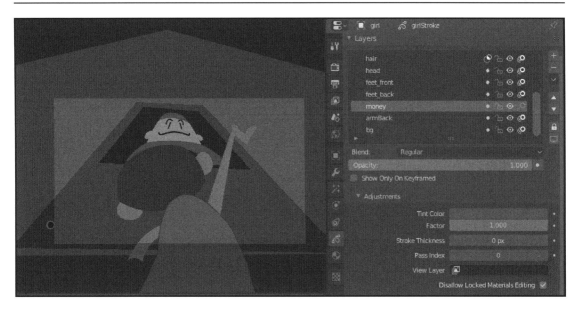

The cold hard cash

4. Add some tween keys, so the take happens over five frames. Retime these to your liking. I have the initial hunch go slow and the reaction fast. Then, fill in the animation on 2s until you like the motion.

5. Animate a take for the **usher**. I drew him blinking, then returning to his original pose. The motion is simple enough that I didn't bother tweening or pencil testing.

The pose with onion skins for both the usher and the girl are shown here:

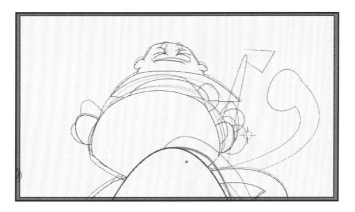

The onion skin feature helps us visualize the frames

Lastly, push the character acting even further by animating a camera angle shift before the take, animating the GP objects in Object Mode:

1. Select your theater, then insert a keyframe for **Location**, **Rotation**, and **Scale** in frame **1**. Do the same on the Girl GP object.

2. Go to frame **11**. Move the character down on the z-**axis** and the theater up. Scale the theater down to .7 and insert keyframes. Test the animation. Although we're working with 2D objects, it implies the camera turning to look at the usher.

3. Switch the **Dope Sheet** to the **Graph Editor**. This shows the keyframes broken down into their individual components. On the left, channels can be locked or hidden. In the editor, the view can be panned and zoomed just like the 3D view. Based on the active channels, you can grab keyframes and move them or adjust their bezier handles.

4. Select all of your keyframes. Right-click and select **Interpolation Type | Bounce**. This creates instant bounciness makes the fake camera shift extra plucky.

The Bounce interpolation creates sophisticated animation, with only two keyframes, as shown here:

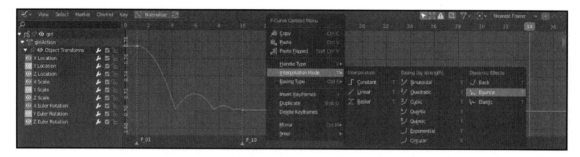

The Graph Editor, showing the Bounce interpolation

Finally, add the ponytail in the foreground. I animated quick, hand-drawn poses that have a secondary animation bounce from the crouch and spring. Our next cut will be to the theater interior, where we'll finally meet the popcorn.

The theater, crying, and triumph

Now inside the theater, the girl walks past a concessions stand with an attendee and a large, sad-eyed bag of popcorn, who looks even sadder upon being rejected. Cut to the popcorn, who sobs at rejection, while the narrator talks about how the popcorn wants to see the movie too. Cut to the girl, who considers this information, then gleefully pulls out more cash to make it happen. At this point in production, the animation goes quicker thanks to the reuse of existing work. See an example of this at `https://github.com/PacktPublishing/Blender-3D-By-Example-Second-Edition/blob/master/Blender3DByExample_ch10/ch10_animatedshort.blend`, using the concessions scene.

Reusing the walk with the concession stand

The techniques used for **Grease Pencil** are now under your belt. Next, we'll be utilizing the same ideas, with occasional changes:

1. Before animating, set the stage. Duplicate the Walk scene. Reuse and remix your theater objects to set a new static stage. I redrew the usher as a concessions' woman, redrew the theater as a concessions stand, and redrew the posters as a door and title section.

2. Delete any leftover object keyframes on the theater; in this scene, it will be static while the character moves through.

3. Add a Text Object with **Add | Text**. Set its alignment to **Center**.

4. In **Edit Mode**, type THEATER 1 on the first line, and the movie title, BRAIN EATER, on the second line, foreshadowing the popcorn's grizzly fate. Orient this object in 3D so it fits the flat perspective of the title section.

5. Move and scale the character to walk across the stage, starting off screen in frame **1**. Keyframe her position in frame **1**, then in frame **90**, move her to the entrance as she walks right past the popcorn, and keyframe the new position.

6. In the **Dope Sheet**, select these basic transform keyframes. Right-click to change their Interpolation type to Linear.

7. Give the concession stand lady a simple take: smiling to the right as the girl approaches (the start pose), a middle squinting frown (anticipation), and frowning sadly to the left as the girl walks right past her.

The combined layout is seen here:

The concessions stand

This shot should come together quickly based on how much we can recycle. The only new element left is the popcorn.

The popcorn

The popcorn deserves a fresh setup with fresh layering. He has unique design challenges and needs a face that can carry lots of emotional weight: sadness (when he'll miss the movie), joy (when the girl decides to get popcorn), horror (when she eats the popcorn in the movie), and a slapstick death:

1. Create a new **Grease Pencil** object and name it Popcorn. Give it a layer named **Box** with a full red tint, and a layer named **stripes** with a full pink tint.

2. In **Draw mode**, use the **Draw Curves** tool with a flats material to make a simple rectangle with jagged edges on the top for the popcorn bag. Make sure to draw near the object origin, so that later, parenting objects doesn't cause problems.

3. On the **stripes** layer, turn on **Masking**. Using the **Draw Curves** tool with a **Strokes** material, turn the **Thickness** Profile off, and draw a stripe down the bag. Resize it with *F* to your liking, then repeat this for three total pink stripes.

4. Because the stripes are dependent on the box shape for masking, do the popcorn kernels on a new GP object. Create a material with a black stroke and a yellow popcorn color. Use the **Draw Pen** tool with no pen pressure or thickness profile, and draw a squiggly line in a circle for the popcorn. Parent this to the popcorn bag object.

The popcorn bag so far looks like this:

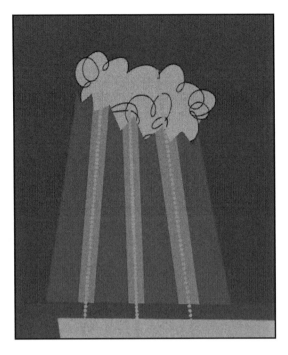

The initial popcorn layout

Now, for the face, I used a new separate **Grease Pencil** object, as the eyes and mouth will rely on masking:

1. Create a new GP object and name it `eyes`. Create the following layers in order: **eyes** (with a bright yellow tint), `pupils` (with a black tint), and `eyelids` (with a purple tint and masking turned on).

2. Draw two big circles on the eyes layer, then use curves on the eyelids layer for some lower eyelids. The pupils can be done with lines or shapes. Use the **Draw Curves** tool on the mouth layer for a frown. With all of these shapes, emphasize sadness, and adjust them in **Sculpt Mode**.

3. Create a new GP object and name it `mouth`. Create the following layers in order: `Mouth`, `Mouth Shadow` (with a red tint, masking, and a blend mode set to Multiply), `Teeth` (with a light white tint and masking), and `Outline`. On the `Mouth` layer, draw a frowning face with a black stroke material.

The popcorn's initial facial expression is shown here:

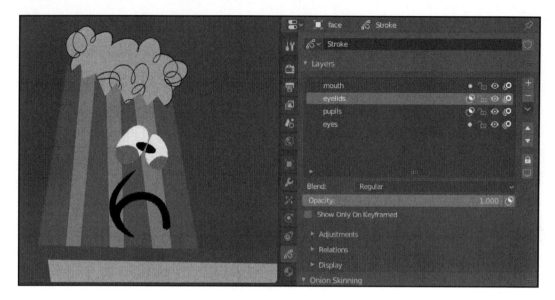

The popcorn's face object

Next, we'll animate a take as the sad popcorn watches the girl pass by:

1. Animate key poses on the face object for the following takes: looking sadly at the girl in frame **1**, looking up at the movie sign (frame **17**), looking back to the girl, then turning to watch her go past.
2. Two frames before each transition, key the middle pose with onion skins.
3. Animate a smear on the popcorn's eyes. In animation, smears help to show fast movement by stretching between the start and end.

The smear's eyeball transition from right to left can be seen here:

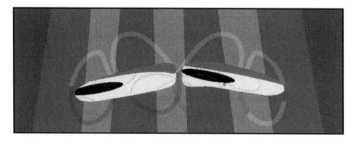

Smeared eyeballs

Facial animations such as blinks are a terrific example of animating once, then copying and pasting keyframes to speed up your workflow. Animate some quick transition blinks, and use duplication to reuse them. Next, we'll zoom in on these characters for a closer sense of their emotional state.

The change of heart

We'll start by making simple backgrounds while zooming in on the popcorn's sad face, then the girl's change of heart. This animation can be found in `https://github.com/PacktPublishing/Blender-3D-By-Example-Second-Edition/blob/master/Blender3DByExample_ch10/ch10_animatedshort.blend`, using the `crying_buying` scene:

1. Create a duplicate of the concessions scene, and name the new scene `crying_buying`. Do the usual retooling of assets for the new shots.

2. Reuse the theater background to save time, but drastically change layers. To add dramatic spotlights, create a series of layers set to **Add**, with shapes for spotlight cones or their impact on the ground. The additive blend mode lightens the layer below it.

3. In frame **1**, scale the popcorn for a close-up. Delete all of the **Grease Pencil** keyframes except the last pose, and move the last keys to frame **1**.

4. Change the eyes on frame 1 to look upward, pleading, with a downward frown.

5. In frame **21**, make a new pose with the eyes closed. Next, duplicate frame **1** keys to frame **24**. Duplicate these keys out to frame **41**, adding a second blink.

6. Create a new layer on the face. Name it tears, then give it a light blue layer tint. In layer **1**, use the **Draw Noise** brush to make long, goopy tears running down both sides of the popcorn's face.

7. Switch to the **Modifiers** panel. Assign a Build modifier with tears assigned to the layer option. Change **Start Delay** to **15**, and **Length** to **30**.

By using a Build modifier on the tears layer, now the tears drip down, as shown here:

Tears slither down the popcorn's face

8. Keyframe the camera's location in frame **1**. In frame **41**, zoom in on the popcorn's face and insert a keyframe again.

9. Repeat this process for the girl as she does a slow take. First, she considers popcorn, then springs up with money in hand, face full of joy. See whether you can animate her take the same way we've done before.

    The more you make, the more you have available to reuse, but redrawing things by hand is often faster. An example of the girl's new pose is shown here:

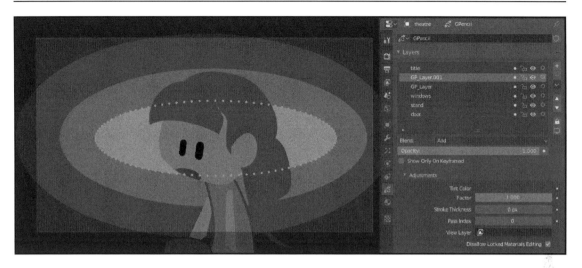

The girl with a background

Extending 2D animation with 3D transitions such as the camera zoom lets you turn a static frame into dynamic content.

The ending

The girl walks down the aisle to her seat. She and the popcorn watch the screen with anticipation. She begins to eat the popcorn, at which point the popcorn realizes its horrible mistake. It screeches in agony as his kernels disappear, sticks his tongue out, and gets Xes for eyes. Cut to the back of the girl's head, where we see the credits roll on the movie screen. You can find these last few scenes in ch10_animatedshort.blend, using the seats, eating, and credits scenes.

Entering the theater

This next scene (found in the project file as the seats scene) retools the walk cycle and backgrounds, so start with a duplicate of the concessions scene. A quick layout of the theater is shown here:

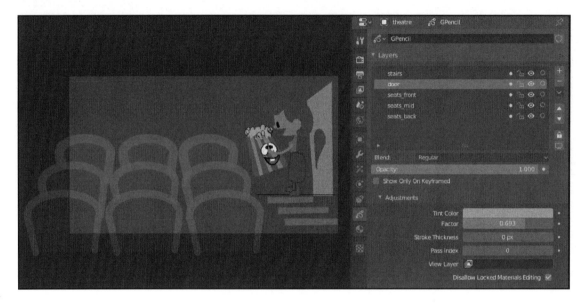

The girl enters the theater

Create the theater background like the other sets we've used: minimal, with flats materials and custom tints, and reusing a duplicate scene from a previous shot. The character walk is similarly reused; the only edits are changing the hands to hold popcorn as she walks, and changing the popcorn to follow along by parenting it to the girl. For the last scenes (the close-up popcorn eating and the credits), only a few new concepts are introduced.

Animating the girl's eating and the popcorn's death

When entering the theater, the popcorn is elated, but then his joy turns to terror. We'll start with a new scene based on an old scene, and modify the mouth layers for additional work:

1. Duplicate your **seats** scene. Change the camera and object locations for a close-up on the popcorn and girl in their seats.

2. In frame **1** of the entrance, draw a big half-circle, open-mouthed smile on the popcorn feature's **Mouth** layer, using a material with red fill and black stroke.

3. On the **Mouth Shadow** layer, draw an overlapping shape for a cast shadow inside the mouth. **Multiply** darkens the existing elements.

4. Draw a shape for the teeth, which gets masked by the mouth layer, but also overlaps the former mouth stroke. To fix this, switch to **Edit Mode**, then hit *L* to select the mouth shape. Duplicate it with *Shift + D*, then hit *M* to move it to the Outline layer. In the **Materials** tab, assign it a black stroke material with no fill.

For clarity, I staged the popcorn on the armrest next to the girl; if she held it on her lap, it would make it difficult to read them both while they overlap. Frame 1 is shown here:

The girl and her popcorn sit down for the movie

Now, let's animate the popcorn's end:

1. Animate the following key poses on the popcorn: joy, more joy as he settles into the movie, confusion and pain at the girl's first bite, an accusing stare, more pain on the second bite, agony on the third bite, and mortal peril on the fourth bite. I did these in frames **10**, **20**, **30**, **40**, **50**, **60**, and **80**.

2. Animate the following key poses on the girl: sitting, grabbing some popcorn, eating the popcorn, mouth open for chewing, mouth closed for chewing, a gulp, and rest. Much like the blinks, repeating the mouth open and closed poses makes for instant chewing.

3. Re-time these keyframes for pose-to-pose animation to your liking. Like earlier, start with a single anticipation keyframe for each change. Then, slow motion down by tweening between the transition and key poses.

4. Fill up the space between your key poses with additional frames animated every two frames.

For some secondary action, add some additional popcorn carnage whenever the girl grabs a handful or takes a bite. Here, he's shown realizing his mistake:

The first bite of popcorn

As the popcorn succumbs to a grizzly doom, the girl enjoys her tasty snack. Now, we'll fade to dark, and roll the credits on the theater screen.

End credits

The camera angle cuts to behind them, where the girl keeps eating the popcorn in silhouette, and we hear its macabre slapstick screams. The lights dim in the theater, brighten on the movie screen, and the credits for the short roll by.

We'll use a new layer with the **Multiply** blend mode to darken everything evenly:

1. Create a new scene that harvests a previous scene as a start point. The set dressings are just a single row of chair backs, backs of the characters' heads, and the movie screen.
2. On your popcorn object, add a new layer called `Shadow`, with **Masking** on and a black tint. Draw a shape over the whole character.
3. In frame **10**, set the layer's **Opacity** to `0`, and right-click on opacity to insert a keyframe. Then, in frame **20**, turn **Opacity** to `1`, and insert another keyframe. The popcorn darkens as the movie starts.
4. Repeat this darkening layer on all of your GP objects.
5. Create a text object with *Shift + A* | **Text**. Hit *Tab* to edit the text object and type in credits for your finished animated short.
6. Insert a location keyframe on frame **31**, then on frame **30**, move the text entirely offscreen, and keyframe it again.
7. Keyframe it again on frame **90**, then on frame **91**, move it offscreen, and keyframe it again.

This rapid transition is a quick, lazy way to make objects cut in and out of a scene. Do this for as many end credits as you like, as shown here:

End credits

Now all that's left is to edit your animations together.

Rendering the finished animation

All of the scenes are in place to go through the whole short. There are plenty of places you can simplify the animation even further to cut corners and plenty of places where the animation can be expanded.

Finish your animation by using the Video Sequence Editor techniques discussed in `Chapter 9`, *Animating an Exquisite Corpse in Grease Pencil*. An example of editing these together is in `ch10_animatedshort.blend`, using the edits scene. You'll also want to use the Video Editing workspace. This scene links in the other scenes and edits them together in the Video Sequence Editor. It also uses audio tracks provided in the `Ch10` files, using the `Sounds` folder. Use these or record your own. Finally, render it to a video, and that's a wrap!

Summary

You've successfully completed an entire animated short. We started with storyboards and a simple premise. By organizing our character in layers, we utilized **Grease Pencil** features such as layer masks, modifiers, and layer tints, and we retooled our walk cycle animation on a case-by-case basis. By reusing our animation cleverly, a walk cycle and a few characters takes got us from start to finish. Think about how you might animate a short that has a similar scope to this and bring that project to fruition next.

Questions

1. Think about an animated short you might like to do next. Draw out some storyboards for your idea.
2. What is the purpose of a pencil test?
3. How do onion skins help you to plan out an animation?
4. What are some important considerations when animating a walk cycle?
5. How can multiple parts on separate layers be different colors while still using the same material?

6. Which modifier lets an animation loop on repeat?
7. Which modifier can modify a layer's location for secondary animation?
8. How do layer masks affect decisions when setting up GP layers?
9. What are the three go-to stages of animating a take?
10. What are some ways that a layer's blend mode can be used?

Further reading

We've looked at a combination of Blender's tools and animation principles. If you want to delve further into the art of animation, a classic book on the subject is *The Animator's Survival Kit* by Richard Williams.

11
Creating a Baby Dragon - Part 1: Sculpting

We've made it to the final project in this book. This is a very large project spanning five chapters. We will be going through every step of the character creation process to create a fully realized beastie suitable for a fantasy video game or movie! Our finished creation will look like this:

Our example baby dragon at the end of this five-part project

The content in these five chapters covers real-world techniques that will be useful for creating almost any type of character you can think of! We will be using these techniques to create a baby dragon because dragons have all sorts of details, such as hard surfaces for horns, teeth, claws, and eyeballs, as well as organic forms across the body. Also, dragons are super cool! Some parts of this project will get tough, but we'll start with one of the most fun parts first: sculpting.

In this chapter, we'll unlock the power of Blender's sculpting tools to create a highly detailed sculpture of the baby dragon. This sculpture will serve as a foundation for all of the subsequent chapters. For organic subjects such as characters and creatures, Blender's sculpting functionality allows for rounded shapes, fleshy details, and intricate wrinkles. This pipeline begins with the freedom of high-poly sculpting, using the **dyntopo** feature to create and destroy polygons where we need them. We'll refine the ferocious little scamp down to the muscles, claws, and scales with textural details while pushing your computer to the max.

In this chapter, we will cover the following topics:

- The sculpting UI preset
- Overview of the sculpting brushes
- Creating the starting point of the baby dragon with **Speed Sculpting**
- Adding intermediate details for common organic elements, such as muscles and bony landmarks
- Special techniques for the teeth, eyes, and claws
- Sculpting tricky areas with masking
- Adding fine details with stencils and textures for dragon scales and skin

The sculpting UI preset

Blender includes several preset scenes to choose from under the **File** | **New** menu. Each of these scenes comes with a preset layout of the UI, preset viewport shading options, and preset objects present in the scene. These presets are a tremendously fast way to get started with whichever type of project you're trying to create. Since we are going to be sculpting, we'll use the sculpting preset:

1. Open the **File** menu.
2. Choose **New** | **Sculpting**.

Great! Now we can dive into sculpting. This scene comes with a sphere mesh object in the middle, which is ideal for beginning our sculpture. Instead of the usual **Object Mode**, we have automatically started this project in **Sculpt Mode**. While we are in **Sculpt Mode**, the toolbar has a completely new list of tools called brushes, and the header of 3D Viewport includes a **Tool Settings** section that we can use to modify our brush settings:

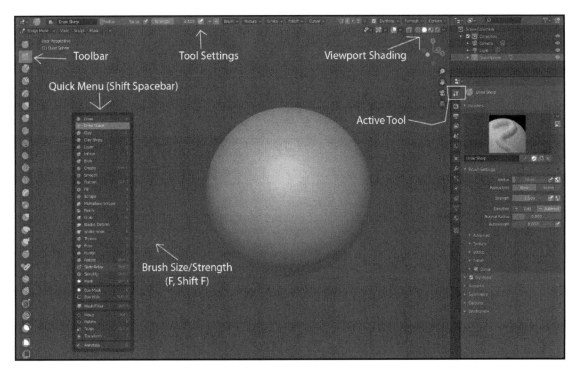

The user interface as it appears in the sculpting preset

The tool settings at the top have options for the **Strength** and **Falloff** of our brush. The menus let us change how our brush behaves, such as adding smooth strokes, textures, or a custom falloff. We can switch between our different brushes by using the toolbar, or by opening the **Quick Menu** with the *Shift + Spacebar* hotkey (as shown in the preceding screenshot).

On the far right of **Tool Settings**, we have an option called **Dyntopo**, which we will use frequently on our baby dragon. We'll learn more about this feature later in this chapter.

This project preset also comes with viewport shading options that are well suited for sculpting. Let's take a look at some of those settings now.

Viewport shading and MatCaps

The 3D Viewport has been set to **Solid** shading with a special type of lighting called a **MatCap**. MatCap stands for "Material Capture." This mode gives us a high-quality preview and does not require the software to compute the lighting in the scene, so more resources can be devoted to high-resolution sculpting. The result is that the viewport looks nice and keeps our computer running fast!

Let's have a look at how we can further customize the **Viewport Shading**:

1. Click on the **Viewport Shading** option to open the pop-over menu (see the preceding screenshot).
2. Click on the little gray sphere inside of the viewport shading pop-over menu.
3. Click any of the multi-colored sphere images to choose a new MatCap.

Some of the MatCaps look nice, like the red clay MatCap. Others are there to help us visualize how lumpy the surface of our sculpture is, such as the horizontal stripes MatCap. You're welcome to choose any MatCap for this project, but for our example, we'll stick with the default gray clay since it looks nice and it's easy to work with.

As long as we have the **Viewport Shading** option open, we can combine the MatCap with other viewport shading options:

1. Click on the button labeled **Random** under the **Color** section.
2. Check the box labeled **Cavity** to enable screen-space contact shadows.

The random colors will assign different color tints for every object in the scene. The **Cavity** option gives us nice highlights and shadows that can make the details of our sculpture visually stand out. It's up to you if you want to use these features or not; they don't change the sculpture, they just make it easier to work with.

Now that our shading is set up, let's have a quick look at the difference between high-polygon models and low-polygon models.

Low poly versus high poly

Up to this point, the modeling projects in the book have used techniques such as box modeling. These techniques produce models with low polygon counts, which we can refer to as **low-poly** models. Low-poly models are typically made up of large polygons, which means we only have enough **resolution** to represent large forms. Low-poly models are often referred to as **low-res** because of their low resolution.

To get small forms and fine details into our models, we need considerably more polygons. Models with a high amount of polygons are called **high-poly** models and have a high resolution for detail. Because of this high resolution, we can refer to these models as **high-res**.

The terms "low-poly" and "low-res" are used interchangeably. "High-poly" and "high-res" are also interchangeable.

Sculpting is a process that requires our mesh to be high resolution. If we only have a few polygons, we won't have enough resolution to do anything interesting. However, if we start with too many polygons, it will be difficult to block out the major forms of our sculpture. To get the best of both worlds, we use a **low-to-high** workflow where we start with just enough polygons to block out the major forms, then add polygons where needed so that we can sculpture the high-frequency details.

Blender has several features for a low-to-high workflow, but for this project we will be sticking with the easiest-to-learn option, called **Dynamic Topology**, which is also known as **Dyntopo**.

Normally, when we use our sculpting brushes, all we're doing is moving around the existing polygons. We aren't creating new polygons, and we aren't adding any resolution to the mesh. In fact, we often run out of resolution by pulling our polygons too far apart from each other, and eventually, we need to add more polygons in order to add more details. That's where **Dyntopo** comes in. The **Dyntopo** feature dynamically creates new polygons wherever we need them in order to support the details we're trying to sculpture.

We will be using the **Dyntopo** feature for most of this project. Go ahead and activate it now:

1. Find the checkbox next to the word **Dyntopo** in **Tool Settings** at the top of the 3D Viewport.
2. Click the checkbox to activate **Dyntopo.**

Up next, we'll try out some of our brushes on the sphere to get a feel for the tools we'll be using to create the baby dragon.

Overview of the sculpting brushes

The best way to learn sculpting is simple: sculpture! Experienced sculptors still make a habit out of doodling, even if it's just 15-minute experiments starting with the preset sculpting scene. Before starting on the dragon, let's have a look at some of the brushes that we'll be using for this project, and we'll just doodle for a bit!

Each brush manipulates the geometry of the mesh in a different way. We will need a combination of several brushes to sculpture properly. All of the sculpting brushes share a few hotkeys while we are in **Sculpt Mode**, which are as follows:

- *F*: Adjusts brush radius
- *Shift + F*: Adjusts brush strength
- Hold *Shift*: Temporarily switches to the **Smooth** brush
- Hold *Ctrl*: Reverse brush direction (add/subtract)

We'll use these hotkeys for all brushes. Let's practice with the **Draw** brush.

The Draw brush

The default **Draw** brush pulls geometry out along a stroke. It's a good way to quickly build up lumpy forms on the model. Let's give it a try:

1. Activate the **Draw** brush from the toolbar.
2. Try drawing a few strokes along the sculpting sphere to pull the geometry outward (left-click and drag).
3. Try reversing your brush direction to pull the geometry inward (*Ctrl* + left-click and drag):

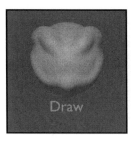

Strokes were added to the sculpting sphere via the **Draw** brush

There, now that's a bumpy sphere! Now let's try adjusting the size of the brush:

1. Press the *f* hotkey to begin adjusting the radius of the brush.
2. Move the mouse inward or outward to increase or decrease the circle that represents the size of the brush.
3. When you've got the size where you like it, left-click to confirm the new radius.

Lastly, we'll adjust the strength of the brush. A strength of **1** means the brush will have 100% influence and make very large changes with each stroke. A strength of **0** means the brush will have 0% influence and make no change at all:

1. Press the *Shift + f* hotkey to begin adjusting the strength of the brush.
2. Move the mouse inward or outward to increase or decrease the brush strength.
3. When you've got the strength where you like it, left-click to confirm the new radius.

 If you're using a drawing tablet with pressure sensitivity (always recommended for 3D sculpting), you can activate the **Strength Pressure** button, which will automatically increase the strength as you press the pen harder onto the tablet.

Now that we know how to use the **Draw** brush, let's learn about the **Smooth**, **Slide Relax**, and **Simplify** brushes to fix some of the lumpiness of our sculpture.

Smooth, Slide Relax, and Simplify brushes

The **Smooth** brush is used to iron out the details and mistakes that we make while using the other brushes. A common technique is to over-draw with a brush, then follow up by smoothing, then repeat: draw-smooth-draw-smooth-draw-smooth, and so on. The **Smooth** brush is such a commonly used brush that there is a special hotkey to access it so that we don't have to activate it from the toolbar over and over again:

1. Keep the **Draw** brush active.
2. Hold down the *Shift* hotkey to temporarily switch to the **Smooth** brush.

3. While the *Shift* key is held down, try drawing over some of the lumps we made previously with the **Draw** brush:

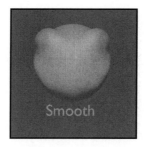

The lumpiness has been smoothed via the **Smooth** brush

The amount of smoothness is dependent on the resolution of our mesh; on a mesh with few polygons the effect will be very strong, but on a mesh with many polygons the effect will be very subtle.

 As we add more polygons and smaller details to our mesh, smoothing will become less and less effective. This is one of the reasons we use a low-to-high workflow, meaning that we block out our major forms first, smooth out the lumpiness, then add more polygons when we're ready to add small details.

Similar to the **Smooth** brush is the **Slide Relax** brush. It uses geometry across your stroke to average out the smoothing. This prevents the over-smoothing that can occur on a low-poly mesh, and the under-smoothing that can occur on a high-poly mesh.

The **Simplify** tool actually does nothing. However, when combined with the **Dyntopo** feature, it can be used to apply a greater or lower resolution to a mesh depending on our **Dyntopo** settings. Use it like a polygon eraser when you want a simpler mesh, or to increase detail without actually deforming the mesh.

Next up, let's learn about the clay brushes.

The Clay and Clay strips brushes

The **Clay** brush functions a lot like the **Draw** brush, but it limits the thickness that can be piled up in a single stroke. It's called **Clay** because it's like adding wet clay a little at a time in real-life sculpting. It's good for filling in concave angles where the **Draw** brush would have a more difficult time, and it's also better for a gentle buildup:

Use the **Clay** brush to build up an even thickness

The **Clay strips** brush is similar, but with more aggressive edges. Many sculptors rely on the **Clay strips** brush to quickly lay down tubes of clay and build up forms. It also gives a great muscle-like texture:

Use the **Clay strips** brush to add strips or tubes of clay

The **Clay strips** brush is a firm favorite among sculptors. Try playing around with these brushes, then we'll have a look at some brushes that let us shove around large sections of our sculpture.

The Snake Hook, Grab, and Elastic Deform brushes

The **Snake Hook** brush pulls a tapering section of our mesh along the stroke. When used aggressively, it's a phenomenal tool to quickly draw out horns and limbs. When used with subtle strokes, it allows minor alterations to geometry placement. Combine it with the **Dyntopo** feature for maximum effect:

The Snake Hook brush makes snake-like shapes, as well as things like horns

The **Grab** tool is very similar, but moves geometry from the start to the finish of your stroke without the tapering effect. Unlike the **Snake Hook** brush, the **Grab** brush doesn't use the **Dyntopo** feature:

The Grab tool pushes around large sections of the mesh

The **Elastic Deform** tool mimics the **Snake Hook** tool in some ways, pulling geometry from the start to the end of a brush stroke. However, it attempts to maintain volume as you use it, stretching the entirety of the form when pulling outward, or bulging a form when pulling inward:

Elastic Deform tries to maintain volume

Using a combination of these brushes will be very useful for making large changes to the form of our sculpture. Next, let's learn how to mask sections of the sculpture so that we only affect specific sections of the model with our brushes.

Mask brushes

The **Mask** brush paints a black mask on our mesh, locking the masked polygons in place. When we try to use our other brushes, the masked polygons will not be affected. Masking out the silhouette of new features (like the nose on a face or the arm socket for an arm), inverting the mask, then extruding the new feature with **Snake Hook** is a fast way to create forms that can then be refined further with other brushes:

The Mask brush prevents the masked polygons from being affected by other brushes

There are also the **Box** and **Lasso** mask brushes that have the same effect, but they let us create masks by dragging a box selection or drawing a lasso respectively:

Box and Lasso are two additional ways to mask our sculpture

Masking becomes very helpful for many parts of our sculpting workflow. You can always clear a mask to get back to normal. Several helpful mask-related hotkeys are as follows:

- *Ctrl + I*: **Invert Mask** (flips the black and white areas of the mask to have the opposite affect)
- *Alt + M*: **Remove Mask** (clears away the mask to get back to normal)
- *Ctrl + Shift* + left mouse button: **Lasso Mask** (a quick way to draw lasso masks without switching tools)
- *B*: **Box Mask** (A quick way to draw box masks without switching tools)
- *Shift + A*: **Mask Expand** (increases the size of the blacked area to enlarge the mask)
- *Ctrl + M*: **Show/Hide Mask** (the mask will stay active, but the black will be invisible so we can see our sculpture clearly)

Next, let's see some fun brushes for creating bulbous shapes.

The Inflate and Blob brushes

The **Inflate** brush functions in a similar way to the **Draw** brush, but it pushes polygons out rather than up. This is useful for bulging muscles. When you have two chunks next to each other, such as an upper and lower lip, the **Inflate** tool can plump them into one another:

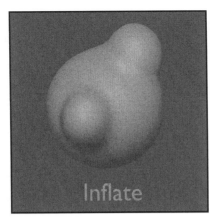

The Inflate brush pushes geometry outward

The **Blob** brush is a very aggressive way to add large blobs to the form of the sculpture and pushes even more outward than the **Inflate** brush:

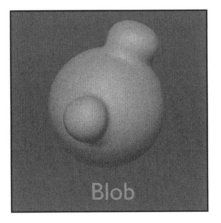

The **Blob** brush adds big old blobs

Next, let's see some brushes for creating crisp edges.

The Crease and Pinch brushes

The **Crease** brush cuts a sharp groove when sculpting or, when reversed with the *Ctrl* key, it adds sharp ridges:

The Crease brush creates sharp grooves

The **Pinch** brush pulls geometry toward the center of the stroke:

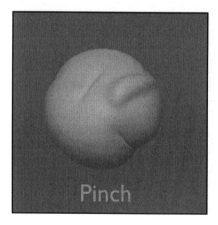

The **Pinch** brush pulls geometry together

Combine these two brushes for wrinkles and seams. First, cut a groove with the **Crease** brush, then second, zip it shut by pinching along the same stroke.

Sometimes we want to scrape away sharp edges instead of creating them, so let's see a couple of brushes for that next.

The Scrape and Flatten brushes

The **Scrape** brush uses your initial click to determine a planar basis, then chisels away to make everything the same flatness. It can be used subtly, or with an aggressive chisel-like setup. For strong chiseling, set it to max strength, then set **Curve** to the final full option. Holding *Ctrl* reverses this, increasing the contrast between two areas of mesh. The entirety of polygons touched by the stroke enter into the averaged stroke, so to obtain a flat polished look, use several brush strokes that don't touch the chiseling border:

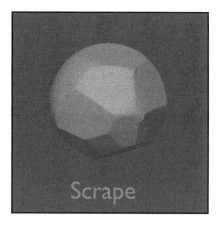

The Scrape brush cleaves off edges

The **Flatten** brush is a less aggressive tool for flattening out the lumpiness of an area:

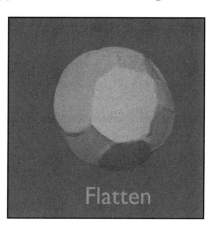

Use the Flatten brush to flatten out lumps

We have a couple more ways to nudge around our sculptures, so let's see those next.

The Nudge and Thumb brushes

The **Nudge** and **Thumb** brushes are close equivalents of the **Snake Hook** and **Grab** brushes. **Nudge** aggressively moves polygons, but won't pull them outward along their normal beyond a certain distance from their origin:

The Nudge brush gives the geometry a nudge without moving outward

The **Thumb** brush's first click sets a plane based on the normals of the polygons under the brush, then moves polygons based on the **X** and **Y** positions of that plane:

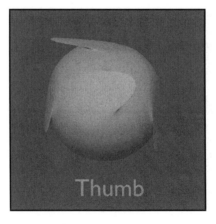

The **Thumb** brush slides geometry along the plane of polygons

Next, let's learn about the **Layer** brush.

The Layer brush

In the **Layer** brush's settings, you can set a **Height** attribute. Once set, when sculpting with this brush, it will never extend beyond that height value, allowing for plateaus of geometry. Setting the height attribute affects its functionality much more than your brush strength:

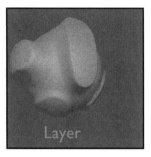

The Layer brush creates layers based on the height setting

Sometimes we want to be able to rotate our geometry, not just shove it around. Next, we'll see some brushes for rotating and posing our sculptures.

The Rotate and IK Pose brushes

The **Rotate** brush spins polygons from the center of the brush. This can limit its functionality, but when used at the end of a long taper, careful use of the **Rotate** brush can make graceful horns or tails. Use **Grab** to pull a chunk of mesh out, then use **Rotate** while clicking on the very end of the taper:

Use the Rotate brush to make curly horn shapes

The **IK Pose** brush dynamically creates temporary bones based on your cursor placement, then uses that to deform the bone with a hinge joint, making it ideal for things like posing or adjusting limbs. The volume of your sculpture helps the **IK Pose** brush simulate a limb, so it works best on areas that are longer than they are wide. The center of your cursor acts like the hand of an arm, while the border of the brush determines the elbow-like hinge. Increasing the **Pose IK Segments** in the tool settings adds segments; for instance, at a value of **2**, the **Pose IK** brush can mimic an arm and forearm, with the edge of the brush acting like a shoulder, the cursor center acting like a hand, and the midpoint interpolating an elbow when you click to sculpture:

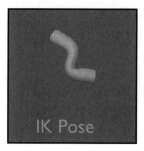

The **IK Pose** brush is useful for posing sculpted characters

Lastly, let's learn about a few utility brushes.

Utility brushes

The **Move**, **Scale**, and **Rotate** sculpture tools function just like these commands do in **Object Mode** or **Edit Mode**, but without leaving **Sculpt Mode**. When a sculpting project is in the later complex stages, basic transforms in **Edit Mode** can face significant slowdowns, and doing so in **Object Mode** will require applying those transforms. In these cases, use the **Move**, **Scale**, and **Rotate** sculpture tools instead, and try combining them with a mask to only affect specific areas on your sculptures.

The **Mesh Filter** tool also provides a global sculpting utility, applying a filter type chosen in the tool settings across the entire mesh. For instance, when the **Mesh Filter** tool is set to **Inflate**, organic sculpts can be made skinny or bulky across the entire form, or in specifically unmasked areas.

Whenever you discover a new brush, take the time to play around on the default sculpting preset to learn its charms. Once you've had a chance to play around with a bunch of these brushes, let's get into creating the basic form of the baby dragon.

Creating the starting point of the baby dragon with speed-sculpting

The process of creating our baby dragon sculpture begins with roughing in the forms and getting all the body parts in their approximate positions. This early stage of a sculpture should allow you to make quick and sweeping changes and new additions. Whole body parts should snake-hook out quickly, and little mind should be paid to their poly cleanliness. Avoid sculpting the intricate details to start, as detailed work will be lost as we make adjustments to the major forms. To comp out the basic form of our dragon, we will look at several approaches, test out big design changes, and work on segments individually. Lastly, we can combine them when we're happy with the design and ready for fine detail. A baby dragon design presents many artistic challenges for us to tackle in our sculpting project. It calls for real-world anatomical references from lizards, chickens, bats, and other critters; it allows cartoonish styling; and it includes textural details such as scales and horns:

Scales and horns

Using the Grease Pencil techniques outlined in `Chapter 8`, *Illustrating an Alien Hero in Grease Pencil*, we've provided some quick concept art for the baby dragon's design. Keep ample reference images handy as well; while sculpting, the occasional glance at condor wings, dragon art, lizards, and dinosaur skeletons can aid you in making sculpting choices. Open up the `ch11_babyDragon_sculpt_start.blend` file and let's get started.

This file has a collection called `Reference`, which has this image loaded as a reference image, the default collection with a sphere ready to sculpture on, and several collections with the prefix `rough`. These collections include initial sculpting attempts using the rough draft techniques outlined in this section. Use them to compare with your own work, or start with them to skip ahead to intermediate and advanced sculpting. If you want your reference directly in your scene, use **Add | Image | Reference**, and import `C11_dragonConcept.PNG` from the `Chapter 11/Textures` folder.

We have several approaches we can use to speed-sculpture our baby dragon. There's no "right" way of creating a sculpture, but some techniques will be better suited for certain areas than others.

Approach 1: Dynamic topology – head, jaw, and horns

For sculpting an organic creature like a dragon, nothing feels as free and fast as Blender's dynamic topology feature: **Dyntopo**. As we learned earlier in this chapter, **Dyntopo** dynamically adds or removes the geometry needed to realize a stroke, letting us forget about polygons. Sometimes the entirety of a sculpting project can go from beginning to end using *only* this feature.

Dyntopo has several parameters that we can set by opening the **Dyntopo** pop-over menu on the right side of **Tool Settings** at the top of the 3D Viewport, as seen here:

The **Dyntopo** pop-over menu

Let's start by using Dyntopo to sculpture just the dragon's head:

1. Start a new Blender default sculpting scene.

2. In the sculpture header, activate **Dyntopo** with *Ctrl + D*. **Dyntopo** changes sculpting so that the polygons in your sculpture are recreated on the fly. In the **Dyntopo** settings, the **Detail Size** determines when new geometry is added or subtracted, and as your sculpture gets more detailed, this number can be lowered.

3. Dyntopo's **Refine Method** should be set to **Subdivide/Collapse**. Refining with **Subdivide** will add extra polygons whenever there's not enough for your sculpture stroke. **Collapse Only** will *remove* polygons if there are too many for your sculpture stroke. This means that you can zoom in and add fine detail, or zoom out and destroy detail. Setting the **Refine Method** to **Collapse Only** with a high **Detail Size** can act like an eraser.

4. Activate **Smooth Shading** in the **Dyntopo** settings to better highlight artifacts that need fixing:

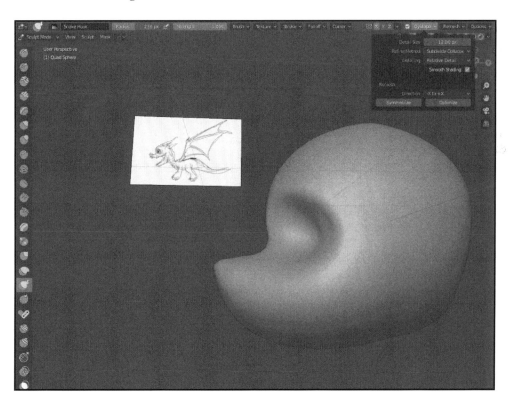

Highlighting artifacts

5. With **Dyntopo** on, use the **Snake Hook** brush to pull out your dragon's snout, and use smaller motions to gently push the eye socket in. Use the **Clay Strips** brush along the lips and nose ridge to build the form up gradually. From a near front view, the **Snake Hook** brush can pull an eye socket hole inward. Do this for the nostril as well, then from a different view, push one part in. Smooth frequently after your strokes with *Shift* + left-click.

6. Once you've got a rough skull shape, click **Symmetrize** and **Optimize** in the **Dyntopo** settings to clean up your mesh. **Symmetrize** fixes mirroring issues. **Optimize** fixes under-the-hood issues in your mesh, making **Dyntopo** sculpting faster and cleaner. Do this whenever you see polygon artifacts that can't be smoothed out.

7. **Dyntopo** subdivides and collapses based on your view. Whenever **Dyntopo** collapses too much geometry, it's time to lower the **Dyntopo** detail size. Over the lifetime of a sculpture, a **Detail Size** of **12 px** at the beginning, **7 px** while refining the form, and **3 px** for details and texture works well.

8. Whenever artifacts appear that can't be sculpted away, increase the **Dyntopo** detail size. At **12** to **15 px**, the detail can then be cleaned with the **Simplify** brush. The Simplify brush doesn't actually sculpture anything, but it will count as a stroke for **Subdivide/Collapse** purposes.

9. Return to **Object Mode**, then add a new sphere for a jaw, and reenter **Sculpt Mode** with **Dyntopo** activated. Sculpting separate chunks of anatomy next to each other is useful in this early stage. The bone structure of the jaw and skull can be modified separately from one another, allowing looser brush strokes. Extend the jaw out with **Snake Hook**, then refine it with **Clay Strips**, **Scrape**, and **Smooth**. Create new separate objects and sculpt them to your liking for additional big chunks, such as horns and the neck. Avoid too much detail at this stage.

10. Use the **Move**, **Scale**, and **Rotate** brushes to roughly position your skull and jaw together, then supplement them with brushes such as **Snake Hook**, **Elastic Deform**, and **Clay Strips**. In **Shading Options**, change the **Solid Mode** color to **Random**. Add other mesh chunks for the horns and neck, and sculpture in relation to the skull.

11. The **Remesh** tool resets a sculpture to a uniform base with good topology. We'll forge our mesh chunks together. In **Object Mode**, select your different chunks and combine them with *Ctrl + J*. Next, switch back to **Sculpt Mode**, and click **Remesh** in the **Remesh** panel. Lowering **Voxel Size** will preserve more details.

12. Since the head and neck base is complete, take a moment to use the **Scale** and **Move** brushes to get accurate scale for your dragon. I measure my reference image and remeshed dragon to fit inside a 2 m default cube, about the size of a baby horse.

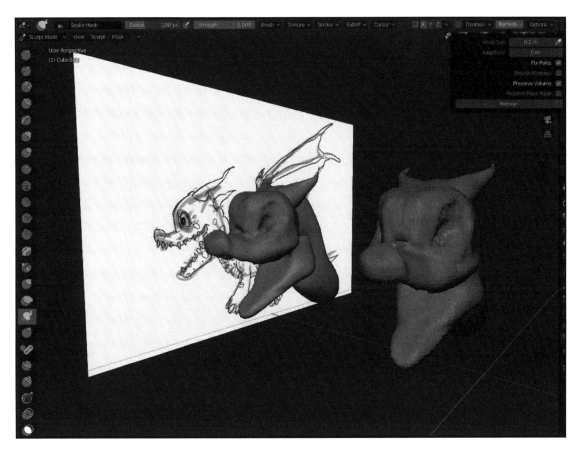

Remeshing the dragon

Dynamic topology could be used to snake-hook out your entire dragon body, followed by the limbs and wings. If that appeals, skip approaches 2 and 3. As more components of the dragon fall into place, you can combine them and remesh.

Approach 2: Skin modifier – wings, arms, and legs

Our dragon's wings are made of long, spindly wing bones, with thin membranes stretched between them. **Dyntopo** sculpting such fragile forms is bound to cause problems. The arms and legs are also arenas that would ideally be blocked out and positioned as easily as a single vertex, *before* we add layers of muscle and scales. The **Skin** modifier can turn a string of edges into a quick skeletal frame. We'll use it to create a flexible setup to block out limbs and adjust their placement:

1. The **Skin** workflow starts with a single vertex that we'll extrude out, effectively **1** edge per bone. Create a cube, then delete all the edges except one.
2. Move the first vertex to around the dragon's shoulder and originating at **0** on the **Y axis**, and move the second vertex out for the first wing bone. **Extrude** out a forearm (e) and four long fingers and a thumb for the wing.
3. Add the following modifiers to the wing object: **Mirror**, **Subdivision Surface**, **Skin**, and another **Subdivision Surface**. When the skin modifier is added, the edges are given a mesh thickness.
4. Turn on **X-Ray** in the 3D Viewport header, so that you can see the individual vertices inside the skin modifier.
5. Select all the vertices, then resize the skin modifier with *Ctrl + A*. Repeat this on individual vertices so that the arm and sternum are thick, and the fingers of the wings taper toward the tips of the wings.
6. Select the first vertex at the shoulder, then in the **Skin** modifier click **Mark Root**. Skin setups can only have one root, and this changes how branches grow out from it.
7. Select the palm-like vertex where the wing splits into fingers, and click **Mark Loose** in the skin modifier, which smoothes the connection. Don't worry about perfect flowing geometry; later, we'll use **Dyntopo** on a collapsed version of this mesh, and skin artifacts can be simplified with a click.
8. Duplicate your root vertex out to the shoulder, and extrude out the front leg with **e**. Repeat for the hind leg as well:

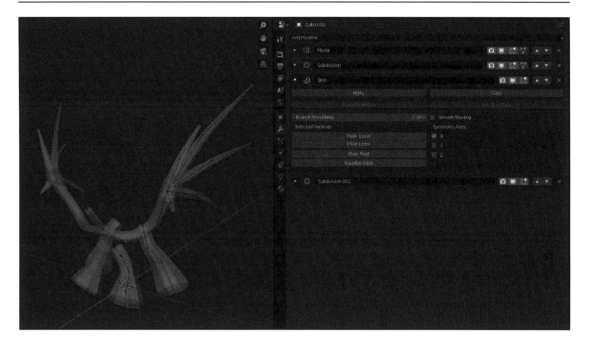

Duplicating root vertex

Whenever a sculpting project has long fingers, tendrils, or tentacles, I consider the **Skin** modifier as a way to get started.

Approach 3: Metaballs – torso and tail

We'll assemble the baby dragon's neck and torso with a goop-like approach that emulates building a sculpture out of wads of clay, via metaballs. **Metaballs** are an object type in Blender that congeal together into a single form, making them great for building up organic forms. By duplicating and scaling a metaball along the chest and down the tail of the baby dragon, we can quickly get an organic baseline. For the body and tail, use the following steps for a metaball workflow:

1. Switch to the side view, then use **Add** | **Metaball** | **Ball**. Move and scale the metaball to the dragon's chest.
2. Duplicate this metaball, and move it further back. The two metaballs congeal together to create a singular metaball mesh. Duplicate a few more along the torso.

3. Try some of the other metaball types. Use **Capsule** metaballs for the tail, scaling them on their local axis to be long and thin. Add an ellipsoid metaball and scale it to be a large, thin disc, then position it under the belly to form a hanging abdomen.

4. Instead of duplicating metaballs, you can tab into **Edit Mode** and instead duplicate individual nodes for one metaball object.

5. In the **Metaball** tab of the **Properties** window, the resolution can be adjusted. If your metaballs lack enough geometry to congeal together, lower the number, and if you want a simpler mesh when this is converted, set it to a higher number.

6. Once you are happy with your dragon's neck, torso, and tail, use **Object | Convert to | Mesh**, or do so later when all the parts are assembled where you like them. Regardless of the metaballs you have selected, a single mesh appears. If there are leftover empty metaballs, they can be deleted:

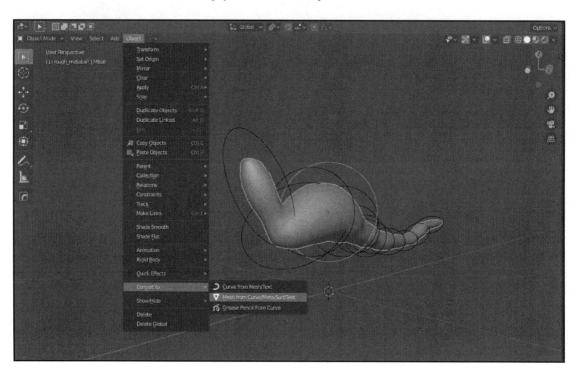

Adding metaballs

Move your converted duplicate to the same collection as your other **Dyntopo** mesh chunks.

Approach 4: Meshes – eyes, teeth, claws, and horns

The baby dragon's eyes show a mix of adorable cuteness and capacity for destruction. The pointy teeth form a cohesive jaw. These intricate structures require a new approach; the spherical eyeballs should *stay* spherical, while the skull and skin deform around them. The teeth stay put, protruding from the jaw, while his slobbering gums puff around the roots of the teeth. By having a set sphere for the eyes, geometry for the teeth, and other separate meshes, we can sculpture around these without worrying about artifacts.

The other rough draft methods can be combined into one mesh and remeshed at this point. The eyes, teeth, claws, and horns, however, will require their own meshes made with the following steps:

1. Create a **UV sphere** with **Add | Mesh | UV Sphere**. Add a mirror modifier, and in **Edit Mode** move all the vertices to the left eye. **Position** and **Scale** them to fit inside the base socket. Later, you can resize it to fit your preferences, then jump back to your head sculpture and reposition the eye sockets.

2. For the eyes, reference images regularly show the nictitating membrane, or secondary eyelid, as present by default. To avoid a messy sculpture, the best solution is another separate object. Create a cube, then position the polygons to squish against the eye mesh in the front corner, and duplicate it for another one in the back corner. Mirror it to the other eye with a mirror modifier. Using the same **Dyntopo** sculpting techniques from the head, sculpt these thin membranes to organically wrap the eye, but make sure they disappear beneath the main eyelid.

3. For the first tooth, create a sphere, scale to an elongated shape, then vertex-snap it and move it to part of the jawline.

4. In **Edit Mode**, select a single vertex for the point of a tooth. Activate falloff (o) and pull this vertex down to create a tooth point. The tooth can also be sculpted with **Dyntopo**.

5. In **Edit Mode**, duplicate all the vertices over to make the next tooth, scaling and adjusting them for individual character. Repeat this all along the dragon's upper and lower jaw. Check a variety of reference materials when placing the teeth: dinosaur skulls, baby alligators, even your own teeth:

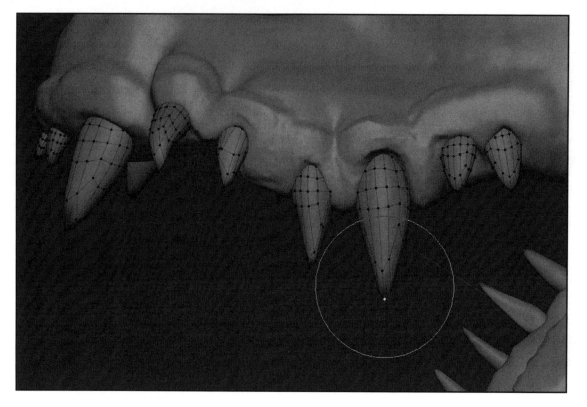

Duplicating all the vertices to make a new tooth

6. Create other single-area meshes for things like the horns, the fingernails, and even the mouth's main biting muscle, which on things like snakes and crocs is heavily exposed, but works best as an overlapped separate ridge. The tongue also works well as a separate mesh, allowing its placement and scale to be adjusted independently.

7. Return to your starting mesh, then in **Sculpt Mode**, sculpt dragon flesh around the teeth and eyes with **Snake Hook**, **Clay Strips**, and your own personal favorites. I also recommend using the **Draw Sharp** and **Crease** brushes along wrinkles, then increase a wrinkle's sharpness by using the **Pinch** brush along the wrinkle afterward.

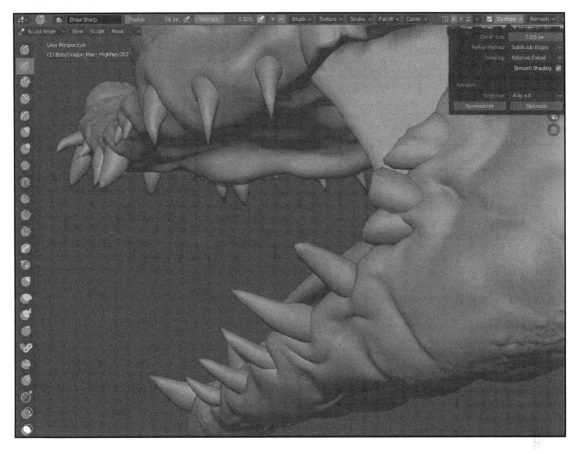

Increasing a wrinkle's sharpness

8. For the wing membranes, we'll use a simple mesh with **Solidify**. Add a **Plane** object, then use vertex-snap to stretch the plane's vertices between the first two wing fingers.

9. Add edge loops and extrusions, until there is enough geometry to fill the whole section of the membrane. Repeat this on the other fingers until the whole membrane is finished.

10. Add the following modifiers: **Mirror**, **Subdivision**, and **Solidify**.

11. On the edge loops corresponding to the wing finger bones, use *Ctrl + E* | **Edge Crease**. This prevents the subdivision surface from affecting the peak points:

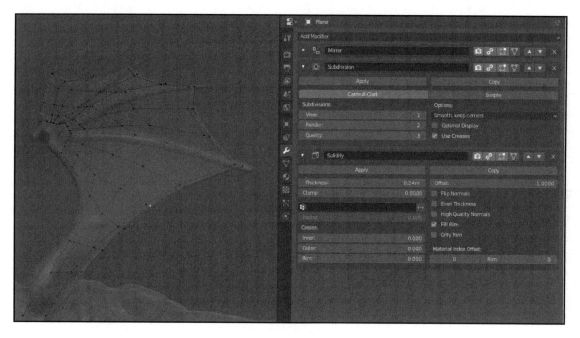

Preventing peak points

The eyes, eye membranes, horns, claws, and teeth can be kept separate so that **Dyntopo** and **Remesh** respect their object intersections. An archived duplicate of your wing is also useful, as its existing polygons can help later during retopology. The rest of the rough draft meshes can be combined and remeshed when you're ready for more complex sculpting.

Brute-force sculpting

Every increase in detail limits your ability to go back and make large changes, so upon completion of the baby dragon's overall form, take one last break to move components around in new directions.

Because of how quickly sculpting lets you try options out, you can explore different head sizes, overall shapes, and creative head modifications before committing. Then, proceed as follows:

1. Select the head, jaw, neck, body, and leg rough draft objects. Combine them all with *Ctrl + J*. Switch to **Sculpt Mode**, and use **Remesh** to merge them into a single mesh with a **Voxel Size** of .05. Adjust this number if the result has too much or too little detail – no more than 200,000 vertices.

2. Duplicate this new mesh, and move it forward in space. Repeat this with *Shift + R*.

3. Use these duplicates with **Dyntopo** to try out some alternative dragon heads, with heavy use of the **Snake Hook** brush. With a variety of references, push the dragon alternates toward various extremes. At times, my dragon looked too much like the baby crocodile reference images, and at other times too much like dragons in other games and media. The best iteration captured the baby cuteness better than the others, with a short snout and big eye sockets, but still had a dangerous-looking, toothy smile.

4. Repeat this process for other areas. In an earlier version, the dragon had longer legs and individual toes. By staying comfortable with this destructive "rough draft" stage, these get sculpted into a simpler, chubbier leg without toes.

5. Use the **IK Pose** brush on things like the limbs, tail, and head to reposition them in a way that mimics bones. On some alternates, I use it to repose the neck and spine for an alternative posture.

6. Move the eyes, toes, teeth, and other meshes back into place. The new head changed where all these secondary meshes need to be located:

Reposition of limbs, tail, and head

At this early stage, sculpting offers a fluid workflow that traditional editing doesn't. Make sure to take advantage of it, and try out new ideas with abandon. You can worry about the polygon counts or edge loops later.

Sculpting intermediate details

Now that our preliminary sculpture is in place, we'll work on intermediate details. These encompass forms including muscles, bony landmarks, major wrinkles, and fat folds. Take a moment to make any final sweeping changes to your baby dragon, such as changing the size of the head or position of the limbs.

Organic forms tend to be made of three main categories: rigid structures such as bones and cartilage, the muscles and flesh attached to them, and surface details such as skin and scales that wrap around the overall form. While sculpting, keep that hierarchy in mind; muscles will deform around unchanging bones, and the skin around the muscles. When sculpting, break the form down into convex versus concave forms, and hard versus soft transitions.

As you gain confidence with how the brushes work, sculpting becomes a stream-of-consciousness activity. Using the **Snake Hook** brush for big adjustments, **Clay strips** for building forms gradually, along with constant smoothing, are the most common tools for these remaining brute-force sculpting moments. With **Dyntopo Collapse**, the **Inflate** tool is also great for eliminating mistakes. For convex areas such as the nasal ridge, build up the form with **Clay strips**. For sharper transitions, the **Crease** tool can cut into concave areas, and when reversed with *Ctrl* can pull out ridges. Repeat your strokes with the **Pinch** brush to pull the ridge inward, and whenever you go overboard, use the **Smooth** brush. There is no single correct approach. Here are some potential workflows for the sculpting tasks involved with our baby dragon.

Chiseling with the Scrape, Pinch, and Smooth brushes

Chiseling has the excellent feel of rigid marble, with chunks coming off in flat slabs. This technique is enjoyable for its ability to make quick changes, and also for its appealing geometric look, especially around the bony ridges seen at the hips and snout, where it comes in handy:

1. Chiseling often requires a ridge first, so that there is something to chisel at. On the snout or other areas, use the **Clay** brush to build up ridges if there's not enough geometry to chisel away at.

2. Switch to the **Scrape** brush. Set the strength to 1, and in **Falloff**, choose **Constant**.

3. In **Brush Settings**, change **Radius Unit** to **Scene**. Now, instead of the brush orienting to the mesh, it will use the view for the entire stroke, creating uniform flatness with the **Scrape** tool.

4. Set **Dyntopo** to between **5** and **8**, with **Refine Method** set to **Subdivide Edges**. Finer detail here will create sharper chisels as well.

5. Use the **Scrape** brush in small strokes, and cut away until you have two areas on opposite sides of the hard angle. Once two neighboring "planes" are established, try to avoid your brush strokes crossing that border.

6. Neighboring areas can be protected with the **Mask** brush. If you're chiseling along the snout, masking out the nearby nostril or eye can let you work more freely.

7. Deactivate **Dyntopo** to protect the chisel seam as you refine it. Switch to the **Pinch** brush, and draw along the chisel seam. Large strokes help straighten the seam as it pulls to a sharp point. Finish with light smoothing:

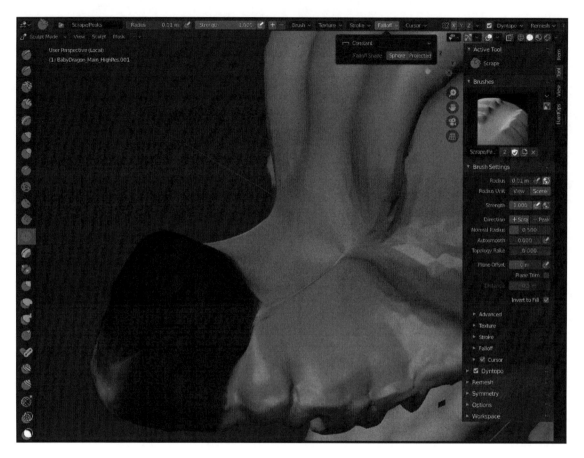

Deactivating Dyntopo

Let's try to understand bulging seams next.

Bulging seams

Whenever two forms push against each other like bulging muscles or bent joints, they create a seam as they begin to bulge against each other. This sculpting challenge happens around the baby dragon's eyebrows, nostrils, and muscles, and is good to emphasize at any sharp joins with the legs and wings where remesh added a sharp joint.

Let's use a combination of brushes to emphasize these features now:

1. Enable **Dyntopo** with *Ctrl + D*, with only **Subdivide** active for **Refine Method**.
2. Use the **Crease** brush along the seam between two bulges, deepening the crevice.
3. Switch to the **Pinch** brush and draw along the seam. The deep crease sharpens closer and closer together.
4. With the **Inflate** brush, set a low strength and large radius, then gently brush along the seam. The left bulge will inflate toward the right bulge, and vice versa. Do this just enough that they intersect.
5. Use the **Smooth** brush along the seam. The previous **Inflate** brush damage goes away:

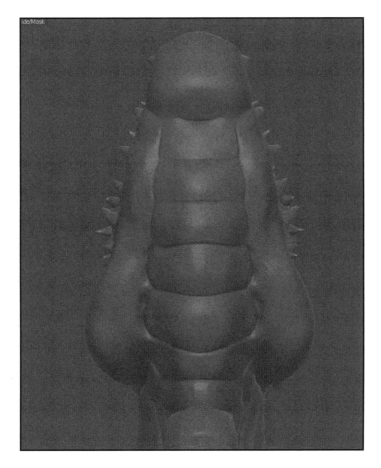

Using the Smooth brush along with the seam and removing Inflate brush damage

When working with multiple bulging seams, you can mask out areas as you finish them, then work loosely on the next section. The banded large scales on the underside of the dragon were all done using the bulging seams technique, then were later masked out to increase the jaw ridge surrounding them.

Overlapping muscles via masking

On areas like the shoulders and flanks, our dragon has sheet muscles that layer one on top of the other. For these challenges, masking out lower muscles means we can sculpture these layered overlaps, then smooth to emulate skin wrapping around them. Use this mask-based workflow when refining muscles on your dragon:

1. Activate **Dyntopo**, with a **Detail Size** of **7px** and **Subdivide Edges** for **Refine Method**.
2. On an area with layered muscles, such as the shoulders for the wing and the front leg, mask out protected areas such as the biceps or collarbone.
3. Use the **Grab** or **Snake Hook** tools to pull geometry over the mask, as if pulling a blanket over it.
4. Clear the mask and smooth any extra artifacts.
5. Masking is also useful for clearing up a cluttered view. While sculpting difficult areas like the inner thighs or the chest near the wings, you can mask the part of the mesh that's blocking your view, then hide those polygons with **Hide/Mask | Hide Mask**.
6. For the hole of the nostril, paint a mask where the hole should be, invert the mask, and sculpture the hole inward. Afterward, inflate around the nostril to plump it closed.
7. When you feel ready to move to fine-detail brushes, use the **Remesh** command, with a low-enough **Voxel Size** to avoid oversimplification. Use the **Remesh** eyedropper on your mesh and it will automatically choose a size relevant to your detail. As shown here:

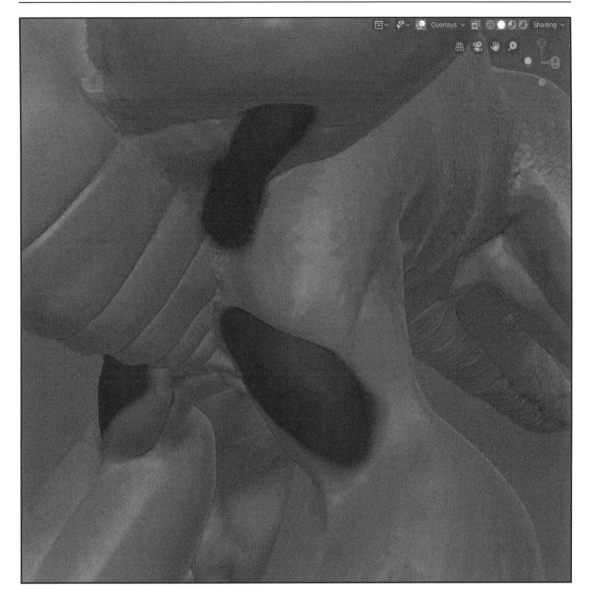

Avoiding oversimplification using Voxel Size

Use masks frequently while sculpting, until it becomes second nature. You'll find many instances when sculpting where masking out a protected area frees up your sculpting workflow for the other brushes.

Sculpting the fine details

The baby dragon's mottled scales and final details are essential when viewed from close up. It's important to polish the dragon's intermediate shape as far as you can before going into details. The polygonal density of these last touches will be so heavy that previous techniques, such as using the **Smooth** brush to de-lump muscles, won't be effective. So far, our example looks like this:

Mottled scales and final details

n this section, we'll look at techniques for these fine detail challenges. Scales, pores, bumps, and wrinkles are so intricate that we'll rely on textures to bring them out in our dragon. There are two main methods to utilize these textures: First, as a stencil, in which the texture details limit where brush strokes create new **Dyntopo** geometry. Second, as a brush tip, which will add textural detail along a stroke.

Stenciling in scales

The intricate patterns found in a dragon's scales would be a nightmare to carve individually. By stenciling, we can easily achieve that detail. Stenciling uses a static image as a mask, allowing fine details. For much of the dragon's back and flanks, a single simple stencil can cover the whole character. Once you're familiar with the stenciling workflow, you'll find both procedural and image textures can work great when adding your final details. Let's get started:

Stencil hotkeys
Right-click: Move the stencil.
Shift + right-click: Scale the stencil.
X or *Y*: During scaling, constrains the scale to the x or y axis.
Ctrl + right-click: Rotate the stencil.

1. Change your **Dyntopo** | **Detail Size** to **3px**. This is where our mesh will explode in poly count. If your computer's good, you might be able to use a lower detail size, but if your computer's not so fast, you might need to limit your sculpting to a higher detail size. From here on out, avoid using *Ctrl* + *Z* for undo; the time it takes to process an undo operation when you're at over 2 million polygons can get so slow, you'd be better off fixing errors by temporarily turning on **Dyntopo Collapse** and using the **Simplify** brush.

2. Select the **Clay** brush, then in the **Texture** menu, click **New** to create a brush texture data block. Name this texture `scales` and change its mapping to **Stencil**.

3. A black square for our stencil appears. Using the stencil hotkeys, adjust the box to cover a close-up chunk of the dragon's back.

4. In the **Brush Texture** properties window, change the type to **Voronoi**, then set the **Voronoi** settings listed in the following screenshot. The result is a scaly procedural texture. Change its size to `.05`, and in the viewport, scale the stencil so that it covers a patch of dragon skin accurately.

5. With the **Dyntopo Detail Size** of **3 px**, the dragon scale details can be added a little at a time. If you don't get the level of detail you wanted, zoom in closer and scale the stencil up as you can see in the following:

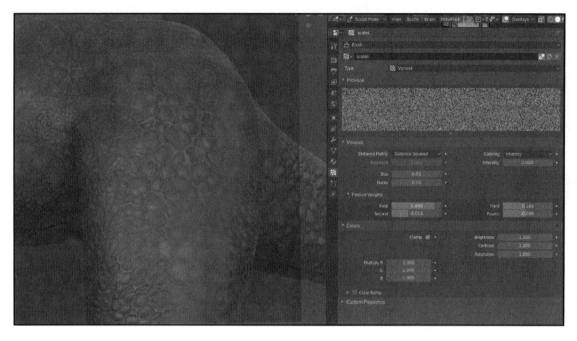

Dragon scale details

6. Next, we'll add occasional large scales, then mask them. For the large scales, scale the stencil way up, then sculpture in two to five scales at a time.

7. As you add large scales, use the **Mask** brush to paint them out. Paint in these larger scales on areas that are on bulges or protrusions, such as the jawline, knee, or spine.

8. The stencil can be scaled on one axis for longer stretched scales. Use *Shift* + right-click, then hit *X* to scale them into long rectangular scales. Paint these along curving areas such as the jawline or tail, so they don't all look round and even.

9. Scale the stencil up, and zoom in close for the smaller scales in between the larger ones. These finer scales gather particularly around joints, wrinkles, and creases.

10. Fine details might lead your mesh into the millions of polygons, and depending on your computer hardware, sculpting can get cumbersome. Avoid using undo, and instead, when you make mistakes, revert back to a higher **Dyntopo** pixel value, then collapse mistakes with the **Simplify** brush.

11. When the scales are in place, their textural qualities can be further emphasized. Switch to the **Fill** brush, then hold *Ctrl* and paint in reverse, deepening the severity of the scales. The scales can also be plumped with the **Inflate** brush for more intense borders, as shown here:

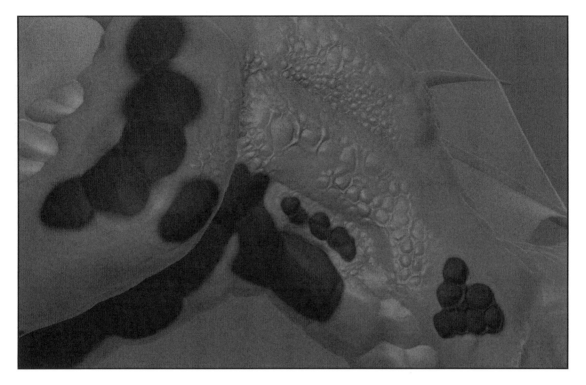

Emphasizing textural quality

The other texture options can create very different looks. Experiment with **Magic**, **Noise**, **Voronoi**, and even image textures you paint by hand as stencils.

Stamping ridges along the wing and spine

The baby dragon's spine repeats the same ridge, tapering from thick to thin from the neck to the tail. Creases repeat along the wing fingers. For fine details along a natural stroke, we'll use stamping. In this mode, the texture is drawn once for each length of the radius, like a stamp. This can add a constant rough sculpture to your brushwork, and also be used to stamp a texture every certain distance, even following the brush stroke orientation. We'll use this to add repeating molting bands along the wing fingers and arms.

Add textures as a repeating brush element with the following steps:

1. Switch to the **Clay** brush. Make sure **Dyntopo** is enabled, with a 2- or 3-px **Detail Size**, and **Subdivide** for its **Refine Method**.
2. In the **Texture** menu, create a new texture, name it Bands, and change the brush's **Texture Mode** to **Area Plane**.
3. In the **Texture** properties panel, change the texture's **Type** to **Marble**, with **Second Basis** set to **Saw**, and a **Size** of .8. We want this band to leave tapering sharp ridges going along the wing.
4. The marble texture is, by default, rotated by 45 degrees. To offset this, in **Texture settings**, change the **Angle** to **45**. Now when you sculpt, the texture is always oriented horizontally.
5. Turn on **Rake**, which will make the texture draw perpendicular to the stroke direction. In the **Stroke** menu, set **Spacing** to 50%, which will only draw a band when it's gone half the length of the texture.
6. Draw these bands along the spindly fingers of the dragon's wings, starting at the tip. With **Rake** turned on, the ridges turn to follow along the stroke. Repeat this on the other side of the wing:

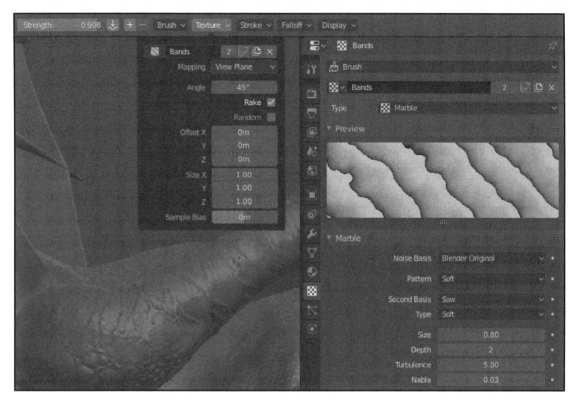

Spindly bands scraped along the dragon's wings

With the right image texture and brush spacing, you could add repeating spines, stripes, or ridges, and add them along your dragon's back with one graceful brush stroke using this technique.

Refining the details

Once your textured detail sculpting is done, the skin detail can be tweaked in ways that adhere to the overall form. Here are some final steps for your baby dragon sculpture:

1. Turn off **Dyntopo**, which will make your sculpting of existing details faster.
2. The texture that created the scales mostly pushed polygons up or down, but organic areas usually bulge, bump into each other, and spill over. Use the **Inflate** brush with a weak strength on areas of scale. The scales grow outward while the Voronoi "grout" swells as well.

3. The **Nudge** brush conforms its target to an averaged normal. In other words, the skin can be pushed and pulled along the dragon, and it will act as if it's wrapping around the muscles beneath it. Use it along muscle divisions, and skin areas that would stretch during movement. On a number of the bigger scales, I pull outward to make them rounder and shapelier. Even a handful of nudges can also disguise a repetitive stencil pattern.

4. There's always one more thing to sculpt. Focus your efforts on the area's viewers will see the most.

And there we have it! We've gone through many stages of our sculpture and learned many interesting ways to add both major forms and details. Our example baby dragon sculpture turned out like this:

Our final baby dragon sculpture complete with scales

Compare your final sculpture with the results in `ch11_babyDragon_sculpt_final.blend`, where the final sculpture is in the collection `BabyDragon_HighRes`. This mesh was remeshed to lower the file size, but you're under no such obligation to do so on your home computer. If slowdowns begin to impact your workflow, limit how much new detail you're adding.

Summary

The baby dragon's sculpted final form ripples with cuteness and ferocity. By starting with rough, destructive sculpting and low-commitment drafting methods, lots of ideas could be explored quickly. We then refined muscles and bones, increasing the amount of detail at every step. Lastly, the final patina of scales, wrinkles, and ridges were added with stencils, brush textures, and polygon counts soaring into the millions.

Unfortunately, the huge poly count limits this sculpture's usefulness. Animation rigs will strain to move, rendering engines will choke on the complex details, and real-time game engines are way out of reach. In the next chapter, we'll fix that by creating a usable mesh with a reasonable poly count, then bake important details from our high-poly sculpture to our medium-poly production mesh.

Questions

1. How do you change the size and strength of your sculpting brush?
2. What mouse hotkey do you use to lasso select a mask?
3. What brush would you use to rapidly pull out and position limb geometry?
4. How can you seamlessly combine **Dyntopo** rough-draft sculpts, meshes created in **Edit Mode**, and metaballs into a single sculpting base?
5. What are some character elements that would work best *not* being combined into a single sculpt mesh?
6. When using **Dyntopo**, what sculpting scenarios would correspond to a detail size of 12px, 7px, and 3px?

7. When using **Dyntopo**, why would you set the **Refine** method to **Collapse Edges**?

8. How do you add a stencil texture, and how do you adjust it in the 3D Viewport?

9. What brush settings are needed to draw repeating elements along a brush stroke?

10. What brushes and settings would you use to adjust fine patterns on a mesh without adding or subtracting geometry, and respecting the overall mesh volume?

Further reading

Pablo Dobarro's work on Blender's sculpting interface has added massive improvements, with new brushes and features pouring out every week. In addition to providing the Blender community with excellent tools, he is also a skilled sculpting artist. Follow his development on `https://code.blender.org/author/pablodp606/`, and on Twitter at `https://twitter.com/pablodp606`.

12
Creating a Baby Dragon - Part 2: Retopology

We have finished sculpting the baby dragon, but there are a handful of things that still need to be done before it's ready for production, and right now this model is not optimized for any of the upcoming steps: texturing, rigging, and animating.

During the sculpting process, we had the luxury of ignoring the technical parts of three-dimensional modeling. We got to use organic and artistic workflows to create the shape of the model without having to get caught up on technical things such as the individual placement of polygons, edge flow, or valence of vertices.

This is a typical workflow when it comes to sculpting, especially while using the **Dynamic Topology** feature as we did in the previous chapter. However, generating polygons dynamically turns the model's **topology** into an uncontrolled mess. Topology is a broad term we use to describe how the vertices, edges, and faces of a model are connected to one another.

So now it's time for the technical side of making the baby dragon model. We have to fix the topology through a process known as **retopology**. Before we start, we will cover some of the basics of topology so that we know what to look for in a finished model. Next, we will cover the basic setup for the retopology workflow in Blender. Once the project is set up, we will use a combination of four methods for retopologizing the baby dragon: the Poly Build tool, manual extrusion plus F2, Shrinkwrap, and Bsurfaces.

The following topics will be covered in this chapter:

- What is topology?
- What are the rules of good topology?
- Setting up Blender for the retopology workflow
- Retopologizing the baby dragon

What is topology?

Topology refers to how the components of a mesh are connected to one another. Topology is not the same thing as shape – it is possible for multiple models to have identical shapes but different topology, as you can see in the following image:

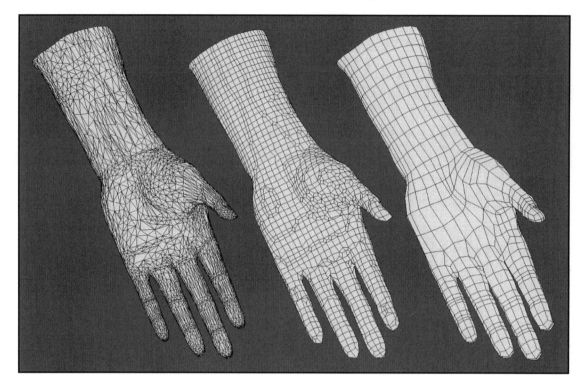

These three hand models have the same shape, but each one has different topology

In the preceding image, the hand model on the left has very messy topology. It's made up of triangles that are randomly scattered around its surface. There are no clear patterns in the arrangement of the topology, so it requires approximately 7,000 polygons to represent the shape of the hand. This is not very efficient, but even worse is the fact that the surface of this model looks jagged. Just like a crumpled piece of paper, it will be nearly impossible for the surface of this model to look smooth again once it's got all of those jagged edges creased into it, which will become especially apparent when trying to animate this model.

The middle hand is better; it uses quadrilaterals that form a grid pattern along the surface. However, the grid pattern is far from perfect, and its edges don't flow through all of the details of the hand's shape. In particular, the ball of the thumb is a mess with random patterns. Even though this model looks cleaner than the first one, it's still far from the most efficient implementation of topology and it still requires approximately 6,000 polygons to represent the shape of the hand. A lot of the "crumpled paper" effect has been solved, but it will still be difficult to animate this version of the hand.

The hand on the right uses much better techniques to control the topology. We can see that the grid patterns flow nicely down the arm, across the palm, around the fingers, and the grid pattern even switches directions in order to flow across the thumb and the fingertips. This is an efficient model, using only about 2,000 polygons to represent the shape of the hand, and it will be much easier to animate this version of the model.

It would be fair to say that the hand models on the left and in the middle both have "bad topology," while the hand model on the right has "good topology." Ideally, all meshes will have good topology before they are used in a final product. Up next, we'll take a look at how we can create good topology.

What are the rules of good topology?

Let's take a closer look at some of the rules of topology that will help you create high-quality, 3D models.

A 3D model isn't a real object, it's just a representation of an object. In order for a model to best represent a given object, the model's topology ought to work in conjunction with the shape of the object. A model with bad topology has polygons that work *against* the shape of the model, which makes it hard to work with in production and can cause lots of problems.

A model with bad topology usually has far more polygons than necessary because the polygons aren't forming efficient patterns. These unneeded polygons don't benefit the end result, and can even lead to shading errors. In the following image, you can see what ought to be a smooth surface (on the left side), but the poorly placed polygons (visible on the right side) are causing it to look rough and make some spots show up dark:

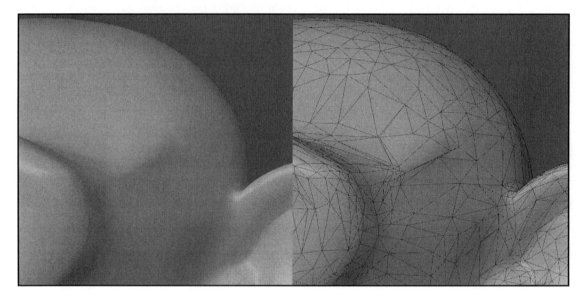

Shading errors caused by bad topology result in a visually rough surface and form a dark spot in the middle of the surface

A model with good topology uses several concepts to optimize the polygons in a way that best represents the shape of the object. This lets the computer draw the model efficiently and gives us a result that is exactly the way we intend it to look. Let's focus on four of these concepts: **polygon density**, **edge loops**, **face loops**, and **poles**. First up is polygon density.

Polygon density

Polygon density refers to the relative size of polygons in a particular area of a mesh. Areas of high detail usually require a higher polygon density than areas of low detail. Examine the polygon density of the character model in the following screenshot:

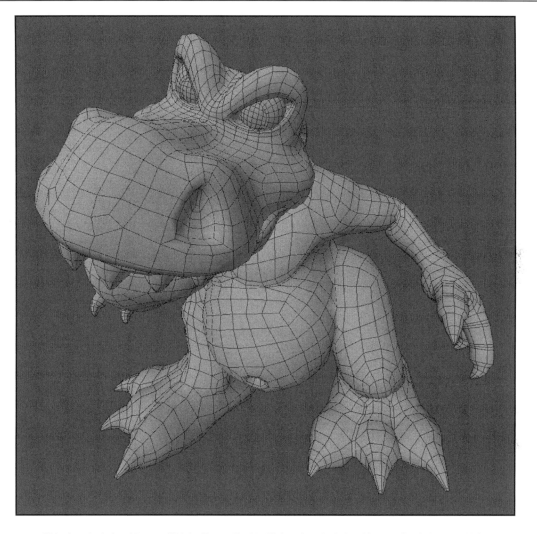

High polygon density is used for areas of high detail (eyes and hands), while low polygon density is used for areas of low detail (snout and belly)

As we can see, the character has a higher polygon density near the eyes, but a lower density on his belly.

Within any given area, polygons should all be approximately the same size as one another so as to avoid shading issues.

Now, let's have a look at edge loops.

Edge loops

Edge loops are one of the most powerful tools we have at our disposal as 3D modelers. An edge loop is a series of connected edges that form the columns and rows of the grid-like patterns in a model's topology. They are useful for many things:

- Controlling the deformation of a character (blinking eyelids, bending elbows, and so on)
- Adding new details to a model (most notably when using the Loop Cut tool)
- Providing good places for sharp edges and seams (more on this in the next chapter)

When used properly, edge loops will flow through the form of the model, creating what is sometimes referred to as **edge flow**. A mesh with good edge flow will help the details of the model stand out, and won't cause shading errors. In the following diagram, you can see two versions of a model; one with bad edge flow (left side), and the other with good edge flow (right side):

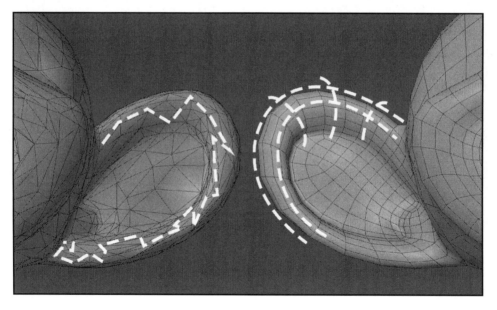

Two versions of a model

The model on the left doesn't use edge loops properly and lacks edge flow. The model on the right uses edge loops to form a grid pattern that flows through the shape of the model. Good edge flow supports the shape of the model, resulting in good topology.

Now, let's have look at a similar concept – face loops.

Face loops

Face loops are almost exactly the same as edge loops, but with one obvious difference: face loops are comprised of connected *faces* instead of edges. A pair of adjacent edge loops can be connected to form a face loop, as you can see in the following diagram:

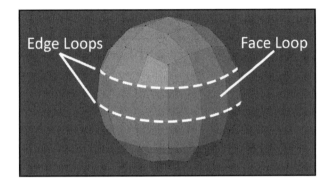

Edge loops are a series of connected edges; face loops are formed between pairs of adjacent edge loops

As we already know, faces are the part of the mesh that the computer uses to draw the final image, so face loops are arguably more important than edge loops. One of the best ways to determine whether your model's topology is good is to highlight the face loops and see whether they flow with the shape of the model. If they don't follow the shape, we may want to make some adjustments and redirect the edge flow.

Speaking of redirecting the edge flow, let's learn how to do that with poles.

Poles

Poles are a special type of vertices defined by the number of edges they are connected to. The number of edges connected to a vertex is called its **valence**. Within a standard grid pattern, all vertices have a valence of **4**. However, some areas of the mesh require a vertex to have a valence of **3**, **5**, or more. In those cases, we call that vertex a pole.

 Its is not very common to hear the term "valence" in 3D modeling; instead, we simply classify a vertex as a pole, or not a pole, which is usually all the information we need.

Poles should be placed sparingly within a mesh to avoid breaking up the grid pattern, but used properly, they can redirect the edge flow of a model so that the edge loops align with detailed areas properly. Poles aren't something you have to constantly worry about; they will naturally start to show up in the topology where they are needed during the retopology process.

Highlighted in the following diagram, you can see that *27* poles are used to redirect the face loops around the contours of the smiley face. The grid pattern still flows through the majority of the mesh because most of the vertices still have a valence of **4**. Using these techniques, face loops are perfectly formed around the eyes and mouth:

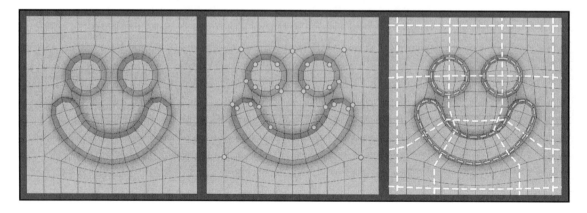

Poles are used to redirect edge flow and support details of this smiley face shape

Without these poles, the mesh would just be a grid, and would be incapable of supporting the smiley face's shape. In the following diagram, you can see what it would look like without the poles:

Two models of a smiley face shape, one without poles (left) and the other with poles (right)

As you can see, the version without the poles is not very effective. Although it has even polygon density and has lots of edge loops, it would still be considered bad topology in this context, since it's working against the shape we are trying to represent.

As mentioned in `Chapter 1`, *Introduction to 3D and the Blender User Interface*, there are several types of polygons and they are classified by the number of sides:

- Three sides make a triangle (often abbreviated to **tri**).
- Four sides make a quadrilateral (often abbreviated to **quad**).
- A polygon with more than four sides is simply referred to as an **n-gon**.

Quads are usually the best choice for creating good topology. Face loops are only formed between adjacent quads. Triangles and n-gons terminate face loops, so they should be avoided. An all-quad mesh allows us to control edge flow through the model most effectively.

Sometimes, triangles are an appropriate choice; we just need to be careful not to place them in the middle of our grid patterns. Some artists avoid them altogether, but they should always be used sparingly so we don't accidentally break our grid patterns and terminate edge loops.

N-gons should be avoided altogether. This is because we can't control them. When you tell a 3D modeling program to create a polygon with more than four sides it has to guess what that surface looks like, and when we are defining a shape we **never** want the computer to be guessing. Some software won't even let you produce n-gons in the first place. Blender only started including support for n-gons a few years ago. They are very useful while we are in the middle of working on a model (for instance, using the knife tool to cut through a polygon could result in n-gons). We can always fix an n-gon afterward, but the general consensus is that they should never be used in the final result of a mesh.

So now we know the most important rules for creating good topology:

- Keep polygon density as even as possible.
- Use edge loops and face loops to support the shape of the model.
- Use poles to redirect the edge flow through the details of the mesh.
- Use quads to form grid patterns.
- Avoid triangles and n-gons whenever possible.

Up next, we will prepare our scene for the retopology workflow so that we can fix the topology of our baby dragon model.

Setting up Blender for the retopology workflow

To fix the topology of the baby dragon, we will go through the process of retopology. **Retopology** (also known as **retopo**, or sometimes just **retop** for short) is the process of building new topology on top of a model that has bad topology. This is almost always necessary after completing a **high-resolution** (thousands or millions of polygons) sculpture.

The process is not particularly complicated: we create new polygons and snap them to the surface of the high-res model. When we're finished, we will have constructed a new version of the model that has good topology at a **low resolution** (a few hundred or a couple of thousand polygons). You can see the results of this process in the following diagram:

The baby dragon before and after the retopology process (left side 1,882,102 tris; right side 23,868 tris)

After we create the low-resolution version of the model, we have a technique for bringing back all of the high-resolution details. This technique is called "baking", which will be covered in Chapter 14, *Baby Dragon – Part 4 – Baking and Painting Textures*. Suffice it to say that the end result will have all the benefits of a low-res model with good topology, while retaining all the detail of the high-res model.

Now, let's start setting up our baby dragon project files so that we can retopologize the dragon.

Downloading the source files

If you followed along with the previous chapter, you can begin this process with your own sculpted dragon. If you would like to use the example dragon from this book, download the ch12_BabyDragon_HighRes.blend file.

The high-resolution baby dragon sculpture contains millions of polygons, so Blender will run extremely slowly if you try to *Tab* in or out of **Edit Mode** (it might even freeze for a moment while it processes the data). Avoid Edit Mode while working in this file.

The demo file has already been prepared for you, but if you're working on your own sculpture, you'll want to clean up the file a little bit before getting started on the retop:

1. Delete all unnecessary work-in-progress pieces.
2. Rename all of the remaining pieces so it's obvious which piece is which (it's helpful to include _HighRes in the name of each piece).
3. Move the pieces so that the dragon stands right on top of the grid:

High-resolution model centered above the grid (the feet should be approximately touching the ground)

4. Apply the transforms to all objects (*Ctrl + A* | **All Transforms**):

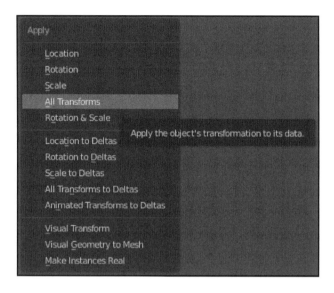

Access the **Apply** menu with the *Ctrl + A* shortcut

Applying transforms will make sure that the dragon stays centered and will eliminate any odd behavior due to the non-uniform scale. Once you've finished these steps, you should be left with a clean Outliner, which will make the rest of the retop process easier. Your Outliner should look similar to this:

The Outliner for the high-res baby dragon

Once you've finished cleaning up the Outliner, save your file. We're done working on this `.blend` file. That might sound a bit odd, but up next we'll see how we can link the data from this file into a fresh scene.

Linking the sculpture to a new scene

Sculpted models often have thousands or millions of vertices, which means the file size on your computer will be quite large (the example baby dragon sculpture is about 140 megabytes, but some sculptures can be over a gigabyte). As you work on projects like this, it's a good idea to save multiple work-in-progress versions in case you make a mistake or the file becomes corrupt.

 Blender doesn't usually have problems with file corruption, but it's always smart to plan ahead and be on the safe side.

The trouble is that saving multiple versions of a file that's this big will fill up your computer's storage extremely fast. So what can we do? Blender supports a way to **Link** data from one file to another. This process will not make a copy of the data; instead, it will be referenced from the original .blend file into the new one. That way, each time we save a copy of our retopology scene, the data from the sculpting scene doesn't have to be duplicated.

Start a new Blender scene, and let's link the data with the following steps:

1. Go to **File | New | General**.
2. Select and delete the default objects (the Cube, Camera, and Light).
3. Go to **File | Link...**.
4. Navigate to the ch09_BabyDragon_HighRes.blend file.
5. Click on the .blend file to look inside it.
6. Click on the Object folder to look through the objects contained in the .blend file.
7. Click and drag over all of the HighRes objects to highlight them.

8. Click the **Link from Library** button:

With all of the _HighRes objects highlighted, click the **Link from Library** button in the top right

This could take a moment to process since the sculpture has so many polygons to load, but when it's done, you'll see all of the objects appear in the Outliner with a little link icon. Rename the collection that contains these linked objects to `BabyDragon_HighRes`:

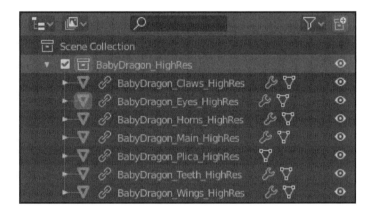

The new BabyDragon_HighRes collection contains all of the linked objects – notice the chain-link icons

Next, we want to make these objects unselectable:

1. Click the **Filter** button in the top right of the Outliner (marked as **1.** in the following screenshot).
2. Enable the **Selectable Restriction Toggle** to activate the **Disable selection** in the viewport column in the Outliner (marked as **2.** in the following screenshot):

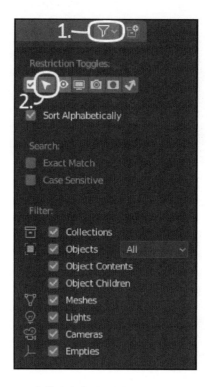

Enable the Outliner Restriction Toggles filter

3. Click the little arrow icon (marked as **3.** in the following screenshot) for the BabyDragon_HighRes collection to disable selectability for the collection:

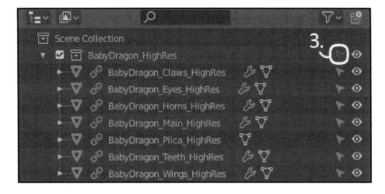

Disabling selectability of the collection

This will prevent us from accidentally clicking on the high-res objects in the Viewport.

Save your file as `ch09_BabyDragon_Retopology.blend`. Notice that this new file doesn't take up more than a megabyte on your computer, even though we can see the high-resolution model in the scene.

 Another benefit to linking the sculpture to a new file is that you can always go back to the original scene and edit the sculpture, and once you save the file, those changes will propagate to the other `.blend` files that have linked data.

Setting up viewport shading

Before we go any further, we should make a quick adjustment to the viewport shading settings. Blender 2.8's viewport is immensely customizable, and some options have better performance than others. Since our high-res model has millions of polygons, we should use a shading option that will keep the software running quickly while we work:

1. Make sure we're set to **Solid** mode.
2. Open the **Viewport Shading** pulldown in the 3D Viewport Header.
3. Change the **Lighting** mode to **MatCap**.
4. Change the **Color** mode to **Object**.

5. Check the box for the **Backface Culling** option:

Use these viewport shading settings

 MatCap stands for **Material Capture**. This mode gives us a high-quality preview and does not require the software to compute lighting in the scene, so it looks nice and runs fast! You can click on the colored sphere to change to a different style of **MatCap**. It's up to you which one you want to use, but some might be easier to work with than others.

Great! Now that we've got our shading set up, let's enable our snapping settings to allow us to snap our new topology onto the surface of the HighRes model.

Setting up the snap settings

The retopology workflow is heavily dependent on snapping to the surface of the high-res mesh, so we have to get our snap settings right:

1. Turn on snapping by clicking the magnet at the top of the viewport.
2. Open the **Snapping** pop-over menu by clicking the icon next to the magnet.
3. Set the type of element to snap to as **Face**.
4. Turn on **Project Individual Elements**.
5. Enable **Rotate**, and **Scale** in the **Affect** section (keep **Move** enabled):

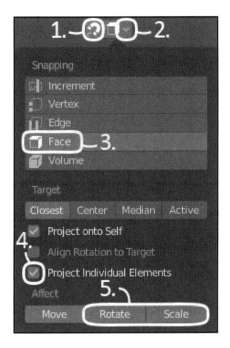

Your snap settings should look like this

Perfect – we've played with some of the snap settings in previous chapters, but these settings are key to the retopology workflow since most of what we'll be doing is snapping vertices to the surface of the sculpted model. Next, we'll create a new mesh object, and we'll snap its vertices to the surface of the sculpture to begin the retop.

Setting up the retopology object

Since we've disabled the selectability of the `BabyDragon_HighRes` collection, we need to create a new collection to store our retopology objects in:

1. Click the **Scene Collection** in the Outliner to make it active.
2. Click the **New Collection** button in the top-right corner of the Outliner.
3. Name the new collection `BabyDragon_Retop`.
4. Click on the `BabyDragon_Retop` collection in the Outliner to make it active.

 Blender will place all newly created objects in the active collection.

Now, let's set up the object that we will use to create the low-res mesh:

1. Make sure the 3D Cursor is at the world origin via the **Snap** pie menu (*Shift* + *S*) | **Cursor to World Origin**.
2. Open the **Add** menu (*Shift* + *A*).
3. Choose **Mesh** | **Plane**.
4. Open the **Object Context Menu** and choose **Shade Smooth**.

This will be our retopology object inside which we will create the low-res mesh. Let's snap the first four vertices to the surface of the baby dragon to make sure everything is working:

1. With the plane selected, *Tab* into Edit Mode.
2. With all four vertices selected, press *G* to grab them.
3. Drag the vertices onto the high-res mesh (any place will do):

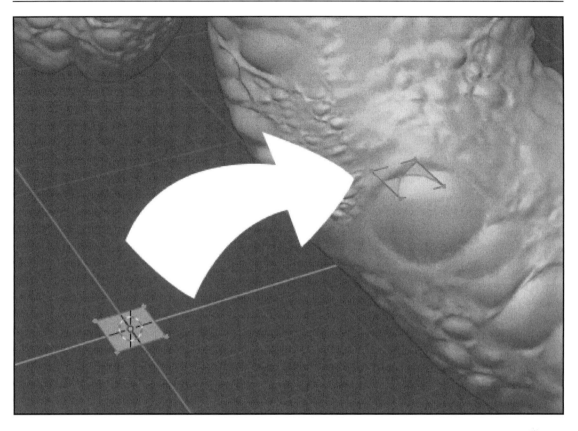

Use the *G* hotkey to drag the vertices onto the high-res mesh

If it worked, the vertices should now be snapped to the surface of the high-res mesh. If it didn't work, make sure your snapping settings are set correctly.

There are a few things we can do to improve the visibility of the retopology object. Let's adjust some settings for the object:

1. Go to the **Object** tab of the **Properties** panel.
2. Rename the plane to `BabyDragon_Main_Retop`.
3. Under the **Viewport Display** options, set the color to a bright green (or any color that stands out).

4. Optionally, you can check the **In Front** box:

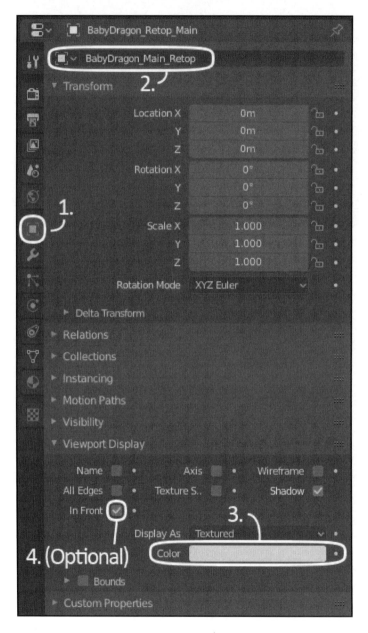

Viewport Display options

The **In Front** option was called **X-Ray** in previous versions of Blender, but it was renamed so that it wouldn't be confused with the viewport shading option of the same name.

In Front forces Blender to always draw this object in front of other objects. This feature can be useful for retopology, but it can also make the viewport confusing to look at, so it's up to you if you want to turn it on.

Without the **In Front** option, the high-resolution mesh will tend to poke through the surface of the low-resolution mesh. This is called **clipping**. Clipping can make it difficult to see what's going on. There are some premium retopology add-ons for Blender that offer a built-in solution to fix this issue, but for the purposes of this book, we assume that you don't have access to those premium add-ons. Instead, we can use the **subdivision-shrinkwrap** method as a work-around, shown here:

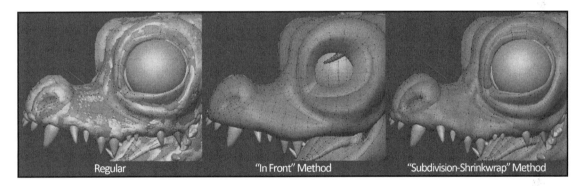

Retopology visualization methods

If you're happy with the regular or **In Front** methods, you can skip ahead to the *Enabling add-ons* section, but if you want to use the more advanced subdivision-shrinkwrap method, then read on, as that's what we'll cover next.

Subdivision-shrinkwrap method (optional)

This method is completely optional. If you're willing to put up with the high-res model poking through the surface of the low-res model, as seen in the **Regular** method, or if the **In Front** method works for you, then you can skip this step. This method can also run a little slowly, so you might want to skip it if you don't have a fancy computer.

The subdivision-shrinkwrap method makes the retopology process easier to visualize than either of the other methods. This method uses the versatility of Blender's modifier stack. With just a couple of settings, we make the polygons always draw on top of the high-res model almost flawlessly.

When using this method, make sure to turn off the **In Front** option.

First, we need to add a **Subdivision Surface** modifier, which will provide more polygons for Blender to project onto the surface of the high-res model. This will be a big help in reducing the areas where the high-res mesh clips through the low-res mesh:

1. Go to the modifier tab of the **Properties** panel.
2. Click **Add Modifier**, and choose **Subdivision Surface** under the **Generate** section.
3. Switch from the **Catmull-Clark** algorithm to the **Simple** algorithm.

Normally, we use the subdivision surface modifier to smooth out a mesh with the *Catmull-Clark algorithm*. But for this retopology workflow, we don't want all that fancy stuff.

Next, we need to set up the **Shrinkwrap** modifier, which will project the low-res mesh onto the surface of the high-res mesh:

1. Click **Add Modifier** again and choose **Shrinkwrap** under the **Deformer** section.
2. Toggle on the **On Cage** setting for the modifier.
3. Set **Target** to `BabyDragon_Main_HighRes`.
4. Set **Offset** to `0.1m`.
5. Make sure **Mode** is set to **Nearest Surface Point**.
6. Set the subsection of **Mode** to **Above Surface**.

If the high-res mesh is still clipping through the low-res mesh, try setting the **Offset** value slightly higher.

Enabling add-ons

There are a lot of fancy plugins that can help with the retopology process, and there are even some premium third-party plugins available online. However, for the purposes of this book, we will only be using tools and add-ons that ship with Blender. There are three that will be very useful, so let's enable them:

1. Go to **Edit** | **Preferences...**.
2. Go to the **Add-ons** tab.
3. Type the letters `F2` into the search box.
4. Check the box to enable the **Mesh: F2** add-on.
5. Search for `LoopTools`.
6. Check the box to enable the **Mesh: LoopTools** add-on.
7. Search for `Bsurfaces GPL Edition`.
8. Check the box to enable the **Mesh: Bsurfaces GPL Edition** add-on.

F2 gives us a powerful way of connecting polygons with the *F* hotkey. The *F* hotkey already gives us some ability to "fill" in areas by adding new faces, but the **F2** add-on takes it to the next level. **Loop Tools** will help us make perfect circles and clean up our edge loops. **Bsurfaces** will give us a powerful set of topology creation tools as an extension of the **Annotations** tool.

Great! Now that we're all set up, we're ready to retopologize.

Retopologizing the baby dragon

Finally, all of our setup is finished and we can start retopologizing. There is a lot of repetition in this process, and many of the steps will be specific to your exact model. So, rather than taking you through every single step, we will be covering five methods of retopology, and offering a guide on how to build your edge flow around different types of details. In the end, it doesn't matter which methods you use, so long as the resulting geometry follows the rules of good topology.

Method 1 – the Poly Build tool

Let's start off with a new tool in Blender 2.8: the **Poly Build** tool.

First, let's move those four vertices up to the baby dragon's face so we can begin the retop:

1. Position your 3D view so that you can see both the nose of the baby dragon and the `BabyDragon_Main_Retop` object (refer to the following screenshot).

2. *Tab* into Edit Mode on the `BabyDragon_Main_Retop` object.

3. Select all four vertices.

4. Press *G* to grab and drag them to the dragon's face:

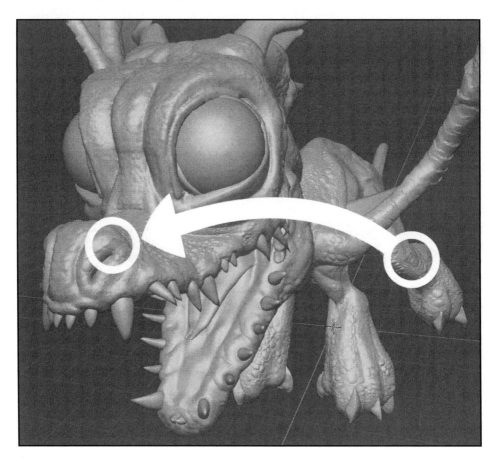

Position your camera to frame the nose and the verts of the retop object

5. Use the **View Selected** option (~ | **View Selected**) to zoom in on the dragon's nose. Select the vertices one at a time, and drag them into position near the nostril, as shown in the following screenshot:

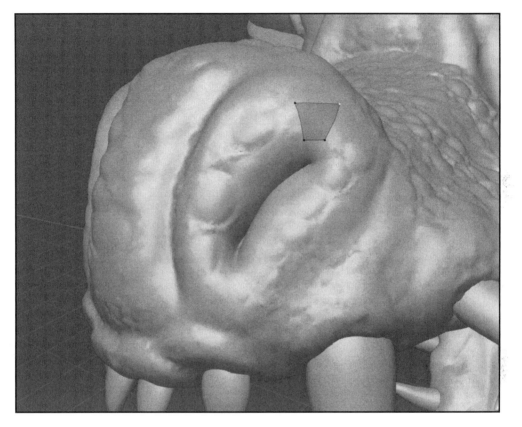

Position the four vertices as shown here

If you can no longer see the green color of the retop object, it might be inside-out. Select all four verts, and then recalculate the normals with the *Shift + N* shortcut.

Now we have our start, the best way to think about how to proceed is to identify the detail we want to capture with the new topology. In this case, it's the nostril (yuck!). Once you've identified the detail, think about what face loops are required to represent that detail.

Using what we learned at the beginning of this chapter, we can imagine that the face loop we need looks like the example in this image:

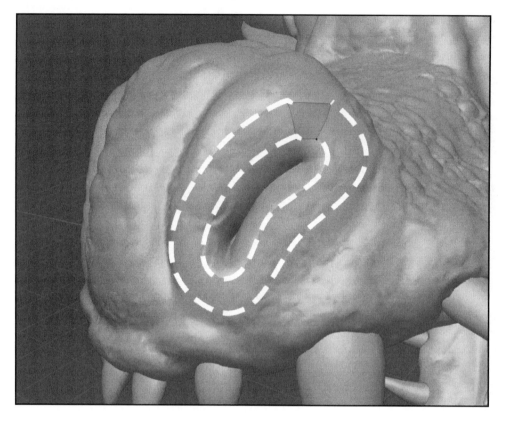

The approximate shape of the face loop we need to make around the nostril

Now that we know what we're trying to do, let's use the **Poly Build** tool to create this face loop. Find the **Poly Build** tool on the Toolbar. It looks like this:

The Poly Build tool

Blender 2.80 and 2.81 each have different default settings for the **Poly Build** tool. This example was created with 2.81, which uses the new **Create quads** option. Additionally, in Blender 2.80, edges will be highlighted in pink, whereas in 2.81, they will be highlighted in blue.

Poly Build is an easy way to get started with retopology. Let's give it a try:

1. Click on the **Poly Build** tool to activate it.
2. Hover over an edge of the quad to highlight it.
3. Hold down *Ctrl* to see a triangle preview (refer to the following screenshot).
4. Click to create the triangle shown in the preview:

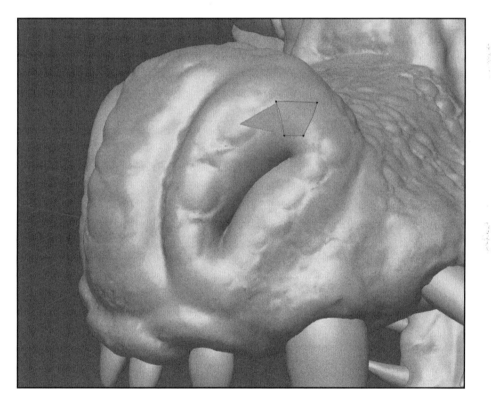

Holding down the *Ctrl* key draws a preview triangle

Excellent! Now expand that triangle into a starting quad by means of the following steps:

1. Make sure the **Poly Build** tool is still active.
2. Hover over the edge of the new triangle to highlight it.
3. Hold down *Ctrl* to see a triangle preview (refer to the following screenshot).
4. Click to create the triangle shown in the preview:

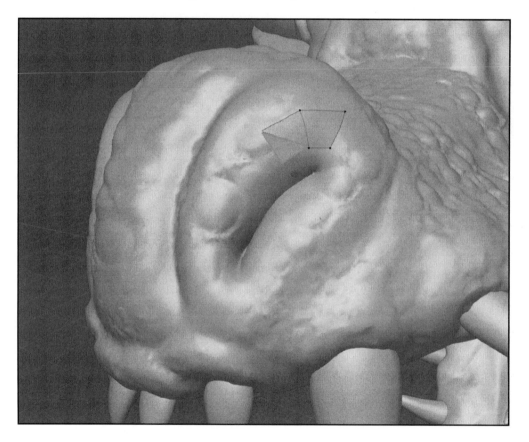

Preview of the second new triangle

Since the **Create quads** option is enabled by default, the two triangles will have merged into a quad. And as we know, quads help us make good topology!

Repeat this process until you've made a loop around the nostril (refer to the following screenshot):

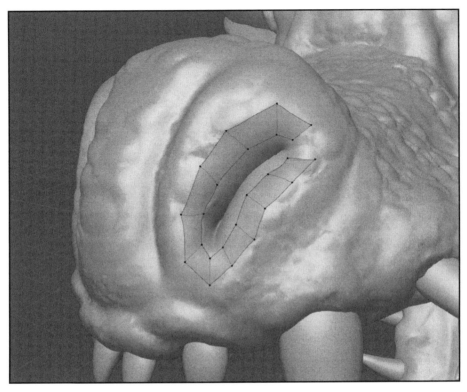

An almost complete face loop around the nostril

 If you need to move the vertices around after the polygons have been created, you can hover over a single vertex and then click and drag to move it into position.

This loop is almost complete – now we just have to bridge the gap. The **Poly Build** tool is still a new addition to Blender and it doesn't support any features for bridging such a gap, so, for now, we need to switch back to the default selection tool:

Standard select tool

If you like using the **Poly Build** tool, you may continue to use it for most of the retopology process, including most of the following steps. But for now, we'll introduce the next method so that you have as many options at your disposal as possible!

Method 2 – Manual extrusion and F2

This method is very similar to using the **Poly Build** tool, but with a bit more flexibility and without the pretty blue highlights:

1. Switch to Edge Select mode by pressing the *2* key on the keyboard.
2. Select the two adjacent edges that have the gap between them (highlighted in the following screenshot).
3. Press the *F* hotkey to **Fill** a new face in the gap:

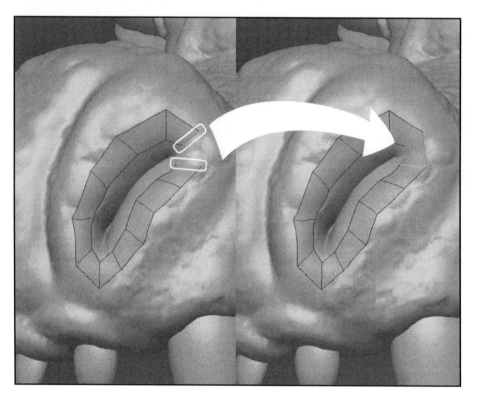

Fill the face between two edges by pressing *F*

So far, so good! Now we need to start building outward from these polygons. First, let's identify the next detail we want to represent with a loop. There is a ridge up and to the left of the piece we've already made and it looks like the perfect place to put an edge loop. Generally, creases and sharp edges ought to have an edge loop flowing through them, so let's make one for that ridge in the nose:

1. Select the edges along the left side of the face loop that we made a moment ago.
2. Press the *E* hotkey to extrude these edges.
3. Move the mouse up and to the left to drag out the new polygons (as seen in the next image):

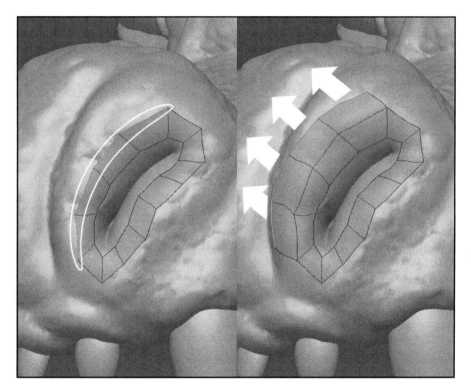

Extrude the polygons on the left side of the nostril

Now that we have some new geometry to work with, let's refine it a bit and nudge it into place:

1. Rotate your view to get a better angle on the ridge of the nose.
2. Switch to vertex select mode by pressing *1* on the keyboard.
3. Select one of the new vertices that came from the extrusion and press *G* to grab.
4. Drag the selected vert toward the ridge of the nose, as shown here:

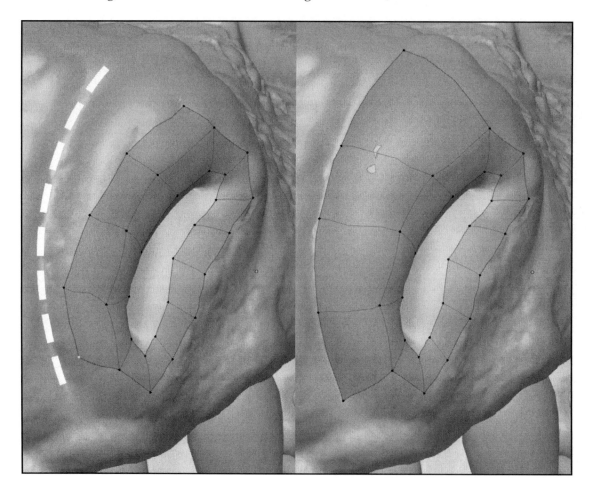

Move the new verts into the highlighted nose ridge

It is important to rotate your camera to an appropriate angle while working your way through this process. This is because the snapping setting we are using uses the camera angle as the direction to project the vertices along, so if you are working at an off-angle, you will get poor results.

This approach probably felt familiar. It's no different than our standard modeling workflow. The difference is that we already have the shape the way we want it, so we can focus on the edge flow to capture the existing details.

The nose topology is starting to take form. Let's now fill in that nostril so it isn't just an open hole:

1. Select the vertices that line the left side of the inner edge loop (circled in the following screenshot).
2. Press *E* to extrude and pull the verts inward to the centermost point of the nostril.
3. Press the *S* hotkey to scale the verts down a little (also seen in the following screenshot):

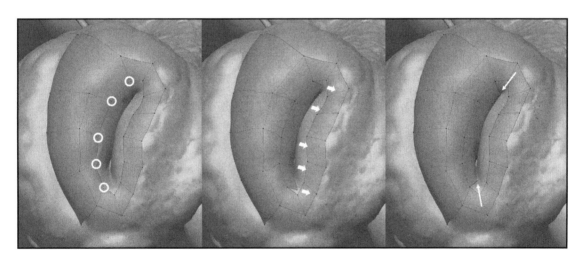

Select, extrude inward, and then scale down the verts to form the innermost edge loop of the nostril

Manual extrusions like this allow for very precise placement of vertices, but we have a gap again. That sounds like a problem we can solve with the *F* hotkey. But let's crank it up a notch and use the power of the F2 add-on:

1. Select the two verts at the top of the gap.
2. Press *F* six times:

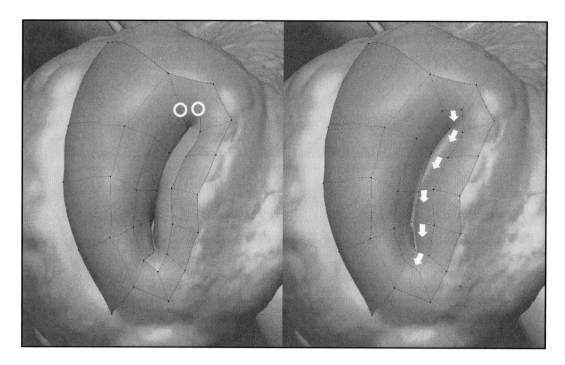

Using the F2 add-on to fill the gap

Wasn't that cool? F2 uses the rules of good topology to flow through grid patterns and helps you fill in faces without having to make lots of selections by hand. It can only do this if you set it up with clean grid patterns though, so make sure you're following the rules of good topology that we learned at the beginning of this chapter.

Practice with these tools. Can you identify more areas that would be good places to put face loops?

Save your work before moving on.

Method 3 – Shrinkwrap

This method is pretty simple and is usually just used as a jumping-off point. You may want to refine the polygon placement afterward.

Earlier in this chapter, we saw one use of the **Shrinkwrap** modifier that helped us visualize our retopology object. But now we're going to take a look at a more traditional use for it. When it comes to retopologizing simple forms of a character, such as the tail on our baby dragon, we can start by box-modeling a basic shape with clean topology, and then shrinkwrap that object to the surface of the high-res model:

1. Make sure your 3D cursor is at the world origin.
2. *Tab* back into **Object Mode**.
3. Add a cylinder (*Shift + A* | **Mesh** | **Cylinder**).
4. Set **Vertices** to 16.
5. Change **Cap Fill Type** to **Nothing**:

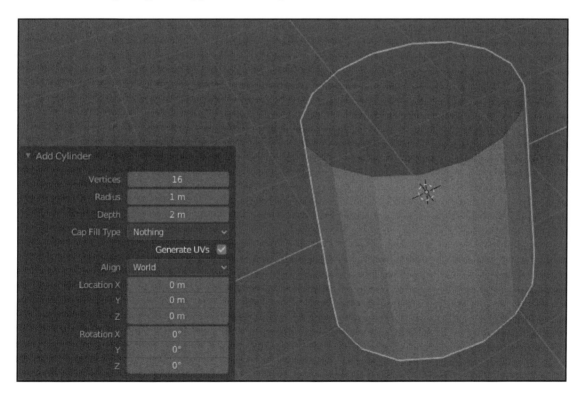

Settings for adding the new cylinder

When making circles in topology, you will get the best results by using vertex counts that are multiples of 4 or 6: **4, 6, 8, 12, 16, 24, 32, 48, 64**, and so on. These will result in good grid patterns.

Good. Now we have our cylinder that we can use to make the tail:

1. Click the magnet at the top of the screen to turn off snapping.
2. *Tab* into Edit Mode on the cylinder and go to a side view (~ | **Right**).
3. With all of the verts selected, press the *R* hotkey and type 90.
4. Press *Enter* to apply the rotation:

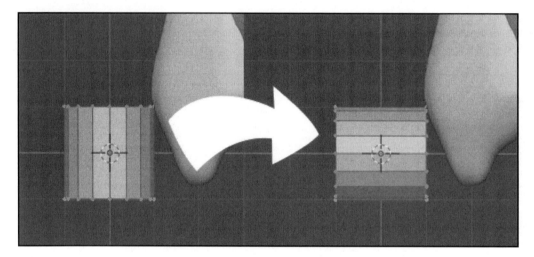

Rotate the cylinder by 90 degrees

5. Zoom out so you can see the baby dragon's tail.
6. Press *G* to grab the verts.
7. Move the cylinder over to the tail.

8. If needed, press the *S* hotkey to scale up the cylinder so it surrounds the tail, as seen in the following screenshot:

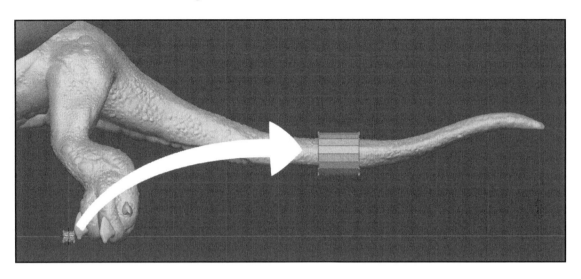

Move (and, if necessary, scale) the cylinder so that it surrounds the tail

Now that we have our first segment in place, we can extrude outward from either end to start forming the tail. It's going to get a little difficult to see, so let's enable X-Ray mode:

1. At the top of the screen, click the **Toggle X-Ray** button.
2. Hold down the *Alt* key and click on one of the vertical edges along the right side of the cylinder to select the whole vertical edge loop.
3. Move your mouse along the tail a short distance.

4. Hold down the *Ctrl* key and click to extrude the selected edge loop to the cursor position (refer to the following screenshot):

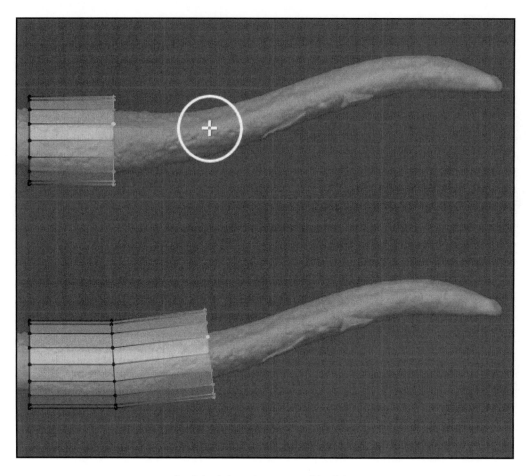

Extrude the edge loop to the cursor to extend the cylinder

Repeat this process until you have enough segments to cover the length of the tail. When you reach the end, select the edge loop on the other side of the cylinder and repeat these steps until you have connected up to the base of the tail as well. When you're finished, you should have something resembling the following screenshot:

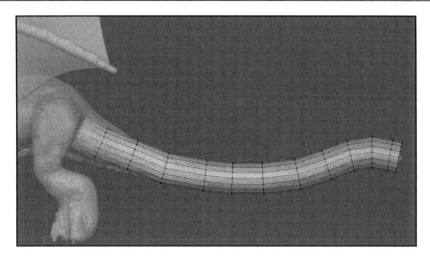

All tail segments in place

Now, we need to taper the tail so that it more appropriately lines up to the high-res model:

1. Keep the edge loop at the base of the tail selected.
2. Turn on the **Proportional Editing** feature at the top of the 3D View.
3. Press the *Alt + S* hotkey to scale the edge loop outward from its own center.
4. Use the scroll wheel on your mouse to increase the area of effect so that more segments of the tail begin to scale along with the selected segment:

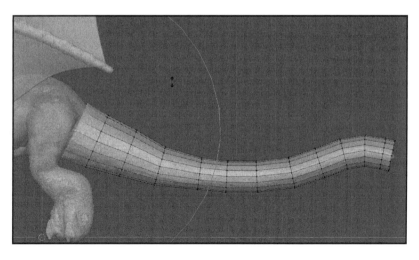

Proportional editing at the base of the tail

5. Do the same thing toward the tip of the tail:

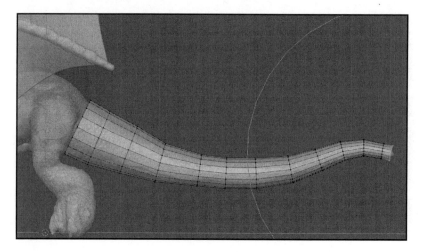

Proportional editing at the tip of the tail

Awesome! One last thing before we add the **Shrinkwrap** modifier – let's put an end cap on the tip of the tail:

1. Make sure you still have the edge loop around the tip of the tail selected:

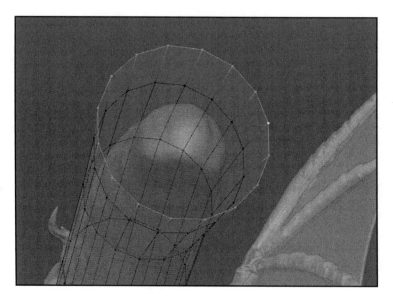

Select the edge loop around the tip of the tail

2. Open the **Face Context** menu (*Ctrl + F*).

3. Choose **Grid Fill**.

4. If needed, adjust the **Offset** so that the grid lines up better:

Grid Fill the tip of the tail

Great! Now that all of our polygons for the tail are in place, we can get ready to add the **Shrinkwrap** modifier:

1. Turn off the **Toggle X-Ray** button and **Proportional Editing**.
2. *Tab* back into **Object Mode**:

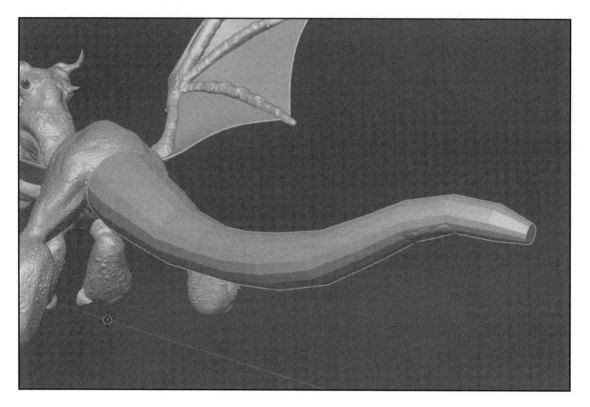

The tail as seen in Object Mode

Now, let's add the modifier:

1. Go to the **Modifiers** tab of the **Properties** panel.
2. Click **Add Modifier** and choose **Shrinkwrap** under the **Deform** section.
3. Set **Target** to BabyDragon_Main_HighRes:

The tail with the **Shrinkwrap** modifier

If you're not happy with the result, you can go back into Edit Mode and move some of the vertices around. When you've got the tail the way you like it, you can merge it with the other retopology object we made earlier:

1. Press **Apply** on the **Shrinkwrap** modifier.
2. Open the **Object Context** menu and choose **Shade Smooth**.
3. Hold *Shift* and click to add `BabyDragon_Main_Retop` to the current selection.
4. Press the *Ctrl + J* hotkey to join the two objects.

By joining the tail to the retopology object, the tail should have acquired all of the settings of the other object. In our case, that means the tail should have turned green:

The tail merged with the retopology object

Save your work and let's move on to Bsurfaces!

Method 4 – Bsurfaces

There are, of course, more advanced methods for retopology that involve a little less manual work than what we've seen so far. Earlier, we enabled the **Bsurfaces** add-on, which will provide us with a really cool way of doing retopology.

It works by letting us draw *annotations* on the surface of our high-res mesh, and when we're ready, it will generate polygons using those annotations. Let's get started:

1. Go into Object Mode.
2. Snap the 3D cursor to the world origin (*Shift + S* | **Cursor to World Origin**).
3. Add a plane (*Shift + A* | **Mesh** | **Plane**).

This will be the object inside which the **Bsurfaces** add-on generates new polygons.

1. Open the sidebar (press the *N* key).
2. Switch to the **Edit** tab.
3. Expand the **Bsurfaces** section.

> If you don't see this section, the add-on might not be enabled. Refer to the *Enabling add-ons* section of this chapter.

4. In the **Mesh of BSurface** section, choose the **Plane** that we just created.
5. Click the **Initialize** button.
6. Check the **In Front** box.
7. Under the **Initial settings** section, set **Cross** to 6 and **Follow** to 2:

Settings for the Bsurfaces add-on

Mesh of BSurface is the object that the generated polygons will be added to. **Initialize** sets up the chosen object and prepares the annotation tool settings for us to use. **In Front** is the same option we've talked about earlier in this chapter that will help us visualize the new polygons. **Cross** and **Follow** are essentially the horizontal and vertical lines of the grid pattern that will be generated.

Alright. Now we're ready to use the add-on, so let's use it to retopologize the eye:

1. You should already be switched over to the **Annotate** tool because you clicked on the **Initialize** button.
2. Zoom in on the eye of the baby dragon.
3. Click and drag to draw two annotations along the surface of the eyelid (as seen in the following screenshot).
4. After drawing both annotations, click the **Add Surface** button:

 Make sure you draw all of the annotation strokes in the same direction as each other. If you draw one stroke from left to right, but another from right to left, then **Bsurfaces** won't be able to generate a proper surface.

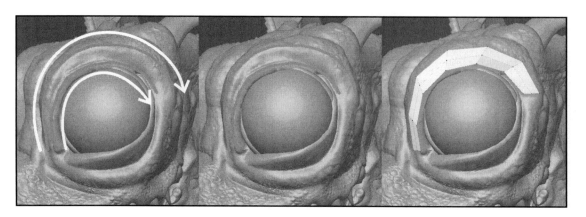

Draw two strokes across the upper eyelid

 If you need to erase annotations, you can hold down the *D* key and then right-click and drag over the annotations you want to erase.

Excellent! Now let's do the same thing for the lower eyelid:

1. Click the **Add Annotation** button to get back to the **Annotate** tool.
2. Click and drag to draw three annotations along the surface of the eyelid (as seen in the following screenshot).
3. After drawing all three annotations, click the **Add Surface** button:

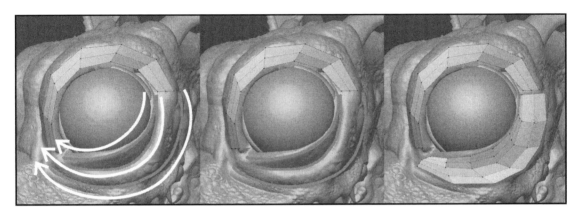

Draw three strokes across the lower eyelid

Wonderful! Now we can merge these polygons back into the retopology object:

1. *Tab* into Object Mode.
2. Switch back to your main selection tool.
3. Select the **Plane** object.
4. Open the **Object Context** menu and choose **Shade Smooth**.
5. Hold *Shift* and click to add `BabyDragon_Main_Retop` to the current selection.

6. Press the *Ctrl* + *J* hotkey to merge the eyelid with the retop object:

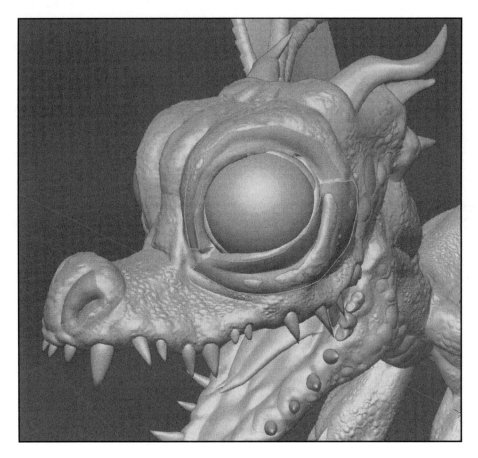

The new eyelid merged with the retop object

Alright! Now we have one more method at our disposal for retopology. Save your work and let's move on.

Method 5 – QuadriFlow remeshing

 This method is exclusive to Blender 2.81 onward. If you're using Blender 2.80, this feature will be missing.

The last method for retopology that we're going to take a look at is an automated approach. This feature is brand new to Blender, so it's far from perfect, but it's a very exciting tool that falls under the **Remesh** category.

QuadriFlow is a lot like retopology, except the computer figures out where the polygons should go for you. Unfortunately, it doesn't have the intelligence to figure out all the complexities and its choices for polygon placement often leave a lot to be desired. However, it is very well suited to remeshing areas such as the horns on our baby dragon, so let's give it a try!

Let's start by making a duplicate of the high-res horns:

1. Re-enable the selectability of the BabyDragon_HighRes collection.
2. Select the BabyDragon_Horns_HighRes object.
3. Press *Shift + D* to duplicate the horns.
4. Press *M* and move them to the BabyDragon_Retop collection.
5. Once again, disable the selectability of the BabyDragon_HighRes collection.

Now we have a local copy of the horns that are no longer linked to the high-res sculpture file:

1. Rename the horns to BabyDragon_Horns_Retop.
2. Go to the **Object Data** tab in the **Properties** panel.
3. Expand the **Remesh** section.
4. Change **Mode** to **Quad**.

 Remeshing is an intense process for the computer, and it's a somewhat experimental feature. Save your work before remeshing a model in case Blender crashes.

5. Uncheck **Use Paint Symmetry**.
6. Set **Number of Faces** to 1500.
7. Click the **QuadriFlow Remesh** button.

You should see a progress bar at the bottom of the screen. Be aware that this process could take a little while. When it's done, you'll have a brand-new, all-quad mesh!

Unlike the previous pieces, it's okay to leave the horns as a separate object.

It's far from perfect, but this might be a good start for retopologizing several parts of your sculpted character.

Finishing up

Now that we've learned these methods of retopology, we can finish retopologizing our model. Use a combination of the techniques we've learned to finish the job. Our example turned out like this:

The finished baby dragon retop

Sometimes, it's helpful to see the important face loops highlighted in bright colors to show off the patterns and topology structure. You can see an example of this on our baby dragon model in the following screenshot. If it helps, you can use it as a guide for where to place your face loops:

Highlighted face loops on the retopologized mesh

There's plenty left to do, so if you would like to move onto the next chapter before finishing this retop, you can download the finished retop model from the next chapter's source files.

Congratulations on making it through this section! It may not have been as fun as our sculpting session, but it's a necessary part of the 3D modeling production pipeline. Who knows – maybe you really enjoyed retopologizing your sculpt. It can be a bit like working out a jigsaw puzzle; tedious, perhaps, but a fun challenge and rewarding in the end.

Summary

So now you know the difference between good and bad topology. We know that good topology supports the shape of our models and lets us use fewer polygons to achieve the same shape. We also learned that bad topology is a scattered mess that can be hard to work with and can cause shading errors. This new topology for our baby dragon will help us tremendously in the remaining chapters of this project.

You've learned some techniques for controlling edge flow, including polygon density, edge loops, face loops, and poles. You've learned how to set up a Blender scene in preparation for retopologizing. You've also learned five methods of working your way through the retopology process, including the **Poly Build** tool for quick and easy polygon creation, the F2 add-on for quickly bridging our extrusions together, and the **Shrinkwrap** modifier for shrinking the pre-existing topology onto the surface of our retopologized model. The other methods we looked at were the use of Bsurfaces for drawing the edge flow we want and to generate polygons to follow that edge flow, and QuadriFlow remeshing for a more automatic approach.

Now, our baby dragon sculpture is ready for the next part of production: UV unwrapping. Hang in there – we're almost back to the fun part, but UV unwrapping is a necessary step before we can add materials and textures to color the dragon.

Questions

1. What is edge flow?
2. Why do we prefer to use quads instead of triangles and n-gons?
3. What's the difference between retopologizing and remeshing?
4. How do you decide where to place a face loop?
5. What were the five retopology methods we covered in this chapter?
6. How do we use poles in topology?
7. What's the difference between an edge loop and a face loop?
8. What's more important to the end result; edge loops or face loops?
9. How do triangles and n-gons interact with face loops?
10. What are some of the problems that can be caused by bad topology?

Further reading

Topology is a vast subject that could fill a book all on its own, but if you would like to research topology further, here is a list of terms that you can investigate on your own:

- *Topology*
- *Polygon density*
- *High-poly*
- *Low-poly*
- *Edge flow*
- *Edge loop*
- *Edge ring*
- *Perimeter loop*
- *Detail loop*
- *Holding edge*
- *Face loop*
- *Pole*
- *Junction*
- *Spiral*
- *Diamond quad*
- *End cap*
- *Star pole*
- *High-valence pole*
- *Triangulate*
- *Quadrangulate*
- *Concave face*
- *Non-planar face*
- *Non-manifold geometry*
- *Non-contiguous parts*
- *Valence*

13
Creating a Baby Dragon - Part 3: UV Unwrapping

Now, the hardest part of creating the baby dragon is over, but we have another small step to take care of before we can paint textures—unwrapping the model to create UVs. Creating UVs won't take anywhere near as long as retopology (thank goodness!), but this is still a very technical and important part of the process.

Ultimately, our goal is to make our model look fantastic and we can't do that without colors, materials, and textures. UVs will give us a sort of canvas to paint our textures onto. In this chapter, we will make UVs for our baby dragon so that it will be ready for texture painting in the following chapter.

The following topics will be covered in this chapter:

- What are UVs?
- Setting up Blender for the UV unwrapping workflow
- Marking seams and UV unwrapping
- Laying out the baby dragon's UVs

What are UVs?

A common misconception is that **UV** stands for ultraviolet. But, in the context of 3D, UV actually doesn't stand for anything. As we learned earlier in this book, we use the *X*, *Y*, and *Z* coordinates to describe where a model is in three-dimensional space, but we also have a *U* and a *V* coordinate to represent a model in two-dimensional space.

Why do we need to represent a model in two-dimensional space, you ask? Because that is how three-dimensional software attaches textures to a model. The two extra coordinates, *U* and *V*, are used to locate areas of a two-dimensional texture and map them onto a model's three-dimensional coordinates. However, before we can map a texture, we have to **unwrap** the model to create UVs.

A fun way to visualize this is with holiday candies:

This snowman candy can be unwrapped to see the texture

Pretty cool, right? Who knew you could eat candy and learn at the same time. Unwrapping a 3D model is a little more complicated than unwrapping a piece of candy, but it has the same basic idea.

When we unwrap something more complicated than the previous example, we run into a problem—3D objects don't want to be flat; they want to be 3D. When we try to force a 3D object into a 2D space, we end up with **distortion**. Let's take a look at this cube made from paper as an example:

A paper cube next to its crushed cube counterpart

On the left, in the preceding photo, is a three-dimensional cube. On the right side of the photo is that the same cube crushed flat into two dimensions. Technically, the crushed cube could count as a two-dimensional representation of its former three-dimensional self. However, this representation has too much distortion to be useful in any way—each side of the cube is not equally represented within the two-dimensional space. The underside is completely covered by all the other crushed parts that overlap it, and what used to be six clearly defined squares are now mashed-up nightmares.

In order to alleviate this distortion and get a better two-dimensional representation of the model, we have to cut some of the edges so that the mesh can be laid out flat. Let's use the paper cube as an example again:

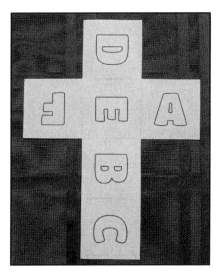

The paper cube cut and laid out flat

That's a much better result than the previous, crushed cube. If you've ever made paper dice before, the shape in the preceding photo may look familiar. The pattern in the preceding photo needs to be drawn onto a piece of paper, cut out, folded, and taped together to make the paper cube. UVs for a 3D model work in the same way, but in reverse—we start with the model (in this case, a cube), we figure out which edges to cut, we cut them, and then we can unfold the cube. Once we have our UVs, we can paint textures onto the flat version of the model. You can see what unwrapping a 3D cube looks like in this image:

Unfolding the 3D cube

In Blender, the edges that need to be cut are called **seams.** We will learn how to mark the seams of a mesh in an upcoming section of this chapter. A good set of UVs finds a balance between the number of seams and the amount of distortion; too much distortion and all of our textures will come out warped when we paint them, too many seams and our model will be cut up into tiny pieces instead of being a clean 2D representation of our 3D object.

 When working on 3D characters, the UVs end up looking a lot like a bearskin rug, so some 3D Artists call this process "pelting," although it is much more common to hear it simply called "UVing", "UV mapping", or "UV unwrapping."

Now that we understand what UVs are, let's set up Blender for the UV unwrapping workflow.

Setting up Blender for the UV unwrapping workflow

As with any workflow in Blender, it's easiest if we adjust the user interface to fit our needs. UV unwrapping requires us to have a 3D Viewport and a UV Editor open at the same time, so let's learn how to easily set that up.

Downloading the source files

If you're working from your own retopologized mesh, then open the scene with your low-res mesh.

If you would like to work from our example model, download the `ch13_BabyDragon_LowRes.blend` file.

Open the file and let's get started!

Setting up the interface

Blender 2.8 now comes with an easy-to-use feature called **workspaces**, which provide a quick way to rearrange the user interface to the needs of our current workflow. Workspaces show up as little tabs at the top of the screen. So far, most of our projects have used the **Layout** workspace. To create UVs, we need to switch over to the **UV Editing** workspace after selecting the model:

1. Select all of the baby dragon objects:
   - `BabyDragon_Main`
   - `BabyDragon_Claws`
   - `BabyDragon_Eye_L`
   - `BabyDragon_Eye_R`
   - `BabyDragon_Horns`
   - `BabyDragon_Plica`
   - `BabyDragon_Teeth`
2. *Tab* to **Edit Mode**.
3. Select all of the geometry by pressing the *A* hotkey.

4. Click on the **UV Editing** workspace:

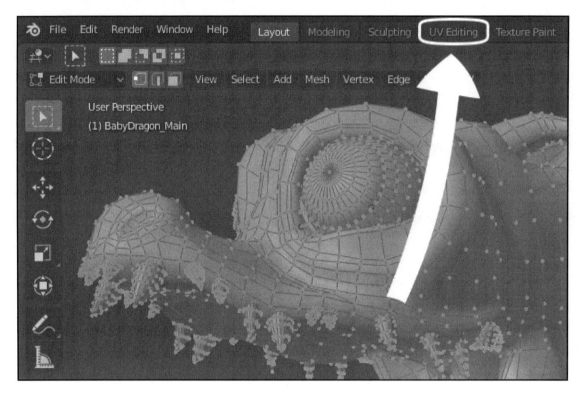

The tab for switching over to the UV Editing workspace

You should now have two views open—a 3D Viewport on the right side and a UV Editor on the left side. The UV Editor is where the UVs will be displayed. If you need to, you can use the **View Selected** (~ | **View Selected**) option in the 3D Viewport to frame the baby dragon in the new viewport.

On the left side, you should see one of two things—first, you might see a bunch of junk that looks like this:

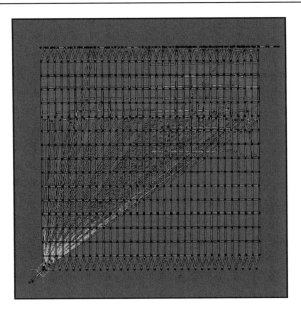

Junk in the UV Editor

Alternatively, you might see a blank white area with four dots on the corners (you may also see a diagonal line running through the middle):

Reset UVs in the UV Editor

Whichever one of those layouts you have in your **UV Editor**, that is the 2D representation of your baby dragon—or as we say in 3D modeling terms: the baby dragon's UVs.

Neither one of these is going to offer a good result when we get to the texture painting stage, so we're going to make a brand-new unwrap and all of those junk UVs will be cleared away.

Setting up the preview checker pattern

Before we start making our UVs, we should set up a new preview material that will help us visualize the UVs with a checker pattern:

1. Change the **Viewport Shading** mode to **Material Preview**.
2. Go to the **Materials** tab of the **Properties** panel.
3. Add a new material by clicking the **New** button.
4. Rename the new material `Checker Test`.
5. Scroll down to the **Surface** section of the material.
6. Click the dot next to **Base Color** to add an input node.
7. Choose **Checker Texture** under the **Texture** section.
8. Click the dot next to **Vector** to add an input node.
9. Choose **UV** under the **Texture Coordinate** section.
10. Underneath **Color1** and **Color2**, set **Scale** to `100`.

 If you're using Blender 2.80, the **Material Preview** shading mode is called **Look Dev**, while in 2.81, it is called **Material Preview**.

Excellent! Now, we can see a checker pattern on our baby dragon. This pattern will help us see the distortion of the UVs, so let's make sure we apply it to all of our baby dragon objects:

1. *Tab* to **Object Mode**.
2. Select all of the baby dragon objects.
3. Select the `BabyDragon_Main` object last so that it is the active object (outlined in a yellowish orange instead of a reddish orange like the other objects).

4. With your mouse in the 3D Viewport, press the *Ctrl + L* hotkey to bring up the **Make Links** menu.
5. Choose **Materials**.

Now, all of the baby dragon objects should have the `Checker Test` material applied. Now, we're ready to mark seams!

Marking the seams and UV unwrapping

As we saw earlier, your model might have started with junk UVs from the retopology phase. When we're done marking the seams, all of these temporary UVs will be replaced with new, better UVs. The edge marking process is easiest in **Edge mode**:

1. Select the `BabyDragon_Main` object.
2. *Tab* into **Edit Mode**.
3. Press 2 on the home row to go to **Edge Select** mode.

Now, we need to determine which edges to cut. This can be a little bit difficult to do if you're new to the process, but over time, it will become intuitive. Because we did such a good job in our retopology phase, we now have lots of edge loops to work with on our baby dragon model. These edge loops will help us figure out where to mark seams.

Marking the first seams

The finished UVs of a character are not likely to be in one solid piece as was the case with the cube in the previous example. Instead, we will end up with lots of separate chunks of the model, called **UV islands**. Each of these islands is used to separate areas of high complexity into sections with minimal distortion. Since our character's head is the most complex area, let's start by marking a seam around the neck to separate it (don't worry, it won't hurt the dragon):

1. Select an edge loop all the way around the dragon's neck (refer to the following screenshot).
2. Press the *Ctrl + E* hotkey to bring up the **Edge Context** menu.

3. Choose **Mark Seam**:

Hold *Alt* before clicking on an edge to select the whole edge loop; edge loops make marking seams easy!

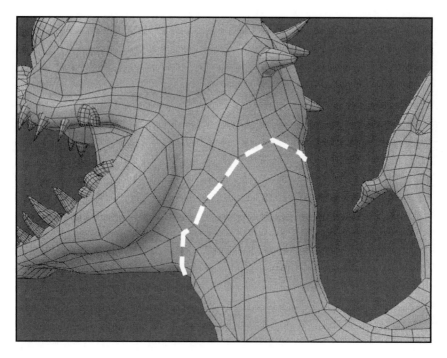

Mark the seam on the neck at the base of the head

Marking seams is just that easy. Edges with marked seams will show up red in the viewport. Now, let's see what our UVs look like when we try to unwrap them:

1. Press the *A* hotkey to select the entire model.
2. Open the **UV** menu by pressing the *U* hotkey.
3. Choose the **Unwrap** option.

There you have it—your UVs are started. However, we have a long way to go. There is distortion-galore happening with these UVs. It's hard to tell what's going on just by looking at the UVs in the UV Editor, but have a look at the checker pattern on the baby dragon in the 3D Viewport:

The distorted checker pattern

As you can see, the checker pattern is really distorted. The edge we marked alleviated the distortion around the neck, but as a whole, these UVs aren't much better than the crushed cube example we gave at the start of this chapter. We need more seams to alleviate the distortion across the whole character.

Before we mark any more seams, let's turn on the **Live Unwrap** feature so that our UVs will continuously unwrap when new seams are cut into the geometry:

1. Hover your mouse over the 3D Viewport.
2. Press the *U* hotkey to bring up the **UV** menu.
3. Check the **Live Unwrap** option box.

We also have an option to always display our UVs in the UV window, as long as we are in **Edit Mode**, even when the components of the mesh aren't selected. In the top-left corner of the UV Editor, click the **UV Sync Selection** button.

Excellent—now, let's mark our next seam. This time, let's mark the edge loop around the base of the tail:

1. Select an edge loop all the way around the base of the tail (refer to the following screenshot).
2. Press the *Ctrl + E* hotkey to bring up the **Edge context** menu.
3. Choose **Mark Seam**:

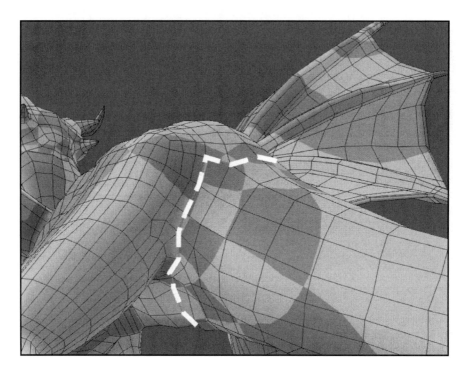

Mark the seam around the base of the tail

Since we have the **Live Unwrap** feature turned on, you won't have to tell Blender to unwrap the model again; it automatically unwrapped it the moment you marked a new seam. Now, let's cut two more seams to finish off the tail.

We've cut the tail away from the rest of the body, but the tip of the tail is causing the UVs to bunch up together in one spot; so, lets cut off that end cap of the tail with another seam. This time, we don't want to completely cut off the section of the mesh, so don't mark the very bottom edges of the tail tip, but mark a seam around the rest of the loop:

Mark the seam around the tip of the tail

Alright, one last seam for the tail! The first two seams have effectively turned the tail into a long tube. Once we have a tube such as the one in the following screenshot, there's only one seam left before it can lay out flat. Select an edge loop that runs along the length of the tail:

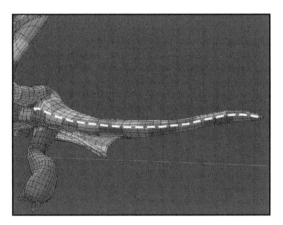

Mark a seam along the length of the tail

That last seam was all we needed to eliminate the distortion on the tail. We now have an even checker pattern along the tail—excellent! Don't worry about the size of the checkers compared to the rest of the character for now. At the moment, we just want them to be an even size within a single island—in this case, the tail.

Just as with the tail, the limbs of the dragon are causing the UVs to bunch up, so let's mark seams around the areas where each limb attaches to the body. Don't bother marking the seams on the opposite side if your character is perfectly symmetrical; we will learn how to mirror over the seams at the end. Here are the places where we marked seams in our example:

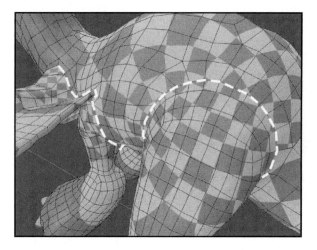

Mark the edge loops where the limbs connect to the body

Remember to check the model from all angles, including the underside. We need to make sure that the marked seams connect all the way through, as you can see here:

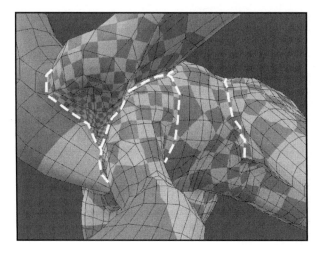

The same edge loops, seen from the underside

Excellent! Marking the edge loops where the limbs attach to the body alleviates a lot of distortion and is the best way to mark seams on a character. We can already see our checker pattern starting to come back. Let's keep going.

The legs are a lot like the tail; all they need is one long seam that runs along the length of the tube shape to alleviate the distortion. Any one of the vertical edge loops will work; however, seams can cause small issues with our textures from time to time and, just like seams on our clothing, they will stand out (under certain conditions). So, we should try to hide the seams from view whenever possible. We can hide the seams on our legs by choosing the edge loops that are closest to the center of the character's body:

1. Select an edge loop along the inside of each leg.
2. Press the *Ctrl + E* hotkey to bring up the **Edge** context menu.
3. Choose **Mark Seam**:

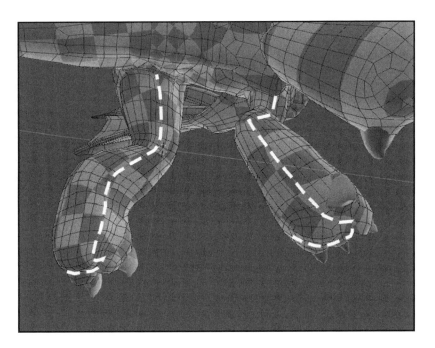

Mark seams down the length of the inner legs

In our example, we chose to continue these seams downward around the base of each foot to alleviate as much distortion as possible without having to completely cut off the base of each foot. This may not be necessary for your character. We will go over another way to visualize distortion later in this chapter.

We can judge our progress by the even distribution of the checkers, and after those last two seams, we can see that it's really coming together (refer to the following screenshot):

Major progress on the baby dragon's UVs

Next, let's tackle the wings. The wings are a very large, flat shape that we basically just have to cut in half. So, just as with our legs and tail, we can mark one long seam up the length of the wing, down the webbing of the wing, and all the way to the tip, which ought to be enough to get a solid start:

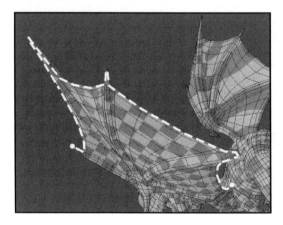

One long seam across the webbing of the wing, ending at the tip

Very good—now, let's move on to the head. The mouth is a concave area of the mesh, so it's going to be very hard for the unwrapping algorithm to make good UVs while it's still attached—so, let's mark it:

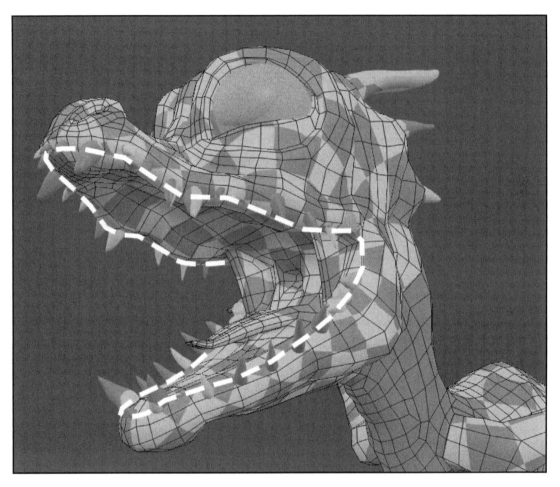

A seam marked around the mouth

Very good—all of our main seams are in place; so, let's mirror them:

1. Select any edge that has been marked as a seam (it doesn't matter which one).
2. In the 3D Viewport, go to the **Select** menu.
3. Go to **Select Similar | Seam**.
4. Deselect the seam that runs along the length of the tail (this one is supposed to be asymmetrical).

5. Once again, go to the **Select** menu.
6. At the bottom, choose **Mirror Selection**.
7. Press the *Ctrl + E* hotkey to bring up the **Edge** context menu.
8. Choose **Mark Seam**:

Most major seams are in place

We're really close now, but we're still getting distortion around the neck, so let's separate the top of the neck and the back from the underbelly. Mark the seam indicated in the following screenshot on both the left and right side of the dragon:

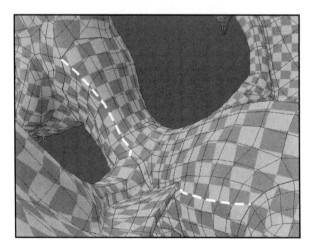

Marking the seam marked

Alright, now the checkers are looking pretty good! However, there is another way we can check for distortion that will help us visualize and then fix the last few areas of our UVs.

Visualizing the distortion

Our checker pattern has been very helpful for finding areas that have a lot of distortion, but another way to visualize it is with the stretch display in the UV Editor:

1. Open the sidebar of the UV Editor (press the *N* hotkey with your mouse in the UV Editor).
2. Go to the **View** tab of the sidebar (usually active by default).
3. Expand the **Display** section (usually expanded by default).
4. Expand the **Overlays** section.
5. Check the box for **Stretching**.
6. Expand the **Stretching** section.
7. Set the **Type** drop-down option to **Area**.

Now, you will see that the UV islands in the UV Editor have colored tints to them. These colors will help us visualize the areas of our UV islands that have stretching:

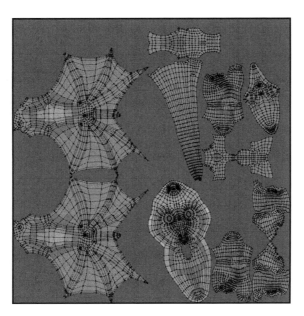

The baby dragon's UVs with the area stretching overlay enabled

Blue areas have the least distortion, green areas have a little distortion, and red areas have a lot of distortion. These colors are all relative, so as we reduce the amount of distortion, the colors will try to redistribute themselves across all of the UV islands. Don't worry about trying to remove all the distortion; we just need to fix the worst areas.

In this case, the worst areas are on the head and on the little claws on the wings. These problem areas are caused by them not having enough room to unfold. If we look at the claw on the wing, we can see that it's highlighted red and all of the vertices of the claw are crammed into a tiny space in our UVs. This results in the claw receiving very little texture space to sample from, so we see a big gray blob instead of our checker pattern:

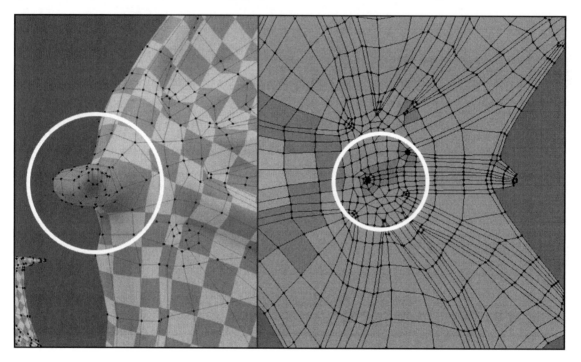

The claw has a lot of distortion

Let's fix this with a few more seams—one around the base of the claw to separate it from the wing, and one up the length of the claw to unfold it as with the rest of our limbs (mark these seams on both wings):

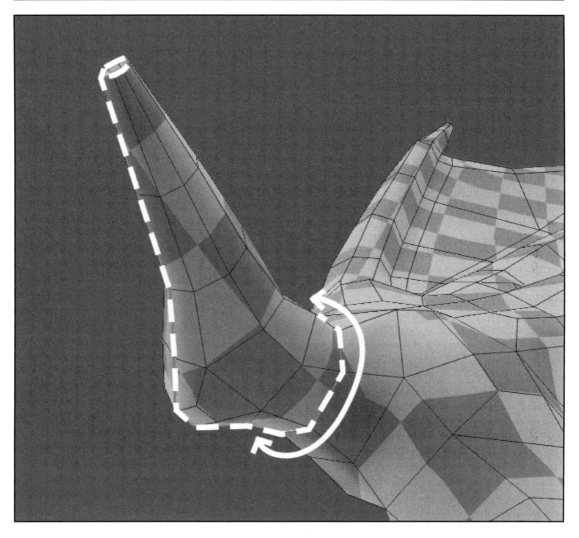

Seams for the baby dragon's claw

Much better—those extra seams helped us to solve a major **texel density** issue.

Fixing texel density issues

Texel density refers to how many pixels on our texture map are dedicated to each area of our UV islands. It's another way to think about distortion in our UVs; if our UVs don't have even texel density, then we will get distortion.

We want our UV islands to have even texel density as often as possible, especially for important areas of the character, such as the head. The claw was very problematic and easy to notice since it was a big gray blob, but the baby dragon's head is also problematic. The texel density changes from the forehead to the snout to the jaw:

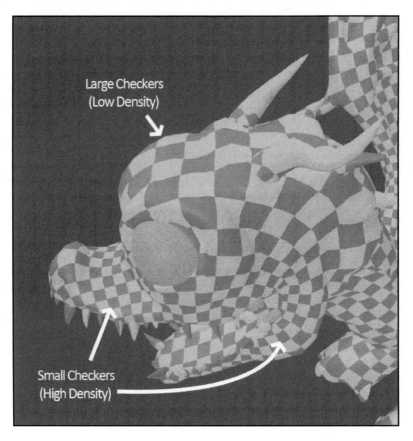

Large Checkers
(Low Density)

Small Checkers
(High Density)

Texel density issues on the baby dragon's head

These issues are caused by the same thing that was causing trouble with the dragon's claw. Since this character's mouth is so huge, keeping the jaw attached to the rest of the head causes distortion. Let's fix this with a few more seams:

Cut this seam on both sides to separate the jaw

Similarly, there are a couple more small areas inside the mouth that need our attention. Let's cut these seams to fix the tongue and webbing of the mouth:

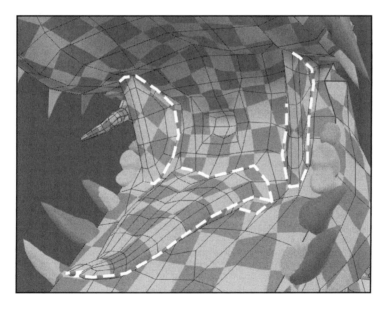

Fixing the tongue and webbing of the mouth

Sometimes, we don't have to cut a seam all the way through in order for it to help with our distortion. Let's cut an extra seam up the side of the head that will help the head's UVs spread out for a more even texel density:

Cutting a seam up the side of the head on both sides

Look at what happened to the head's UV island before and after that seam was added:

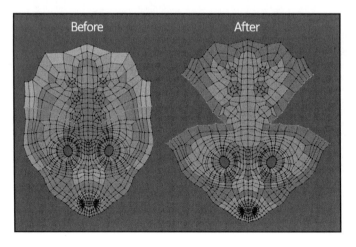

Distortion on the head's UV island before and after the seam was added

Notice how the distortion in the center of the island has been alleviated. It's like loosening your belt after eating too much at a Thanksgiving meal. All that pressure and stretching can relax and spread out evenly instead of being bunched up.

We still have some red spots on the head and other islands, but we have to decide whether it's worth cutting more seams. In this case, we've hit a pretty good balance between the number of seams and the amount of distortion, so we can move on to the final stage of our UVs.

Before we move on, take a moment to use these techniques to UV unwrap the eyes, inner eyelids, horns, teeth, and claws. These pieces will be much simpler to unwrap than the rest of the character; think back to how we unwrapped the tail and the other limbs.

Laying out the baby dragon's UVs

Now that we have all of our UV islands, we need to lay them out so they fit nicely in the UV area:

1. Select all of the baby dragon's pieces in **Object Mode**.
2. *Tab* to **Edit mode**.
3. Press the *A* hotkey to select all of the components of all of the objects.
4. Press the *U* hotkey and choose **Unwrap**.

At this stage, you may want to turn off the **Live Unwrap** feature so that Blender doesn't overwrite your UV layout.

This final unwrap has done three things for us:

- It unwrapped each object into a UV island based on our seams.
- It averaged the UV island scales so that the texel density is as even as possible between all the islands.

- It laid out the UVs within the UV space as best as it could:

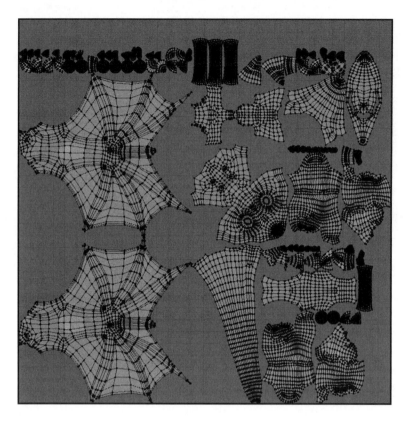

The resulting unwrap

The resulting unwrap is very close to done. In a final set of UVs, all UV islands must be packed into this square area; otherwise, we will have problems when we go to paint our textures. We also need to make sure that none of the pieces overlap each other; this, too, would cause problems. However, we also don't want to waste space in our texture area and, unfortunately, Blender's default packing algorithm isn't very smart and wastes a lot of space.

Let's move these islands around by hand to save space:

1. Hover your mouse in the UV Editor and press the *A* hotkey to select all of the UVs.
2. Turn off the **UV Sync Selection** button at the top-left side of the UV Editor.
3. Change **UV selection mode** to **Island** (press the *4* hotkey).

Now, all we have to do is select our islands and use our familiar transformation tools—move, scale, and rotate—to make the islands fit better within the space.

 Try not to scale individual UV islands as this will cause them to have a different texel density than the other islands.

We look for several things in our final layout:

- All the islands are contained within the UV area.
- There are no overlapping parts.
- Related parts are clumped close together (see all the teeth at the bottom-left side of the following screenshot).
- We are utilizing the UV space as efficiently as possible (there are no huge blank areas).

Keeping these things in mind, try to fit all of the pieces together like a jigsaw puzzle:

A much better layout

Excellent—the baby dragon's UVs are done; the checkers on the model should look something like this:

The baby dragon with a checker pattern showing off the finished UVs

Now, those are some good UVs! It might not have been a particularly fun part of the process, but creating UVs was a necessary step to carry out before we can create materials and textures for our dragon.

Summary

In this chapter, we learned what UVs are and that they are necessary for creating textures. We learned how to mark seams to help Blender unwrap a model and how to visualize and fix distortion issues. We also found a balance between the number of seams and the amount of distortion. We learned how to lay out the UVs and we finished off by unwrapping our baby dragon model.

It's been a long journey since we started sculpting this character, but it's all going to pay off in the next chapter, where we'll finally get to paint textures and see the dragon come to life in full color!

Questions

1. What does UV stand for?
2. Why do we need UVs?
3. Can we paint a texture without UVs?
4. What's wrong with the "crushed cube" as a two-dimensional representation?
5. What are seams?
6. Where can you place a seam on a tube-like shape to make it unfold?
7. What is texel density?
8. Is it okay if the checkers are huge on one part of the character but are tiny on other parts?
9. What happens if we don't cut enough seams?
10. What happens if we cut too many seams?

14
Creating a Baby Dragon - Part 4: Baking and Painting Textures

The baby dragon is ready for reptilian camouflage, spiny scales, calloused claws, and glowing runes. All of these will come through the little scamp's textures and material setup. The high-poly dragon sculpture will come back into play as we recapture its details using a process called baking. Next, we'll create new textures through Blender's texture painting tools and supplement them with external painting programs. With good bakes and textures, we'll have the ingredients necessary to build an organic creature's materials and render them out in Eevee. An example of the final baking and materials setup can be found in the project file

The following topics will be covered in this chapter:

- Getting set up for texture baking
- Baking texture maps from high poly to low poly
- Texture painting the base color in Blender
- Using external programs for image editing
- Setting up the remaining BSDF textures

Technical requirements

In this chapter, you'll bake and paint massive high-resolution textures, often adjacent to your high-poly dragon sculpture. Depending on the quality of your computer, creating these textures can end up taking forever or even result in Blender crashing. It's recommended that if your machine is struggling, instead opt to bake straight from the low-poly model and use textures at a lower resolution, such as 2,048, 1,024, 512, or even 256. Even on my good computer, I reduce samples in Cycles to 8 when struggling with repeat crashes.

You'll also paint on your textures and a painterly interface is ideal. Refer to `Chapter 8`, *Illustrating an Alien Hero with Grease Pencil,* for advice on tablet and stylus hardware.

Now, let's get set up for texture baking!

Getting set up for texture baking

Before this baby dragon gets any final textures, we'll need a preliminary material setup. This should approximate the texturing setups with flats and get a proxy set up for the texture maps that will be used in the final dragon. We can then supplement this lay-in with some starting lights and rendering for Eevee. First things first, we need to prepare the scene.

Preparing the scene for baking

Our starting process consists of a high-poly mesh for details, a low-poly mesh with UVs to capture that detail, and a cage mesh that helps determine the boundaries for their interaction. We'll be starting off where we ended with the previous chapter, so we need both the high-poly and retopologized baby dragons handy. It's a good idea to organize the models into different collections and to have an extra collection for rendering stuff. Since we'll want to see our textures in a production setting, start with some moderate rendering setup steps:

1. In the **Render** panel, change your renderer to the Cycles engine. Eevee doesn't support baking, but also, we'll need Cycles for its full rendering power.
2. Load the **Shading**, **Texture Painting**, and **UV Editing** workspaces, all of which will be used in this chapter.

3. Organize your models. Keep your low-poly mesh on one collection, your high-poly assets on another, and all your leftovers in another collection. Except for the eyes, join all your low-poly meshes (such as horns, nails, teeth, and the body) into one object with the *Ctrl + J* hotkeys.

4. Duplicate your low-poly mesh and rename it `cage`. Add a **Displacement** modifier and increase the strength until it sits over the low-poly mesh (about 2). Add a **Smooth** modifier, with enough **Repeat** to smooth any clipping errors from the **Displacement** mod. Apply the modifiers and pull vertices out in **Edit Mode** until the cage completely overlaps the low-poly mesh.

5. In the outliner, use the filters icon, , to turn on the render restriction toggle, . Disable rendering for the cage, as we'll only need it for spatial data.

A selection you'll make over and over while baking is right-clicking on your high-resolution dragon collection, selecting objects in that group, and then shift-selecting the low-poly baby dragon so that it's the active object in your selection.

Material baking setup

The **Shader** editor will be integral to our baking process. Before working on the actual shader, we'll need some basic setup for all the textures that will get baked out:

1. Add a new material to the low-poly dragon.

2. Add an image texture node by going to **Add** | **Texture**. Create a new image, named `lowRes`, with the **Width** and **Height** values set to 256 px and a generated type of **Color Grid**. Baking textures can take a long time and it's better to test on a low-resolution texture. Only spend time baking finalized maps if you know the bake will be successful.

3. Add another image texture node. Create another new image, this time with the **Width** and **Height** values set to 4096 and, once again, with a color grid and 32-bit float. Name it normal. Some textures need 32 bits to function correctly, which means your files will have bigger sizes but store more data. Normal and bump maps usually require 32 bits or 16 bits, while something such as metal (only black or white) can be heavily compressed for game engine optimization.

4. Repeat the creation of 4096 x 4096 textures for all the textures we'll end up baking, but without 32 bits activated and without alpha—**Ambient Occlusion**, **Subsurface**, **toplight**, **softlight**, **Convexity**, and **Cavity**. Some of these will end up as their own final map, while others serve as ingredients for other eventual textures. I think of baking like "mise en place," where you gather all your ingredients in the right place before making a cooking recipe. It never hurts to save extra maps if you bake something that looks like it could be useful later in texture creation.

5. Although we'll be hand-painting our **Base Color** and **Bump** textures, you might as well create them now. Make a 4096 x 4096 texture, set to **Blank**, for each, with a .5 gray color and no alpha channel.

6. Add a **Texture Coordinate** node and a **Mapping** node with UVs as the vector for all of the following maps: ambientOcclusion, cavity, lowRes, subsurface, bump, normal, convexity, and light.

As maps are baked out, the image texture node that is currently selected will be our target. The results of the bake will be a specific output chosen in the **Bake** dialog. In the project file, the material BabyDragon_bake provides an example layout. The relevant bake settings can be assigned to the material output, and the target texture selected, right before baking, as shown here:

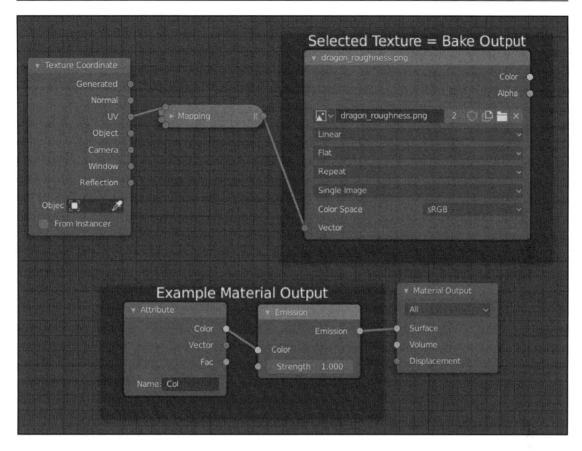

The node setup with all of our texture maps hooked up and ready to be baked

In the event of that output being something such as a render of a material setup, we'll choose that by running it in **Material Output**, which will bake the material output to the selected node.

Now that we're all set up, let's begin baking our texture maps for the baby dragon!

Baking texture maps from high poly to low poly

Baking is the process of translating mesh information into image textures. All sorts of data can be extracted in this process and can be applied in a number of conventional and creative ways. Even if you're painting a texture by hand, a baked map provides a helpful guide for where model details are. A big part of the baking workflow is to bake from a high-poly mesh to a low-poly mesh; the high-poly mesh is usually unusable in production due to size. By baking that detail to maps, we get the functionality of the low-poly mesh with the details of the high-poly mesh. Some of the maps we create will immediately be used in our dragon's final material. Others will serve as auxiliary textures, creating images that we'll use for starting points and masks when painting the final textures. The first map we need to bake is called **Ambient Occlusion (AO)**.

Your first bake – AO

Once our baby dragon has some initial textures baked out, we can get to work with making its material. I think of this as a hoarding stage. First, we get as much useful data as we can in texture format. Then, we can dispense with our high-poly model and get to work with plugging maps into inputs and adding to them with a painterly touch. Let's start by just seeing how a map is generated and what we need to do to get the right output.

This first texture is AO. AO is darker, based on contact shadows where light won't penetrate, even if it comes from every direction. AO is a useful auxiliary map, which we'll use for selections and for modifications to other textures:

1. Hide your high-poly collection and select just your low-poly dragon. Switch to the **Shading** workspace.
2. Select the **lowRes texture** node in the **Shader** editor. Blender will bake to a selected image texture node. Also, load the **lowRes** image in the image editor.
3. Navigate to the **Properties** window, then go to the **Render** panel, and then the **Bake** tab. Again, if you don't see it, switch your renderer to Cycles.
4. Set **Bake Type** to **Ambient Occlusion**. Each bake type generates something different. Sometimes, we'll get a result by choosing a bake type. Other times, we'll choose **Combined**, **Shadow**, or **Emit**, and instead get a particular result by modifying our materials or the lights and scene around the dragon.
5. Hit **Bake**. After the process is done, we have an **Ambient Occlusion** texture that is darker in the nooks and crannies of your mesh.

If it turned out correctly, your AO map should look like this:

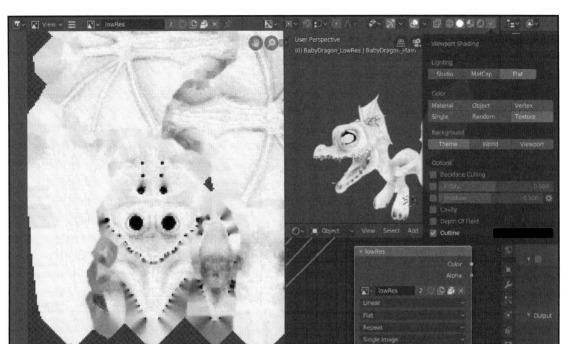

The baked ambient occlusion map for the baby dragon

View your AO texture on your low-poly mesh; if the **Node Wrangler** add-on is enabled, this can be done by pressing *Ctrl + Shift* and clicking on the AO texture. I do this to inspect bakes after every time. However, afterward, disconnect this material output (or replace it with **Principled BSDF**) and return to having the texture selected. If the texture is connected to the final output *while* you are baking, circular dependencies can cause errors. Next, we need to use the high-poly mesh as our source:

1. Turn on both your **highRes** and **lowRes** collections. Right-click on your **HighRes** collection and select **Objects**, then press *Shift* and select the low-poly mesh so that it's the active object.
2. In **Bake Settings**, turn on **Selected** to **Active**. Set **Extrusion** to 1M and hit **Bake**.

3. A cage mesh can improve the baking quality by limiting what Blender considers for the bake. Duplicate your low-poly mesh and rename it `dragon_cage`. In the outliner, disable rendering for it. Add a **Displacement** modifier and increase **Strength** until the faces completely cover the high-poly mesh. For extra fidelity, use a **Smooth** modifier, apply the modifiers, then use the **Edit** mode to clean up the remaining mesh artifacts.

4. In **Bake Settings**, turn on **Cage** and choose `dragon_cage` as your cage object. Set **Extrusion** to `.1m`.

5. Once more, select objects in your **High Poly** collection, followed by the **lowRes** mesh, and hit **Bake**. If the results look good, select your **Ambient Occlusion** texture node and bake the full-resolution version.

Now that the cage is set up, we'll use these settings for all the other baked textures, as well. Our next map will capture all of the bumpy surface details into a normal map.

Normals

Normal maps change the normal angle of a mesh at the pixel level and can make it look like it has many more polygonal facets than it actually has. Your best bet, compression-wise, for normal maps is half-float (16 bits) with PIZ compression. Upping them to 32 bits will create a much higher file size with a negligible increase in quality. Lowering them to 8 bits or other file formats will create compression problems and loss of data.

The blueish color of normal maps comes from the data it stores, with the red and green channels equating to a normal's angle on an X and Y axis. The pixel value (0 to 255) corresponds to -1 and 1 for X or Y and so at 128 (gray), there's no distortion. The blue channel corresponds to Z, or the face's normal direction, and so defaults to 1 (out). So, this creates an overall light-blue look.

1. In **Render Settings**, set **Bake Type** to **Normal**.

2. Turn on both your **HighRes** and **LowRes** collections. Right-click on your **HighRes** collection and select **Objects**, then press *Shift* and select the low-poly mesh so that it's the active object.

3. In the **Node** editor, select your **Normal** texture and hit **Bake**.

4. On the normal map texture node, change **Color Space** to **Non-color** so that it will be interpreted correctly.

5. Save this image as a targa called `dragon_normal.exr` and in the **Save** dialog, change the codec to PIZ compression. If the file size is a concern, you can instead use DWAA compression. In the image editor, you can check whether the image is a 32-bit float in the Sidebar's **Image** tab. (Press the *N* hotkey to open the Sidebar).

You can always tell which map is the normal map because it's bumpy and purple-looking, as you can see from our result here:

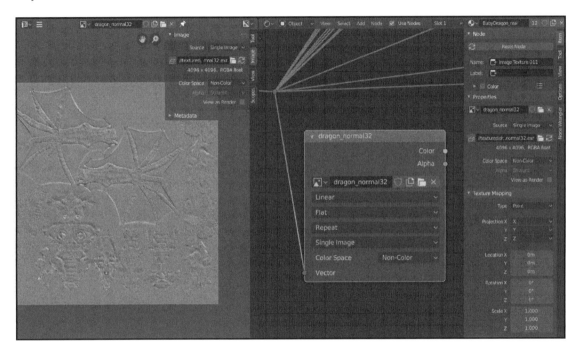

The baked normal map for the baby dragon

Once the normal map is applied to the material, it will provide the illusion of far more polygons on our low-poly mesh than we actually have.

Despite normal maps making a powerful illusion, we still need to get back some of our other surface information in a cavity map and a displacement map, which is what we'll do next.

Cavity and displacement

A cavity map is similar to AO but it focuses more on acute detail. We can map out the cavities through the mesh's pointiness:

1. In **Node Editor**, add a **Geometry** node, **ColorRamp**, and an **Emit** node, then connect them together and feed the result into the material output.
2. View the material in **Render** mode on the high-poly sculpt mode. As you pull the black and white stops on **ColorRamp** in, the pointiness is more visible. Set the white input to .45 and the black input to .55.
3. In **Render Settings**, set **Bake Type** to **Emit**.
4. Turn on both your **HighRes** and **LowRes** collections. Right-click on your **HighRes** collection and select **Objects**, then press *Shift* and select the low-poly mesh so that it's the active object.
5. In the **Node** editor, select your **Cavity** texture and hit **Bake**.

These maps look really neat and can be used to mask out crevices in our creature's texture. Ours turned out like this:

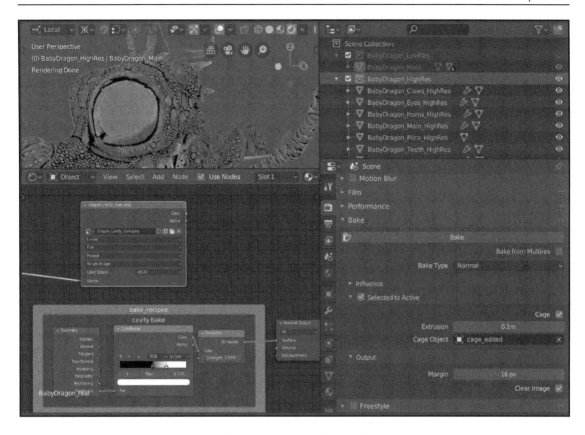

The baked cavity map for the baby dragon

Varying the color ramp provides different looks that we can use as stencils. I also baked a map out, called `dragon_cavity_dark.png`—with the black stop at `.48` and the white stop at `.8`—and another, called `dragon_displacement.exr`—with 32 bits on, and no color ramp.

Up next, we have a very similar map that we need to bake, called the convexity map.

Convexity

The dragon's convexity map represents details closer to the surface. Convexity is useful for showing things such as wear and tear, where the scales face exposure to elements more than the crevices, and also color variance:

1. Set your **Viewport Shading** mode to **Solid**. In the pulldown, change **Lighting** to **Flat** and **Color** to **Vertex**.

2. Select your high-poly sculpt and switch to the **Vertex Paint** mode. In the **Properties** window's **Mesh** panel, the **Vertex Colors** tab automatically creates a value called `Col` that stores a color value for each vertex.

3. Go to **Paint | Dirty Vertex Colors**. This generates black and grayscale vertex data based on the polygon angles. Repeat for all the high-poly objects.

4. In the **BabyDragon** material, add an **Attribute** node and type `Col` for the name. Add this to an **Emission** shader and feed it into the material attribute.

5. Select all your high-poly objects. Add the low-poly dragon to the selection as the active object.

6. In the **Properties** window, go to the **Render** panel and then the **Bake** tab. Change the bake type to **Emit**, with the usual settings—**Selected** to **Active**, **Cage**, and **Extrusion .1m**.

7. Select the **lowRes** image node and hit **Bake**. Check whether the map turned out alright. If it did, select the **Convexity** image node and hit **Bake**.

You can see the results of our example convexity map here:

The baked convexity map for the baby dragon

Note that the pointiness node won't work in Eevee. We don't use Eevee to bake anyway, so it's not an issue for our workflow. Up next, we'll have a look at subsurface, which we can use to capture details under the dragon's skin.

Subsurface

The dragon's subsurface map will control the amount of light that permeates the dragon's skin and scatters back out. The thin skin of the wing membranes will let light through, just like putting your hand over a flashlight, while thicker parts, such as the limb and torso, will create less subsurface scattering.

An inverted AO hack will let us measure this distance into starting map bakes. Other areas will require an artistic touch; the horns and teeth will be as thin as the wing in certain areas, but bone is denser than skin. Since the bake will differ based on the distance we set, we can bake out multiple results to mix and match later:

1. For the initial shader, add an **Ambient Occlusion** node by going to **Add | Input**. Check the options of **Inside** and **Only Local**. This will generate AO from inside the mesh; thin crevices, such as the wing membrane, will have more AO, and appear black, while AO near the chest has lots of room to bounce around and so will appear lighter.

2. Set the **Ambient Occlusion** node's distance to .01. This will cause the AO to fall away based on unit proximity. The size of your dragon plays a major part here. The example dragon is scaled to fit roughly inside Blender's 2 m default cube, to give you context for the **Distance** attribute.

3. Run this in an **Invert** node, then in an **Emission** node, and use the result for the material output.

4. Select all your high-poly objects. Add the low-poly dragon to the selection as the active object.

5. In the **Properties** window, go to the **Render** panel and then the **Bake** tab, change the bake type to **Emit**, with the usual settings—**Selected to Active**, **Cage**, and **Extrusion .1m**.

6. Select the **lowRes** image node and hit **Bake**. Check whether the map turned out alright. If it did, select the **Convexity** image node and hit **Bake**.

You will get very different results based on the **Distance** attribute of the **Ambient Occlusion** node, which can come in handy later as auxiliary maps when making creative choices. I bake and save multiple subsurface maps at distances of .1, .05, .01, and .005. Combining these maps later resulted in the following Subsurface texture:

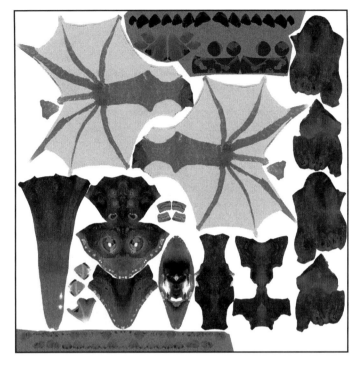

The baked subsurface map for the baby dragon

Alright, we're getting close now, just a few more maps and we'll be done.

Top lighting, soft lighting, and facing maps

As a bonus auxiliary map, we can bake out some lighting scenarios and normal data. These can be handy for masking just the back and can add a pleasant transitional glow for a mesh:

1. Add a **Sun** object to the scene. Have it point straight down. Set its energy to `100`.
2. Select all your high-poly objects. Add the low-poly dragon to the selection as the active object.
3. In the **Properties** window, go to the **Render** panel and then the **Bake** tab, change **Bake Type** to **Shadow**, with the usual settings—**Selected to Active**, **Cage**, and **Extrusion .1m**.

4. Select the **lowRes** image node and hit **Bake**. Check whether the map turned out alright. If it did, select the **toplight** image node and hit **Bake**.

5. A softer look can be made by upping your **Sun** object's angle in the light properties. Bake out and save a version of lighting with angles at 0 and 90 and save both textures.

Similar to this is a map that represents the upward-facing normals:

1. Add the **Texture Coordinates**, **Separate XYZ**, and **Emit** nodes. Hook the **Texture Coordinate** node's normal to the **Separate XYZ** input, then map the Z channel to the **Emit** node and the **Emit** node to **Material Output**.

2. Bake this to a new material, called `dragon_up.png`.

You can see the results of our example here:

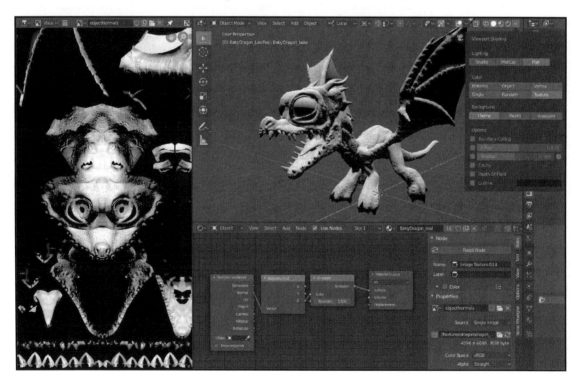

The baked auxiliary map for the baby dragon

We can experiment with other baking outputs when combining them into diffuse patterns, later.

That's enough baking for one day; now, it's on to the fun stuff—texture painting!

Texture painting the base color in Blender

This young hatchling is ready to put his arsenal of maps to use. We'll use these bakes both as initial textures as well as masks when creating the final **Base Color**, **Specular**, **Roughness**, **Subsurface**, **Normal**, **Bump**, **Displacement**, and **Emit** textures. Blender's Texture Paint interface uses many tools similar to the sculpting and Grease Pencil interfaces and lets us paint our maps by hand.

First up, we'll paint some base color onto our baby dragon so that it won't look so bland anymore.

Painting the base color

We'll start our first pass on the **Base Color** texture by painting in Blender. If you're only allowed one texture, **Base Color** is the most important:

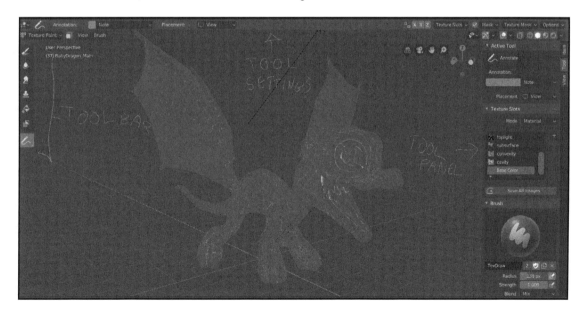

The areas of the UI we will use to paint our base color map

The following are the texture paint mode hotkeys:
F: Brush size.
Shift + F: Brush strength.
S: Sample color.
E: Change the stroke method.

To begin painting our base color map we mush hook in up in the Shader editor, then we can paint:

1. Plug your **Base Color** image texture node into the **Principled BSDF** node's **Base Color** attribute. While working on the base color, I frequently switch between **Principled BSDF** as my final output and previewing the base color via the node wrangler shortcut of *Ctrl + Shift*, clicking on a texture to preview it.

2. Switch your mode to **Texture Paint**. This interface should look familiar after using Blender's other brush-based interfaces. There is a toolbar on the left, **Tool Settings** on the header, and a panel on the taskbar or in the **Properties** window that more details.

3. Set your texture to **Base Color** in the **Paint** mode tool settings and in the image viewer. Brush strokes will affect the tool settings' texture, even if we're viewing or editing it in the image editor or the **Shader** editor.

4. Turn on *X* **Symmetry** in **Tool Settings**, then try out the painting brush in the three-dimensional view, painting directly onto the dragon's three-dimensional model. With reference images handy, color-pick with *S*. You can clear the base color back to the starting color by clicking on the paint bucket.

5. Using a mask from another bake, let's differentiate between scales and crevices. In **Tool Settings**, click the **Mask** pulldown and choose **Cavity texture**. Pick a green color and fill the whole dragon with the fill tool, You may need to invert, the mask in its settings. The scales are now green, while the cracks are ignored. I regularly toggle overlays to double-check my mask, then paint without seeing the mask:

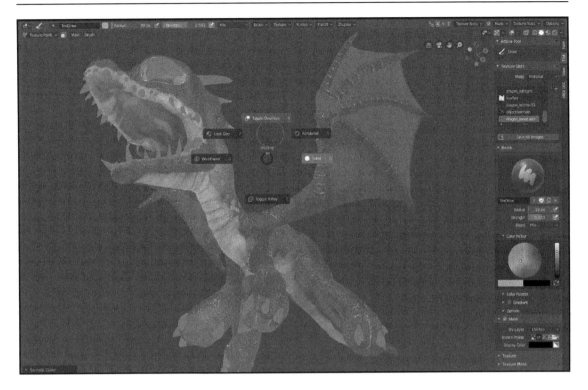

The base color map is coming along nicely

6. Use broad strokes with the brush to paint colored areas, such as a pink mouth, a light-yellow underbelly, and other areas of local color. Check your reference often to maintain realism; for instance, a quick look at bat wings revealed that when we don't consider subsurface scattering, they tend toward lighter skin over bony fingers and darker skin for the wing membranes.

7. To simplify your color workflow, use a color palette. Open the sidebar's **Tool** panel and scroll down to the **Color Palette** tab. Pick a color in **Color Picker**, then hit the **+** icon. This swatch can now be clicked for quick color. I used around seven colors on the palette—dark-green scales, light-green scale crevices, a yellow underbelly, brown underbelly crevices, light pink and dark red for the mouth, and dark purple for accents.

8. Sample new brush colors by hitting *S* while hovering your mouse over the color you want. You can also click while holding down *S* to add to your palette. This allows a painterly approach; for instance, I used dark purple on the wing skin, but it was overkill. I then just sampled over a transition between dark purple and middle green and used that mixed color to correct things. Toggle between this and the secondary color by pressing *X*.

9. Painting on crevices, such as around the mouth or horns, can be difficult due to geometry occlusions. Solve this with a **Smooth** modifier on the dragon and increase the settings until your baby dragon is a smoothed-out blob. Toggle this on and off as needed:

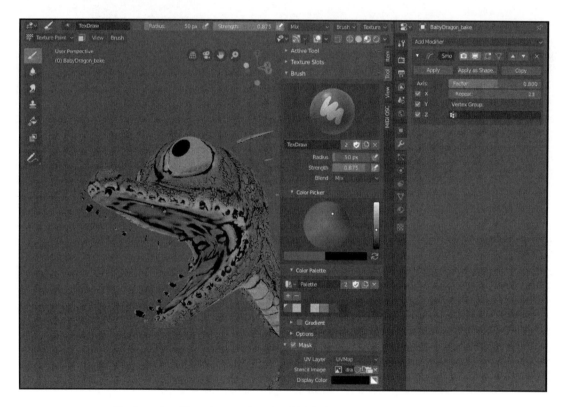

Using the smooth modifier to gain access to the crevices of the baby dragon so they can be painted more easily

10. Load your `toplight_soft` texture as a mask. Choose a dark color and use the paint bucket with .3 opacity to fill with this color. Follow this with a large brush, toggling the stencil to see your progress. I also changed the stencil color to bright red so that I could easily tell what was masked.

11. Load your toplight texture as a mask. Use a darker color to paint a stripe that follows the scales. Based on my reference, I added other stripes and patterns, as well. Coloring in nature often follows the same logic from lizards to insects to fish—light areas for the underbelly, inner legs, and around the eyes and mouth, then a medium color above that, with patterns of stripes or dots inside that, starting from dark on the borders to slightly lighter inside.

12. The smudge ( ) and blur ( ) tools can soften your details. A great place to use them is along harsh border seams that might occur due to masking or along UV borders, when painting both over seams causes problems. Additionally, use *Ctrl* with the blur tool to sharpen instead; with a light brush, this can make scales and details pop.

13. Use blend modes once your base colors and patterns are added, which allows color variation while respecting the fine detail you've worked on. In the **Brush** settings, set the blend mode to **Overlay**, then use the pinks and reds from the mouth with a large brush to add in warmth. Based on reference, I do this in areas with major visibility (such as the back) and areas where more blood would be close to the surface (such as joints and area with thin skin).

When you're satisfied with your base color, save your changes. Make sure you save the textures externally; just saving the blend file isn't enough to save your textures.

Up next, we're going to make some stencils to add little details, such as scattered spots.

Creating stencils in the image editor

These painting tools translate over to the image editor, where we can work on the texture in its flattened UV layout or on new images to use as stencils. Parts such as the teeth, nails, and horns are mapped to separate areas of the texture, so painting them in the image editor is much easier, as you don't have to worry about accidentally painting on the dragon's mouth. On the other hand, you'll need to be careful painting near seams; while painting over seams in the three-dimensional view automatically goes across borders, it can cause artifacts when you do so in the image editor:

1. Switch to **Edit Mode**. Select your dragon's body by pressing *L*, then hide these faces.
2. View your `dragon_basecolor.png` texture in the image editor.

3. The UV map overlay shows where the claws, teeth, and horns are. Turn off pressure sensitivity for the brush strength and paint all these areas in with bone and teeth colors.

4. There might be artifacts around the dragon's gums that previous strokes couldn't paint due to the teeth faces occluding it. Do the same for the pink eye membranes.

5. Search for problem areas on the unwrap that might be more easily painted on the unwrap than on the model.

You can give your brush some more visual interest by creating brush stencils in the image editor:

1. Create a new image named `mask` with a height and width of `128` pixels and no alpha.

2. Use the brush tool to paint some white dots in an organic pattern. Go to **Image** | **Pack** to store this image inside the blend file.

3. In the sidebar's **Texture** tab, add a new brush,  , and name it `maskBrush`. In the **Texture Mask** tab, select the mask image. Set **Mask Mapping** to **Random**, with **Stroke Spacing** set to `50%` and **Jitter** set to `5` px. The brush paints with more organic randomness.

You can see how our stencil turned out in the following screenshot. Notice how the stenciled pattern shows up under the brush:

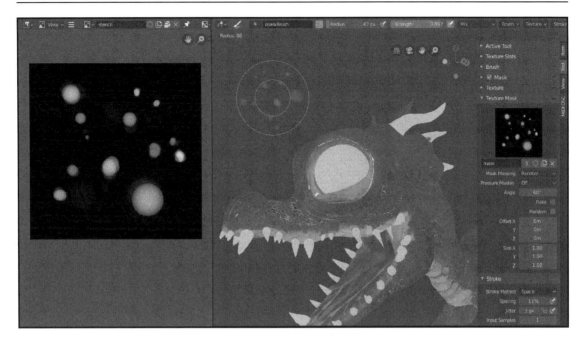

The stencil pattern controls the shape of the brush

For more stencils to customize your brushes, load them from the folder in the project directory.

Now that we've made some real progress on the color, we can add some bumpy details, next.

Normal maps and sculpting with a bump map

At this point, we'll set up the normal map. By combining this with a bump map, we'll paint even more details using **Texture Paint Mode**:

1. Switch back to the **Node** editor. Hook **Principled BSDF** in as **Material Output**.

2. Add a **Normal Map** node by going to **Add | Vector** and attaching your normal map as the input. Run this in the **Normal** input on **Principled BSDF**. Change your viewport render mode to see the effect. If all the settings were correct (32-bit texture, non-color data), the normals distort for much finer detail.

3. Add a **Bump** node by going to **Add | Vector** and drop it in between this connection so that the **Normal Map** node feeds the bump's **Normal** input and the **Bump** node drives the BSDF input, now.

4. Add a new texture called `dragon_bump`, with `4096 x 4096` and 32-bit float activated. Set it to **Blank**, with a `.5` gray for its starting value, and save it as `.EXR`. In the image node, change the texture interpolation to **Cubic** and put the **Bump** texture's color in the **Bump** node's height.

5. Create a new texture mask and load the `singlecut.png` image. Set **Mask Mapping** to **View Plane**, with **Rake** activated, so that the mask follows your stroke. Use this brush with white and black to paint grooves on `bump.exr`.

You can see the bumpiness starting to come through in the following screenshot:

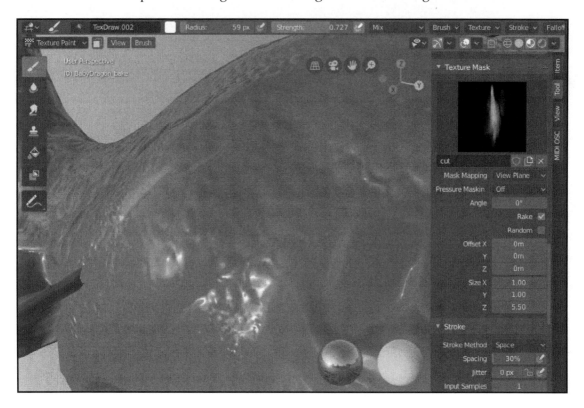

The normal map and bump map combine to create the details in the surface of the baby dragon

The result is a general start on the normals via the normal map, while still allowing painterly edits with bump maps.

Up next, we will need to use a different piece of software to edit some of our images externally.

Using external programs for image editing

As you paint your baby dragon's textures, you might recall tools from drawing and some programs that you'd love to integrate into texturing. There are many programs devoted to a two-dimensional image editing workflow and they possess functionality that Blender users can put to use. For our purposes, we'll use Krita—the industry standard for digital illustration. It's free, open source, and has a terrific brush-centric interface. Download and install Krita at `https://krita.org/`. Many of the stencils were also made in Krita, as well. If you have another professional image editor you prefer to use, such as GIMP or Affinity Photo, these workflows can translate over to those editors, as well.

Setting up an external program

We'll start by making sure Blender and Krita talk friendly to each other; then we will put Krita's tools to use:

1. Go to **Edit** | **Preferences** | **File Path**, and for the image editor, navigate to the location of your image editor application. In my case, it's `C:\Program Files\Krita (x64)\bin\krita.exe`, but this may differ based on your OS, software of choice, and the install location.

2. Unpack your images by going to **File** | **External Data** | **Unpack into Files**, and write them to the directory. So far, we've made textures in Blender and so we have saved them there. When this happens, the textures are zipped with the rest of the blend file. Unpacking the textures places them in a folder called `textures`, next to where the Blender file is saved.

3. In Blender's image editor, load your base color texture, then go to **Image | Edit Externally**. The file opens in Krita. Do this for your `toplight_soft` texture, as well.

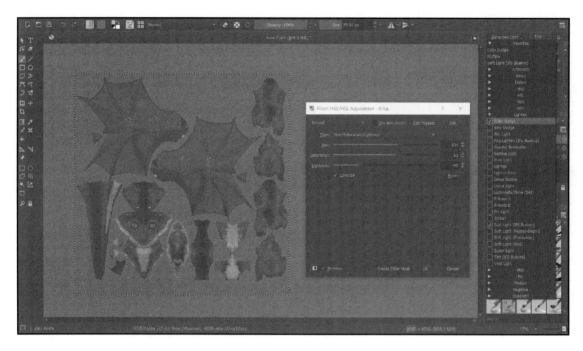

The base color texture as seen inside of the Krita painting software

4. Copy and paste the toplight texture into the base color texture. On the **Layers** docker, change its blend mode to **Color Dodge**, which will saturate and lighten it. Next, go to **Filter | Adjust | HSV Adjustment** and turn on **Colorize**. Adjust the settings to bring in a touch of cartoonish brightness, as well as the layer's opacity.

5. Right-click on the **Layers** docker and choose **Flatten Image**. Save and close the file. In Blender, reload the image by pressing *Ctrl + R* in the image editor and your changes will load.

6. Open your **Cavity** texture in Krita in the same way. This time, go to **Filter | Adjust | Threshold**, then use the slider to get a mask for the creases between scales. Save this as `dragon_scaleMask.png` in the texture's directory. Load it as a mask in the **Texture Paint** dialog and use it for more accurate, sharp painting. When utilizing filters in a secondary program, limit yourself to things that remap colors evenly, rather than distorting pixels; otherwise, UV seams will show the distortion and you'll waste time fixing it:

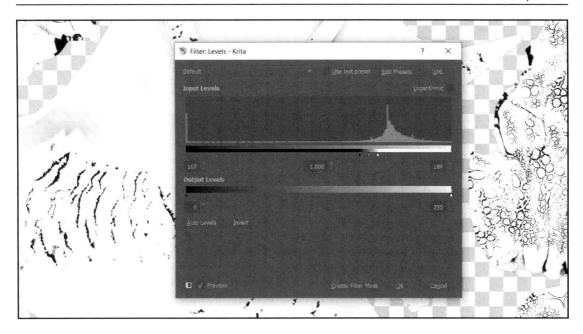

The levels adjustment in Krita can be used to fine tune our masks

7. As another example of the fancier tools available in an external image editor, edit `dragon_basecolor.png` externally. In Krita, duplicate the layer, then go to **Filter | Color | Color Transfer**. In the dialog, select a photo. The filter remaps the textures to relative colors based on the photo. I did this with several photos, then modified their layer opacity until the dragon's look felt more natural.

Save the layered document as a Krita file and save over `dragon_basecolor.png` with your new texture. Next, we'll do some projection painting.

Image edit projection painting

Image edit projection painting takes a screenshot of your model, then opens it in a different program that can edit images more comfortably:

1. Align your view to a problem area that you want to paint over in Krita. Do not move the view until the process is complete or the image won't be aligned.
2. In the sidebar's **Options** tab, expand the **External** tab. Set the **Screen Grab** size to `1024` by `1024`, then hit **Quick Edit**. The image opens in Krita as `.png`, saved in your temp directory.
3. Create a new layer and paint on this layer until your content with the edits.

4. Delete the original projection, merge all other layers, then save the file.

5. Return to Blender and hit **Apply**. The paint-over fixes are projected onto the mesh.

Here is a screenshot of our workflow:

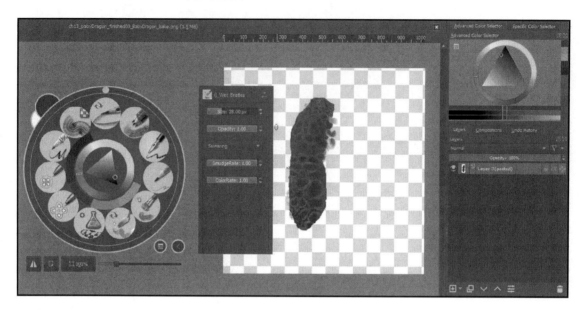

The projected section of the texture can be painted independently in the external software

Image edit projection painting is especially handy when cleaning up UV seams where the texture doesn't line up. Edit it externally, paint a hotfix on a new layer, then apply that change to automatically clean up the seams.

Now that we have most of our main maps taken care of, we need to set up our other textures that will plug into the **Principled BSDF** shader and complete the look of our dragon.

Setting up the remaining BSDF textures

Our dragon's base color and normal setup are working and it's time to get the rest of the final shader set up. It's always worth thinking through a shading problem before solving it. We won't need a metallic map, as this cutie pie is all organic. The specular map will be shiniest near the wetness of the eyes and mouth and the roughness will be at the lowest value.

The horns, teeth, and claws will be less rough than the dragon's skin. Beyond these major areas, we can get a varying level of detail on specular and roughness with our auxiliary maps. Subsurface scattering will breathe a lifelike glow into the baby dragon. Lastly, we'll add some glowing runes to the dragon's back. Let's get started.

Making specular and roughness maps from a master file

The specular and roughness maps will be combined from the various maps we have created so far. Because of this, we'll jump directly into Krita to combine them. Having an organized file for all your textures makes it easier to mix and match the result you want. The specular map is one-part artistic license and one-part material logic. It should be lightest at the wet mouth and teeth and darker on the horns and claws. The majority of the skin will be dark but will have varying details pulled from maps:

1. Open Krita. Create a new `4096 x 4096` texture.

2. Drag and drop all the maps we've used so far into the Krita window or go to **Layer** | **Import/export** | **Import Layer** and select all your various maps at the same time. These are all loaded as layers in a single document.

3. Select all the layers in the **Layers** docker, then go to **Layer** | **Quick Group**. Double-click on the group name and call it `all maps`. When building a specific texture, we can keep a backup of all our bakes in this group.

4. Start by duplicating the `dragon_cavity` and `dragon_convexity` maps. Move them into a new group and rename the group `specular`. Set the cavity layer's blending mode to **Multiply**, darkening the **Convexity** map below it.

5. Add a new layer by going to **Layer** | **New** | **Paint Layer**. Set its blending mode to **Overlay**. Choose a dark-gray color and fill this layer via **Edit** | **Fill with Foreground Color**.

6. Use the polygonal lasso tool to select around the teeth and then press *Ctrl + U* to increase the lightness for the teeth. Repeat this for the horns and nails, as well.

7. Add another paint layer called `Mouth`. We need to increase the overall strength of the specular map on the mouth, but avoid crossing over UV seams in a way that will be noticeable. Use the polygonal lasso tool to select the overall area. Reset your colors to the default black and white by pressing *D*, then fill this selection with white by going to **Edit** | **Fill with Background Color**. Switch to the brush tool and use `Airbrush_soft` to paint over the white section to make a soft transition. Set the blend mode to **Addition**, and lower its opacity. Go to **File** | **Export** and save your finished specular as `dragon_specular.png`.

8. Create a new **Image Texture** node in your material. Load your specular map and use it for the specular input on the **Principled BSDF** node:

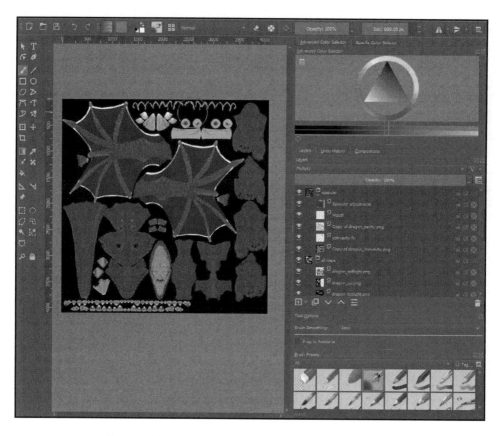

Our texture editing process in Krita lets us customize our specular map to our specific needs

The roughness map will follow a similar workflow. First, think through the problem—the teeth and claws will have dark roughness values, while the skin will be rougher. The mouth, wet with saliva, is also less rough, and so it will be darker:

1. Right-click on your specular group layer and choose **Duplicate Layer or Mask**. Rename this group Roughness.

2. Start with a mixture of convexity and cavity that approximates a 30% dark-gray value, while retaining details from these maps for visual interest. I did this by inverting the convexity map by going to **Filter | Adjust | Invert**, setting the cavity map layer above it to a **Multiply** blend mode, and adjusting the levels on both of these by pressing *Ctrl + L*.

3. Recycle the overall adjustment layer from the specular group by inverting it, setting its blend mode to **Multiply**, and adjusting its levels, as well.

4. Invert the **Mouth** layer and set it to **Multiply** so that the mouth is darker (and therefore less rough) than the rest of the body.

5. Go to **File** | **Export** and save your finished specular as dragon_roughness.png.

6. Create a new image texture node in your material. Load your roughness map and use it for the roughness input on the **Principled BSDF** node:

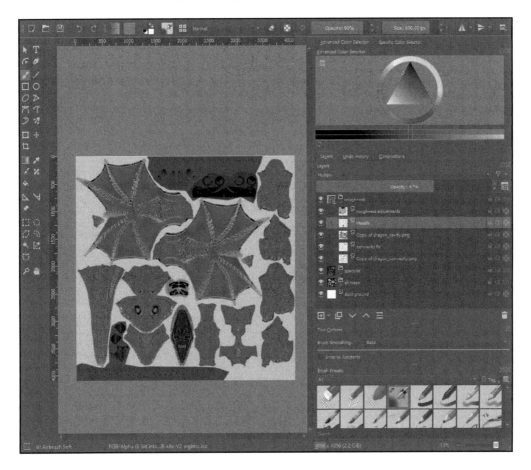

The finished roughness texture as in appears in Krita

You can see how I layered maps in the dragon_textures.kra example file, as well as how all the textures are in one place. Once these exports are set up in the material, you can adjust your specular and roughness composites more, varying their overall values and textural details by modifying these layers and exporting them once more.

Subsurface scattering

We'll give the baby dragon a blush of health with **Subsurface Scattering** (**SSS**). Some light hits these scales and bounces right back. Other light permeates inward and bounces around, eventually absorbing or bouncing back out. If organic matter is thin enough, that light transmits through, but unlike light easily passing through glass, it scatters through the blood vessels, skin, fat, and other organic matter. We see this when light shines through thin skin, such as backlit ears, or when a hand is held over a flashlight. We'll use a hand-painted subsurface color map to represent those internal colors and our subsurface bakes to control.

The subsurface attribute of the BSDF controls where SSS occurs. The subsurface radius approximates how the scattering occurs; as the light splits into a spectrum, RGB usually has a ratio of 1 to .2 to .1, respectively. The subsurface color represents the interior color of the dragon—blood, muscles, fat, skin, and bone—rather than the exterior scales:

1. In the **Options** panel of your shader, activate **Subsurface Translucency**.
2. In your Krita master document, create copies of the subsurface maps you baked at a distance of .05 and .01, respectively, and put them in a new group. These maps have the closest approximation of how much light permeated the skin. At .01, almost everything is dark except the wing membrane, while .05 allows more light through.
3. Put the .01 subsurface map as your top layer, set its blend mode to **Multiply**, and put its layer opacity to 60%. We could combine these in Blender with a MixRGB mode, but combining these two maps externally means one less 4k map.
4. Add a new layer and use Krita's selection tools to select the tooth, claw, and horns. Fill this with black and lower the layer's opacity to 60% to control these areas' subsurface translucency.
5. Export this map as dragon_subsurface.png. Load this as an image texture node and plug it into the **Subsurface** attribute on **Principled BSDF**.
6. Change the subsurface color to a fleshy red.
7. Now that SSS is all set up, we can control its overall strength. Drop a **Math** node onto the noodle of the final subsurface output. Set it to **Multiply**, with a value of .2. I also use a **Sun** object as my only light, with 10 energy, and rotated to backlight the wings so the subsurface effect can be seen. Both the **MixRGB** multiply node and the math **Multiply** node can be adjusted to control how much light permeates the wings.

8. For a more advanced subsurface color, you can add a new image texture and save it as `dragon_subsurface_color.png`. Plug this into the **Subsurface Color** attribute of the **Principled BSDF** node. Using texture paint and projection painting, paint an approximation of what the dragon looks like under its skin—mostly red muscles, bony protrusions at joints and the face, fatty yellow tissue on the underbelly, and light pink epidermis for the wing skin. Anatomical images from the internet of skinless anatomy can also be edited onto this when projection painting:

The subsurface texture looks gross, but helps color bleed through to the surface of our baby dragon

The subsurface glow permeating the dragon's wings adds a blush of life, which is especially needed to make the wing membrane believable.

Next, we have a fun addition to our baby dragon's textures—we're going to add a glowing rune to its back.

Rune magic with object projection

Positioning a magic rune on the baby dragon's back is best done with a separate rune texture. By using an empty object to position it, we retain a lot of flexibility; the rune can be repositioned easily and it can be replaced and recolored when using different kinds of magic:

1. Use an image editor of your choice to design the runic symbol mask for your dragon on a `1024 x 1024` texture, using white for the symbol and black for the background. We've provided one—`dragon_runes.png`.
2. Add this as an image texture node in the **Shader** editor, with the tiling set to **Extend**.
3. Add a UV map node (**Add | Input**). Create a new UV layout for this node on the dragon in the **Properties** window and name the UV map `rune`.
4. In the **Modifiers** panel, add a **UV Project** modifier. Select the new UV map.
5. Create an empty object and name it `rune_empty`. Use this in the **UV Project** modifier's object input.
6. Move the empty object around in the three-dimensional space. It now aims and places the rune.
7. **UV Project**, unfortunately, puts the runes on the dragon's belly as well, so we'll subtract those faces with vertex colors. Add a new vertex color called `runeFaces`. In **Vertex Paint** mode, use a face mask, , to limit painting to selected faces, then set **Vertex Colors** (*Shift + K*) to make a white mask for the correct faces. In the **Shader** editor, use an **Attribute** node and multiply it over the stencil image with a **Math** node.
8. Set up an addition to your node tree to change the base color to green where the rune is, and also add a green **Emission** output. Use a **MixRGB** node with the base color as `Color1`, your rune color as `Color2`, and the stencil as the factor, and run this in the **Base Color** attribute. Use another **MixRGB** node set to `Color`, with the rune set to `Color1` and the rune color set to `Color2`. Run its output in the **Emission** attribute. Lastly, add an **RGB** node by going to **Add | Input | RGB** and use this on both **MixRGB** nodes' `Color2` attributes, so that a single value controls both colors.

You can see how the rune is projected onto our baby dragon's back in the following screenshot:

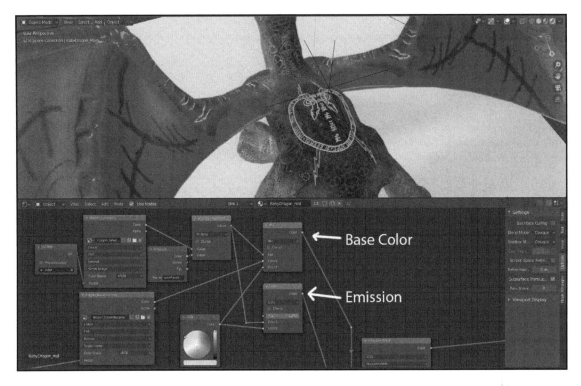

Our rune is projected onto the baby dragon's back and glows with emissive color

The color of the rune can be controlled with the RGB node and its placement can be controlled with the empty object.

Alright, now our dragon just needs some texture for its eyes and we'll be done!

Painting the eye

The dragon's eyes are best painted as their own separate texture for the same reason that we organize them as their own separate object. This will make the eye easier to reuse in your future projects and standardizes it so the pupil is in the center of a square texture. We'll paint the individual sections for the pupil, iris, sclera, and blood vessels in Krita as flat layers, then use filters to make the finished texture look like an eyeball.

Note the mesh modifications to the eye mesh in the demo file, including an outer mesh with a glass/transparent shader and the additional modeling for the sclera, iris, and pupil. For an example of the eye texture layers, see `dragon_eye.kra` in the project files:

1. Open up Krita and create a `512 x 512` document. Fill the first paint layer with the default black foreground color by pressing *Shift + Backspace*. Double-click on the layer and rename it `Pupil`.

2. Create a new paint layer (go to **Insert**) named `Iris`. Use the rectangular selection tool (*Ctrl + R*, select the middle third part of the texture, and fill it with a dark-red eye color. In the **Layers** panel, click the transparency lock icon for the iris so that painting is constrained to the currently opaque pixels.

3. Do the same for a new sclera layer on the upper third part of the texture, filling it with a cream color.

4. Go back to the iris layer. Select the wet bristles brush, then paint some gold on the iris band near the pupil and darker red near where it meets the sclera. Adjust your brush opacity by pressing *I* and *O* and push the pixels until you're pleased with the transition.

5. Select a hard brush, such as the `Basic-6_details` brush, and color pick by pressing *Ctrl* and left-clicking on your red eye color. In the brush settings, change your **Blend mode** from **Normal** to **Multiply**, which will darken as you paint. Add some strokes of darker color going up and down the iris.

6. Color pick on your gold eye color. In **Brush Settings**, change your **Blend mode** from **Normal** to **Color Dodge**, which will both lighten and saturate when you paint. Add some streaks of glowing motes up and down the iris.

7. On the sclera layer, use the wet bristles brush to mix a transition from the white sclera to the dark reds near the top.

8. Add another paint layer called `blood vessels` and use the basic details brush to paint dark-red lines for the blood vessels, with more blood vessels near the top.

9. Go to **View** | **Wrap Mode** to loop the texture. Next, use a blending brush to clean up any seams that might have happened from the right and left edge.

10. Click on your top layer, press *Shift* and click on the bottom layer so that all layers are selected, then duplicate them all by pressing *Ctrl + J*, and merge the duplicates by pressing *Ctrl + E*, so that you have one layer with all the layers combined.

11. Go to **Filter** | **G'MIC-Qt**. This launches a vast library of image filters. Go to **Deformations** | **Sphere filter**. Set the **Background** mode to **Mean Color** and adjust the dilation to modify the ratios of the eye sections.

12. Save this as `babydragon_eye.kra` to keep the layered Krita file. Next, export it for use by going to **File** | **Export** and set the file type to `.png`.

Our example eyeball texture turned out like this:

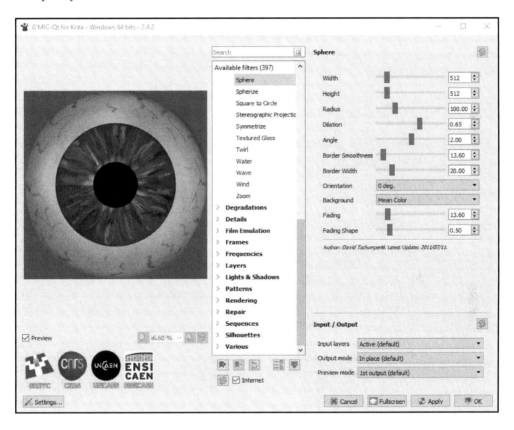

The eye texture for the baby dragon

Next, we'll set this up on the eye object, with personal shaders for both the eye and the reflective sphere surrounding it:

1. Select your eyeball mesh. Create a new material for it called `Eye`.

2. Add an image texture node by going to **Add** | **Texture** | **Image** and open the `Eye` texture. Use it as the base color for **Principled BSDF**.

3. Select your eye reflection object and create a new material for it, called `Eye_reflection`.

4. Delete the **Principled BSDF** node and add the `Transparent BSDF`, `Glass BSDF`, and `Mix Shader` nodes. Plug the **Transparent** and **Glass** nodes into the mix shader's two shader inputs and use the mix shader for the material output. Give the **Glass** BSDF shader `0` roughness and an IOR of `1.4`.

The dragon's eye can be further adjusted by scaling rings of UVs to dilate or contract the pupil:

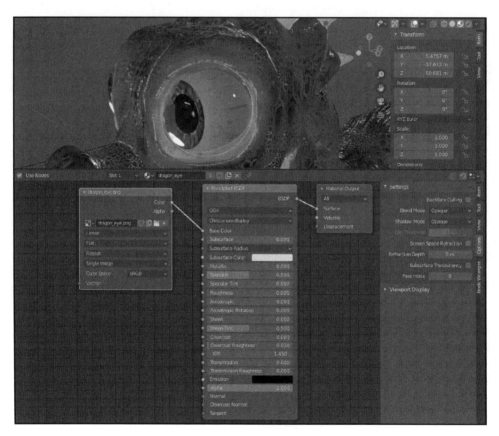

The eyeball texture applied to the baby dragon in Blender

With this final texturing hurdle done, the baby dragon's peepers are ready to go out and view the world.

Summary

This adorable hatchling is finally ready to take to the sky and rain down fireballs. Think about the next steps you could carry out to make this setup even better. A detailed texture, much smaller in scale via mapping, could be overlaid for the specular, roughness, and normal maps so that it retains an organic fidelity even when zoomed in. Clever textures might save the specular, roughness, and subsurface maps as R, G, and B channels in a single .png. The color choices for the top and underbelly could be made modular with a mask for the pattern. The various auxiliary maps we baked, saved externally now, could be removed to speed the shader up. A sophisticated node tree could even break down the dragon's elemental powers into a single node group attribute.

Next up, we'll set the baby dragon up with a customized character rig. At last, our fully realized baby dragon will hop, walk, chomp, and come to life.

Questions

1. How do you determine which texture Blender will bake to?
2. Why should you bake to a low-resolution texture first?
3. What map types should a 32-bit float be to function correctly in Blender?
4. How does an auxiliary map differ from a map used in the final shader?
5. How do masks aid in Blender's texture painting interface?
6. How do you create and use a custom stencil for your brush tip in Texture Paint mode?
7. What requirements are needed to edit a projection painting successfully?
8. Why would you create a specular map from your auxiliary maps in an external program, rather than combining them with nodes?
9. What is the difference between the subsurface and subsurface color attributes?
10. What are some examples you can think of where you'd position textures with a **UV Project** modifier?

Further reading

To learn more about Krita, visit https://docs.krita.org/.

15
Creating a Baby Dragon - Part 5: Rigging and Animation

In the previous chapter, we added materials and textures to our baby dragon. Now, we can set it up for animation! The process for preparing a character for animation is called rigging. Like the strings of a puppet, a rig provides controls that can move mesh with bones. Some of the bones physically bind the mesh to them, weighting vertices between targets. Other bones act as controllers for these weight bones, providing animators with a clean user interface. Many other bones exist just to create a necessary parent/child hierarchy or to create complex functionality in between the control and weight bones.

Rigging your baby dragon from scratch might be impossible, but the **Rigify** add-on can get any character up and running quickly. This add-on uses anatomical templates that can be adjusted for any character and generates a production-ready rig. We'll then attach our mesh to the rig, using weight painting to transition deformation from one bone to another.

Lastly, we'll put this rig to use. We'll use the same animation principles discussed in `Chapter 9`, *Animating an Exquisite Corpse in Grease Pencil* and `Chapter 10`, *Animating a Stylish Short in Grease Pencil*, for some dragon poses and walk cycles.

The following topics will be covered in this chapter:

- What is a rig?
- Practicing with a simple tentacle rig
- Using the Rigify add-on to rig the baby dragon
- Modifying armature weights
- Animating a flying cycle

What is a rig?

The dragon needs a rig to fly. A rig is a set of joints, controls, and features that lets us control and animate a three-dimensional character. In claymation, a clay character is built on top of a wire armature to give it structure and make sure its limbs bend at the elbows, knees, and other joints. In three dimensions, the process is the same but backward. We make the character first, then we place an armature inside it with joints and bones.

The **Armature** object type stores a rig composed of these bones. Bones utilize parental hierarchies to move correctly; rotating your chest will move your arm, which moves your forearm, which moves your hand. Before working on the dragon, let's play around with armatures to control the simple tasks of a basic tentacle rig.

Armatures and bones in Edit Mode

Let's create an armature with some simple bones to explore the basic components of rigging:

1. Start a new scene and delete the default cube. Add an armature by going to **Add** | **Armature**. This object includes a single bone with a root, body, and tip. The root is the bone's origin and functions like object origins. The body stretches between the root and tip and can serve as the range of influence that a bone exerts. The tail at the end is the literal or metaphorical point where the bone's children will come from and, combined with the root, determines the bone's default angle.
2. Change to **Edit Mod**e (*Tab*). An armature's components can be moved and adjusted in **Edit Mode**, just like vertices in a mesh object. Select the bone's root and tip, in the same manner, to move them around, or move the whole bone by selecting the bone body. When adjusting an armature in **Edit Mode**, you're modifying its default state.
3. Select just the tip and extrude a new bone upward by pressing *E*. Rename it `child` by pressing *F2*. This new bone is the child of the original bone and has an explicit connection; the tip of the first bone is also the root of `child`.
4. Select the body of `child` and duplicate it to the side by pressing *Shift + D*. This duplicate inherits the parent/child relationship of its sibling, shown by a dotted line. Like a tree branching outward, bones can have multiple children but only one parent.
5. With the newest bone selected, right-click and subdivide it, then in the operator panel (labeled **Subdivide Multi** for this operation), set **Number of Cuts** to 4.

6. Select a connected bone and disconnect it from its parent by pressing *Y*. This removes the root/tip connection and the parent/child relationship. Add the previous parent to your selection and parent it by pressing *Ctrl + P*, choosing **Keep Offset**. It has now become a child that inherits transforms from the parent but also can be moved out in space.

7. In the **Viewport Display** tab, turn on **In Front**, **Names**, and **Axes**, which can provide useful info.

8. Select a bone, then adjust its roll by going to **Armature | Bone Roll | Set Roll** (or pressing *Ctrl + R*). This, plus the **Recalculate Roll** options, are vital to making bones turn the right way. For example, a neck bone rotated on its local *x*-axis should nod its head up and down and rotating bones on the *y*-axis should explicitly rotate the bone along its axis. Joints such as your knees will often only bend on their local *x*-axis, unless they're broken or sat on. While animating, I frequently hit *R*, *X*, and *X* or *R*, *Y*, and *Y* to animate with one axis only.

9. Move a bone to a new bone layer by pressing *M*. In the **Properties** window's Armature object panel, the **Skeleton** tab shows the bone layers. Click on a layer to see its bones or use multiple layers by pressing *Shift* and clicking your mouse.

These are the basic methods for connecting a bone hierarchy. Now, to use it on a tentacle rig.

Practicing with a simple tentacle rig

We'll walk through the entire process of building a rig from scratch with a simple tentacle. This use case involves using three different methods of control—major controls for the whole tentacle, smaller controls for individual segments, and an alternate control for positioning the tentacle tip. The first two categories will use **Forward Kinematics** (**FK**) and the tip-oriented control will use **Inverse Kinematics** (**IK**). All of these will need good naming conventions and layer organization for ease of use. We'll make the rig more user-friendly with widgets for easier navigation, plus a custom attribute to switch between IK and FK.

The hierarchy for all of this will also require intermediate bones for parenting and deforming:

1. Start a new default scene. Model a quick tentacle that's 4 m tall, with plenty of subdivisions on both the *X* and *Y* axes, with the base at the world origin.

2. Create a single bone armature by going to **Add | Armature | Single Bone**. In the **Properties** window, go to the **Object Data Properties** panel and open the **Viewport Display** tab. Activate **In Front** so that we can see the rig through the mesh. Also, change it to **Display As B-Bone**. Next, go to the **Viewport Display** tab in **Object Properties** and change it to **Display As Wire**.

3. Switch to **Edit Mode** and move the bone tip up on the *Z* axis by 3 m so that the bone is the same length as the tentacle. Right-click on the bone, choose **Subdivide**, and in the **Tool options** panel, increase the subdivision to 7 so that there are 8 bones in total.

4. Select all 8 bones. Press *Ctrl + F2* to batch rename the bones. Change **Data Type** to **Bones**, with **Set Name** as **New**, and the **Name** as **tentacle**. Click the **+** icon to add another name with a prefix of DEF. and a suffix of .001. The first bone is now named DEF.tentacle.001:

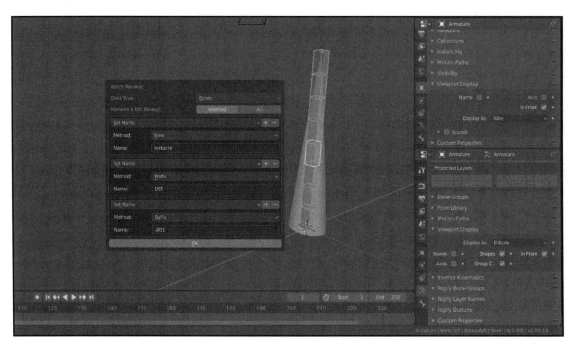

Batch renaming the bones

5. Select all these bones, duplicate them, and move them to the second bone layer by pressing *M* and choosing the second square. Activate this bone layer in **Object Data Properties**. Use **Batch Rename** once again with the following bone renames—find and replace DEF with ORG, strip the characters and digits from the end, and set the name with a suffix of .001. The bones are renamed ORG.tentacle.001 through .008. Lastly, scale the bone radius down by pressing *Ctrl + Shift + S*.

6. Repeat this process two more times with three more sets of bones. You should eventually have 8 bones per layer, named along the lines of tentacle.001 on the first layer, DEF.tentacle.001 on the second layer, MCH.IK.tentacle.001 on the third layer, and ORG.tentacle.001 on the fourth layer. All four layers should have their bones scaled to different sizes by pressing *Ctrl + Alt + S* in **Edit Mode**. By doing so, multiple layers can be active at the same time, with different bone types identifiable by their radius.

7. On the first layer, duplicate tentacle.001, name it tentacle.main, and scale its radius larger. Duplicate it again, name it Root, and scale its radius even more. Grab the tip of tentacle.008, extrude a new bone up by pressing *E*, and rename this new bone tentacle.IK. Select tentacle.001, duplicate it by pressing *Shift + D*, and move it 2 unity to the right along the x-axis. Rename this bone tentacle.IK.target.

The ingredients for our tentacle rig are now all in place. Now, we need to get it to function by using parenting, modifiers, drivers, and widgets.

Setting up the tentacle rig's controls

In our basic hierarchy, the Root controller is the parent to everything and will be used to place the whole tentacle rig. Root will have many children, some control bones (tentacle.main, tentacle.ik, and tentacle.001), and some independent hierarchies (DEF.tentacle.001 and MCH.IK.tentacle.001). The trickiest parent/child chain will be the layering of the FK controls. MCH.tentacleMain.001 will have ORG.tentacle.001 and tentacle.001 as sibling children. ORG.tentacle.001 will contain the next layer of the hierarchy, with MCH.tentacleMain.002 as a child, which then contains the siblings, ORG.tentacle.002 and tentacle.002, again. This repeats all the way up until the .008 bones. We'll then put bone constraints on the ORG bone to its sibling control bone's transforms. This creates a layer of protective hierarchy, leaving the ORG bone with clean transform values, even though it's still posable via the control bone.

Over on the IK bones, an IK constraint will deform the whole chain to bend between the first IK bone's root and the tentacle.IK controller, pointing the IK chain at the target. The deform bones will copy the transforms of both the ORG and IK bones and we'll use a custom property as a driver for these, transitioning between the two options. An informal rule of rigging is that bone should only be used to do one thing at a time. The sum total of their purposes (deformation, organization, the IK controls, the FK controls, and so on) can be created through parenting and constraints:

1. Go to **Edit Mode** and parent
   DEF.tentacle.001, ORG.tentacle.001, MCH.IK.tentacle.001,
   tentacle.IK, and tentacle.main to Root, with **Connected** turned off for all
   of them.

2. Select tentacle.IK.target. Change its parent to tentacle.IK.

3. Select MCH.IK.tentacle.008 and give it an IK constraint in the **Properties**
   window's **Bone Constraints** panel. For the target, choose **Armature**, with
   tentacle.IK for the bone. Set **Pole Target** to **Armature**,
   with tentacle.IK.target for the target. For **Weight**, turn on both **Position**
   and **Rotation**. You can test the IK by moving the tentacle.IK
   and tentacle.IK.target controls, which can be moved and rotated to control
   the whole chain.

4. Change the parent of tentacle.002 to ORG.tentacle.001, with **Connected**
   turned off. Repeat this for tentacle.003 through .008, so that each
   ORG.tentacle instance contains two siblings—the next ORG bone and its
   equivalent control.

5. Select ORG.tentacle.001. In the **Bone Constraints** properties, give it a **Copy
   Transforms** constraint. Set **Target** to **Armature** and **Bone** to tentacle.001. It
   now copies the bone's moves, but ORG.tentacle.001's transforms remain
   clean.

6. Add another **Copy Transforms** constraint to ORG.tentacle.001. Set this one to
   target the armature, with tentacle.main for the bone. Set **Mix** to **After
   Original** and change both of the **Space** evaluators to **Local** with **Parent**.

7. Repeat this constraint on ORG.tentacle.002 through .008, with tentacle.002 through .008 as the bone target. You can speed some of this up by selecting all the ORG bones, with ORG.tentacle.001 as the active bone, then use **Copy Constraints** via **Pose** | **Constraints** | **Copy Constraints** to **Selected Bones**. Go through each bone and update the first constraint's target bone to the correct target, but leave the second constraint on tentacle.main.

8. Select DEF.tentacle.001. Add two **Copy Transforms** constraints, with the first targeting ORG.tentacle.001 and the second targetting MCH.IK.tentacle.001. If you set **Influence** for both of these to .5, the DEF bone will blend between the two when the control bones move them.

9. Select the tentacle.IK controller. In the bone properties in the **Custom Properties** tab, add a property with a property name of IK/FK. This will drive the influence of the two constraints on DEF.bone.001. In the sidebar (press *N*) under the basic transforms; the IK/FK property is now visible. Right-click on its value, then **Copy Data Path**.

10. Return to DEF.tentacle.001, right-click on the first **Copy Constraints** influence, and then on **Add a Driver**. Drivers are a different means of controlling properties and allow more sophisticated math. Right-click again and open it in **Drivers Editor**. Change **Type** to **Sum Values**, then use the **Type** pulldown to change it to **Single Property**. Set the **Prop** ID type to **Object** and choose the **Armature** as the target object. Paste the IK/FK data path into **Path**. Now, the **Copy Transforms** constraint duplicates whatever your IK/FK property is set to.

11. The second constraint should be the opposite of the IK/FK value. Create a driver for this constraint's influence as well, also using **Single Property** targeting the armature, with the IK/FK bone's data path pasted in once more. Change this driver's type to the **Scripted** expression and change **Expression** to, say, 1 - var. Animating the IK/FK property now switches the transform copying from IK to FK on bone.001.

12. Select all your DEF bones, with DEF.tentacle.001 as the active object. Go to **Pose | Constraints | Copy Constraints to Selected Bones**. The driver doesn't copy over, so on DEF.tentacle.001, right-click on the first copy transform's influence and on **Copy Driver**. Right-click and choose **Paste Driver** on the first copy transform's influence for DEF.tentacle.002 through .008. Do the same with the driver for the second constraint:

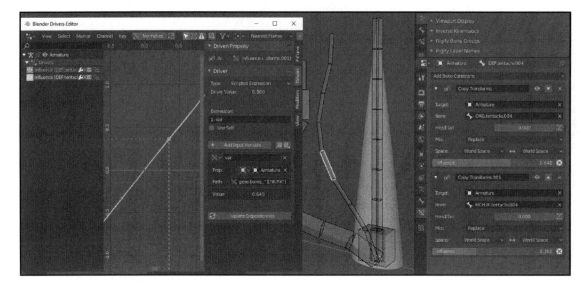

Editing drivers for the blend between IK and FK

The technical setup for the tentacle rig is complete. Now, all that's left is to make the control UI prettier and attach the mesh.

Finishing the tentacle rig

The final step in making the tentacle rig is to make the mesh controlled by the rig. We can then make the rig's interface prettier, adding prettier controls to the rig and hiding all the layers except the things we want to hand to an animator:

1. In **Object Mode**, add a circle by going to **Add | Mesh | Circle**. Rename it WGT_tentacle.fk. Switch to **Edit Mode**, select the two vertices at opposite ends of the y-axis, and scale them on the *y-axis* outward. This notch will help us visualize the bone orientation.

2. Select `tentacle.001`. In the **Properties** window's **Bone Properties** panel, go to the **Viewport Display** tab. Select `WGT.tentacle.fk` as its custom object. You might need to return to `WGT.tentacle.fk` and rotate everything in **Edit Mode** for proper orientation. Use this custom object for `tentacle.002` through `.008` as well, reducing the scale so that they're close but outside the mesh. When you're done, move the widget to a new collection called `Widgets` by pressing *M* and deactivate that collection in the outliner.

3. Repeat this widget process for `tentacle.IK`, `tentacle.IK.target`, and `Root`. You can use empty objects for some custom object shapes as well.

4. In **Bone Properties**, make sure **Deform** is deactivated for all the bones except the **DEF** bones.

5. In **Object Mode**, select your tentacle mesh, then add the armature to your selection. Parent the mesh to the armature by pressing *Ctrl + P*, choosing **Armature Deform** with **Automatic Weights**:

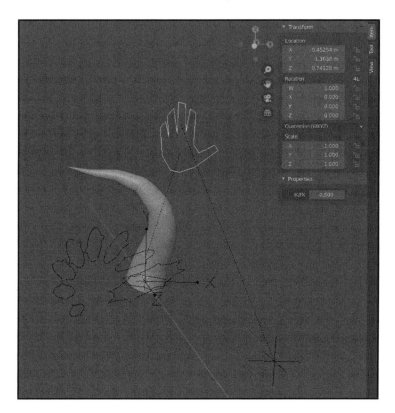

The final tentacle rig

The tentacle rig is complete. `tentacle.main` lets us pose the whole tentacle in FK, with the individual controls (`tentacle.001` through `.008`) providing a second layer of control. This can then switch to IK using the `IK/FK` custom property and the tentacle can be posed to land on an exact spot with the IK controls.

Using the Rigify add-on to rig the baby dragon

The baby dragon will require lots of complex rigging setups, far beyond the simple hierarchies we've seen so far. We'll take a shortcut by using the **Rigify** add-on. **Rigify** uses templates of anatomy—arms, legs, tentacles, a tail, and so on. It requires us to merely align the templates with our character. Then, at the click of a button, all of them are available for use. The only task for the user to carry out is to place the bones correctly inside their mesh and, in the event of unusual anatomy, set up a correct hierarchy of parent and child bones.

Before rigging the dragon, let's dig around in **Rigify** and understand its basic workflow. To use it for your characters, you'll need to understand the difference between a meta-rig and a completed rig, how the **Rigify** bone types work, and how to customize the add-on for different anatomical layouts:

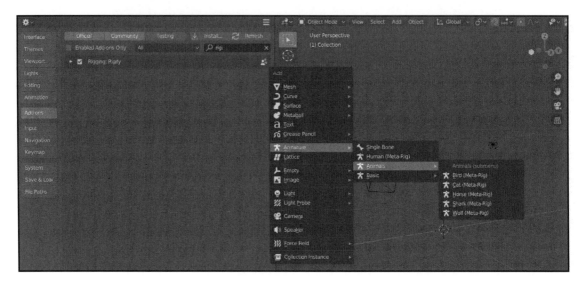

The Rigify add-on's meta-rig templates

To get started with Rigify we need to activate it:

1. Activate Rigify by going to **Edit** | **Preferences**, then select the **Add-ons** panel. Search for `Rigify`, enable it, and save your settings.
2. Add a meta-rig by going to **Add** | **Rig** | **Human (Meta-rig)**.
3. Switch to **Edit Mode**. Go to **View** | **Tool Settings**, then in the **Tool Settings** bar, enable **X Mirror**. Select an arm bone and move it to a different location. Move some other bone locations on the meta-rig around, as if customizing it to a differently shaped character.
4. Switch to **Object Mode**. In the **Properties** window's **Rig** panel, open the **Rigify** tab and click **Generate Rig**. A new rig appears, complete with built-in controls and ready for a mesh. Move it to a new collection (press *M*) so that we can view the meta-rig and the finished rig individually.

It's that easy! But how does it work? First, the meta-rig came with a starting bone hierarchy. Go to **Pose Mode** on the meta-rig in the **Properties** window's **Bone Info** panel and examine how it's parented. The first spine joint is at the top of the hierarchy; its children include the rest of the spine, which leads to the arms and head children, and also the pelvis bones, which lead to the leg children, with a mix of connected and loose child bones.

In the **Bone Info** panel's **Rigify Type** tab; you'll also notice that the first meta-rig spine bone has a rig type—`spines.super_spine`. The other spine bones don't have a type as they inherit this type down the chain until a new rig type is assigned, creating a new chain. This allows for spines, fingers, tentacles, and other features that have any number of segments.

As an example of this, switch to **Edit Mode** on the meta-rig, select all the arm and hand bones, duplicate them upward by pressing *Shift + D* on the first arm bones, and change their parent to the final spine bone (the head). Repeat this with the lower bones and change the first arm bone's parent to `spine.001`. Return to **Object Mode** and hit **Generate Rig** once more.

The generated rig updates to the new changes, now with a functioning six-armed freak rig:

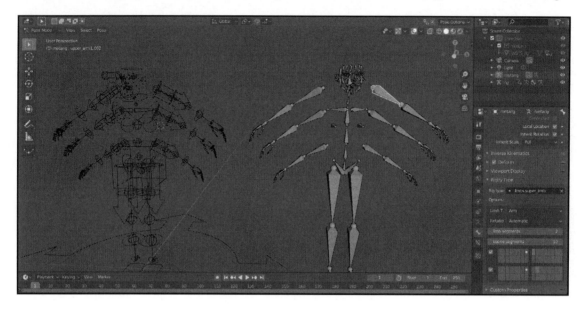

Modifying the meta-rig, which changes the rig that is generated

Certain **Rigify** types have to follow rules, such as the children requiring specific naming conventions or having to have a minimum or a maximum number of children. Other types, such as tentacles or fingers, can have any number of children and will successfully extend the generated rig to the new length. To accommodate these issues, when building a new rig from the rig types, use **Edit Mode** and start building it from samples via the **Add Sample** dialog in the **Rigify Buttons** tab.

Return to the generated rig, switch to **Pose Mode**, and open the sidebar (press *N*). This contains the view buttons for part of the rig UI. The sidebar's **Rig Main Properties** tab also has custom controls for each bone type, such as switching between the IK and FK on the arms and legs.

In the **Properties** window, the generated rig organizes the bones in the bone layers. Note the three final hidden layers—the DEF, MCH, and ORG bones. The DEF bones will occasionally come into use when weight painting, where you might activate only this layer. The MCH bones provide specialized functions and targeting. The ORG bones are a vital stage of the hierarchy for each new addition down a bone chain. Ideally, you should never need to touch these bones when the rig is in use.

The rest of this chapter will focus on getting a **Rigify** rig up and running for the baby dragon. To learn more about the under-the-hood way that **Rigify** builds a rig, examine the modifiers, constraints, and drivers that are on the generated rig's bones, especially the hidden DEF, MCH, and ORG bones.

Setting up the baby dragon's meta-rig

We'll use a quadruped meta-rig to approximate our dragon quickly, then we will add some additional bones for the wings and generate the finished production rig. Start from ch14_babyDragon_texturing_final.blend or carry on from where you previously progressed to. There's a handful of under-the-hood updates from previous chapters, such as mild positioning changes. To save time on positioning the meta-rig, you can append the metarig_simple or metarig_advanced collections from ch15_babyDragon_animation_final.blend. Reference these when positioning your own meta-rig, double-checking the bone names, the parents, the **Rigify** rig types, and the bone rolls. Mistakes in your initial layout are often only discovered once you start animating; if this happens to you, adjust your meta-rig and re-generate. The metarig_advanced collection uses the robust **Quadruped (Wolf)** template, which has many more bones to weight and animate. The metarig_simple collection is less intimidating, removing bones for toes, lips, ears, and so on. If you want to jump ahead to weighting and animation, simply generate a rig using one of the aligned meta-rigs in the start file:

1. In your baby dragon file, add a **Quadruped (Wolf)** rig. Activate **In Front** in **Viewport Display**. For a less complex rig, use a **Basic Quadruped** rig instead.
2. Switch to **Edit Mode** and turn on **X-Mirror**.
3. Scale all the bones in **Edit Mode** to generally match the dragon. Avoid moving the rig forward or backward; instead, move the baby dragon's polygons in **Edit Mode**.
4. Start moving the leg bones to fit the mesh, checking both the front, side, and top views. For exact placement, select the mesh edge loops, set the 3D Cursor to **Selection** (*Shift + S*), select the bone joint, and snap to the cursor by pressing *Shift + S* again.

5. Align the spine from the side view. As long as you understand the **Rigify** add-on's meta-rig system, you can even completely redraw it. Right-click and subdivide bones if you need extras. Re-parent the limbs to their closest spine bone. When you're happy with the placement, select all the spine bones by hitting *L* while the cursor is over the spine. Next, batch rename them by pressing *Ctrl + F2* and set **Data Type** to **Bones** and **Rename** to **Selected**, add **Set Name**, and set **Method** to **New**. Rename them with a proxy name first (cat), so they're named in order of the bone chain, then batch rename them again to the original name (spine):

Batch renaming for the dragon's additional spine joints

6. For the face, use vertex snapping to move bone joints to their best location, then move them inside the mesh bounds. Change the snap target to **Face** (*Ctrl + Shift + Tab*) and hold *Ctrl* to snap. For bones on lines of symmetry, such as the tongue, change their location from the side view. Hide bone chains after placing them to avoid clutter. Avoid deleting or renaming bones; missing bones can throw exceptions during generation, so it's better to do so after the final rig is generated.

7. Build the wing using the **Rig Button** samples in the **Properties** window. Add a basic.super_copy sample, position it from the spine to the left shoulder, rename it wingshoulder.L, and parent it to the nearest spine bone. Add a limbs.super_limbs sample, move its joints to the arm, and parent the first bone to wingshoulder.L. Add a limbs.super_palm sample for each of the five palm starts of the fingers, clean up their names to read as palm.01.L, palm.02.L, and so on, and parent them to the hand bones. Add a limbs.super_finger sample for all five left fingers. Use **Batch Rename** (*Ctrl + F2*) to rename them quickly; with the first finger joint renamed to w_pinky_01.L. The find/replace function quickly changes pinky to ring and **Batch Rename**'s **Remove Characters** function strips off digits and punctuation from the end, cleaning up uses of .001 and .002.

8. Mirror your finished wing bones from left to right, duplicating and scaling with the 3D Cursor from the world origin at -1. Use **Batch Rename** to change .L to .R. If your renaming was successful, the X axis mirror should work on all the wing bones.

9. Position the finger and toe bones similar to how we approached the face. To simplify the rig, I deleted some of the ends so that the hands and feet only have a palm and two finger joints each.

10. The bone roll should be set to the correct angle. In the **Properties** window's **Viewport Display** tab, enable **Axes** to help visualize this, then press *Ctrl + R* to adjust the bone roll. This orientation should usually be such that if we rotated a bone only on the *x-axis*, its arc would be in the correct direction. For example, the S-shaped bend of the leg bones, when rotated only on the *x-axis*, would end up collapsing like a neat spring. Every spine bone, when rotated on the *x-axis*, should go up and down, without any drift to the left or right. The wing bones will be different than the finger bones, as their default X axis rotation should fold the wing inward and outward.

Now for the scary part—generating the rig! Remember that if your template had any errors, such as bones with incorrect names, rig types, parents, or orientations, you could adjust the meta-rig and regenerate it.

Creating and modifying the Rigify rig

The final rig for the baby dragon is just a click away:

1. In **Object Data Properties**, hit **Generate Rig**. The new **Rigify** rig is created, with custom controls to match the dragon.

2. Switch to **Object Mode** and select the old meta-rig. Move it to a new collection by pressing *M* and hide that collection in the outliner as we won't need it anymore.

3. The only custom bones we made were the wings, which need to be assigned to correct layers and start off on multiple layers. Use **Rig Layers** on the sidebar (press *N*) to turn on `Arm.L` (IK). Select the wing's relevant left `IK` controls, including `wingShoulder.L`, `upper_arm_parent.L`, `upper_arm_ik.L`, and `hand_ik.L`. Move them to only be on the `Arm.L` (IK) layer by hitting *M* and choosing the active layer.

4. Repeat this process with the right IK wing and use the same process to get the wing's FK bones to their relevant layers. The `wingShoulder` bones, which are used for both IK and FK, can be assigned to both layers.

5. Repeat this process once more with the wing's finger and palm bones, moving them to the `Paws` layer.

6. Look for custom problems that may have occurred in other areas you customized. For instance, by extending the chain of lip bones on the top and bottom to `4`, their modifier targets were assigned incorrectly.

Don't feel locked into the finished rig that **Rigify** produces for the baby dragon. Instead, think of it as a shortcut that gets 98% of the rig made ASAP and allows modifications once it's complete. For instance, later, when animating, we'll create custom controls for shape keys. You can also think of **Rigify** as a library of good rigging tricks. If you want to build rigs from scratch, use the setups in **Rigify** and reverse engineer them. You may also need to modify areas that generate incorrectly due to modifications; for instance, the lips from my meta-rig generated incorrectly and I solved this by recreating the parenting and constraints of its neighboring lip bones.

Modifying the armature weights

Once your baby dragon is parented to the rig, it finally comes to life and you can move it around the rig to fly, pounce, walk, or anything you can dream of. Weight painting is an intermediate step between building the rig and animating it, where vertices are assigned influence to individual bones. Areas such as the eyes and claws are easy; they'll have a single bone influencing them. The body will be parented with automatic weights and the initial estimate will get you 90% of the way there, as areas such as the elbow blend between the forearm and arm bones. However, we'll also have problems with the initial weights, where the generated weights got them wrong, and a personal touch is needed.

We'll create our first animation to address this—a simple series of movements that stretch the rig's extremes, making it easy to find weighting problems. The approaches we'll use include explicit assignment, manual entry by bone, and weight painting.

Parenting (everything) with automatic weights

When a mesh (such as a baby dragon) is parented to an armature, the most commonly used option is **Automatic Weights**. When this happens, every vertex on a mesh is assigned weights based on the closest deform bones. These numbers can then be massaged for more accurate deformation. We'll start by using automatic weights for everything except the eyes:

1. Select the baby dragon mesh, then add the rig to your selection by pressing *Shift* and clicking with your mouse. All the selected objects will serve as children and the active object (the last one selected) will be the parent.
2. Press *Ctrl* + *P* to parent. Choose **Armature Deform with Automatic Weights**.
3. Select just the mesh and dig around in the **Properties** window to see what happened when we parented it. First, in **Object Properties**, the rig object is set as the mesh's parent. Second, in the **Modifier** properties, an **Armature Deform** modifier has been added, with the rig as its target and the **Vertex Groups** option active. Third, in the **Object Data** properties, the **Vertex Groups** tab has added a vertex group for every bone in the armature that has **Deform** activated in **Bone Properties**, labeled by **Rigify** with the DEF prefix.
4. Repeat this parenting workflow for all the meshes except the eyes.
5. Switch to **Pose Mode**. Select the hip controller and wiggle it. The baby dragon moves with the rig and has taken the next big step toward animation:

Setting the parent with automatic weights that both parent and add an Armature modifier

The baby dragon deforms with the rig, but problems with the deformation abound. Each section will need to be uniquely tweaked to follow the rig correctly.

Parenting to bones (eyes and stencil)

The eyes of the dragon are a special circumstance; rather than dealing with the whole rig, we only need one bone to drive them. Objects can be parented to a single-bone, ignoring the need for weights. On mechanical rigs, where things such as pistons and gears don't stretch between two bones, you might use single bone parenting a lot. We'll also use it on the empty object we used for the stencil, parenting it to a single bone:

1. Select the rig. In the **Properties** window's **Object Data** panel, the **Skeleton** tab lists the bone layers, used to organize bones by their type. Most hold the rig's control bones, but the three final layers contain prefixed bones for **Deform (DEF)**, **Mechanical (MCH)**, and **Organizational (ORG)** functionality.

2. Activate the ORG bone layer.

3. In **Pose Mode**, select the ORG-eye.L bone, then return to **Object Mode**. The rig currently retains ORG-eye.L as its active bone.

4. Select the left eye reflection mesh, then add the rig to your selection by pressing *Shift* and clicking on it. Parent the mesh to the bone by pressing *Ctrl + P* and choosing **Bone**.

5. Repeat this on the left eye mesh. Next, do this on the right eye and the reflection, using ORG-eye.R.

6. Repeat this on the rune_empty object, using the closest spine DEF bone:

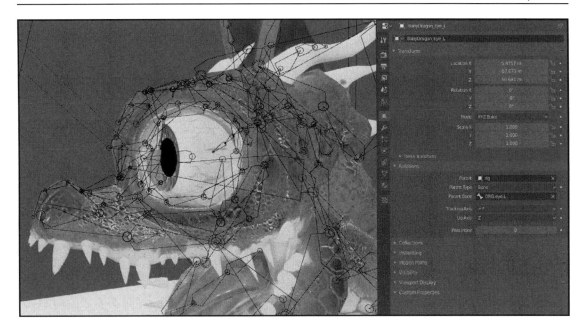

Parenting the eye object to one specific bone

The eye control mesh now moves the dragon's eyes around. The master control can be scaled, rotated, and moved in or out to make the dragon cross-eyed or lazy-eyed, or make it zero in on a target.

Assigning weights manually (to the horns, claws, and teeth)

The dragon's horns, claws, and teeth are bony and don't flex like the dragon's flesh and skin. By using the manual entry of vertex weights, we'll assign them explicitly to their bone of choice:

1. Select the rig. In the **Bone** layers, select the third-to-last layer, which holds all the DEF deform bones.

2. Switch to **Object Mode**, select the horn's mesh, and enter **Edit Mode**. Hit L over the first left horn to select all the linked vertices of a single horn. Next, press *Shift* and select one of the selected vertices so that there's an active vertex.

3. Open the sidebar by pressing N and on the **Item** panel, open the **Vertex Weights** tab. This lists the vertex weights of every vertex, which we can use for manual entry.

4. Enter a value of 1 for the group with the highest value. Enter a value of 0 for all the other groups or remove them entirely by clicking **X**.

5. Press the **Copy** button. This moves the active element vertex's weights to all the other selected vertices, unifying the horn.

6. Repeat this on any other left horns as well.

7. Hit *L* over all your left horns. Copy their weights to the right side of the mesh by going to **Mesh** | **Weights** | **Mirror**.

8. Repeat this process for the claws and teeth:

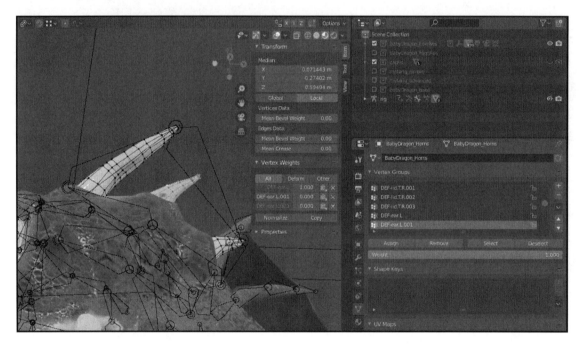

Claws and teeth

The manual entry of vertex weights is handy for a number of other problems. The list of names can tell you whether **Deform** was accidentally activated on a bone. Rogue wiggles in the animation can be investigated by the problem vertex and you'll sometimes find a distant ear weighted to a finger bone at .01. Game engines sometimes optimize by cleaning out the fourth, fifth, and sixth deforming influence. Later on, when using weight painting, if you just can't get two neighboring vertices to play together nicely, some of those conundrums can be fixed with manual entry; for instance, the seam between the dragon's legs will need perfectly equal weights between the two leg bones (.4 and .4), plus some influence from the spine (.2).

Weighting the animation

The baby dragon's other weight problems will be fixed when painting or by manual assignment, but we only notice the weighting problems when the rig moves. The solution is to create the dragon's first animation—a simple cycle through several extreme poses—which will reveal the troublesome areas through movement. We don't need to worry about animation principles, the acting, or the physics behind this; all we care about is extreme movements that show when the bone weights need fixing:

1. Switch to the **Animation** workspace. This includes the dope sheet, which lets us store and move keyframes per bone, a timeline for playback options, and a second three-dimensional view with overlays turned off for cleaner viewing.

2. Select the rig and switch to **Pose Mode**. If you have any control bones out of place from messing around, clear them by selecting them all with *A* and clearing their transforms by pressing *Alt + G*, *Alt + S*, and *Alt + R*. On the sidebar's **Item** panel (press *N*), turn on the **Face**, **Spine**, **Arm IK**, **Arm FK**, **Leg IK**, and **Tail** rig layers. Turn the other layers off.

3. In Dope Sheet, move to the first frame. Select all the visible bones and insert a keyframe by going to **i** | **LocRotScale**. This clean default keyframe appears on the first frame for all the bones.

4. Move to frame 11. Select `front_foot_ik.L`, which controls the IK foot, and move it to a forward stretched position using **Grab** and **Rotate**.

5. Copy this bone's pose to the clipboard by pressing *Ctrl + C*, then paste it onto the opposite foot by pressing *Ctrl + Shift + V*.

6. Carry out this process with the back feet as well. Select all four feet's IK controllers and insert another keyframe by pressing *I*. The feet animate from frame 1 to 11, allowing us to see tricky areas, such as the armpits, at their trickiest angles.

7. Go to frame 21. Select all the bones, clear them out, and insert another keyframe by pressing *I*. This holding frame is often necessary as a default for us to return to. Without it, when we animate something later, it would drift to the new frame all the way from frame 1.

8. In the timeline's **Keying** pulldown, click on **Active Keying Set** and choose **LocRotScale**. Now, when we press *I* to insert keyframes, it will automatically assume we want to keyframe the basic transforms.

9. Activate auto-keyframing by clicking on the record icon on the timeline.
   Auto-keyframing is an alternative to manual keyframe entry.

10. We'll test auto-keyframes by returning to frame 11 and animating the spine. Jump between keyframes with the ↑ and ↓ arrow keys to get back to frame 11. Rotate the spine, chest, hips, and head controllers on the *x-axis* to curl upward. Just by moving the controllers, the auto-keyframe generates new keys.

11. Go to frame 31 and make the next extreme pose—the legs pulled inward with the neck, head, spine, and tail all curling downward. Auto-keyframes are once again generated.

12. Continue alternating between the extreme poses and return to the default poses after every 10 frames. Some should be asymmetrical, with the left feet facing forward and the right feet facing backward. I created some poses that only deal with the more refined controls as well, such as the fingers and toes on the Paws layer and the bones on the Face (Primary) and Face (Secondary) layers. Using more poses doesn't hurt, but don't worry about rig-breaking crazy poses you'll never use.

Hit the *Space bar* key to play your animation and you'll find areas of the baby dragon that look incorrect at certain extremes. These moments in the animation will be crucial for finding mistakes when weight painting.

Painting weights

The baby dragon's weights are best tweaked with a painterly approach. **Weight Paint Mode** in Blender allows you to fix errors with a brush-based interface and if you're familiar with the other brush modes (such as sculpting and Grease Pencil), much of the workflow will be second nature to you. Weight painting displays weights of the selected bone from 0% to 100%, with a color ramp where blue is 0% and red is 100%. Problems can then be solved with an immediate click or a gradual buildup with a weak brush, masked via selected faces, or combined with direct vertex selection in **Edit Mode**:

1. Switch your rig to just the DEF bone layer. Scrub through your weighting animation until you find a weighting problem. The automatic weights created some problems near the legs and back.

2. Go to **Object Mode**, then add the dragon mesh to your selection by pressing *Shift* and clicking on it.

3. Switch to **Weight Paint Mode**. The mesh changes to display the colors of the active bone, with blue representing no influence, red representing a full 1.0 influence, and gradients of green, yellow, and orange representing the transition between them. Change Viewport **Shading** to **solid** as well so that the dragon's textures don't distract you.

4. Select one of the DEF bones by pressing *Ctrl* and clicking on it (assuming the rig was also in your selection). You can also switch to the active bone by clicking through the vertex groups in the **Properties** window's **Object Data** panel.

5. Scrub through your animation and look for problem areas. For instance, the automatically generated weights incorrectly made the tongue bones deform the neck of my baby dragon. Having found an error, press *Ctrl* and click on the problem bone.

6. The draw brush assigns weights directly. The default blend mode (**Mix**) will replace the existing weights on the selected bone to match the weight. Painting with a weight of 1 will give you 100% influence while painting with a weight of 0 will give you 0% influence. I selected the first tongue bone, set the weight to 0, and painted away any influence on the neck.

7. Your workflow will tend toward two setting extremes. The first is full-strength painting. Set the strength to 1 and in the **Falloff** pulldown in the **Brush** settings, choose the last falloff so that the brush is on full power. Use this when explicitly removing problem weights, erasing them to a weight of 0, or when explicitly granting a bone full control, mixing them to a weight of 1. The other method is a more painterly brush-based approach. Set your strength to .05 and return to the default falloff. Use these settings when slowly painting your weights up or down over multiple strokes:

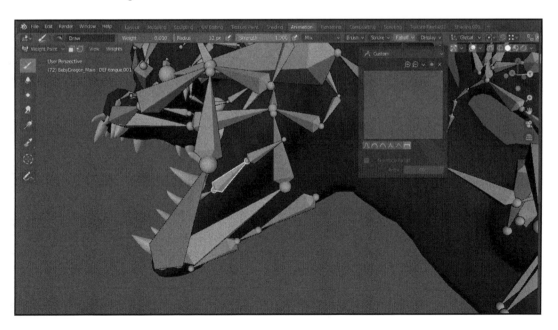

Erasing weights with a weight of 0, hard falloff, and the Mix blending mode

8. Search for problems near pinch points with many neighboring problems, such as the chest and legs. Sometimes, the issue might be a matter of too much or too little influence. The baby dragon is slimmer and more snake-like and as a result, the breast and pelvis bones don't need as much control. Normally, these come into play due to the large distance between the belly and the source of motion (that is, the spine) and on a more rotund character, they might have more influence.

9. If you are unsure of the exact weight you need during a problem keyframe, use the blend modes of **Add** or **Subtract**. These will use the **Weight** setting to always increase or decrease the influence.

10. Mask the area you're painting on by choosing the face or ve mask buttons. After activating the face mask, go to **Edit Mode**, select a ring of faces around the eyelids, then grow the selection two or three times. Return to **Weight Paint Mode** and these faces can be adjusted without worrying about throwing accidental weights onto a distant wing or tail. Faces can be added or subtracted from the mask by pressing *Ctrl* and clicking on them or using the marquis tool. Turn it off when you want to select from bone to bone by pressing *Ctrl* and clicking instead.

11. When the weighting animation plays through with minimal errors, go to **Weights** | **Mirror** to make sure they're correct on both sides.

Usually, I prefer to make the weights as acceptable as possible before jumping into the actual character animation. The weighting animation serves as a good test case for what problems will occur during production animation and when unforeseen weight problems occur during a talking, walking, or flying animation, those animations can be scrubbed while problems are fixed just as easily.

Animating a flying cycle

The baby dragon now has everything it needs to truly animate it. Some of the core concepts used in Chapter 9, *Animating an Exquisite Corpse in Grease Pencil* and Chapter 10, *Animating a Stylish Short in Grease Pencil*, such as using references, blocking in keyframes, making the animation repeat in a cycle, and testing the motion. Other animation problems will require new approaches to suit the complexity of three-dimensional objects and using a rig.

Creating a flying animation allows us to skip over the frustrations that come with creating a walk cycle. The flapping motion is mostly up and down, meaning our initial animation lay-in can mirror poses from left to right. Additionally, with the feet off the ground, we won't need to worry about correctly placed footfalls. Let's look at the rig controls.

Understanding the rig controls

With the wings flapping and the legs off the ground, IK will be turned off for flying and almost all of our keyframes will be done using **Grab**, **Scale**, and **Rotate**. Test out these functions on the various bones and once you have started to animate, try to follow these best practices:

- Using **Scale** on the finger bones will curl all of the finger's joints at the same time.
- If you select every part of an FK chain (for instance, each individual finger joint or every part of the tail) and change your transform pivot point to individual origins with the key, you can then rotate them all at once for another curling method.
- Utilize the control's default angle of movement by rotating locally on only the x or *y-axis* (pressing *R*, *X*, and *X*, or *R*, *Y*, and *Y*). For things such as the forearm, its natural movement might only be the *x-axis*, followed by the *y-axis* for the radius/ulna twisting of the twist.
- Most of the FK joints allow animating their location and scale for cartoony squash and stretch. Use this sparingly and try to animate their changes using **Rotation** first.

- Animating on FK will look better for the interpolated motion, but you might miss the freedom of posing the paws in space with IK. If an IK or FK limb is selected, the sidebar's **Item** tab has a series of FK/IK buttons that copy the pose from one control setup to the other:

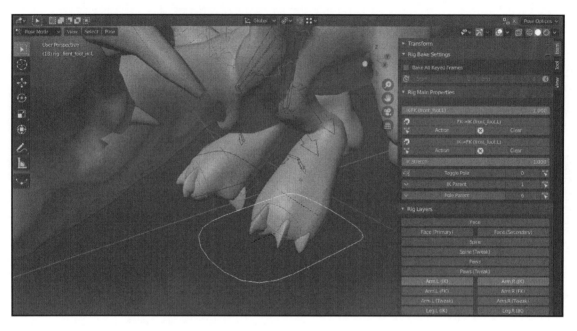

Using custom rig controls in the Item panel

- Act it out as a reference! Get out your webcam or cell phone and actually pantomime a dragon flapping its wings. You need to feel the animation and understand when the wings snap, when the head bobs up and down, and how secondary animation will distribute to the tail and feet. Pretend one arm is the dragon's tail and the other arm is the dragon's head.
- I prefer having a default keyframe on frame 1 for every control, as well as on key poses. Otherwise, if you position a bone without a keyframe, it can throw off all future keys. Start animations by pressing *Shift* and clicking and dragging over all the animation rig layers, selecting them all in **Pose Mode** by pressing *A* and inserting a keyframe for **Location**, **Rotation**, and **Scale** by pressing *I*.
- Getting the right view is key to animation. Turn the rig layers off if they're cluttering your view and in the **Action Editor**, use the **Only Selected** button to show keyframes to only the selected control bones.

- Save yourself some time and effort by copying keyframes and mirrored keyframes by pressing *Ctrl + C*, *Ctrl + V*, and *Ctrl + Shift + V*.

- A **Resting** hold is the sort of place where copy and pasting helps. Poses need to linger for impact, resulting in a keyframe rhythm key pose 1 start and stop and a key pose 2 start and stop. If pose 1 is on frame 1 and pose 2 is on frame 10, I often copy frame 2 and paste it for a resting hold on frame 7. The result is a subtle animation from frame 2 to 7 for the holding frame, followed by animating into pose 10. This is different from Grease Pencil, where a frame sticks around (an automatic resting hold) until the next frame occurs, without interpolation.

- See how far you can get on a pose using the major controllers, such as the head or hand bones. Only use subordinate bones, such as the tweak controllers, after you have got the poses for the heavy-duty controllers 90% right.

- Sometimes a bone's motion doesn't look right. To better visualize why, go to **Object Data Properties** and then the **Motion Paths** panel, and with a problem controller selected, hit **Calculate**. A motion path visualizing its journey over time can help spot the point where a natural arc has gone wonky and you can position the pose correctly:

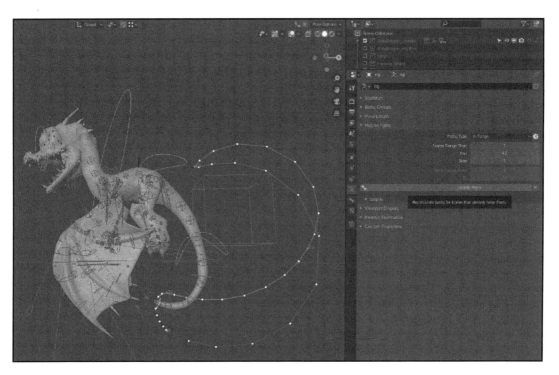

Using motion paths to visualize animation arcs

Of course, the only way to learn about animation is by animating!

Blocking in keyframes

The rig and weights are in place and we've looked at how the rig controls work. Now, we'll create a flight animation that will loop every 40 frames:

1. Set your timeline to 40 frames. Turn on all the layers and adjust the rig controls for a down-flap keyframe. Make heavy use of *Ctrl + C/Ctrl + Shift + V* to mirror a controller's pose to the opposite side.

2. Select all the bones and insert a keyframe.

3. In the **Action Editor**, select the summary keyframe at the top and duplicate it (by pressing *Shift + D*) to frame 41. The **Action Editor** holds similarities to the other interfaces in Blender—press *A* to select all/none, *B* for box selection, and press *Shift* and click to add or remove something from your selection. **Grab** and **Scale** also work here. Frame 1 and frame 41 must be identical so that the animation loops correctly. If you update one of them, remember to paste the pose onto the other.

4. Go to frame 21. Pose the dragon in the other extreme, with his wings up in the air. The major masses of the head, chest, and tail should reflect the necessary weight of the character. For instance, on frame 1, the tail should be down, pulled by the upward force from the down wings. If you are using auto-keyframe, keyframes are generated. If not, you'll need to select all the bones and insert a keyframe.

5. Go to frame 2, select all the controllers, copy the pose, and paste the interpolated pose from frame 2 onto frame 11. With this pose as a starting point, adjust the controllers to improve the pose based on your reference, either by acting it out again or by instinct. I think that if I had wings, the force of returning the wings to an upward position would be led with the elbows.

6. Go to frame 23, copy the pose for all the bones, and paste it onto frame 31. This pose is the first hint of downward thrust from the wings, so I gave the wingtips some snap as they go from relaxed to upward.

7. These four poses comprise the core of the flying animation. I keyframed all the bones on them, but for poses on other frames, I only keyframed the adjusted bones. Using the summary keyframe at the top, you can adjust the movement to land on different frames, then see how it looks when you play the animation. My adjusted poses landed on 1, 10, 19, and 28, and the pose from 1 repeated on 41.

8. Add additional keyframes to flesh out the animation. Sometimes, as a secondary animation, areas such as the fingers, tail tip, and jaw might lag behind.

9. Another method for creating a secondary animation can be used once the animation is nearly complete. Something such as the paws might be the last chain of the arm. You could then select the keyframes for just the paws and move them forward by one or two frames. Lastly, you'd need to paste frame 41's pose into the now-empty frame 1. Use this sparingly, as the offset frames won't now be included in the earlier frame's summary frame:

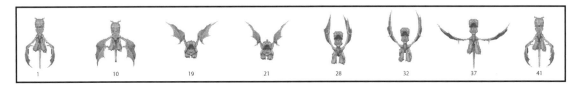

A final flying animation

Your baby dragon now flaps through the air. Take a break from time to time and you might return to the keyframes with a new perspective on how to solve things.

Summary

We've completed the full life cycle of the character pipeline, starting with the dragon's initial sculpture and culminating in him being brought to life. You might follow your flying animation with walks, runs, attacks, spit takes, and anything you can dream of. You might also now dream up your *next* character project. Every new beginning is an opportunity to grow your skills. The baby dragon we created is a culmination of the skills we built up over many chapters, starting with the basics of Blender, the materials and lighting, the building environments, using Grease Pencil for concept art and animation, and finally, utilizing sculpting to get high-quality textures and meshes.

But what about adding smoke and fire to our dragon? How about making structures crumble from a rough draconic landing? What about Python scripting the hair and all the other aspects of three dimensions? There's so much more to Blender than what we've covered so far. In our final chapter, we'll look at a variety of extra three-dimensional skills that we haven't yet covered.

Questions

1. What mode would you use to position the default settings of an armature and what mode do you use to animate the armature?
2. What are some example jobs that bones might have that would mandate splitting them into separate bones?
3. What is the difference between the **Rigify** add-on's meta-rig versus the rig that is *generated* by the meta-rig?
4. Imagine a mutant character with a giant finger coming out of its head. How would you set these bones up so that **Rigify** includes animation controls for the head finger?
5. When assigning weights manually in **Edit Mode**, which selected vertex will you need to use when copying to all the selected vertices?
6. What purpose does a weighting animation serve?
7. Where in Blender's interface does a **Rigify** rig let you toggle control layers, switch between IK/FK, and use other custom rig attributes?
8. On a walk cycle where the dragon's feet switch from step to step, how would you mirror a pose from left to right?
9. What are the benefits and drawbacks of using auto-keyframing?
10. As a follow-up to your flying cycle, animate a take of your dragon landing to investigate your Viking helmet from `Chapter 2`, *Editing a Viking Scene with a Basic 3D Workflow.*

Further reading

If you're ready to add your baby dragon to a game engine, check out *Unreal Engine 4 Game Development Quick Start Guide* by Rachel Cordone (Packt Publishing). A variety of books on the Unity game engine are available at `https://www.packtpub.com/tech/unity`.

16
The Wide World of Blender

In this final chapter, we'll explore a variety of smaller projects that deal with 3D skills that didn't fit into other projects. So far, we've only scratched the surface of Blender's amazing capabilities. Your task now is to keep learning, join the larger Blender tribe beyond this book, and, above all else, make something.

Perhaps it's games. Perhaps it's an animated film, 2D or 3D. Maybe it's live action, with Blender as your VFX and video editing toolset. Even if you just use Blender to make memes, you're doing the right thing! Animation is not just a skill, it's a lifestyle. Your best Blender art doesn't end with this book, it merely began here.

Out in the Blender community, the skillsets and purpose of peoples' projects vary wildly. From 3D printing to physics simulation, the possibilities are endless. With this farewell chapter, we hope to send you down the right path for continuing your work with Blender, and joining a worldwide community of incredible people and talents. You can find the project files for this chapter at `https://github.com/PacktPublishing/Blender-3D-By-Example-Second-Edition/tree/master/Blender3DByExample_Chapter16`

In this chapter, you'll do the following:

- Learn snippets about all the other Blender skills we couldn't cram into this book: writing code, physics simulations, hair, smoke, photoscanning, the list goes on!
- Try out some of these disciplines via sample blends.
- Combine Blender with other software.
- Tour the amazing projects Blender users are executing around the world, and connect with the Blender community.

Blender skills to learn next

The list of Blender-related skills we didn't cover is longer than the list of topics we can include here. Some of these involve venturing into other programs or using skills such as Python scripting that, although not as visually exciting, can dramatically extend Blender's tools. For things such as physics, hair, and smoke, Blender provides shortcuts that can get a simulation up and running fast.

Photogrammetry

Let's say you've reached the final chapter of this book, and despite our best efforts, you've decided you can't stand 3D modeling and texturing, and plan to swear off of it forever. Never fear! Through the power of photogrammetry, you can make terrific models with just photographs.

Photogrammetry, also referred to as photoscanning, means *measuring from photographs*, and in the modern context it involves turning lots of photos into a 3D model. It's a major aspect of modern film and game pipelines; museums are using photogrammetry to preserve human culture, and insurance companies are using photogrammetry to assess how weatherproof your house is. You can photo-scan all kinds of things! To see an example of the results you can achieve with a few clicks, open up `ch16_photogrammetry_end.blend`.

Photoscanning requires some additional software and tools:

- **Camera**: Your phone will do in a pinch. A modern DSLR can provide much higher quality photos that result in a better scan.
- **Photos**: All photos in a dataset need identical lighting, so turn off any automatic features and flashes when shooting. We've provided you with a dataset to test with in `ch16_photogrammetry.zip`.
- **Meshroom**: This open source program is the best free option on the market. You can also use commercial packages such as Agisoft Metashape and Reality Capture. Meshroom can be downloaded from `https://alicevision.org/`.
- **Agisoft De-Lighter**: This freeware is a terrific tool for removing daylight from your finished output, resulting in clean diffuse textures. Download it from `https://www.agisoft.com`.
- A good computer.

We'll use a deer skull that I scanned while on vacation visiting my friend Jacob. The mossy texture and diffuse lighting made it a perfect subject:

1. Unzip the photos in `ch16_photogrammetry.zip`. This dataset shows some of the shooting issues with photogrammetry. My camera had a shutter speed of 1/200, fast enough that I could free shoot while walking around the skull. I shot with a high aperture (*F11*) to maintain sharpness, and then rounded out my exposure with my ISO.

2. Open up Meshroom. Drag and drop all the photos into its photo window. Save the project and hit the **Start** button. While your computer churns the data, go outside and try shooting your own photoscanning experiments. Meshroom performs a number of processes: tying camera angles together, then mapping the data to a point cloud, then generating a mesh from the points, and lastly generating a texture for the mesh:

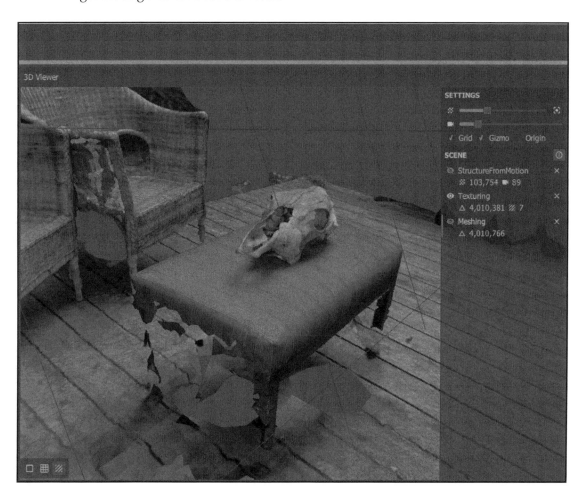

The photogrammetry skull output in Meshroom

3. Open up Blender. Use **File | Import | Wavefront(Obj)**, and navigate to `texturedMesh.obj` in the `Texturing output` folder of your Meshroom project.

4. Adjust the position of your mesh so that the skull is in the middle with the correct orientation. Delete any faces not connected to the skull, and then reset the origin of the object. Export this as a new `.obj` file.

5. Open up **Agisoft De-Lighter**, hit **import**, and navigate to your new `.obj` file. Use the **Shadow brush**, and paint just a little of the shadow under the skull. Use the **light brush** to also paint lit areas. You don't need to fill the whole thing in, just enough to give an impression of the lights.

6. Hit **Remove Cast Shadows**. De-Lighter uses the shadow and light inputs to create a diffuse texture. Export the results to another new `.obj` file.

7. Open Blender and once again import the `.obj` file.

As shown here, the lights and shadows were loosely painted, which helped De-Lighter remove them from the texture:

The skull with de-lighting painted in

Our next task is to translate the high-poly mesh with horrendous UVs into a usable mesh with a clean texture layout. Since the whole benefit here is to get rid of all that pesky modeling homework, we'll use Remesh to clean things up. At this point, you could create a low-poly version of your mesh using the techniques in `Chapter 12`, *Baby Dragon – Part 2 – Retopology*. Once it's unwrapped, bake the diffuse and normal textures from high to low:

1. Duplicate and hide your skull mesh; later, we'll bake from the hidden one.

2. Add a Remesh modifier. Set it to **Smooth**, with an **Octree Depth** of `10`, and apply the modifier.

3. The new streamlined mesh removes the previous UVs. To regain them, use **U|Smart UV Project**, which will make an automatic layout.

4. Bake the textures from the high-poly to the low-poly mesh, using techniques outlined in `Chapter 14`, *Baby Dragon – Part 4 – Baking and Painting Textures*.

Here, the low-poly and high-poly meshes have been set up for texture baking:

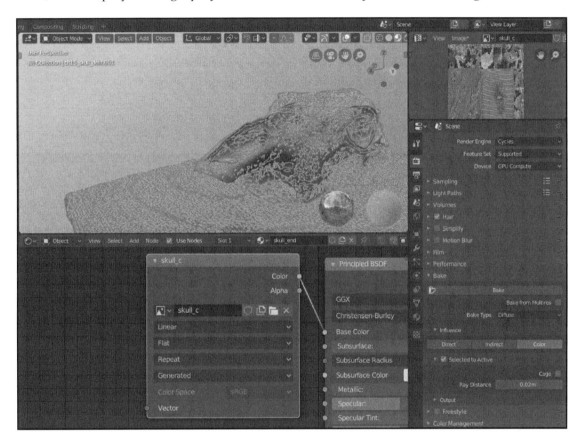

Baking the maps from high poly to low poly

The completed skull has fewer polygons and a single texture map. With more aggressive retopology and UV layout, the skull can be streamlined even further. Next, let's use physics to bash 3D objects together.

Physics

Physics in Blender can be used to simulate crumbling buildings, falling boulders, or randomly scattered objects, as shown in the project file `ch16_physics.blend`. We'll smash through a cube of cubes to test this out:

1. In a new scene, add an Array modifier. Set a **Count** of `10`, and **Relative Offset** *X* of `1.01`. Add another Array modifier, this time with **Relative Offset** *Y* of `1.01`, and another Array modifier with **Offset** *Z* of `1.01`. This cube made of cubes now looks like this:

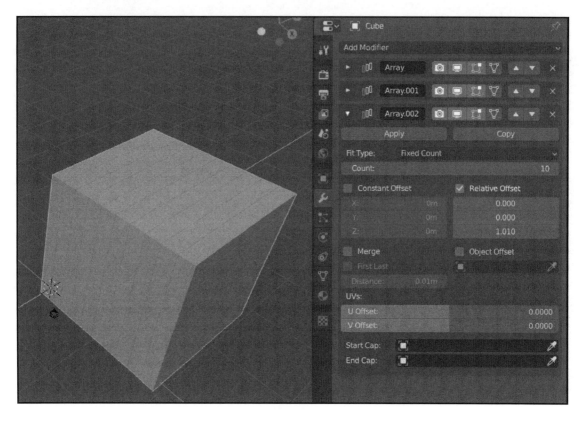

A cube of cubes using Array modifiers

2. Next, we'll make each cube its own object. Apply all three modifiers, and then, in **Edit Mode**, separate the cubes with **P|Separate|By Loose Parts**. Return to **Object** mode, and with all the cubes selected, set their origins with **Object | Set Origin | Origin to Geometry**.

3. Switch to the **Properties** window's **Physics** tab and click **Rigid Body**. Hit *Space bar* to play, and only the active cube falls endlessly. As you change your physics settings, you can reset it by returning to frame 0 and playing again.

4. On the **Collisions** tab, change the shape to **Box**. Physics are calculated based on an envelope around the object bounds. The envelope choice is a matter of speed and accuracy. The **box** option is low poly and speedy and, since it matches our shape, won't cause clipping issues.

5. In the **Dynamics** tab, turn on **Deactivation**, as well as **Start Deactivated**. The cube won't move until a collision occurs.

6. In the **Object** menu, choose **Object | Rigid Body | Copy from Active**. The physics from the first cube is applied to all the cubes. Change your **Viewport Shading** to **Solid**, and in the **Shading** panel, set the color to **Random** to more easily tell your cubes apart.

7. Now we need a collider. Add an Icosphere with **Add | Mesh | Ico Sphere**. Scale it up in **Edit Mode**, and then move it to be above the cubes in **Object** mode. It's important that the object's scale is at 1/1/1, and that its center of origin stays in the middle of the mesh.

Add Rigid Body physics to this as well, change its **Collision type** to **Sphere**, and change its **Mass** to 1000kg to really smash the cubes:

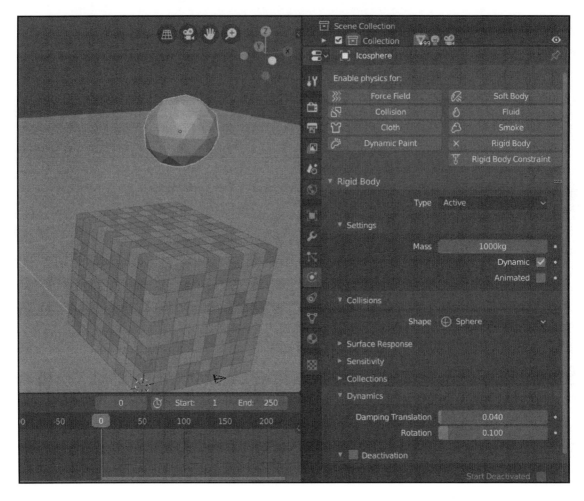

A box of boxes, each with their own origin, position, and rigid body

8. Add a plane, and then position and scale it to sit right under the cube of cubes, with enough area for them to spread out over. Add Rigid Body physics, change its **Rigid Body Type** to **Passive**, and change its shape to **Box**. As a passive object, the plane will sit still throughout the simulation.

9. Go to **Frame 0** and hit **Play**. The sphere smashes through the cubes! Blender stores a cache of the physics simulation by playing through the whole timeline, after which the physics load faster. Set your end frame to 50 to cut out a lot of wasted time.

10. In the **Properties** window's **Scene** panel, expand the **Rigid Body World** tab and set your **Speed** to 5, and play through the animation. The collision is quicker and more toy-like, but loses collision accuracy with the speed-up. To offset this, set **Steps Per Second** to 300, and play through the animation to load the cache:

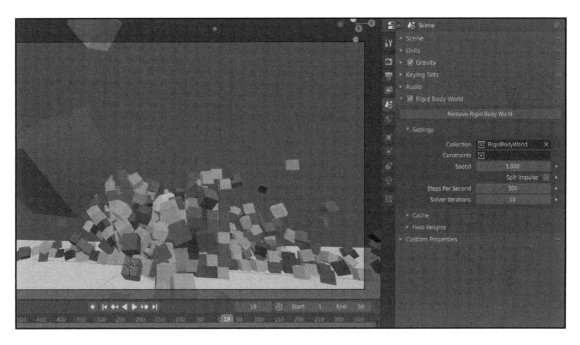

The smashed cubes!

For an even more sophisticated physics setup, use the Cell Fracture Add-on to break one of your models into interlocking sections. You can account for their unique shapes by changing their Collisions Shape to either Convex Hull or Mesh. Next, we'll look at simulating smoke and fire.

Volumetrics

Blender's volumetrics are great for smoke, mist, fire, and other atmospheric effects. The **Volume** attribute of your **Material Output** nodes lets you customize these cloudy things with the node editor. Let's start by seeing how the Volume attribute works with a Principled Volume shader by constructing a smoke ring, and then use a Mantaflow fluid simulation to create realistic burning flames. The finished smoke simulation and materials can be found in ch16_smoke.blend.Let's dive into it:

1. Create a new scene, and choose the Shading workspace. Give the Default Cube a new material called Sphere.

2. Add a Principled Volume shader with *Ctrl + A* | **Add** | **Shader**, and attach it to the **Material Output's Volume** attribute. Like the **Principled BSDF**, the **Principled Volume** shader collects all the attributes that typically affect a volume in one place. The **Color** attributes are for the color of particulate matter in the volume, while the emission, blackbody, and temperature attributes pertain to emissive volumes like fire.

3. Add a gradient texture with *Ctrl + A* | **Add** | **Texture**. Map it to an object with a **Texture Coordinate** and **Mapping** node. Set the gradient texture to **Spherical**, and plug it into the **Principled Volume's Density** and **Emission Strength**. Adjust the **Mapping** node's **Scale** until you get a sphere. This demonstrates how the volume is distributed throughout an object.

4. Shape your volume using math nodes to combine different mappings. Duplicate your mapped gradient texture with a **Scale** of .5, .5, and 0 for a cylinder of smoke. Subtract this gradient texture from the previous gradient texture with a Math node. I also adjust the intensity with an RGB Curve and another Math node. Scale the cube down to a doughnut shape:

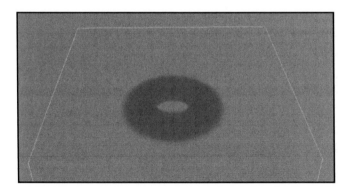

The node setup for a smoke doughnut

To view the complete nodetree for this smoke doughnut material, check the following image [].

5. Now, add some variation to the smoke ring. I combine two Musgrave textures mapped to big and little details, adjust their strengths with some Math nodes, combine them via a **Mix** node with the previous ring, and adjust the overall strength. Duplicate and scale your doughnut object for some example smoke rings.

6. Go to the **Render properties** panel. Under **Volumetrics**, improve the quality of the volume display by setting **Tile Size** to 2px, and **Samples** to 128:

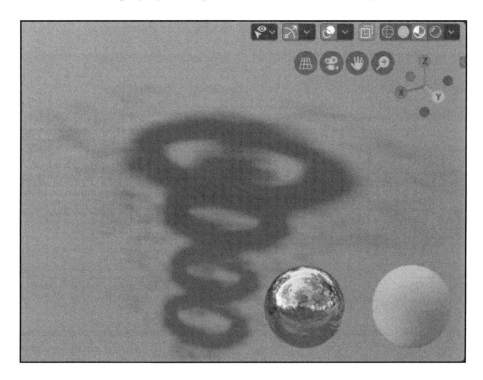

Adjusting the Volumetrics settings

To view the complete nodetree for this volumetrics setup, check the following image [].

This is only one aspect of volumetrics in Blender. Through smoke simulation, the distribution of a gaseous medium is represented in voxels, which simulates a more accurate distribution. Smoke simulations in Blender require two objects: a Flow object to emit the smoke, and a domain, which represents how far it can go.

1. Add a new cube. Hit *F3*, and search for `quick smoke`. This preset creates an automatic smoke simulation, with many of the materials and settings at an ideal starting point. In the **Creation** panel, change **Smoke style** to **Smoke + Fire**. The two objects involved in the scene are a Flow object (the starting cube), which emits smoke, and a Domain object (the newer cube), which determines the bounds in which the smoke is simulated.

2. To see your smoke simulation, save your file, which lets the smoke simulation generate a cache file. Select the outer Domain object, go to the **Properties** window's **Physics** panel, and scroll down to the **Cache** tab. Change its **Type** to **Replay**. When you press **Play**, the smoke simulation now loads.

3. In **Edit Mode**, scale down the Flow cube by `.01`, about the size of a flare's emission. Again, hit **Play**. Once the cache has loaded over the timeline, it plays back much faster.

4. Add a Force Field with *Shift A* | **Add** | **Force Field** | **Force**. A positive strength will push smoke away, and negative strength will attract it. Set the **Strength** to -2, and keyframe some animation where the Force Field moves around over 250 frames. I also keyframe the Strength to vacillate between -2 and 2.

5. Add some additional Force Fields, and play with how they affect the simulation. I use a Turbulence whose Strength is keyframed from -2 to 2, and a Vortex with -2 Strength and 5 Noise.

Adding in force fields gives a much more customized look, as shown here:

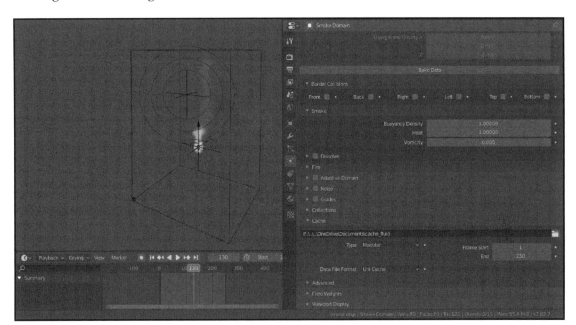

Smoke simulation with force fields

Explore the effects that settings and force fields can have on your smoke and fire simulations. You might use this to add smoke and fire pouring out of the mouth of our baby dragon from `Chapter 15`, *Baby Dragon – Part 5 – Rigging and Animation*. Next up, a Blender tool you should know about that doesn't so much fit with a scaly dragon: hair and fur.

Hair and fur

Blender's hair simulator is great for things like characters and grass, not to mention tasks such as distributing objects. An example of this can be seen in `ch16_hair.blend`. Here's a quick setup for a fuzzy cartoon friend with wild neon hair:

1. Start a new scene. Delete the default cube, and add a UV sphere.
2. Switch to the **Particles** tab, and add a new particle system. Change its **type** to **Hair**. Give it a starting Emission of `5000`, with `.25` Hair Length.

3. On the **Children** tab, set the child particle type to **Simple**, which adds secondary particles while allowing a stylish haircut. For the child roughness, set the **Endpoint** to .05 and **Random** to .05.

4. Switch to **Particle Edit** Mode. You'll find a brush-based interface similar to sculpting. Use the **Comb** tool to move strands, **Add brush** to add hair, and **Cut brush** to remove hair. Comb the hair's direction with the **Comb** tool, and then use the **Puff** tool to add volume. When your haircut is mostly in place, grow and shrink it with the **Length** brush, or by deactivating **Preserve Length** in the **Options** panel, and then combing to get more length. Set the **Path Steps** to 5 in the **Options** pulldown, and, in the particle settings' **Viewport Display**, set **Strand Steps** to 5.

5. For longer hair with some bangs, I lengthen the hair everywhere, comb it all downward, and then puff it with the **Puff** tool. Next, use the **Cut** tool with .25 strength from the side view, erasing away to get the right silhouette.

Give your sphere some cute bangs, such as these ones:

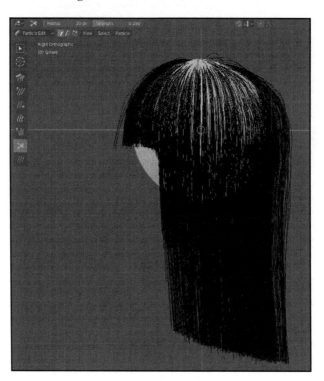

A haircut for our sphere

Switch your view to Rendered mode, and the need for hair-specific materials and rendering becomes clear. We'll give the hair rainbow stripes all the way down, and render it in Cycles:

1. Switch your rendering engine to Cycles. Create two materials named `Skin` and `Hair`. On the **Particles** tab, set the hair as the material, and assign the skin material to the mesh faces.
2. In the **Hair** material, add a **Principled Hair BSDF** shader with **Add|Shader**. In the pulldown, choose **Melanin Coefficient**, and the whole hair material is uses a BSDF model that mimics realistic hair properties.
3. Set the mode back to **Direct coloring**, and then for its **Color**, add a **Magic Texture** with **Add|Texture**.
4. Add a **Hair Info** node with **Add|Input**, which can access the hair values. The Intercept value maps strands from root to tip. Use this as the **Magic Texture**'s vector.
5. Add a **MixRGB** node, and multiply the **Magic Texture** by the random value. Neighboring strands now have minor variations in darkness.

Finish it up with some additional creative tweaks for colorful hair like this:

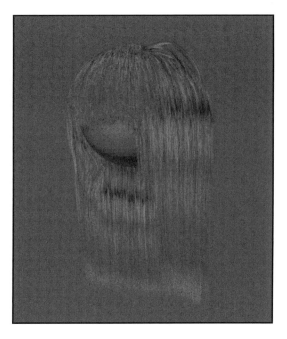

The multicolored hair material

To view the complete nodetree for the multicolored hair material, check the following image [].

Use Hair for long and short haircuts, as well as things like grass. Next, some Python!

Recording a macro in Python

Let's look at using Python in Blender to write a script that makes plant alpha cards. Blender is written in a mix of C, C++, and Python programming languages. It includes lots of tools to let someone experienced in Python write their own code snippets, macros, and add-ons. Even for someone scared of coding, Blender provides everything you need to write macros to automate your task. Let's look at the interface and tools for using Python in Blender, and then walk through a simple code solution for creating alpha cards out of hair. For a deeper dive on Python, We recommend *Getting Started with Python*, by *Fabrizio Romano*, available from Packt.

Start a new Blender scene, and click on the Scripting workspace. This includes all the main areas where you'll interact with Python:

- The Python Console window. Python code can be tested here, and you can explore Blender's Python API.
- The **Info** window. Any time an operation is performed in Blender, the Python code and parameters for the operator will be displayed here. These code snippets can be copied from the info window and pasted into the Python Console so that we can reuse them in our own scripts after performing an action.
- The Text Editor, where your scripts are written.
- The usual Blender windows, so your scripting output can be seen.

We can also enable two extra features to make scripting easier:

1. Go to **Edit|Preferences**, and navigate to the **Interface** panel.
2. Turn on **Python Tooltips** and **Developer Extras**.

Now the Python code snippets can be will be displayed in the tooltips just by hovering over buttons and menu options throughout Blender's user interface. We also have access to online documentation for the operators by right clicking on any item and choosing "Online Python Reference".

Test out some code in the Python Console window:

```
2+2
print('hello world')
for i in 10:
  print(i)
```

Whenever an action is performed, feedback appears in the Info window. Other errors are logged to the Console, found by using **Window | Toggle System Console**. Hide it the same way; if you close the console, you'll close Blender. Add a new object, and then copy and paste the code into the console to perform it again:

```
bpy.ops.mesh.primitive_cube_add(enter_editmode=False, location=(0, 0, 0))
```

This command starts with bpy, the Blender Python API, and then ops accesses the operators, and then a specific operator, performed with certain parameters. Cycle through commands you've typed in the Python Console window with the ↑ and ↓ arrows. Type in bpy., and then hit *Ctrl + Space* to autocomplete. You'll see the modules that make up the Blender Python API. We'll be dealing with context (accessing the current state of Blender), data (accessing Blender's data), and ops (accessing the commands you run.) Use *Ctrl + Space* to autocomplete.

We'll use Python to automate a task that would be tedious to do over and over. When making plants for the kitchen, one technique is to get natural distribution with a hair simulation, and then make that into alpha cards. Open up ch15_python_plants.blend, which has the finished script and a hair simulation ready to run. First, think through the tasks needed:

1. Assume the user's got a hair simulation selected.
2. Convert the hairs to mesh edges.
3. Convert the mesh to curves.
4. Extrude and bevel the curves to make alpha cards.
5. Convert them back into meshes.
6. Assign the plant alpha card material.
7. Set their UVs up for moving around the texture atlas.

In the Script editor, create a new text. In the header, turn on line numbers, word wrap, and syntax highlighting, ⏹⏹⏹. Your script will start with `import bpy`, which lets our script access the Blender API. We can find the Python command we need by hovering over the relevant command. Select the hair system and, on the **Modifiers** tab, hover over the **Convert** button. A Python tip appears. Right-click and choose **Copy Python Command**, and paste it into the script. Click the button, and the command can be seen in third place, printed to the Python Console.

1. We get to a curve with this:

```
import bpy
bpy.ops.object.modifier_convert(modifier="ParticleSettings")
bpy.ops.object.convert(target='CURVE')
```

2. Next, we get the curve from the context. `bpy.context` can tell you things such as the current selection, frame, or window. Assign it to a variable to save time on typing. `selected_objects` is an array of the objects selected, with `selected_objects[0]` being the active one, the curve:

```
plants=bpy.context.selected_objects[0]
```

3. Now `plants` is the equivalent of `bpy.data.objects['plot']`, which was the object in the `plants` array at 0. Next, we do a bunch of stuff to `plants` by assigning values to that object's data. These attributes are all in the **Curves** panel, and their exact commands are found by right-clicking and copying the data path:

```
plants.data.extrude = .1
plants.data.fill_mode = 'HALF'
plants.data.bevel_resolution = 1
plants.data.bevel_depth = 0.2
plants.data.offset = -0.2
```

4. Next, we'll convert it back to a mesh, and separate that mesh by loose parts so the UVs will remap correctly later:

```
bpy.ops.object.convert(target='MESH')
bpy.ops.mesh.separate(type='LOOSE')
```

5. The separated objects are all selected, so we'll create a new list from that to iterate over later:

```
cards = bpy.context.selected_objects
```

6. The rest of the commands will be iterated for every face of every object in `cards`, starting with a clean selection:

```
for card in cards:
  card.data.polygons.active=0
    for face in card.data.polygons:
```

7. And lastly, we'll select all the faces, add a UV set, unwrap using `follow_active_quads`, pack the unwrap to the UV bounds, put the plant material on, and deselect it:

```
face.select = True
bpy.ops.object.mode_set(mode='EDIT')
bpy.ops.mesh.uv_texture_add()
bpy.ops.uv.follow_active_quads()
bpy.ops.uv.select_all(action='SELECT')
bpy.ops.uv.pack_islands()
bpy.ops.object.mode_set(mode='OBJECT')
card.data.materials.append(bpy.data.materials['plants'])
card.select_set(False)
```

8. From here, we scale and rotate the UVs to match, and scale their faces to the correct plant alpha card:

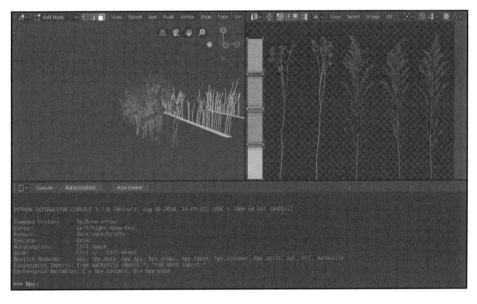

The final alpha card generator

9. The final script is as follows:

```
import bpy
bpy.ops.object.modifier_convert(modifier="ParticleSettings")
bpy.ops.object.convert(target='CURVE')
plants = bpy.context.selected_objects[0]
plants.data.extrude = .1
plants.data.fill_mode = 'HALF'
plants.data.bevel_resolution = 1
plants.data.bevel_depth = 0.2
plants.data.offset = -0.2
bpy.ops.object.convert(target='MESH')
bpy.ops.mesh.separate(type='LOOSE')
cards = bpy.context.selected_objects
for card in cards:
  card.data.polygons.active=0
  for face in card.data.polygons:
    face.select = True
    bpy.ops.object.mode_set(mode='EDIT')
    bpy.ops.mesh.uv_texture_add()
    bpy.ops.uv.follow_active_quads()
    bpy.ops.uv.select_all(action='SELECT')
    bpy.ops.uv.pack_islands()
    bpy.ops.object.mode_set(mode='OBJECT')
    card.data.materials.append(bpy.data.materials['plants'])
    card.select_set(False)
```

10. In the Script editor, browse the Python templates with **Templates|Python** to see other examples of using Python in Blender. Next, we'll look at the wider Blender community, and the resources they can provide.

The Blender community

When two Blender users meet each other, there is often a sense that they are instant best friends. The camaraderie extends to the entire Blender ecosystem—newcomers and professionals, artists and developers, and everything in between. If this book is in your hands, the Blender community means *you*. Explore these groups digitally and in real life as you continue to use this amazing software.

The Blender Foundation and Blender Institute

The heart of Blender development happens in Amsterdam, Netherlands. The Blender Foundation is chaired by Ton Roosendaal, Blender's original creator, who raised funds to make Blender open source in 2002. They released an animated film, *Elephant's Dream* in 2006, directed by Bassam Kurdali, and then established the Blender Institute as a place to continue making Blender-based media, including games, live-action VFX films, 2D animation, and more.

With the Blender Foundation developing the software, and the Blender Institute creating world-class content, Blender has landed on a sustainable and effective strategy of continuous new features. During production, the Blender Institute plans to make their content using features that don't yet exist in Blender. The assets and media are then released to the public under permissive licenses. These projects and Blender development are funded by community members and companies, who reap a terrific reward in the form of cutting-edge Blender features and vast libraries of content to learn from.

You can be a part of Blender's development by joining the Blender Development fund at `https://fund.blender.org/`. Your contributions compound with your fellow Blender lovers, which leads to more full-time developers creating cutting-edge tools.

The Blender Cloud hosts all of the film assets, texture libraries, character rigs, and other goodies created over the decades. Joining the Blender Cloud gives you full access to all this content, allowing you to expand your Blender knowledge even further. You can join the Blender Cloud at `https://cloud.blender.org/`.

Blender user groups

When you're tired of using Blender all alone, and want to talk shop face to face, you can turn to user groups. Blender user groups happen all over the world. They're a great way to learn from others, and also a good venue to show off the projects you complete. If you live in or near a metropolitan area, look up Blender on meetup.com and you'll probably find a group that meets quarterly or monthly. If you can't find one in your city, you might be the person to start one. Many schools will even offer official club funding.

Once a year, the Blender community's various user groups coordinate on World Blender Meetup Day. User groups from all over the world provide video content, generating 24 hours' worth of demos and tutorials in a single day, at `https://www.worldblendermeetupday.org/`.

The biggest Blender meetup is the Blender Conference in Amsterdam. Even if you can't attend, the conference talks are streamed to the rest of the world. To learn more about the Blender Conference, or to support Blender by buying some neat Blender gear, visit `https://store.blender.org/`.

Online Blender communities

A number of digital resources are available to keep you up to date on everything Blender. Find more help at these communities around the internet:

- **Blender Nation**: This is the #1 site for Blender news. Check it daily to see new Blender projects, development updates, and other events, at `https://www.blendernation.com/`.
- **Blender Artists**: This is a forum dedicated to Blender. You can post your projects here, ask questions, and view and learn from the Blender projects other users are sharing, at `https://blenderartists.org/`.
- **Blend Swap:** Hosts a myriad of Blender files that users have released under various permissive Creative Commons licenses. You can download these files and learn from them, or even throw them into production depending on the license. If you have a novel Blender project you think others would benefit from, you can post it for others to see at `https://www.blendswap.com/`.
- **Social media**: Sites such as Facebook, Twitter, and Reddit have many Blender users posting content and helping out fellow users with questions. Tag your content with the `#b3d` hashtag to share it with Blender users, join the Blender Facebook group, and follow the `r/blender` subreddit for more.
- **Blender Stack Exchange**: Here, users can ask questions, and vote on the best answers. If you run into a problem, someone else has potentially faced the same problem and had their question answered. Have a look at `https://blender.stackexchange.com/`.
- **GraphicAll**: This has custom Blender builds, often assembled by developers working on bleeding-edge features. If you want to try the hottest experimental tools, check out `https://blender.community/c/graphicall`.
- **Blender Market**: This is a hub for buying and selling Blender assets. Some of the add-ons for sale here can greatly expand Blender's capabilities, and you can also sell your own Blender creations here as well.

Summary

In this chapter, we've taken a surface-level glance at a number of disciplines in Blender. Photogrammetry in Meshroom showed how other open source programs can assist a Blender pipeline. We set up examples of physics, hair, and smoke that can be further tweaked. We also looked under the hood at how to extend Blender's functionality with Python.

There are still many corners of Blender to explore. Combining Blender with live-action footage can be done through the compositor, movie clip editor, and video sequencer. Your models can be taken over to game engines including Unity, Unreal, and Godot. New features are added every day, whether it's new sculpting brushes, or controlling everything in Blender with Everything Nodes.

I can't predict where you'll take your next steps in using Blender to make great content. But I look forward to seeing it, with great enthusiasm. For Blender users everywhere, the future is bright.

Questions

1. Where does Blender fit in a photogrammetry workflow?
2. When setting up collisions that are both quick and accurate, what collision shapes would you choose for a basketball, a cardboard box, and shards of glass, respectively?
3. Where can you find built-in examples of Blender's smoke, fur, explosions, and liquid capabilities?
4. What `import` statement should Python scripts use to access Blender's API?
5. How is Blender's development funded?
6. What sites can you visit to find Creative Commons Blender files?

Other Books You May Enjoy

If you enjoyed this book, you may be interested in these other books by Packt:

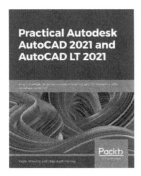

Practical Autodesk AutoCAD 2021 and AutoCAD LT 2021

Yasser Shoukry, Jaiprakash Pandey

ISBN: 978-1-78980-915-2

- Understand CAD fundamentals using AutoCAD's basic functions, navigation, and components
- Create complex 3d solid objects starting from the primitive shapes using the solid editing tools
- Working with reusable objects like Blocks and collaborating using xRef
- Explore some advanced features like external references and dynamic block
- Get to grips with surface and mesh modeling tools such as Fillet, Trim, and Extend
- Use the paper space layout in AutoCAD for creating professional plots for 2D and 3D models
- Convert your 2D drawings into 3D models

Blender for Video Production Quick Start Guide
Allan Brito

ISBN: 978-1-78980-495-9

- Import video and audio footage to Blender
- Use the Video Sequencer Editor to manipulate footage
- Prepare a project related to video in Blender
- Cut and reorganize video footage in Blender
- Create animations and add voiceover and sound to video
- Build infographics based on 3D content
- Blend 3D content with live-action footage
- Export video for YouTube using optimal settings

Leave a review - let other readers know what you think

Please share your thoughts on this book with others by leaving a review on the site that you bought it from. If you purchased the book from Amazon, please leave us an honest review on this book's Amazon page. This is vital so that other potential readers can see and use your unbiased opinion to make purchasing decisions, we can understand what our customers think about our products, and our authors can see your feedback on the title that they have worked with Packt to create. It will only take a few minutes of your time, but is valuable to other potential customers, our authors, and Packt. Thank you!

Index

Printed in Great Britain
by Amazon